Keyboarding with WordPerfect®

6.1 for Windows™

60 sessions

William M. Mitchell, Ed.D.
University of Wisconsin–Eau Claire

Nita Hewitt Rutkosky, M.S.
Pierce College at Puyallup

K.A. Mach, Ed.D.
Irvine Valley College

James E. LaBarre, Ph.D.
University of Wisconsin–Eau Claire

EMCParadigm

Editorial/Production/Design Team

Sonja Brown
Kris Ellis
Margery Meadows
Bradley Olsen
Nancy Sauro
Joan Silver

Cover Design by Bolger Publications/Creative Printing

Illustration on page x was derived from an original illustration courtesy of *U.S. News & World Report.*

Keyboarding with WordPerfect: 6.1 for Windows: 60 seesions/William
M. Mitchell ... (et al.).
p. cm.
Includes index.
ISBN 1-56118-770-4
1. WordPerfect for WIndows (Computer file) 2. Word Processing.
I. Mitchell, William Martin. 1932-
Z52.5.W655K48 1995
652.5'536--dc20

Text and User's Guide
ISBN 1-56118-771-2 Order Number 01236
Instructor's Software Pkg, 3.5"
ISBN 1-56118-773-9 Order Number 41236
Instructor's Software Pkg, 5.25"
ISBN 1-56118-774-7 Order Number 46236

Also in this series:

Keyboarding with WordPerfect 6.1 for Windows (Sessions 1-30) and User's Guide
ISBN 1-56118-842-5 Order Number 01246
Intermediate Keyboarding with Windows (Sessions 61-120)
ISBN 1-56118-923-5 Order Number 01277
Software for the above two texts:
Instructor's Software Pkg, 3.5" ISBN 1-56118-773-9 Order Number 41236
Instructor's Software Pkg, 5.25" ISBN 1-56118-774-7 Order Number 46236

ISBN: 1-56118-770-4

Published by: EMC/Paradigm
875 Montreal Way
St. Paul, MN 55102
800/535-6865
E-mail: publish@emcp.com

Printed in the United States of America.

10 9 8 7 6 5 4

CONTENTS

INTRODUCTION

Learning to keyboard is an important skill that you will use in nearly every kind of career. Another necessary skill is the ability to use a word processing program—WordPerfect 6.1 for Windows, for example—to create a variety of documents, including letters and reports. *Keyboarding with WordPerfect 6.1 for Windows (KWP)* gives you the opportunity to learn both keyboarding and word processing skills at the same time. Students who successfully complete this program gain a valuable jump-start toward mastering the computer competencies required in the modern workplace.

LEARNING OUTCOMES

Keyboarding with WordPerfect 6.1 for Windows: 60 Sessions provides instruction in developing the basic keyboarding skills to key alphabetic, numeric, and special symbols keys as well as instruction in basic WordPerfect features, including creating and printing a document.

When you have completed this book, you will be able to demonstrate a basic-level mastery of keyboarding as well as operating WordPerfect 6.1 for Windows, which includes:

- keying straight-copy alphanumeric material at an average rate of 40 words a minute with two or fewer errors per minute
- keying numeric copy using correct touch techniques on the 10-key numeric keypad at 25 words a minute
- using WordPerfect commands to perform the basic file management activities of creating, saving, deleting, printing, and closing
- using WordPerfect to compose coherent material with correct word usage at the word, sentence, paragraph, and document levels
- using WordPerfect to prepare correctly formatted memos, letters, manuscripts, and reports at 25 words a minute and tables at 15 words a minute with all errors corrected

PROGRAM OVERVIEW

With the program installed, your computer contains both WordPerfect 6.1 for Windows and the Paradigm keyboarding software in the main memory. Whenever you access WordPerfect, the keyboarding software is launched as well. However, the keyboarding software is not activated until you point to the KWP button with the mouse and click the mouse button.

All instruction is offered through a combination of the text and the Paradigm software. New keys and the correct finger positions for striking them are presented by the Paradigm software on the screen, which is the WordPerfect program "window." This window is divided so that approximately the top half is open for keying and the bottom half contains instructions. Drills and timings that you complete are saved by the Paradigm software, and the program moves automatically from one activity to the next.

Instruction in using WordPerfect features such as creating, saving, and printing a document is presented in the textbook, and when you are to complete the instructional activities (called "WordPerfect Reinforcement"), the Paradigm software moves you automatically to the WordPerfect program. In this mode, the window is not divided. It displays as the normal WordPerfect editing window, and you as the user are in charge of creating, saving, and printing documents. On the Main Menu, the WordPerfect mode is called "Freeform."

SESSION STRUCTURE

Each of the 30 sessions ("chapters" or "lessons") follows the same basic pattern:

- **Warm-Up:** As the name implies, this introductory activity has you flexing your fingers and practicing key presses so you are ready to key quickly and efficiently when the new material is presented.
- **New Keys:** The computer keyboard is shown on the screen with the new keys highlighted along with instructions for which fingers to use on the new keys.
- **New Key Drills:** The Paradigm software presents a line at a time of words or sentences using the new keys. You are asked to key the lines so your brain and fingers learn where the keys are and you don't have to look at the keyboard—eventually!
- **Thinking Drills:** This special drill teaches you to compose sentences at the keyboard, or to think and key at the same time, eliminating the need to write down what you want to say on paper first.This skill saves considerable time when you are faced with writing a letter, a research paper, or any kind of document.
  (***Note:*** Not every session includes a Thinking Drill.)
- **WordPerfect Reinforcement:** In this part of the session, you learn WordPerfect features by completing activities offered in the text. You work in the WordPerfect program by itself, just as you would on the job or at home, and you will key a few of the same drills that were presented on the screen earlier. However, you will key from the text. When you finish, you will have created your own WordPerfect document, and you can save the file and print it (directions are included in the text).
- **Timings**: This final session activity is an opportunity for you to determine your keyboarding speed and accuracy. The Paradigm software displays information about the length of the timing and the paragraph and page number in the text. The program's automatic timer begins when you strike the first key. When the time is up, the keyboard locks so you cannot continue. Immediately the software checks the accuracy and length of what you keyed and displays the results in WAM (words a minute) and errors at the bottom of the screen. The software also automatically saves this file to your data disk, and you can print it when required. In addition, the software keeps a record of your timing scores. This record is called the "Student Report," and it has its own button on your WordPerfect Toolbar.
  Note: The KWP program offers the option of correcting errors as you key drills and timings, or this feature can be turned off so that you cannot correct errors. Your instructor will tell you which option to use.

HARDWARE AND SOFTWARE REQUIRED

To use *Keyboarding with WordPerfect 6.1 for Windows*, you will need the following materials and equipment:

- Textbook
- Blank, formatted, high-density floppy disk, either 3.5" or 5.25"
- PC (Personal Computer) with either a 386 or 486 processor, a VGA color monitor, 6 MB of RAM, and a mouse
  Note: The program can be used on a stand-alone PC or on a PC connected to a Local Area Network (LAN). Your instructor will tell you which set-up you are using.
- Keyboarding with WordPerfect software (available to your instructor as a separate package, which will have already been installed for you)
- WordPerfect 6.1 for Windows program (already installed on your computer)

BASIC PARTS OF THE MICROCOMPUTER (HARDWARE)

A microcomputer system contains six basic components: the central processing unit (CPU), the disk drives, the video display (screen), the printer, and the keyboard and mouse (optional for many programs, but recommended for use with Windows programs). These parts provide for input (keyboard and mouse), display (video screen), processing (CPU), output (CPU and printer), and storage (disk drive). Your computer may be linked with the other computers in the room as part of a network, in which case everyone may print from the same printer. Consult your instructor if you have a microcomputer system that you do not know how to operate.

The Processor (CPU)

The CPU is the intelligence of the computer. All the processing occurs in the CPU. Silicon chips, which contain miniaturized circuitry, are placed on boards that are plugged into slots within the CPU. Whenever an instruction is given to the computer, that instruction is electronically processed through circuitry in the CPU.

The Disk Drive

Your microcomputer contains one or more internal (fixed, or hard) drives on which software is stored and one or more external (floppy) disk drives in either a 5.25" or 3.5" size. Your instructor will provide you with information on which type of disk you will be using to store your completed documents and timings. The book will provide instructions on how to store and retrieve the information from the disk.

The Video Display

The video display (monitor) on your computer looks like a television screen and is most likely a color monitor, rather than monochrome (black and white). The monitor displays program messages and the information you key. Data has not necessarily been stored in the computer when you see it on the screen, however. Pressing the appropriate keys or using the appropriate mouse movements will store the data in the computer's memory (the internal, "hard" disk drive) or on the disk inserted in the external "floppy" drive.

The Keyboard and The Mouse

The keyboard and the mouse provide the interface between the user and the microcomputer. Keyboard designs vary, but there are two basic categories: the 87 keyboard and the 101, or enhanced, keyboard, which appears in the illustrations throughout this book. The enhanced keyboard contains function keys, alphabetic and numeric keys, a numeric keypad, and a cursor movement keypad. As you progress through the sessions in the book, you will notice that for space reasons the illustrations usually show only the alphabetic, numeric, and function keys. Look at the illustration below and locate the corresponding sections on your keyboard:

A mouse is a piece of equipment that sits on a flat surface next to the computer and is used with the left or right hand. When using the mouse, there are three terms you should understand—click, double-click, and drag. *Click* means to press a button on the mouse quickly, then release it. *Double-click* or *click twice* means to press the button twice in quick succession. The term *drag* means to press a button, move the pointer to a specific location, then release the button.

If a mouse has been installed with WordPerfect, a mouse pointer will appear in the document window. The pointer changes appearance depending on the function being performed. When the mouse pointer is positioned in the editing window, it appears in the shape of an I-beam (I). This is referred to as the *I-beam pointer*. When the mouse pointer is moved to the Menu Bar, Toolbar, Power Bar, or Ruler Bar at the top of the WordPerfect document window, or to the scroll bars at the right side and bottom of the document window, the mouse pointer displays as an arrow (↖). In this text, this is referred to as the *mouse pointer*. The pointer also appears this way when a dialog box (a box containing command choices or options from which you are to choose) is displayed. For example, to open a new file in WordPerfect with the mouse, you would move the mouse pointer to the File option on the Menu Bar, position the tip of the pointer on the word "File," then click the left mouse button. On the drop-down menu that displays, you would position the tip of the arrow pointer on the desired option, then click the left mouse button. Dialog boxes requiring you to respond with the mouse will also display as part of the Paradigm Keyboarding program. If you have the opportunity, practice using the mouse in the WordPerfect editing window before you work with KWP.

SOFTWARE

The computer programs, or software, provide instructions for the computer on how to complete various functions. As mentioned earlier, the software you need has already been loaded into your computer's memory, including DOS, Windows, WordPerfect 6.1 for Windows, and Keyboarding with WordPerfect. DOS is the basic operating system; Windows provides a graphical (picture) user interface with a variety of software programs, including WordPerfect 6.1 and Keyboarding with WordPerfect. Windows programs are popular because their picture-based menus and features are easy to understand. Another advantage to learning Windows programs is that certain basic features such as opening, saving, and printing files operate the same from program to program.

Another similarity among Windows applications is that all Windows programs are centered around menus with choices (just like a restaurant menu) and dialog boxes (with questions and/or choices for giving more specific information to the program). The menus contain options that display in a list that "drops down" below the menu item when you click on that item.

Windows menus follow certain conventions, as listed below:

1. If an option is dimmed, it is unavailable at the present time.
2. Similar options are grouped and separated from the other options on the menu by horizontal lines.
3. Some menu options are called *toggle switches* because you toggle them on and off by selecting them. You will see a check mark on the left side of a toggle option when it has been turned on.
4. Some of the options are one-step commands.
5. Some options require additional steps, which is symbolized by the dots after the option. When one of these is selected, a dialog box appears so you can give Windows specific instructions.
6. Many options have a key you can press that allows you to execute the option directly, without going through the menu. These are called *hot keys* or *shortcut keys*. The major shortcut keys for WordPerfect 6.1 for Windows are included in the *User's Guide* that is packaged with this text.

PREPARING YOUR WORK ENVIRONMENT

A comfortable and well organized work environment is essential to efficient keyboarding. Your work station should contain only those items necessary for working on the sessions. Here's a checklist to review before you begin (refer to the following illustration as well) :

- ✔ Align the front of the keyboard with the desk's front edge.
- ✔ Adjust the monitor so your line of sight is 10-20 degrees below the horizontal.
- ✔ Adjust your chair so that you sit about 16 to 24 inches from the screen and your chair seat is 16-19 inches from the floor.
- ✔ Sit up straight, back against the chair, feet flat on the floor.
- ✔ Place your fingers on the keys in a curved position. Forearms and wrists should be as horizontal as possible. Do not rest your forearms on the keyboard!

WORKSTATION ERGONOMICS

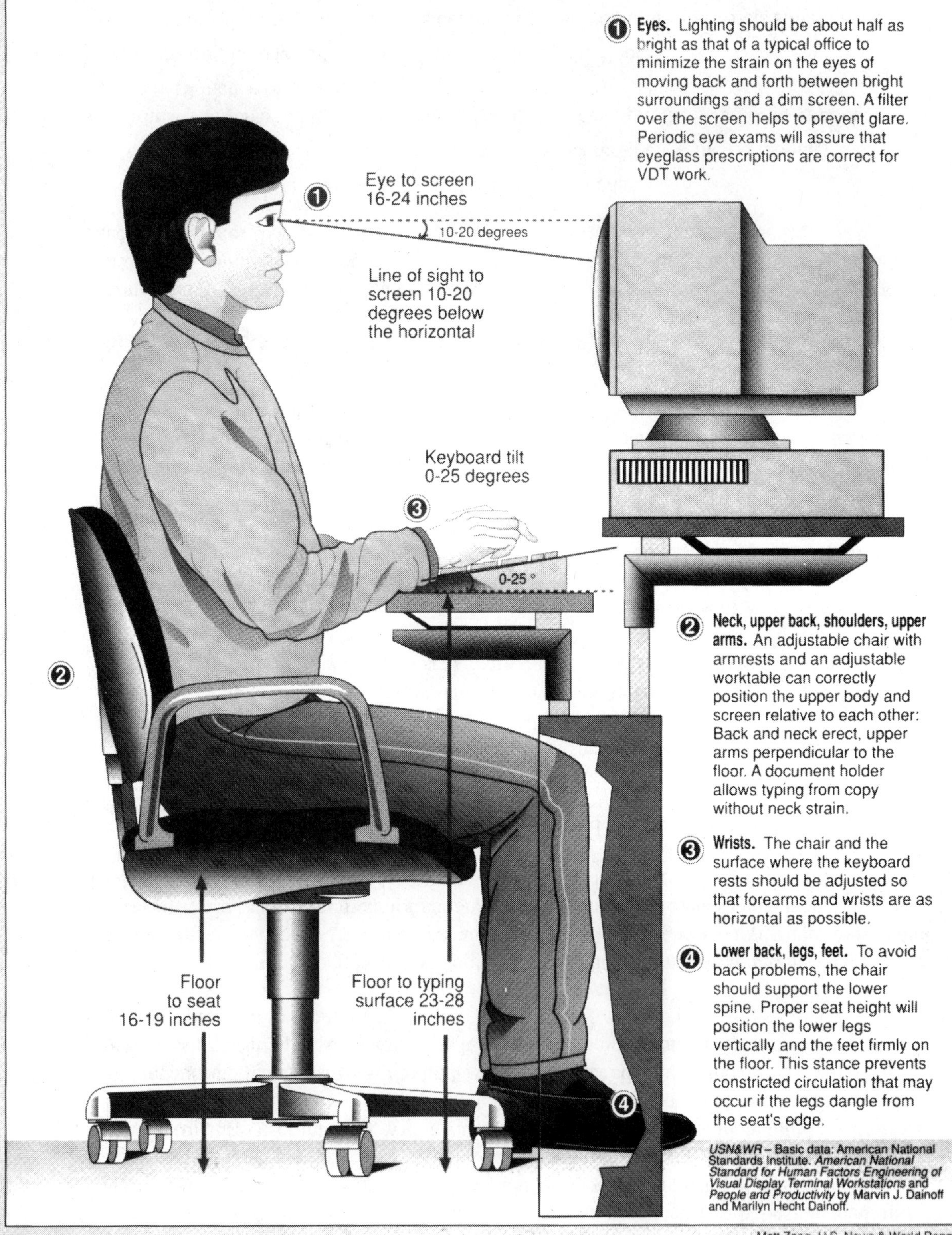

❶ **Eyes.** Lighting should be about half as bright as that of a typical office to minimize the strain on the eyes of moving back and forth between bright surroundings and a dim screen. A filter over the screen helps to prevent glare. Periodic eye exams will assure that eyeglass prescriptions are correct for VDT work.

❷ **Neck, upper back, shoulders, upper arms.** An adjustable chair with armrests and an adjustable worktable can correctly position the upper body and screen relative to each other: Back and neck erect, upper arms perpendicular to the floor. A document holder allows typing from copy without neck strain.

❸ **Wrists.** The chair and the surface where the keyboard rests should be adjusted so that forearms and wrists are as horizontal as possible.

❹ **Lower back, legs, feet.** To avoid back problems, the chair should support the lower spine. Proper seat height will position the lower legs vertically and the feet firmly on the floor. This stance prevents constricted circulation that may occur if the legs dangle from the seat's edge.

USN&WR – Basic data: American National Standards Institute. *American National Standard for Human Factors Engineering of Visual Display Terminal Workstations* and *People and Productivity* by Marvin J. Dainoff and Marilyn Hecht Dainoff.

Matt Zang, U.S. News & World Report

Your Position at the Machine

Before beginning to key, check your position at the workstation. After reading the suggestions above, adjust your position at the workstation so that you are comfortable.

ESSENTIAL PROGRAM COMMANDS AND FEATURES

Keyboarding with WordPerfect 6.1 for Windows is designed to operate easily, without the user having to memorize lots of commands. Dialog boxes and menus containing choices include specific directions for selecting an option. In addition, there are four basic program buttons that appear on the WordPerfect Toolbar:

- KWP Next Activity
- KWP Previous Menu
- KWP Main Menu
- KWP Student Report

The **KWP Next Activity** button allows you to move from activity type to activity type *within* a session as well as from a final session activity to the first activity of the next session. For example, if you already key at a basic level, you may not need to complete all the drills presented within a session. In that case, you could click on the KWP Next Activity button to move to WordPerfect Reinforcement or to the Timings. In another situation, you may have completed a session and have selected Freeform (WordPerfect itself) from the Main Menu to print your work. When you are finished, you would click on the Next Activity button to go to the next session.

The **KWP Previous Menu** button works as its name implies. You can use it to back up to a previous session menu or to return all the way to the Main Menu.

The **KWP Main Menu** button also has a name that probably requires little explanation. You will use it to access the Freeform option (WordPerfect by itself) for completing the WordPerfect Reinforcement activities and for printing session work. You also will use the Main Menu button whenever you want to exit the KWP program.

Clicking on the **KWP Student Report** button accesses the record of your individual timing scores, grouped by timing length. You can check your scores periodically to assess your progress. An important point to remember about this button as well as the other three buttons discussed is that the feature does not work if the program is requiring some other specific response (for example, a dialog box is displayed and the program is waiting for you to respond). However, once the response has been completed, the KWP buttons will function.

PROGRAM HINTS

At this point, you are ready to begin working in the program. Here are some hints to help you move smoothly and efficiently through the sessions:

- **To access the program, you must insert your data disk**. The program will not run without it. The first time you use the program, you will need a blank disk. Insert this disk before clicking on the KWP icon on the Toolbar to start the program. The program will then add your unique student information to the disk, which becomes your identification as far as the program is concerned. From then on, each time you sit down at the computer to access the program, insert your personal data disk before clicking on the KWP icon. You will probably also use this disk to store your work for this class (check with your instructor).
- **Generally, if you see a message telling you to click on OK, you can press Enter and get the same result.** Both options are available because at times, one choice is more efficient than the other.
- **Whenever a dialog box is displayed, you must respond to it before trying to execute another program command.**
- **All printing is done in WordPerfect (Freeform option on the Main Menu).**
- **All session work except for WordPerfect Reinforcement activities is named and saved automatically:**

  New-key drills and Thinking Drills are saved in a file called 000ses.kwp (where 000 is the session number, "ses" stands for session, and kwp stands for Keyboarding with WordPerfect). These are WordPerfect files that can be retrieved and printed.

  Timings are saved in a file called 000tim.kwp (where 000 is the session number, "tim" stands for timing, and kwp stands for Keyboarding with WordPerfect). Again, these are WordPerfect files.
- **Students save their own WordPerfect Reinforcement files, using a naming convention similar to those outlined above.**
- **Certain type conventions have been used in the text:**
  1) Command sequences are shown as follows: **File** → **Exit**, where the bolded letter is the letter WordPerfect shows underlined on the screen. the arrow indicates a drop-down menu, and the next command listed is the option to be selected from the drop-down menu.
  2) Key presses appear in bold italic type.
  3) Dialog box names, prompts, and filenames that appear on the screen are shown in italics.
  4) Command sequences the user keys are shown in bolded type.

UNIT

1

ALPHABETIC KEYS

HOME ROW, SPACE BAR, ENTER
CREATING A DOCUMENT

ASDF JKL;
Space Bar, Enter Key

Create, save, print a document
Insertion Point Keys and Mouse

GETTING STARTED

You will use *Keyboarding with WordPerfect* on a stand-alone microcomputer or on a local area network (LAN). Check with your instructor to find out which setup you will use. The software has already been installed for you.

If you are working on a networked computer, do the following:

1 Ask your instructor or LAN manager for instructions on accessing *Keyboarding with WordPerfect*.
2 Go to step 3 below.

If you are working on a stand-alone computer, do the following:

1 Turn on the computer and monitor.
2 At the Windows Program Manager screen, position the mouse pointer on the WordPerfect icon and double click the left mouse button. You will see the following screen:

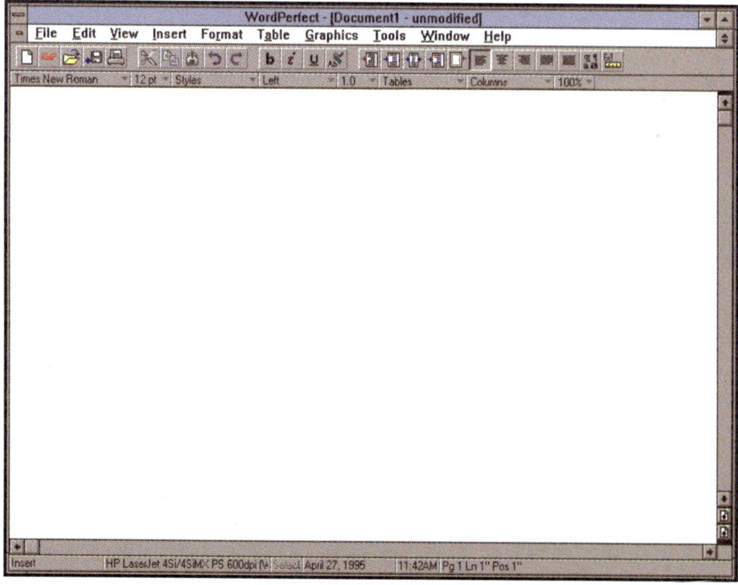

3 Insert a blank 3.5" or 5.25" disk into your floppy disk drive.
4 Click on the KWP button on the Toolbar.

Accessing the Internet

Essentially there are three ways to access the Internet. They are as follows:

1. The business, government agency, service organization, or educational institution has an access to the Internet and as an employee, you are given permission to use Internet.
2. You can subscribe to one of the on-line services such as *America Online*, *CompuServe*, and/or *Prodigy*. These on-line services offer access to applications such as Web connections, FTP, E-Mail, and NewsGroups. The user pays a monthly fee for a limited number of hours on the Net.
3. Companies are springing up throughout the country that provide Internet access to individuals that subscribe to their service. They generally provide a variety of plans based on monthly use.

Conclusion

The Internet is not static. Changes, applications, and the tools being used are constantly evolving. We must not forget that the Internet has a global impact. Never before in history have so many people been able to communicate in an instant with other people around the globe. The Internet brings meaning to the concept that the world is indeed becoming smaller.

Document D — *Evaluation of the Keyboarding Course*

Now that you have completed this keyboarding course, reflect on what you have learned and on how it was presented. At your keyboard, write an evaluation of the course and this textbook. Format it as a memo report to your instructor. Use headings to guide your reader through the report.

Describe what you have accomplished. Did you meet the learning objectives listed in the preface? If not, why? Discuss the strengths and weaknesses of the textbook and the software program. How could they be improved? Then, pick your favorite session or activity and explain why you liked it.

Save the file as **060wprd.kwp**. Then print it and close the file.

ENDING THE SESSION

Congratulations on completing this Keyboarding with WordPerfect course! If you need to print any Session 60 files, do so at this time. Be sure to turn in all required materials to your instructor. Then exit the program.

5 After the copyright screen appears, you will see the following screen:

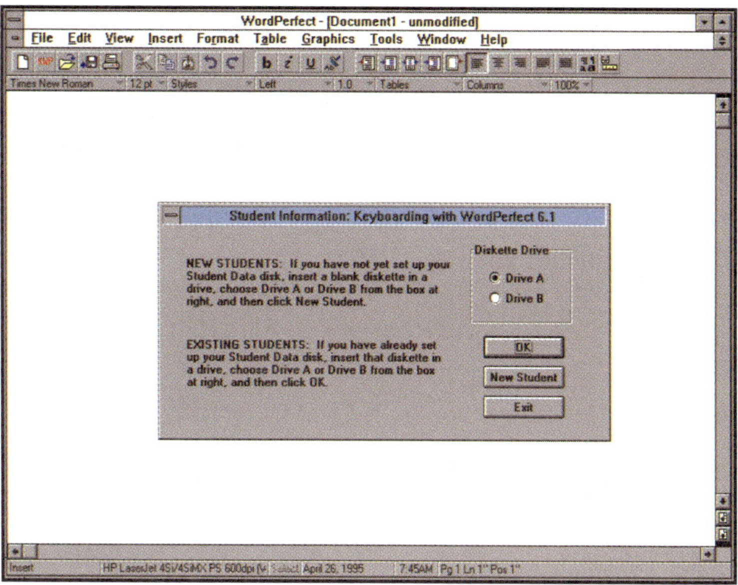

6 Click on New Student. (Hereafter, each time you access the program you will click on OK because you will have entered your Student Information previously.)

7 The following screen appears, asking you to enter your Student Information:

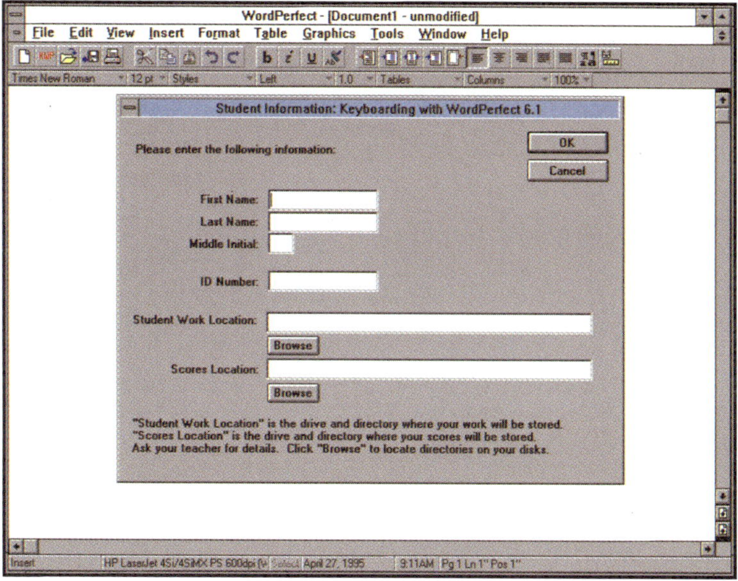

8 Key your name (first name, middle initial [with no period], and last name). Your name will appear in all capital letters.

9 Key your Student ID and any other information requested (ask your instructor if you are not sure what to include). Press ***Enter*** or click on OK.

10 Check the information again. If you need to make changes, follow the instructions on the screen. When all data is correct, click on OK. From now on, the program will add your name, the date, and the appropriate session number to your printed documents. ***Important:*** **Each time you access the *Keyboarding with WordPerfect* program, you must have your data disk ready to insert before clicking on the KWP button to start the program.**

that exceeded 10 trillion characters per month. There are those in the U.S. who look upon the Internet as our National Information Highway with global connections.
The World Wide Web

The Web adds another dimension to the Internet. Initially the Internet has been text based, full of words without pictures that seem dull to many potential users. The Web provides color, images, pictures and motion. Information on the Web is arranged in "pages" as you would expect to find in a magazine. These "pages" can include headlines, images, photos, text, illustrations, and graphics. A term that has evolved in conjunction with the Internet and the World Wide Web is "HomePage" - which can be created by businesses or individuals to provide a variety of information to anyone interested. The World Wide Web consists of four components:

1. The Web client is a multi platform, common presentation Internet navigator and information access front end.
2. The Hypertext publishing language HTML (Hypertext Markup Language) based on ASCII (American Standard Code for Information Interchange) is used for writing programs for the Web.
3. A common network communications protocol TCP/IP (Transmission Control Program/Internet Protocol) provides for an open system so that communication can take place between and among computers of different makes and models.
4. The Web server, which is an Internet-based distributed-processing system used for packaging and transferring files across the net.

Internet Tools/Applications

There are a variety of tools and applications used on the Internet. Browsers for getting around the net to obtain information come in two types: text based and GUI (Graphic User Interface) based. One example of a text-based browser is *Gopher*. Two examples of GUI browser are *Mosaic* and *Netscape*. List servers represent an application whereby individuals can subscribe to special interest topics and receive information related to that topic.

Newsgroups, another application, provide the user with an opportunity to search through information related to a particular topic without having to subscribe to that interest group. FTP (File Transfer Protocol) is a feature that allows individuals to up and download information from the Internet. For example, there are opportunities to obtain software programs available on the net (*shareware* and *freeware*). FTP provides the means to download programs to an individual's computer.

E-Mail (electronic mail) gives Internet user's the ability to send and receive messages to individuals and/or groups of people. All you need is to know the Internet addresses of those with whom you wish to communicate. Communicating via E-Mail puts people in touch wherever they are located without regard to geographic boundaries.

Continued on next page

11 The *Keyboarding with WordPerfect 6.1 for Windows* Main Menu displays with *Keyboarding Sessions* highlighted:

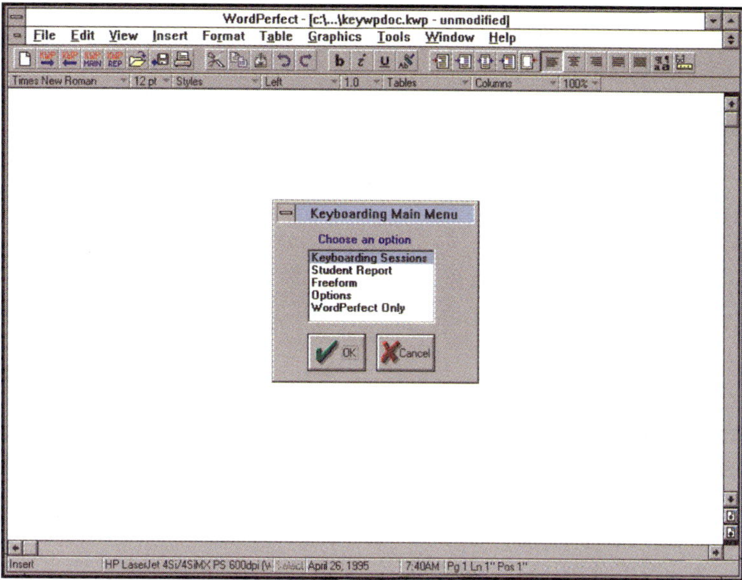

12 Click on OK to access the Keyboarding Sessions part of the program.
13 On the next screen the highlight is on *1-27 Keyboarding Introduction*. Click on OK.
14 The next menu appears with *1-13 Alphabetic Keys* highlighted. Click on OK.
15 The *Alphabetic Keys* menu appears with *1. Home Row, Space, Enter, WPR* highlighted. Click on OK.

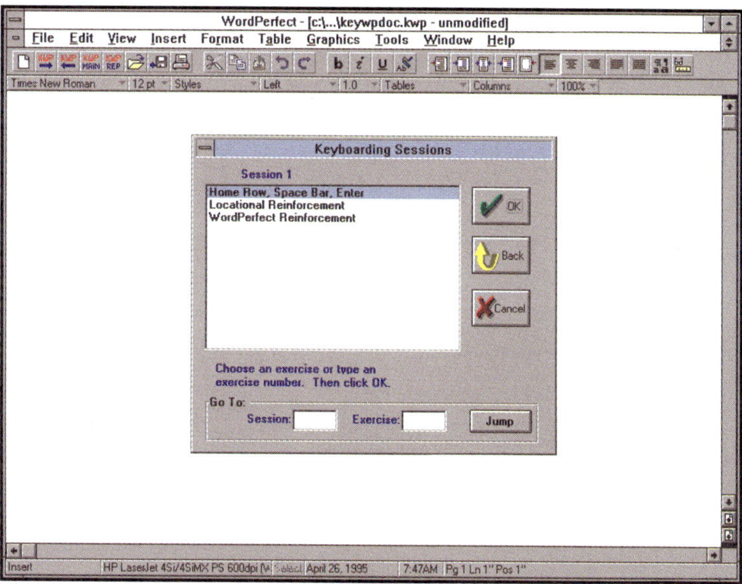

Now you are ready to begin the activities for Session 1. The software will guide you step by step through the session. You do not need the book for now. Follow the instructions on the screen until a message tells you to return to the book to complete the WordPerfect Reinforcement activities.

WORDPERFECT REINFORCEMENT

Welcome back! You have begun building your skill on the home keys, space bar, and Enter key. Everything you have keyed so far has been saved automatically in a WordPerfect file named

Document C ← Memorandum Report

1. At the *Production–Session 60 Document C* screen, key Document C as a memo report. Before you begin, review the document and plan the steps for formatting.
2. Proofread and correct any errors, then complete a spell check.
3. Click on Check to save, name **(060proc.kwp)**, and check the document.
4. To print the letter with errors highlighted, click on the Print button.
5. To correct errors highlighted by the KWP program, click on View Original. Make changes, then recheck the document.
6. Close the document.
7. Click on the KWP Next Activity button to bring up a clear WordPerfect document window.

Document C

current date

TO: Troy Ward
General Manager

Alex Hicks

BACKGROUND INFORMATION ON THE INTERNET

The Internet is a National Science Foundation network that evolved from Arpanet, a Defense Department network that linked computers in a variety of locations so that information could be disbursed. Internet is the largest, fastest growing network in the world thanks in part to the World Wide Web.

Internet Uses

Internet is a network of networks so that allows computer resources to be shared literally around the world. The network provides users with an opportunity to share ideas without regard to geographic location. People are able to "chat" with others from all stations in life and from a variety of cultures. Individuals use the Internet as a source of information, a means to communicate via electronic mail, and more recently as a means of advertising. The Internet is governed by the people and organizations who use it.

Background Data

Currently the Internet sends data up to 45 million bits per second. By 1993 the Internet consisted of 2 million host computers connected by 20,000 networks in 63 countries. The Internet is doubling in size every year. The average U.S. growth rate is 7.5 percent per month. There was a traffic volume on the Internet backbone in 1994

Continued on next page

001ses.kwp. Now you will review the Session 1 keys and learn how to create, save, and print your own WordPerfect document. Whenever you work on WordPerfect Reinforcement (WPR) activities, you will be using the Freeform option (WordPerfect 6.1 for Windows by itself). You can return to the Keyboarding with WordPerfect program at any time by clicking on the KWP Next Activity button on the Toolbar (the KWP button with the right-pointing arrow).

Creating a WordPerfect Document

With a clear WordPerfect editing window on your screen, you are now ready to create a document. The blinking vertical line in the upper-left corner (the *insertion point*, or the *cursor*) indicates where the first character you key will appear. The Status Bar across the bottom of the window indicates the mode (*Insert* is the default) , the printer you are using, the date and time, and the location of the insertion point (page 1, line 1 inch from the top of the page, position 1 inch from the left of the page). Watch the insertion point location information change as you enter text from the following pages.

Reviewing the Home Row Keys

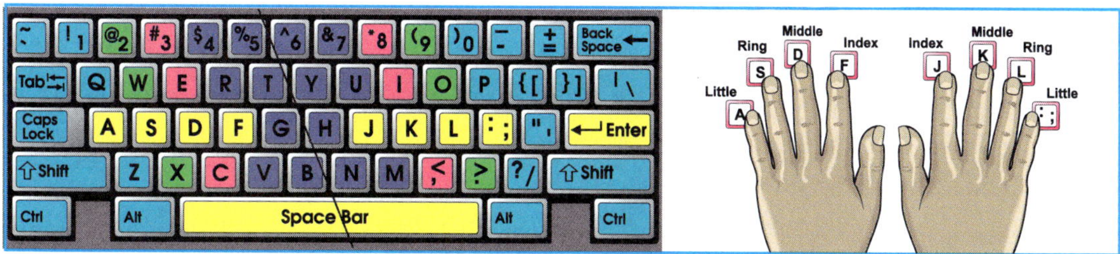

Fingers:

- Left hand on ASDF
- Right hand on JKL;
- Either left or right thumb on space bar
- Little finger of right hand for Enter

Home Row Drill

- Key each line once.
- Keep eyes on copy.
- Press ***Enter*** at the end of each line. Press ***Enter*** twice between groups of lines.
- Repeat any group of 3 lines if you need more practice.

1 a s d f j k l ; aa ss dd ff jj kk ll ;;
2 aa ss dd ff jj kk ll ;; asdf jkl; af j;
3 aaa sss ddd fff jjj kkk lll ;;; sd kl ;

4 a ad a ad add add adds adds a ad add ad
5 a as as a ask ask asks asks a all all a
6 ad add as asd a; a;as adds asls a;; ad

Document B ◄-- *Unbound Manuscript*

1 At the *Production–Session 60 Document B* screen, key Document B as an unbound manuscript. Format the document according to the guidelines presented in the Manuscripts and Reports unit. Be sure to read the document before you make any entries so you can plan how to format headings and verify proofreaders' marks. Think through the steps of formatting before you begin preparing the document.

2 Proofread and correct any errors, then complete a spell check.

3 Click on Check to save, name **(060prob.kwp)**, and check the manuscript.

4 To print the letter with errors highlighted, click on the Print button.

5 To correct errors highlighted by the KWP program, click on View Original. Make changes, then recheck the document.

6 Close the document.

Document B

STUDENT MEAL PLANS Many schools require that students who elect to stay in residence halls must also pay for a meal contract of some type. The meal plan is a contract which provides a student a certain number of meals per week for a particular price. Many institutions offer several different type meal plans. For example, it may be possible to contract for as many meals as 21 per seek. Or, the school also may offer an option whereby it is necessary to pay for as few as 15 meals per week. Regardless of the particular meal plan a student has available many students do not regard the food service at any particular institution too highly. It is quite common to hear a variety of complaints ranging from "the quality of the food is terrible," to "the times a day the meals are served are when I'm not hungry" It seems it is almost impossible to provide the quantity, quality and serving conditions to satisfy every individual. Most institutions allow professional food service companies to offer bids for providing food service to students. Usually, and perhaps this may be part of the problem, the contract is given to the lowest bidder. The service is contracted to the food service company for a certain number of years, usually two to five years. Providing food to students also provides a large number of jobs. Usually the contracting company hires many students as part-time workers. Although the pay is not the highest, it allows the students to earn enough money to help pay for their education. Recent market research suggests that educational institutions could improve their student meal systems by considering the current needs of their customers. For example, students are becoming increasingly knowledgeable about nutrition and health. Schools may need to offer a greater variety of food choices and more meals using fresh produce and low-fat meats. Although these changes may mean increased costs to the school, surveys report that students are willing to pay more if they think they will get higher-quality meals. Whatever direction institutions pursue regarding student meal plans, administrators and planners should bring all the players together to help plan the changes. Wide participation generally assures smooth implementation and acceptance.

7 fads fads fall fall falls falls fad fad

8 lass lass lad lad lads dad dads ask ask

9 falls flask alas fads dads asks all sad

Using the Insertion Point Movement Keys or the Mouse to Edit

The insertion point movement keys (also called the "arrow keys") are located to the lower-right of the alphabetic keyboard. Look for an up arrow, a down arrow, a right arrow, and a left arrow. You can use these insertion point keys to move to any place in the document where you want to edit (insert or delete) text. You can also use the mouse to move the insertion point. To position your insertion point with the mouse, move the ***I** beam* (I) to any place in the document and then click the left mouse button once to set the insertion point. Depending on the task, you will sometimes find the insertion point keys more efficient for positioning your insertion point. At other times, the mouse method will be more practical.

→	right arrow	Moves the insertion point to the right
←	left arrow	Moves the insertion point to the left
↑	up arrow	Moves the insertion point up, line by line
↓	down arrow	Moves the insertion point down, line by line

Remember: You cannot move the insertion point around on a blank screen—only within copy that has been keyed.

Key the following drill. Press ***Enter*** after each line.

DRILL

1 all all

2 sad sad dad dad

3 fad fad alas alas

4 fall fall lad lad add add

Now use the insertion point keys or the mouse to edit your copy (make changes):

1. Change the first *all* in line 1 to *fall*—position the insertion point on the letter *a* and enter the letter **f**.
2. Change the last *dad* in line 2 to *dads*—position the insertion point on the space following *dad* and enter an **s**.
3. Change the second *fad* in line 3 to *fads*.
4. Add an **s** to all the words in line 4.

Your edited copy should look like this:

1 fall all

2 sad sad dad dads

3 fad fads alas alas

4 falls falls lads lads adds adds

A last tip: Before beginning your design work, locate some examples that you like. Look at catalogs from paper makers and suppliers, letters you receive on letterhead you consider attractive and effective, magazines, television, and the world around you.

WP PRODUCTIVITY CHECK

Now that you have completed the instructional activities for creating memos, letters, reports, manuscripts, and tables, it is time to assess how accurately and quickly you can key these documents.

The goal for memos, letters, business reports, and manuscripts is 25 WAM or higher. The goal for tables is 15 WAM or higher. The time used in calculating your WAM rate for all types of documents includes the following:

- Formatting the document.
- Accessing the WordPerfect features.
- Keying the document.
- Correcting any errors.

The completed document must be "mailable." To reach the highest possible WAM rate, be sure to read the instructions for each document before you enter your first WordPerfect command or key any of the material because the clock starts when you strike the first key or click the mouse. If you are to prepare a simplified-style memo, a block-style letter, or an unbound manuscript, make sure you know the formatting elements and guidelines. If you are unsure, check your User's Guide or the appropriate sessions in the text for a quick review.

Document A — *Business Letter*

1. At the *Production–Session 60 Document A* screen, key Document A as a block-style letter. Insert the date automatically and center the letter on the page.
2. Proofread and correct any errors, then complete a spell check.
3. Click on Check to name (**060proa.kwp**), save, and check the letter.
4. To print the letter with errors highlighted, click on the Print button.
5. To correct errors highlighted by the KWP program, click on View Original. Make changes, then recheck the document.
6. Close the document.

Document A

Henry Vosen/Roseville Estates, Apartment 803/Charleston, SC 29402-4680/Dear Hank:/Here is a copy of the canceled check for the Sinclair Electric dividend of $54.44. Since the stock was sold prior to the dividend date, we must remit the payment to the proper owner of the stock. You already have a credit of $57.37 on your account. Therefore, you need only send us a check for $2.93./Hank, since this payment must also be reported on your income tax statement, it is important that you maintain a record of all dividends that you receive./We are always pleased to serve you./Sincerely, Robert E. Truax, President

Working with WordPerfect's Menu Bar

The Menu Bar located at the top of the document window provides you with drop-down menus that give you access to all WPWin features. To choose an option from the Menu Bar, position the mouse pointer (an arrow) on the desired option, then click the left mouse button. Another way to select options from the Menu Bar is to press the Alt key and then key the underlined letter of the desired option. Once you open a drop-down menu, you can access its options by keying only the underlined letters of menu choices or by positioning the mouse pointer on the item, then clicking the left button. In this and following sessions, you may choose Menu Bar options by using either the mouse or the Alt key along with the underlined letter. You can cancel any menu selection and return to the document window by pressing the Esc key one or more times.

Saving a WordPerfect Document

WordPerfect offers a number of ways to save a document :

- File → Save
- File → Save As (or F3)
- File → Close
- Save button on the Toolbar

Choosing either the Save As or Save options the first time a document is saved causes the Save As dialog box to display. WordPerfect then asks you to name the document. Thereafter, choosing the Save command or the Save button from the Toolbar automatically saves the document in the editing window (including any changes you have made) over the original document. If you use the **C**lose option (**F**ile → **C**lose) after creating a document, WordPerfect asks you if you want to save the document first. Assuming you selected the Yes response, you would name the document. Then it is saved and removed from the window. If you have not made any changes to the document since it was saved, you will not be asked if you want to save the document.

To save the material you have keyed in the WordPerfect Reinforcement section, complete the following steps:

1. Choose **F**ile → Save **A**s (or F3).
2. At the *Save As* dialog box, key the filename **001wpr.kwp** in the filename textbox. (Note that 001 is the session number, wpr stands for WordPerfect Reinforcement, and .kwp represents Keyboarding/WordPerfect). Press ***Enter***.

Note: You may key the filename in either uppercase or lowercase letters. WordPerfect displays the name in lowercase.

Naming Files

A WordPerfect document name can be from one to eight characters long. It can contain letters (uppercase or lowercase), numbers, or both. The document name cannot contain spaces. You can extend a name by adding a period (at the end) and up to three more characters (as you did in step 2 above). This is called an extension.

Recently, experts have found that the Crown-of-Thorns variety of starfish has endangered the coral reefs. This fish preys steadily on countless coral polyps. Some experts feel that subtle changes in the water temperature or minerals may have caused the influx of starfish. Regardless of the cause, scientists know that the starfish presents a real danger to the future survival of coral reefs. Experts hope that this underwater warfare will reverse and the reefs will survive.

FIVE -MINUTE TIMING

Goal: 35 WAM/1 error

SI: 1.54

- Take one 5-minute timing.

A letterhead creates an image for a business. It is possible to hire a person, or a design firm, to design a letterhead for you, or you may decide to use a computer to make your own. By making your own, you have the flexibility to make it a "true picture" of you and your firm. There are several things you should keep in mind while designing your letterhead.

Keep in mind that your letterhead will make a statement about your firm. It will give the reader vital data and also create an image in the reader's mind about your firm. Do you wish the reader to obtain the mental image that your firm is "solid as a rock and conservative"? Or, do you wish your firm to be seen as "active, flashy, and fast reacting"? You must decide.

Vital data that must be included on your letterhead is the name of your firm, the address, and phone and fax numbers. There are certain placement guidelines that should be followed regarding the name and address of a business. For example, the firm name, address, phone and fax numbers may be centered at the top of the page. Left- or right-justifying at the top of the page is also very popular. When displaying this data, you may simply block the lines or you may wish to be more creative and try such things as separating the data by bullets, clip art, and so on.

Many businesses have logos and slogans that may be used on the page. These two items may be placed anywhere on the page. A popular method to display a slogan is across the bottom of the page with the logo placed in the left- or right-hand side of the page.

You may wish to use different fonts when displaying your firm's data. Experts warn, however, to not use more than two fonts when designing your letterhead. Consider using both bold and plain fonts for variety. When picking fonts, keep in mind what image you are trying to present. Don't select a "flashy" type font if you are attempting to appear conservative.

The background design also has an impact on the reader. You should know what the background will be before beginning the design of your letterhead. Many people feel that the background and the paper used have more impact than the data contained in the letterhead. If you do select a background, make sure it is simple and does not "hide" the firm data. There is a large selection of preprinted design paper that you can buy on which to print your letterhead. The first step is to select your paper. Then design the letterhead.

Continued on next page

Printing a Document

Before you print, make sure you have saved the document. WordPerfect offers two ways to print a document:

- File → Print (or Ctrl-P or F5)
- Print button on the Toolbar

Choosing either of these options causes the Print dialog box to display with the name of the default printer at the top of the dialog box. You may print the full document or the current page. To print, you would point to the Print button with the mouse pointer and click the left mouse button or press ***Enter***. To print the document currently on your screen, do the following:

1. Choose **File** → **Print** (or F5). (You have already saved the file 001wpr.kwp.)
2. Press ***Enter*** or position the mouse pointer on the Print button, then click the left mouse button.
3. You should see a message box telling you that if you want the KWP program to print your name on the document, you must first save the file, then print using the Document on Disk option (explained below). If you print without first saving the file, you will need to write your name on the document.
4. You have already saved the file, so click on OK and continue with the printing process.

Printing previously saved files requires slightly different steps. To print the session activities you have completed up to WordPerfect Reinforcement (the KWP program has automatically saved them), do the following:

1. Choose **File** → **Print**.
2. At the *Print* dialog box, make sure the Document on Disk option is selected, then click on Print. (To select the option, position the arrow pointer on the option name or on the circle before it, then click the left mouse button once. A bullet should appear in the circle.)
3. At the *Document on Disk* dialog box, key the filename **001ses.kwp** in the filename box. (The file has already been named and saved by the *Keyboarding with WordPerfect* program.) Then press **Enter** or click on Print.

ENDING THE SESSION

If you want to continue with Session 2, do the following:

1. Click on the KWP Next Activity button on the Toolbar.
2. At the Session 2 menu, *Warm-Up* is highlighted. Click on OK (or highlight the next activity, then click on OK) and proceed with Session 2.

If you have finished the WordPerfect Reinforcement activities, or if you must leave your work station before completing the entire session, you should close any open documents (see above section) and then exit WordPerfect by doing the following:

1. Click on the KWP Main Menu button on the Toolbar.
2. At the Main Menu select WordPerfect Only, then click on OK.
3. Choose **File** → **Exit**.
4. You will see the Windows File Manager screen.
5. To exit Windows, click on **File**, then E**x**it. You should see a message saying *This will end your Windows session*. Click on OK.

SESSION 60

DOCUMENT PREPARATION PRODUCTIVITY CHECK

SESSION GOALS

3-Minute: 40 WAM/1 error
5-Minute: 35 WAM/1 error

Writing an assessment of the Keyboarding course

GETTING STARTED

If you are continuing immediately from Session 59, go to the three-minute timing. If you exited the program at the end of Session 59, do the following:

1. Access Windows, then WordPerfect 6.1 for Windows.
2. Click on the KWP icon to access *Keyboarding with WordPerfect.*
3. Go to the Keyboarding Sessions menu and click on Jump to return to your last activity. Or, access the Session 60 menu and click on OK to begin the session.

THREE-MINUTE TIMING

Goal: 40 WAM/1 error

SI: 1.50

- Take one 3-minute timing.

Nature lovers cannot find words that describe the strange beauty of a coral reef. These fragile and dainty aquatic kingdoms have been compared to colorful gardens; the sea animals are the flowers of this classic garden. The strangely eerie sights beneath the waters of the seas have made scientists gasp at the exquisite coral reef beauty.

Some reefs contain hundreds of varieties of coral. The warm and clear water is ideal for the continued healthy existence of all those small stony coral polyps. They are the architects of the coral reef. Others who live in this ocean world are countless invertebrates and a number of different species of fish. The creatures are beautiful and sometimes bizarre in appearance and can be seen in almost every shape and color to be imagined. Each of the tiny creatures has a different and unique form of protective gear. The sea urchin is well fortified with an arsenal of rock-like, blunt spines. The lionfish exudes some of the most powerful and poisonous venom in the world. The stonefish is a near-perfect replica of a rock; but when an unsuspecting fish is nearby, it is quickly captured by the stonefish.

Continued on next page

RIGHT SHIFT, H, LEFT SHIFT, COLON
CORRECTING ERRORS

SESSION GOALS

 **Left and Right Shift, H, Colon**

 **Correcting errors with Backspace and Typeover Using the Mouse, QuickCorrect**

GETTING STARTED

If you are continuing immediately from Session 1, the first item on the Session 2 Menu should be highlighted. Since your fingers are already warmed up, highlight the next activity and click on OK to begin.

If you exited the program at the end of Session 1, do the following:

1. At the Windows Program Manager screen, position the mouse arrow on the WordPerfect icon and double-click the left mouse button.
2. At the WordPerfect editing window, click on the KWP button on the Toolbar.
3. The Student Information screens will appear. Click on OK to move to the Main Menu. ***Note:*** These screens will display each time you access the program.
4. At the *Keyboarding with WordPerfect Main Menu*, the *Keyboarding Sessions* item should be highlighted. Click on OK or press ***Enter***.
5. Now you have two options: (1) you can move through the program until you reach the next session's menu, then click on OK to begin the first activity; or (2) click on Jump to go to your previous location. (Note that the session number and exercise in which you last worked are displayed at the bottom of the *Keyboarding Sessions* menu.)

The program will guide you step by step through the remainder of your current session. When you have completed the on-screen keyboarding instruction, you will see a message telling you to return to the book to do the WordPerfect Reinforcement activities.

Remember: You can click on the KWP Next Activity button (KWP with right-pointing arrow) on the Toolbar to move from one activity type to the next. Or, use the KWP Previous Menu button (KWP with left-pointing arrow) to move backwards through the program menus.

WORDPERFECT REINFORCEMENT

With a clear editing window on your monitor, you will now key some of the same drill lines you keyed earlier. You will work in WordPerfect exclusively to review the key reaches presented during the first part of Session 2. In addition, you will learn several ways to correct errors. The basic skills of saving and printing documents will be reinforced in this section and in the WordPerfect Reinforcement activities throughout the text.

Document D

NORTHWEST PRODUCTS STORE QUARTERLY PROFITS					
Store	**First Qtr.**	**Second Qtr.**	**Third Qtr**	**Fourth Qtr.**	**Total**
Seattle	$32,438.96	$23,483.20	$31,249.45	$34,239.43	
Portland	$19,945.00	$20,435.75	$21,349.60	$23,423.50	
Sacramento	$42,120.46	$41,284.57	$40,342.84	$44,293.90	
Boise	$25,394.55	$20,345.20	$17,345.90	$25,394.00	

ENDING THE SESSION

To end this session, DELETE outdated WordPerfect Reinforcement files, PRINT any files from Session 59 not printed earlier, then CONTINUE with the next session or EXIT the program.

WordPerfect's QuickCorrect

QuickCorrect is a new WordPerfect feature that automatically replaces some common spelling errors and miskeyed words. For example, if you key *teh* and then press the space bar, QuickCorrect changes *teh* to *the.* QuickCorrect can also be used to automatically correct sentence problems such as initial double uppercase and double spacing between words.

To view the QuickCorrect feature, do the following:

1. Choose **T**ools → **Q**uickCorrect (or Ctrl-Shift-F1).
2. At the *QuickCorrect* dialog box, view the words that QuickCorrect will replace. If you want to turn off QuickCorrect, remove the X from the *Replace Words as You Type* option.
3. Choose **C**lose to return to your document.

Note: The QuickCorrect feature is disabled during drills and timings, but is functional when you work in Freeform or in WordPerfect Only.

Correcting Errors

Here are two ways to correct any keying errors you might make as you complete WordPerfect Reinforcement activities:

Backspace: deletes characters as you backspace over them.

Typeover: replaces text letter by letter at the insertion point position. This feature is turned on and off when you press Insert. (This is referred to as a toggle key.)

Correcting with Backspace

Move the insertion point to the right of the letter you want to correct. Press the ***Backspace*** key to delete the letter, then key the correct letter.

To practice correcting with the Backspace key, do the following:

1. Key **saf**.
2. Press the ***Backspace*** key to delete **f**.
3. Key the letter **d**.
4. Press the ***space bar***, then key **lasd**.
5. Press the ***Backspace*** key to delete the **d**.
6. Key the letter **s**.
7. Press the ***space bar***, then key **flasd**.
8. Press the ***Backspace*** key to delete the **d**.
9. Key the letter **k**. Press ***Enter.***

Your line should now look like this:

sad lass flask

Correcting with Insert/Typeover

By default, Insert is on. This means that anything you key is inserted in the text rather than keyed over existing text. If you want to insert or add text, leave Insert on. If, however; you want to key over something, turn Insert off by pressing the ***Insert*** key (located in the cluster above the insertion point movement keys). When you press ***Insert***, the message *Typeover* appears at the bottom left corner of the status line. Typeover stays in effect until you press the ***Insert*** key again or until you exit WordPerfect.

Document C

The Reasons Businesses Use Temporary Secretarial Help	
Reasons	***Usage***
Peak load periods	86.50%
Temporary replacement	48.60%
Vacation replacement	70.30%
One-time projects	54.10%
Specialized work	27.00%
Possible permanent recruitment	18.90%
Lower employee costs	10.80%
Less paper work	2.70%

Document D *Six-Column Table with Column Headings and Formula*

1 At a clear WordPerfect document window, create a table with 6 columns and 6 rows.
2 Join cells A1 through F1.
3 Change the Justification to Center for cell A1, the Appearance to Bold and Small Cap, and the Size to Large.
4 Select cells A2 through F2, then change the Justification to Center and the Appearance to Bold. With cells A2 through F2 still selected, add 10% fill and change the top and bottom lines to Double.
5 Select cells B3 through F6, then change the number type to Currency. With cells B3 through F6 still selected, change the Justification to Right.
6 Add a Shadow border to the table.
7 Key the text in the cells as shown in Document D. (Do not key the dollar signs; these are automatically inserted when you move the insertion point to another cell.)
8 Insert the formula **sum(b3:e3)** in cell F3 and then copy the formula down 3 times.
9 Center the table horizontally on the page.
10 Center the table vertically.
11 Proofread and correct any errors and then complete a spell check.
12 Choose **F**ile → Save **A**s, then key **059wprd.kwp** as the filename.
13 Choose **F**ile → **C**lose to close the document.

To practice correcting with the Typeover feature, do the following:

1. Key the following line:
   Sad All Asks Dads Fads Alas Flask Falls
2. Press the ***Insert*** key. (The message *Typeover* appears in the lower left corner of the window.)
3. Change the uppercase *S* in *Sad* to a lowercase *s*. To do this, move the insertion point with either the mouse or the left arrow key to the *S* and key **s**.
4. Change the remaining uppercase letters to lowercase.
5. Turn Insert back on (Typeover off) by pressing the ***Insert*** key.

Your line should now look like this:

sad all asks dads fads alas flask falls

Reviewing the Right Shift, H, Left Shift, and Colon Keys

Remember: The right shift key is used to make capital letters that are keyed with the left hand, and the left shift key is used to make capitals that are keyed with the right hand.

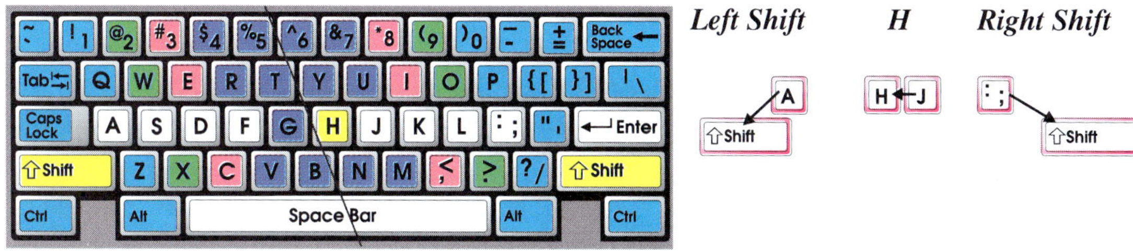

Drill Instructions

- Key each line once.
- Press ***Enter*** at the end of each line.
- Key the appropriate group of lines again if you need more practice.

Right Shift Drill

1 Ad All Asks Adds Alas All Ask As Add Ad

2 Fad fad Falls falls Fall fall Fads fads

3 Sad All Asks Dads Fads Alas Flask Falls

H Drill

1 jh hall hall hall sash sash has sash jh

2 half half half lash lash lash half lash

3 Dads sash Falls Shall Shall Flash Flash

Document B

Overseas Long-Distance Telephone Rates		
Country	***Station-to-Station***	***Person-to-Person***
Australia	$9.75	$13.00
France	$8.50	$12.00
Germany	$6.50	$11.75
Italy	$5.95	$10.50
Japan	$9.50	$13.25
Philippines	$9.50	$13.25
United Kingdom	$5.25	$10.00

Document C — *Two-Column Table with Column Headings*

1 At a clear WordPerfect document window, create a table with 2 columns and 10 rows.
2 Change the justification to Center for column B.
3 Join cells A1 and B1.
4 Change the Justification to Center for cell A1, the Appearance to Bold and Shadow, and the Size to Large.
5 Select cells A2 and B2, then change the Justification to Center and the Appearance to Bold and Italic.
6 Select cells B3 through B10, then change the number type to Percent.
7 Key the text in the cells as shown in Document C. (Do not key the zeros after the decimal point or the percent sign; these are automatically inserted when you move the insertion point to another cell.)
8 Center the table horizontally on the page.
9 Adjust the width of each column by decreasing and/or increasing the width so the text just fits the columns as shown in Document C.
10 Center the table vertically.
11 Remove all lines in the table.
12 Proofread and correct any errors and then complete a spell check.
13 Choose **F**ile → Save **A**s, then key **059wprc.kwp** as the filename.
14 Choose **F**ile → **C**lose to close the document.

Left Shift and Colon Drill

- Shift of semi (;) key produces a colon (:).
- When keying documents, press space bar once after keying a colon.

1 jJ kK lL ;: Jj Kk Ll ;: JL; jK lL :;:; KL

2 Had; Lad; Has; Lass; Half: Lads: Hall:

3 Lass Lad Lads Flask: All: Sad: Lads:

Saving a Document

As you learned in Session 1, you can save a document in WordPerfect by using the File, Save As sequence or the F3 function key. To save the WordPerfect Reinforcement activities you have just completed, do the following:

1. Choose **F**ile → Save **A**s (or F3).
2. At the *Save As* dialog box, in the filename textbox, key **002wpr.kwp** (002 for Session 2, wpr for WordPerfect Reinforcement, and .kwp for Keyboarding with WordPerfect). Press ***Enter***. Your document has been saved to disk, and it also remains on the screen.

ENDING THE SESSION

At the end of each KWP session, you have three options:

- Print any documents you have created.
- Continue with the next session.
- Exit KWP, WordPerfect, and Windows.

PRINT If the document is on the screen:

1. Click on the Print button in the Toolbar or choose **F**ile → **P**rint.
2. At the *Print* dialog box, click on **P**rint.
3. Close the document (**F**ile → **C**lose).

If you want to print previously saved files:

1. At a clear editing window, choose **F**ile → **O**pen.
2. With the mouse, click on the name of the file to be printed.
   Note: You can use the mouse pointer and the Ctrl key together to highlight more than one filename. Press the ***Ctrl*** key as you click on each filename to be printed.
3. Choose File **O**ptions → **P**rint.
4. At the *Print File* dialog box, click on **P**rint.
   Note: If you had highlighted several files to be printed, you would see the question, *Do you want to print the selected files?* Click on **P**rint to print the whole group.
5. Click on Cancel (or press ***Esc***) to close the *Open File* dialog box.

Document A

Care Units *Sacred Heart Hospital*	
Floor	***Type of Care***
Second floor	Neurological
Third floor	Maternity
Fourth floor	Psychiatry
Fifth floor	Medical
Sixth floor	Surgical
Seventh floor	Pediatrics
Eighth floor	Orthopedics
Ninth floor	Rehab/Medical

Document B — *Three-Column Table with Column Headings*

1. At a clear WordPerfect document window, create a table with 3 columns and 9 rows.
2. Change the Justification to Center for columns A, B, and C.
3. Join cells A1 through C1.
4. Change the Appearance to Bold and the size to Large for Cell A1. Add 10% fill.
5. Select cells A2 through C2, then change the Appearance to Bold and Italic. Change the bottom line of the selected cells to Double.
6. Select cells B3 through C9, then change the number type to Currency.
7. Add a Thick/Thin 2 border to the table.
8. Key the text in the cells as shown in Document B. (Do not key the dollar sign; it is added automatically when you move the insertion point to another cell.)
9. Center the table horizontally on the page.
10. Adjust the width of each column by decreasing and/or increasing the width so the text just fits the columns as shown in Document B. (Do not let the column headings wrap.)
11. Center the table vertically.
12. Proofread and correct any errors and then complete a spell check.
13. Choose **File** → Save **A**s, then key **059wprb.kwp** as the filename.
14. Choose **File** → **C**lose to close the document.

CONTINUE

1. Print and close files.
2. If you are currently working in Freeform (WordPerfect Reinforcement), click on the KWP Next Activity button to go to the next session menu. Highlight the desired activity and click on OK to begin.

EXIT

1. Print any files, if necessary.
2. Click on the KWP Main Menu button on the Toolbar.
3. At the Main Menu, select WordPerfect Only, then click on OK.
4. Click on **F**ile → E**x**it.
5. Exit Windows, if necessary (**F**ile → E**x**it).

disease can be spread by airborne spores; a bird, insect, or animal can also carry the parasite. The elm disease is spread by spores also but is only carried by a species of beetle.

A major hope for both types of trees remains in chemical prevention and biological strains. On test plots, the use of chemicals has been quite successful; however, when tested in the major forest areas of our land, chemicals have not been so successful. At this time, control of the diseases seems to offer the best answer to the problem.

For the long term, homeowners should think about preventing mass tree loss by planting a variety of tree types. Certain diseases affect only some species. Thus, if you grow a wide range of trees, your landscape will not have huge holes if an illness invades one species. Pick trees that are hardy in the city as well as on the land.

WP PROGRESS CHECK

You have now completed the activities teaching you how to create a variety of tables using WordPerfect 6.1 for Windows. At this point, you have the opportunity to assess your ability to create this type of production document.

Key each of the following documents as quickly as possible, correcting all your errors. Each document should be "mailable." In other words, when you finish each document, it should contain no errors. It is your responsibility to review each table before it is formatted and keyed to determine column alignment, appearance, number type, and any other formatting considerations.

Your goal is to key tables that are centered vertically and horizontally, correctly formatted, and with all errors corrected at 15 WAM (1.5 lines a minute) or higher. Access the timer by clicking on WAM Only at the bottom of the screen. The timing starts as you begin keying the first line of the table (the heading) and ends when the table is saved (corrections have been made and the spelling check has been completed). Click on Stop WAM to stop the timer.

If your document production rate is below 15 WAM (1.5 LAM) and/or your are missing errors that should have been corrected, your instructor may ask you to repeat one or more of the tables.

Document A — *Two-Column Table with Column Headings*

1. At a clear WordPerfect document window, create a table with 2 columns and 10 rows.
2. Change the Justification to Center for columns A and B.
3. Join cells A1 and B1.
4. Change the Appearance to Bold and Italic and the Size to Very Large for Cell A1.
5. Select cells A2 and B2, then change the Appearance to Bold and Italic and the size to Large.
6. Key the text in the cells as shown in Document A.
7. Center the table horizontally on the page.
8. Adjust the width of each column by decreasing and/or increasing the width so the text just fits the columns as shown in Document A.
9. Center the table vertically.
10. Proofread and correct any errors and then complete a spell check.
11. Choose **File** → Save **A**s, then key **059wpra.kwp** as the filename.
12. Choose **File** → **C**lose to close the document.

PERIOD, T, COMMA, CAPS LOCK
OPENING DOCUMENTS, USING THE CURSOR KEYS

SESSION GOALS

 **Period, T, Comma, Caps Lock**

 **Open a document on disk**
Use insertion point keys

 **Descriptive Words**

GETTING STARTED

If you are continuing immediately from Session 2, the first item on the Session 3 Menu should be highlighted. Since your fingers are already warmed up, highlight the next activity and click on OK to begin.

If you exited the program at the end of Session 2, do the following:

1. At the Windows Program Manager screen, position the mouse arrow on the WordPerfect icon and double-click the left mouse button.
2. At the WordPerfect editing window, click on the KWP button on the Toolbar.
3. At the Student Information screens, click on OK.
4. At the *Keyboarding with WordPerfect Main Menu*, the *Keyboarding Sessions* item should be highlighted. Click on OK or press ***Enter***.
5. Now you have two options: (1) you can move through the program menu to menu until you reach the next session's menu, then click on OK to begin the first activity; or (2) click on Jump to go to your previous location. (Note that the session number in which you last worked is displayed at the bottom of the *Keyboarding Sessions* menu.)

The program will guide you step by step through the remainder of your current session. When you have completed the on-screen keyboarding instruction, you will see a message telling you to return to the book to do the WordPerfect Reinforcement activities.

Remember: You can click on the KWP Next Activity button on the Toolbar to move from one activity type to the next. Or, use the KWP Previous Menu button to move backwards through the program menus.

WORDPERFECT REINFORCEMENT

In Sessions 1 and 2 you learned how to save and print a document in WordPerfect. In this session you will practice opening a previously saved document and resaving it to your data disk. In addition, you will review the key reaches presented during the first part of Session 3. You will use WordPerfect exclusively for the remainder of Session 3.

THREE-MINUTE TIMING

Goal: 40 WAM/1 error

SI: 1.51

- Take one 3-minute timing.

When using binoculars, try to rest the elbows on a firm surface to steady the glasses. A telescope is fairly simple to learn to use. Many telescopes are equipped with a finder. The finder will assist you in focusing on the portions of the sky that you wish to study. Adjusting a finder is a quite simple maneuver. With little practice, you can become an expert at using all types of optical equipment. An image will sometimes seem to shimmer. Any shimmering effect could be due to the fact that you jarred the telescope tube or binoculars; the effect may also be due to a turbulence or an atmospheric disturbance. You will soon discover that the best nights for viewing and observing the stars are those nights when the temperatures have remained fairly steady for several nights.

Within our own galaxy, you can observe many beautiful sights. A lovely domain that you can admire is the satiny stars. It is easy to see all sorts of patterns in the heavens if you simply relax and turn your imagination loose. You can obtain diagrams with which to study, observe, and chart the various star patterns. If you have the equipment to look beyond our own galaxy, you will be able to observe stars and galaxies far out into space. An observatory is a marvelous place to observe the heavens. The starry displays and changing seasons are not to be missed by an astronomer. You can develop a very fine hobby through star-gazing if you care to take the time.

FIVE-MINUTE TIMING

Goal: 35 WAM/1 error

SI: 1.52

- Take one 5-minute timing.

Many of the beautiful and stately elm trees that have covered our huge nation for several decades are in trouble. Spreading chestnut trees, common a few years ago, no longer populate the forests of our nation. Both magnificent species have been the victims of fungal parasites that have invaded our lands. At first, halting the diseases seemed to be quite impossible, but now the prospects are excellent that the ravaging and destructive blight can be arrested. The future of both species seems to look very much brighter.

The bark disease, or chestnut blight, was first discovered on an eastern site in the early nineteen hundreds. Within but a few years, the parasites had spread throughout the entire eastern coastal states and damaged trees. The Dutch elm disease was brought into our nation in the nineteen thirties. Within a period of 45 years, great numbers of mature elm trees have been destroyed throughout the entire nation. Although the two blights are quite similar, there is a major difference. The chestnut

Continued on next page

Opening a Document

After a document has been saved to disk, you may want to bring it back to the screen to add more text, review the document, or make corrections. To open the WordPerfect document you created in Session 2, complete the following steps:

1 Choose **F**ile → **O**pen (or F4 or Ctrl-O).
2 You should see a list of names of saved documents in the left side of the *Open File* dialog box.

Note: If you cannot locate your document, check the *Drives* box located in the lower right and make sure the drive listed in the box is the same drive where you saved your documents.

The *Open File* dialog box lists all documents saved on the disk (or directory) in alphabetic (or numeric) order. If you highlight a filename by clicking on the document name with the mouse pointer, the date and time the document was created (or last edited) and the size of the file is displayed in the lower-left corner of the dialog box.

3 Position the mouse pointer on the filename *002wpr.kwp* and click the left button to highlight the file.
4 Press ***Enter*** or click on OK to open the file.

Note: You can also double-click (two clicks in quick succession) with the left mouse button on the filename to open the file.

5 With the document in the window, use your insertion point keys to move up, down, to the right, and to the left through the text. When you hold the insertion point key down, the insertion point moves very quickly through the document.

Note: You may also use the mouse to reposition the insertion point. Move the mouse pointer to the desired location and click the left mouse button once.

6 Move the insertion point to the end of the document. Now you can either leave the document as is or add or change copy and then resave the file. You will add the text keyed in this section and then save the entire document as a new file. Move the insertion point to the end of the document and position it at the left margin on a new line before you begin keying the following activities. (You may have to press the ***Enter*** key.)

Reviewing the Period, T, Comma, and Caps Lock Keys

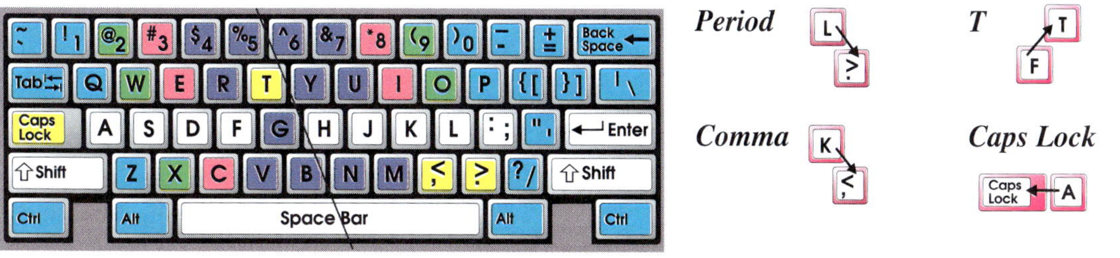

Drill Instructions

- Key each line once.
- If you are not comfortable with a reach, repeat the appropriate group of two lines.

SESSION 59

PRODUCTION PROGRESS CHECK
TABLES

SESSION GOALS

1-Minute: 45 WAM/1 error
3-Minute: 40 WAM/1 error
5-Minute: 35 WAM/1 error

Review of Table feature

GETTING STARTED

If you are continuing immediately from Session 58, go to the one-minute timing. If you exited the program at the end of Session 58, do the following:

1. Access Windows, then WordPerfect 6.1 for Windows.
2. Click on the KWP icon to access *Keyboarding with WordPerfect.*
3. Go to the Keyboarding Sessions menu and click on Jump to return to your last activity. Or, access the Session 59 menu and click on OK to begin the session.

ONE-MINUTE TIMING

Goal: 45 WAM/1 error

SI: 1.52

- Take a 1-minute timing on the following material.
- Use your most recent timing speed to set a speed or accuracy goal.

There is a trend away from the office of today as we know it. The growth of the newer and more efficient office is a result of five trends. First, many businesses are dividing their work tasks into smaller, more cost-effective units. Second, because all firms are pushing to cut costs, the size of the space given to each worker has been reduced. Third, the number of laws and rules for larger firms has grown rapidly. Fourth, firms are cutting their size by doing something called corporate downsizing. This trend results in more people being out of work. The fifth trend is a growing sense of people that the idea of working for oneself may be better than working for a large firm. All these trends, along with the rapid rise in technology, have led to new forms of the office.

Period Drill

Important: Tap the space bar **once** after the period at the end of a sentence. Only one space is required when you use a proportionally spaced font such as the WordPerfect default, Times New Roman. (Proportionally spaced means each character is designed relative to the other letters. The i, for example, is narrower than the t or the r. On the other hand, characters in monospaced fonts such as Courier each take up the same amount of space.)

WordPerfect's QuickCorrect feature can be set to automatically correct the end-of-sentence spacing to either one or two spaces by choosing **T**ools → **Q**uickCorrect → **O**ptions, and selecting the desired "radio" button in the *End of Sentence Corrections* box. **For this text, unless instructed otherwise, enter one space after a period or other sentence-ending punctuation.**

Note: If a period ends a line, press ***Enter*** immediately. There is no need to tap the space bar.

1 All lads shall dash. A lad shall fall.
2 Ask a sad lad. Sad lads fall. Ask Al.

T Drill

1 ft at hat hats sat sat tall tall data data
2 fast fast slat slat halt halt last last

Comma Drill

Remember: Do not space before a comma, but always space once after a comma (except when keying numbers).

1 That tall, fat, fast lad shall ask dad.
2 A flat, half lath falls; all lads halt.

Caps Lock Drill

1 STALK A FAST LAD; A SAD LAD HAS A FALL.
2 DAD HALTS A TALL LAD. A SAD LAD HALTS.

Building Speed with Control

Your mind controls your fingers, so think **speed.** After you practice setting your "mind" goal several times, you should find that your mind eventually controls your fingers automatically.

Key lines 1–3 once. Key lines 1–3 again as fast as you can.

1 Stalk a fast lad; a sad lad has a fall.
2 A lad talks; a lass talks; a dad talks.
3 Dad halts a tall lad. A sad lad halts.

c. At the *Copy Formula* dialog box, choose **D**own.
d. Key **4**.
e. Choose OK or press ***Enter***.

10 Center the table vertically. (Do this at the *Center Page(s)* dialog box.)
11 Proofread and correct any errors and then complete a spell check.
12 Choose **F**ile → Save **A**s, key **058wprd.kwp**, then choose OK.
13 Choose **F**ile → **C**lose to close the document.

Document D

Spreadsheet Activities					
Name	***Act. 1***	***Act. 2***	***Act. 3***	***Act. 4***	***Average***
Hausmann	88.00%	79.50%	91.00%	87.50%	
Lowe	73.50%	68.00%	82.50%	77.00%	
Montgomery	98.00%	95.50%	90.00%	88.00%	
Reynolds	72.00%	69.00%	83.50%	75.00%	
Waterson	85.00%	82.50%	90.00%	91.50%	

ENDING THE SESSION

To end this session, DELETE outdated WordPerfect Reinforcement files, PRINT any files from Session 57 not printed earlier, then CONTINUE with the next session or EXIT the program.

Using Page Up, Page Down, Home, and End Keys

In addition to the arrow keys that move one line or space at a time, the Page Up and Page Down keys can be used to speed movement through a document. They are located directly above the arrow keys.

Note: The same keys are included on the 10-key pad. However, the Num Lock key must be off to use them.

1. The ***Page Up*** key moves the insertion point backward through the document one window of text at a time.
2. The ***Page Down*** key moves the insertion point forward through the document one window of text at a time.
3. The ***End*** key moves the insertion point to the end of the line on which it is currently located.
4. The ***Home*** key moves the insertion point to the beginning of the line on which it is currently located.

Ctrl + Home	Moves to the beginning of the document.
Ctrl + End	Moves to the end of the document.
Page Up	Moves to the top of the window.
Page Down	Moves to the bottom of the window.
Alt + Page Up	Moves to the first line on the previous page.
Alt + Page Down	Moves to the first line on the next page.
Ctrl + →	Moves to the beginning of the next word.
Ctrl + ←	Moves to the beginning of the previous word.
Ctrl + ↑	Moves up one paragraph.
Ctrl + ↓	Moves down one paragraph.

5. Practice moving the insertion point around the window for the activities you have completed in Session 3.

Note: Remember that you can also use the mouse to reposition the insertion point. Move the mouse pointer to the desired location and click the left mouse button once to move the insertion point to a new position.

Saving WordPerfect Reinforcement Activities

Before you leave Session 3, you need to save the text you have keyed during WordPerfect Reinforcement. To save this document, do the following:

1. Choose **F**ile → Save **A**s (or F3).
2. At the *Save As* dialog box, the filename *002wpr.kwp* is displayed in the filename textbox (this is the document you opened and added text to).
3. Key the new filename, **003wpr.kwp**. Press ***Enter*** or click on OK. Your document is saved to disk, and it also remains on the screen. Now you have the previous document, *002wpr.kwp*, on disk as well as the new document, *003wpr.kwp*, which combines the old file and the new material.

Note: If you wanted to replace the existing file with the new one, you would press ***Enter*** at the *Save As* dialog box **without** keying a new filename. When the prompt, *Document already exists. Do you want to replace it?* appears, you would key **Y** or click on the Yes button to replace the existing file with the new document.

14 Center the table vertically. (Do this at the *Center Page(s)* dialog box.)
15 Proofread and correct any errors and then complete a spell check.
16 Choose **File** → Save **A**s, key **058wprc.kwp**, then choose OK.
17 Choose **File** → **C**lose to close the document.

Document C

Sales Account			
Company Name	***Salesperson***	***Total Sales***	***Commission***
DiJon's	Smythe	$15,000.00	
Miss A's	Myers	$13,400.50	
By the C	Talbot	$32,800.00	
Red Bird	McGee	$39,455.80	

Document D — *Six-Column Table with a Formula*

1 At a clear WordPerfect document window, create a table with 6 columns and 7 rows.
2 Change the justification for columns B, C, D, E, and F to Center.
3 Join cells A1 through F1.
4 With the insertion point positioned in cell A1, change the Justification to Center, the Appearance to Bold and Italic, and the Size to Very Large.
5 Select cells A2 through F2, then make the following changes:
  a Change the Justification to Center, the Appearance to Bold and Italic, and the Size to Large.
  b Add a double line to the top and bottom of the cells.
  c Add 5% shaded fill to the cells. (Do this at the *Table Lines/Fill* dialog box.)
6 Select cells B3 through F7, then change the number type to Percent.
7 Key the text in the cells as shown in Document D. Do not key the zeros after the decimal point nor the percent signs. (WordPerfect automatically adds the zeros and the percent sign when you press ***Tab*** to move the insertion point to the next cell.)
8 Insert a formula in cell F3 that computes the averages by completing the following steps:
  a Position the insertion point in cell F3.
  b Choose T**a**ble → Fo**r**mula Bar.
  c Position the I-beam pointer inside the Formula Bar editing window (to the right of the green check mark), then click the left mouse button.
  d Key **ave(b3:e3)**.
  e Click on the green check mark on the Formula Bar.
  f Choose **C**lose to turn off the display of the Formula Bar.
9 Copy the formula in cell F3 relatively to cells F4, F5, F6, and F7 by completing the following steps:
  a Position the insertion point in cell F3.
  b Choose T**a**ble → Cop**y** Formula.

ENDING THE SESSION

Now you may print this session's files, continue to the next session, or exit the program:

PRINT

If the document is on the screen:

1 Click on the Print button on the Toolbar or choose **F**ile → **P**rint.
2 At the *Print* dialog box, click on **P**rint.
3 Close the document (**F**ile → **C**lose).

If you want to print previously saved files:

1 At a clear editing window, choose **F**ile → **O**pen.
2 With the mouse, click on the name of the file to be printed.
Note: You can use the mouse pointer and the Ctrl key together to highlight more than one filename. Press the ***Ctrl*** key as you click on each filename to be printed.
3 Choose File **O**ptions → **P**rint.
4 At the *Print File* dialog box, click on **P**rint.
Note: If you had highlighted several files to be printed, you would see the question, *Do you want to print the selected files?* Click on **P**rint to print the whole group.
5 Click on Cancel (or press ***Esc***) to close the *Open File* dialog box.

CONTINUE

1 Print and close files.
2 If you are currently working in Freeform (WordPerfect Reinforcement), click on the KWP Next Activity button to go to the next session menu. Highlight the desired activity and click on OK to begin.

EXIT

1 Print any files, if necessary.
2 Click on the KWP Main Menu button on the Toolbar.
3 At the Main Menu, select WordPerfect Only, then click on OK.
4 Click on **F**ile → E**x**it.
5 Exit Windows, if necessary (**F**ile → E**x**it).

a Position the insertion point in cell B7, then press the ***End*** key.
b Press ***Tab***. (This inserts a row.)

3 Position the insertion point in cell A8, then key **Total**.
4 Position the insertion point in cell B8, then insert a formula that adds the numbers in column B by completing the following steps:
   a Choose T**a**ble → Fo**r**mula Bar.
   b Position the arrow pointer inside the Formula Bar editing window (to the right of the green check mark), then click the left mouse button.
   c Key **sum(b2:b7)**.
   d Click on the green check mark on the Formula Bar.
   e Choose **C**lose to turn off the display of the Formula Bar.
   f Change the number type to **C**urrency for Cell B8.
5 Choose **F**ile → Save **A**s, key **058wprb.kwp**, then choose OK.
6 Choose **F**ile → **C**lose to close the document.

Document C — *Four-Column Table with a Formula*

1 At a clear WordPerfect document window, create a table with 4 columns and 6 rows.
2 Join cells A1 through D1.
3 Insert a double line border around the table. (You will need to scroll through the list to see *Double*.)
4 Change the bottom line of cell A1 to Thick.
5 Change the Justification to Center for columns A and B and change the Justification to Decimal Align for columns C and D.
6 Change the Justification to Center for cell A1, the Appearance to Bold and Small Cap, and the Size to Very Large.
7 Select cells A2 through D2, then change the Justification to Center, the Appearance to Bold and Italic, and the Size to Large.
8 Select cells C3 through D6, then change the number type to Currency.
9 Key the text in the cells as shown in Document C. Press ***Enter*** once after keying the title in cell A1. Do not key the dollar sign for the numbers in column C. (WordPerfect automatically adds the dollar sign when you press ***Tab*** to move the insertion point to the next cell.)
10 Insert a formula in cell D3 by completing the following steps:
   a Position the insertion point in cell D3.
   b Choose T**a**ble → Fo**r**mula Bar.
   c Position the I-beam pointer inside the Formula Bar editing window (to the right of the green check mark), then click the left mouse button.
   d Key **c3*.15**.
   e Click on the green check mark on the Formula Bar.
   f Choose **C**lose to turn off the display of the Formula Bar.
11 Copy the formula in cell D3 relatively to cells D4, D5, and D6 by completing the following steps:
   a Position the insertion point in cell D3.
   b Choose T**a**ble → Cop**y** Formula.
   c At the Copy Formula dialog box, choose **D**own.
   d Key **3**.
   e Choose OK or press ***Enter***.
12 Center the table horizontally on the page. (Do this at the *Format* dialog box with T**a**ble selected at the top.)
13 Adjust the width of each column by decreasing and/or increasing the width so the text just fits the columns as shown in Document C.

N, E
REVIEW OF CORRECTING ERRORS

SESSION GOALS

N and E

Correct errors with Delete, Backspace, Typeover, and Insert

Word Response

GETTING STARTED

If you are continuing immediately from Session 3, the first item on the Session 4 Menu should be highlighted. Since your fingers are already warmed up, highlight the next activity and click on OK to begin.

If you exited the program at the end of Session 3, do the following:

1 At the Windows Program Manager screen, position the mouse arrow on the WordPerfect icon and double-click the left mouse button.
2 At the WordPerfect editing window, click on the KWP button on the Toolbar.
3 At the Student Information screens, click on OK.
4 At the *Keyboarding with WordPerfect Main Menu*, the *Keyboarding Sessions* item should be highlighted. Click on OK or press ***Enter***.
5 Now you have two options: (1) you can move from menu to menu until you reach the next session's menu, then click on OK to begin the first activity; or (2) click on Jump to go to your previous location. (Note that the session number in which you last worked is displayed at the bottom of the *Keyboarding Sessions* menu.) Once you have returned to your previous location, position the mouse arrow on the activity of your choice and click on OK.

The program will guide you step by step through the remainder of your current session. When you have completed the on-screen keyboarding instruction, you will see a message telling you to return to the book to do the WordPerfect Reinforcement activities.

Remember: You can click on the KWP Next Activity button on the Toolbar to move from one activity type to the next. Or, use the KWP Previous Menu button to move backwards through the program menus.

WORDPERFECT REINFORCEMENT

Some of the drills you completed during the first part of Session 4 are repeated here to reinforce your keyboarding skills. You will also review error correction methods and save a document using **Close**. You will work in WordPerfect exclusively for the remainder of the session.

10 Key the title, **CENTURY CORPORATION,** in cell A1, then press ***Enter***. Key the subtitle, **Yearly Sales Profits**, then press ***Enter***. Press ***Tab*** to move the insertion point to the next cell, then key the remaining text in the cells as shown in Document A. When keying the amounts in cells C3 through C7, do not key the dollar ($). WordPerfect inserts this automatically as soon as you press the ***Tab*** key to move the insertion point to the next cell.

11 Insert a formula in cell C8 that calculates the amounts in cells C3 through C7 by completing the following steps:
   a Position the insertion point in cell C8.
   b Choose T**a**ble → Cell **F**ormula Entry. (This inserts a check mark before Cell Formula Entry.)
   c At the box asking if you want to turn on cell formula entry, choose **Y**es.
   d Key + in the cell.
   e Press ***Shift*** + ***Tab***. (When you press ***Shift*** + ***Tab***, the numbers in column C are calculated, then the total is inserted in cell C8.)

12 Center the table horizontally on the page. (Do this at the *Format* dialog box with Ta**b**le selected at the top.)

13 Adjust the width of each column by decreasing and/or increasing the width so the text just fits the columns as shown in Document A.

14 Center the table vertically. (Do this at the *Center Page(s)* dialog box.)

15 Proofread and correct any errors and then complete a spell check.

16 Choose **F**ile → Save **A**s, then key **058wpra.kwp** as the filename.

17 Press ***Ctrl*** + ***End*** to move the insertion point to the end of the document then choose T**a**ble → Cell **F**ormula Entry. (This removes the check mark before the option.)

18 Choose **F**ile → **C**lose to close the document.

Document A

CENTURY CORPORATION **Yearly Sales Profits**		
Name	***Branch***	***Amount***
L. Snyder	Richmond, VA	$18,345.22
G. Gallagher	Miami, FL	$9,845.75
H. Halpern	Dallas, TX	$14,345.80
M. Carlton	Chicago, IL	$9,234.15
E. Keach	Boise, ID	$15,356.70
Total		

Document B — *Inserting a Row and a Formula in a Table*

1 At a clear WordPerfect document window, open **055wprc.kwp**.

2 Add a row to the end of the document by completing the following steps:

Building Keyboarding Speed

To increase your keyboarding skills, you must key without watching your fingers. Concentrate on keeping your eyes on the copy. When asked to key at a controlled rate or for accuracy, concentrate on making the correct reaches. When pushing for speed, concentrate on making your fingers move faster.

Reviewing the N and E Keys

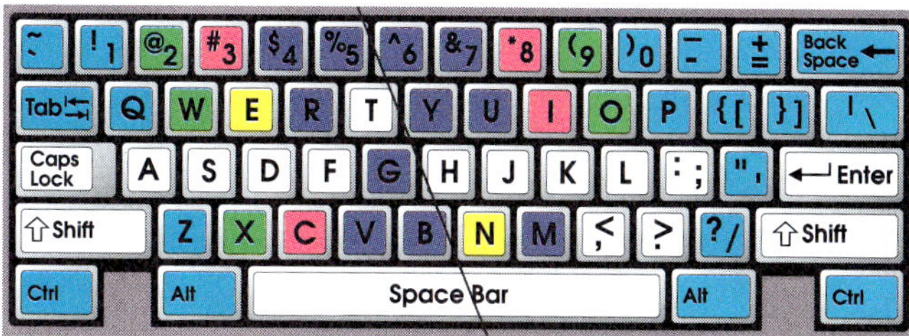

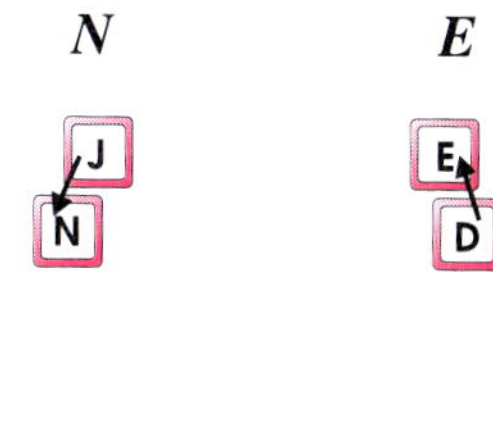

N Drill

Key lines 1–2 once; push for speed.

1 an an and and land land sand sand tanks

2 slant slant shall shall thank thank and

Key lines 3-5 once for control.

3 Jan shall hand a sad lad an atlas fast.

4 Hal shall thank that tall and lank lad.

5 Hats and sandals shall stand as a fad.

E Drill

Key lines 1–2 once for speed.

1 Den den eat eat eel eel ate ate ale ale date date

2 let let she she see see the the fee fee else else

Key lines 3-5 once for control.

3 Taste the lean tea; handle the kettle that leaks.

4 The fat hen left the lake. She landed at a nest.

5 Send the dated lease and halt the endless hassle.

Correcting Errors: Review

There are four ways to correct any keyboarding errors you make:

Backspace — When you backspace over a character on the screen, the character is deleted.

Typeover — This function allows you to replace, or *type over*, existing text. To use Typeover, press the ***Insert*** key. The Typeover mode stays in effect until you press ***Insert*** again.

To cancel a formula as you are keying it, click on the red X on the Formula Bar. This removes any formula you have entered. If you want to key another formula, position the arrow pointer in the Formula Bar edit box (located to the right of the green check mark), click the left mouse button, then key the formula.

Copying formulas: Once a formula has been entered in a cell, that formula can be copied to another cell or a relative version of the formula can be copied down or across to the other cells. The *Copy Formula* dialog box contains three options—*To Cell, Down*, and *Right*. Use the **T**o Cell option to copy a formula to another cell. When you use this option, the formula is copied exactly to the specified cell. Use the **D**own and **R**ight options if you want to copy a relative version of the formula to other cells.

Calculating numbers in a table: When a formula is inserted in a table that contains numbers, the formulas can be automatically or manually calculated (this default may vary) and the answer is inserted in the cell. If the formula does not automatically recalculate, choose Calculate from the Formula Bar or choose the *Calculate* option from the Table drop-down menu.

Document A — *Two-Column Table with Column Headings and a Formula*

1. At a clear WordPerfect document window, create a table with 3 columns and 8 rows.
2. Join cells A1 through C1.
3. Apply the following formatting to cell A1:
   a. Position the insertion point in cell A1.
   b. Display the *Format* dialog box (with C**e**ll selected at the top).
   c. Change the Justification to Center.
   d. Choose **B**old in the Appearancc section.
   e. Change the Size to Very Large.
   f. Choose OK to close the *Format* dialog box.
4. Change the bottom line in cell A1 to Double by completing the following steps:
   a. Position the insertion point in cell A1.
   b. Choose T**a**ble → **L**ines/Fill.
   c. Click on the down-pointing arrow to the right of the **B**ottom option (in the Line Styles section of the dialog box), then click on *Double*. (You may need to scroll through the list to display *Double*.)
   d. Choose OK to close the dialog box.
5. Select cells A2 through C2, then apply the following formatting:
   a. Display the *Format* dialog box (select C**e**ll at the top of the dialog box).
   b. Change the Justification to Center.
   c. Choose **B**old and **I**talic in the Appearance section.
   d. Change the Size to Large.
   e. Choose OK to close the *Format* dialog box.
6. Join cells A8 and B8.
7. Select cells B3 through B7, then change the Justification to Center.
8. Select cells C3 through C8, then change the Justification to Right.
9. Change the number type to Currency for cells C3 through C8 by completing the following steps:
   a. Select cells C3 through C8.
   b. Choose T**a**ble → N**u**mber Type.
   c. At the *Number Type* dialog box, make sure C**e**ll is selected at the top of the dialog box.
   d. Choose the Cu**r**rency in the Available Types section of the dialog box.
   e. Choose OK to close the dialog box.

Insert — When you want to insert letters that were left out of a word, move the insertion point to the spot where the first character will be added. Key the characters to be added.

Delete — Use delete to erase the character at the insertion point position.

To practice the correction methods, go to line 3 in the previous N drill and change *Jan* to *Dan.* In line 4 insert *At last* at the beginning of the sentence and delete *and lank lad*, replacing it with *lass.*

Using the Save and Exit Command

In Session 1 you learned to use Save or Save As to save a WordPerfect document. Either of these methods is especially useful when you are working on a document and need to leave your computer briefly but want to keep the document in the window so you can finish it later. ***Remember:*** Once you have named and saved the document, using Save As provides a reminder that you are replacing the original document and also gives you an opportunity to change the document name. The Save command, however, automatically saves and replaces the original document with the on-screen document, including any editing changes. There is no reminder that you are replacing the original document.

Another way to save a document is with WordPerfect's Close command (**F**ile→**C**lose or Ctrl-F4). The Close command lets you save a document and then clears the screen. To practice using this command, you should now save your WordPerfect Reinforcement activities for this session by following these steps:

1. Press **F**ile → **C**lose (or Ctrl-F4).
2. A *WordPerfect for Windows* dialog box appears with the prompt, *Save changes to Document1?* Click on Yes or press ***Enter.***
3. At the *Save As* dialog box, key **004wpr.kwp** in the filename text box and press ***Enter***.
4. The document is saved and closed, and you are returned to a clear WordPerfect editing window.

ENDING THE SESSION

At this point, you may print Session 4 files, continue to the next session, or exit the program:

PRINT — If the document is on the screen:

1. Click on the Print button in the Toolbar or choose **F**ile→**P**rint.
2. At the *Print* dialog box, click on **P**rint.
3. Close the document (**F**ile→**C**lose).

If you want to print previously saved files:

1. At a clear editing window, choose **F**ile→**O**pen.
2. With the mouse, click on the name of the file to be printed.
   Note: You can use the mouse pointer and the Ctrl key together to highlight more than one filename. Press the ***Ctrl*** key as you click on each filename to be printed.
3. Choose File **O**ptions→**P**rint.
4. At the *Print File* dialog box, click on **P**rint.
   Note: If you had highlighted several files to be printed, you would see the question, *Do you want to print selected files?* Click on **P**rint to print the whole group.

 FORMATTING TABLES WITH FORMULAS

In this section you will continue building your skills with tables. Read the following information then continue with Document A. Once Document A has been completed, proceed with Documents B and C. Read the instructions for each document before you start keying.

Changing Number Type

With the Number Type option from the Table drop-down menu, you can specify how numbers are used (as values or as text), how numbers are displayed, and how numbers are printed in a table.

When you choose Number Type, you can specify numbering type for the current cell, all cells in a column, or all cells in a table. To specify which cells are to be affected, choose the appropriate radio button (they look like knobs on the radio) at the top of the dialog box. The default radio button is C**e**ll.

The Available Types section of the *Number Type* dialog box displays the variety of methods that can be used for displaying numbers. The default number type is *General*. At this setting, numbers display without a thousands separator and no trailing zeros to the right of the decimal point. The other types are: *Accounting, Commas, Date/Time, Fixed, Integer, Percent, Scientific,* and *Text*. As you select different numbering types, the Preview box at the bottom of the dialog box shows the numbering type style.

To change the number type, do the following:

1. Position the insertion point in the cell or select a group of cells.
2. Choose T**a**ble → N**u**mber Type.
3. At the *Number Type* dialog box, choose **C**ell, C**o**lumn, or **T**able as appropriate.
4. Choose the desired numbering type from the Available Types section of the dialog box.
5. Choose OK to close the dialog box.

Inserting Formulas in a Table

WordPerfect contains a wide variety of options that can be used to create a spreadsheet with the Table feature. Using the Cell Formula Entry option from the Table drop-down menu or an option from the Formula Bar, you can insert a formula in a cell that will calculate numbers in rows or columns. You can also copy this formula to other cells in the table.

Four basic operators can be used when writing a formula: the plus sign for addition (+), the minus sign (hyphen) for subtraction, the asterisk (*) for multiplication, and the forward slash (/) for division.

To use the Cell Formula Entry option, choose T**a**ble → Ce**l**l Formula Entry. This inserts a check mark before the option. Key the formula in the cell, then move the insertion point to another cell. When the insertion point is moved, the formula is calculated and then inserted in the cell.

You can also enter a formula in a cell using the Formula Bar. To display the Formula Bar, choose T**a**ble → F**o**rmula Bar. Position the arrow pointer in the Formula Bar edit box located to the right of the green check mark, then click the left mouse button. Key the formula, then click on the green check mark on the Formula Bar. Choose **C**lose to turn off the display of the Formula Bar.

5 Click on Cancel (or press ***Esc***) to close the *Open File* dialog box.

CONTINUE

1. Print and close files.
2. If you are currently working in Freeform (WordPerfect Reinforcement), click on the KWP Next Activity button to go to the next session menu. Highlight the desired activity and click on OK to begin.

EXIT

1. Print any files, if necessary.
2. Click on the KWP Main Menu button on the Toolbar.
3. At the Main Menu, select WordPerfect Only, then click on OK.
4. Click on **F**ile → E**x**it.
5. Exit Windows, if necessary (**F**ile → E**x**it).

FIVE-MINUTE TIMINGS

Goal: 35 WAM/1 error

SI: 1.51

- Take two 5-minute timings.

If you work with a computer, you should have the habit of backing up your computer system. Few computer users, however, understand and use system backup. When a backup for a computer system is done, the files and data from the computer's hard drive are transferred to a storage unit that is separate from the main computer. The data stored on the secondary system is called the system backup. If your machine should "crash" or lose data from the hard drive, the backup system can restore the data to the computer's hard drive in no time.

Most people don't know how important a good system backup is to the user. Just think of losing a week's (or even a day's) data due to operator error, a fire, an earthquake, or a flood that causes water damage. You can see why you should back up your files.

Loss of data is costly in terms of money and time. Studies have shown that a large data loss may cost a business the use of the data for 18 to 20 days. The dollar cost to restore sales data and marketing facts can climb into the thousands of dollars. It is true that the data can be recovered, but there may be a loss of customers due to loss of sales.

The most common backup method for small businesses and home users is to copy the data to floppy disks. To make the backup task easy, most computer stores have many backup software programs from which to choose. Not only is the backup task quicker and easier, but some of these programs use data compression (shrinking the space needed to save data). The one problem with this backup method is that it takes a lot of disks and the user must be on hand to change disks when needed.

Larger businesses do not use the disk method. For larger amounts of data, most owners like to use a tape backup system, which requires a tape drive. Tape drives can either be internal units or external units that are attached to the computer by cables. There are several types of tape drives and cartridges that are in use at present. These systems cost more than the disk system. When this method of backup is used, the user is free to do other tasks while the backup is running.

The latest backup tool, which is not lower in cost at this time, is the optical disk. These disks hold a quite large amount of information that can be read by laser technology. The problem with some optical disks is that they can be used (written to) one time only.

Users should keep one rule in mind when using a backup. Follow a routine for backup and do it daily or weekly. Some users back up their data each hour.

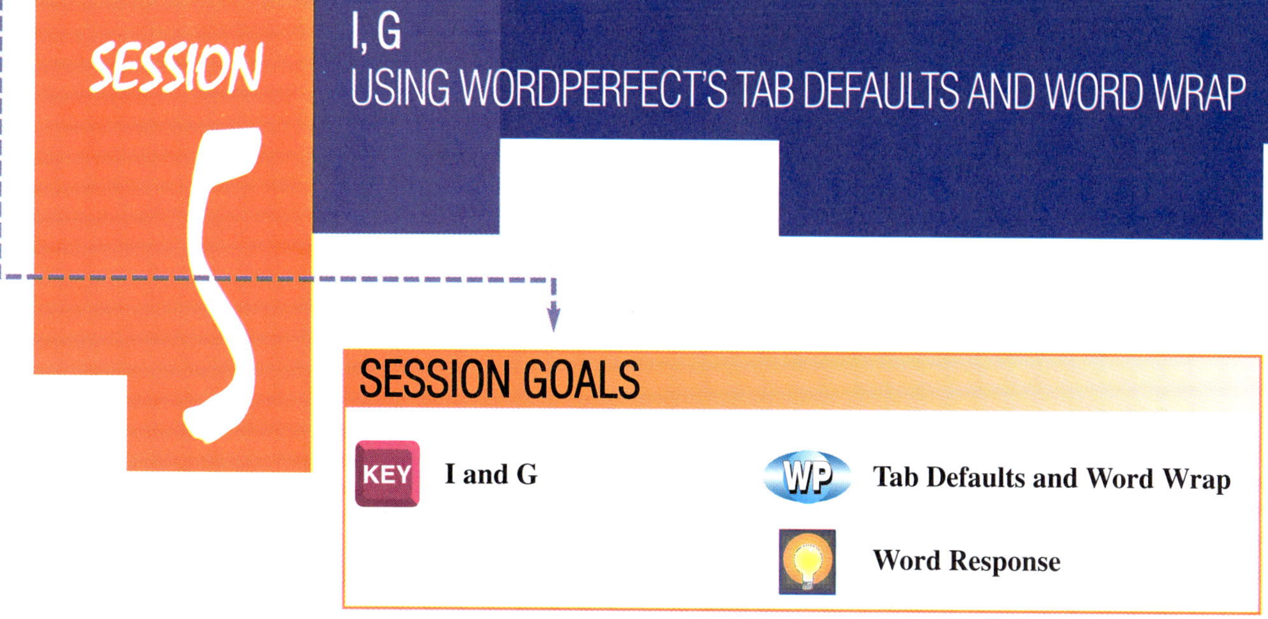

SESSION 5 — I, G USING WORDPERFECT'S TAB DEFAULTS AND WORD WRAP

SESSION GOALS

KEY **I and G**

WP **Tab Defaults and Word Wrap**

Word Response

GETTING STARTED

If you are continuing immediately from Session 4, the first item on the Session 5 Menu should be highlighted. Since your fingers are already warmed up, highlight the next activity and click on OK to begin.

If you exited the program at the end of Session 4, do the following:

1. At the Windows Program Manager screen, position the mouse arrow on the WordPerfect icon and double-click the left mouse button.
2. At the WordPerfect editing window, click on the KWP button on the Toolbar.
3. At the Student Information screens, click on OK.
4. At the *Keyboarding with WordPerfect Main Menu*, the *Keyboarding Sessions* item should be highlighted. Click on OK or press ***Enter.***
5. Now you have two options: (1) you can move from menu to menu until you reach the next session's menu, then click on OK to begin the first activity; or (2) click on Jump to go to your previous location. (Note that the session number in which you last worked is displayed at the bottom of the *Keyboarding Sessions* menu.) Once you have returned to your previous location, position the mouse arrow on the activity of your choice and click on OK.

The program will guide you step by step through the remainder of your current session. When you have completed the on-screen keyboarding instruction, you will see a message telling you to return to the book to do the WordPerfect Reinforcement activities.

Remember: You can click on the Next Activity button on the Toolbar to move from one activity type to the next. Or, use the Previous Menu button to move backwards through the Program menus.

WORDPERFECT REINFORCEMENT

Now you will work in WordPerfect exclusively to review the key reaches presented during the first part of Session 5. But first you will open the document you created in Session 4 (004wpr.kwp) and add text to the file. The new material includes practice with using word wrap and WordPerfect's tab defaults.

SESSION 58

SESSION GOALS

1-Minute: 45 WAM/1 error
5-Minute: 35 WAM/1 error

Using formulas in tables

GETTING STARTED

If you are continuing immediately from Session 57, go to the one-minute timings. If you exited the program at the end of Session 57, do the following:

1. Access Windows, then WordPerfect 6.1 for Windows.
2. Click on the KWP icon to access *Keyboarding with WordPerfect.*
3. Go to the Keyboarding Sessions menu and click on Jump to return to your last activity. Or, access the Session 58 menu and click on OK to begin the session.

ONE-MINUTE TIMINGS

Goal: 45 WAM/1 error

SI: 1.50

- Take two 1-minute timings.
- Use your most recent timing speed to set a speed or accuracy goal.

If you are thinking about setting up an office in your home, you must think about the legal aspect of your new venture. The impact of zoning, insurance, and taxes on home offices is a major one. All cities have some type of zoning law. You must be sure that you know and comply with all laws for the area in which you live. You must also change your personal home insurance policy to include your new business venture. Although the costs are sure to rise, it is a textbook must to insure equipment and protect yourself against any future claims. Most of us fail to study the impact of taxes on a home business. You should hire a good tax lawyer to guide you through the maze of rules on the books today. The other choice is to buy a good book on the subject and take a risk that you have read up on all the laws that apply.

Opening a Document

After a document has been saved on the disk, you may want to bring it back to the screen to make revisions. To open the WordPerfect document you created in Session 4, do the following:

1. Choose **File** → **O**pen (or F4 or Ctrl-O).
2. Click the mouse pointer on the filename *004wpr.kwp* to highlight the file.
3. Press ***Enter*** or click on OK to open the file.
   Note: You can also double-click on the filename to open the document.
4. Move the insertion point to the end of the document by holding down the ***Down Arrow*** key.
5. Move the insertion point to the beginning of the document by pressing ***Ctrl-Home***.
   Note: Pressing and holding the ***Right*** or ***Left*** **Arrow** keys allows you to move horizontally on any line.
6. Move the insertion point to the end of the document by pressing ***Ctrl-End***. Press ***Enter*** twice to move the insertion point below the existing text.

Reviewing the I and G Keys

I

G

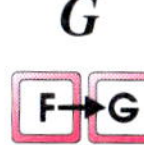

I Drill

Key lines 1–2 once; push for speed.

1 if if in in it it kid kid his fail fine file find

2 The kid thinks I had the idea that he did finish.

Key lines 3-5 once at a controlled rate.

3 Ill Inside Indeed If Illness Island Indeed Inside

4 She is a skilled athlete and likes little detail.

5 He did ski that hill. That is indeed a sad test.

G Drill

Key lines 1–2 once; push for speed.

1 gal gal gas gas get get sag sag egg egg gal glass

2 Dennis and Gene nailed a lath in the fallen gate.

Key lines 3–5 once; concentrate on control—try not to make errors.

3 Giant Giggle Glide Gentle Gene Gain Gift Glad Get

4 The endless agenda had eight legal details added.

5 Al tested his stiff ankle. He gnashed his teeth.

6. Select cells A6 through C6, then add 10% shaded fill.
7. Select cells A8 through C8, then add 10% shaded fill.
8. Key the text in the cells in the table.
9. Remove all table lines, then add a Thin Top/Bottom border.
10. Center the table horizontally. (Do this at the *Format* dialog box with Ta**b**le selected at the top.)
11. Adjust the width of each column by decreasing the width so the text fits the columns as shown in Document B.
12. Center the table vertically. (Do this at the *Center Page(s)* dialog box.)
13. Proofread and correct any errors and then complete a spell check.
14. Choose **F**ile → Save **A**s, then key **057wprb.kwp** as the filename.
15. Choose **F**ile → **C**lose to close the document.

Document B

American Painters		
Audubon, John	Hart, George	Pierce, Waldo
Carle, Ralph	Henri, Robert	Pyle, Howard
Cole, Thomas	Hicks, Thomas	Shahn, Ben
Davis, Stuart	Huhn, Walt	Sloan, John
Fuller, George	Marin, John	Stella, Joseph
Grasz, George	Melchers, Gari	Tiffany, Louis
Harding, Chester	Moran, Edward	Weber, Max

Document C — *Editing a Table*

1. At a clear WordPerfect document window, open **057wprb.kwp**.
2. Insert single lines inside the table and change the border to Double. (To do this, display the *Table Lines/Fill* dialog box with Ta**b**le selected at the top, change the **L**ine Style to *Single*, change **B**order to *Double*, then choose OK to close the dialog box.)
3. Add 10% shaded fill to cell A1.
4. Remove the shaded fill in cells A2 through C2, A4 through C4, A6 through C6, and A8 through C8. (To do this, select the specified cells, display the *Table Lines/Fill* dialog box, change **F**ill Style to <None>, then choose OK to close the dialog box.)
5. Change the Justification to Center for cells A2 through C8.
6. Choose **F**ile → Save **A**s, then key **057wprc.kwp** as the filename.
7. Choose **F**ile → **C**lose to close the document.

ENDING THE SESSION

To end this session, DELETE outdated WordPerfect Reinforcement files, PRINT any files from Session 57 not printed earlier, then CONTINUE with the next session or EXIT the program.

Introducing the Tab Key and Word Wrap

Tab Key

The first line of a paragraph is usually indented five spaces. In WordPerfect, there is a preset tab every 0.5 inches. It is not necessary to set tabs for each document unless you want to change the preset tabs or eliminate them.

To see how the preset tabs work, key the columns of words that follow. Key the first word in the first column; then press the ***Tab*** key twice and key the first word in the second column. Press ***Enter*** to move to the next line of the first column. Repeat the process for the remaining lines.

lane	Feat
tip	Tease
paid	That
nail	Print
leap	Fate

Word Wrap

When you key paragraphs of text (for example, in a letter), you do not need to press ***Enter*** at the end of each line. WordPerfect uses word wrap, a feature that automatically wraps a word to the next line once that word exceeds the right margin. With word wrap, you need to press ***Enter*** only to end a paragraph, create a blank line, or end a short line (for example, a person's name in an envelope address).

Key the two paragraphs that follow. Use the Tab key to indent the first line of each paragraph and let word wrap move the insertion point to the next line. Press ***Enter*** twice at the end of each paragraph to leave a blank line between paragraphs.

An idle lad finishes last. He is shiftless as he sits and tells his tales. He needs an insight in the elegant things in life.

Allan is attaining a skill in legal defense. The giant task is thankless. He insists that all the details heighten his thinking.

Saving WordPerfect Reinforcement Activities

To save the WordPerfect Reinforcement activities completed in Session 5, follow steps 1-3 below. (***Remember***: The session activities you keyed up to the WordPerfect Reinforcement section have been saved automatically.)

1. Choose **F**ile → Save **A**s (or F3).
2. At the *Save As* dialog box, the filename *004wpr.kwp* is displayed in the filename textbox (the document you opened and edited).
3. Key the new filename: **005wpr.kwp**. Press ***Enter*** or click on OK. Your document is saved to your data disk; it also remains on the screen.

Note: If you wanted to replace the existing file with the new one, you would press ***Enter*** at the *Save As* dialog box without keying a new filename.

CREATING TABLES WITH ENHANCEMENTS

In this session you will continue to develop your table formatting skills. As you prepare Documents A-C, be sure to read the instructions in the text for each document.

Document A — Four-Column Table with Shaded Fill and a Shadow Border

1. At a clear WordPerfect document window, create a table with 4 columns and 8 rows.
2. Join cells A1 through D1.
3. Change the Justification of cell A1 to Center, change the Appearance to Bold and Italic, and change the Size to Very Large.
4. Add 10% shaded fill to cell A1.
5. Add a shadow border to the table.
6. Center the table horizontally. (Do this at the *Format* dialog box with T**a**ble selected at the top.)
7. Key the text in the cells in the table.
8. Adjust the width of each column by decreasing the width so the text fits the columns as shown in Document A.
9. Center the table vertically. (Do this at the *Center Page(s)* dialog box.)
10. Proofread and correct any errors and then complete a spell check.
11. Choose **F**ile → Save **A**s, then key **057wpra.kwp** as the filename.
12. Choose **F**ile → **C**lose to close the document.

Document A

Words Indicating Happiness			
prosperous	favorable	fortunate	successful
bright	wealthy	optimistic	healthy
refreshing	victorious	triumphant	secure
nice	pleasant	charming	elated
cheerful	satisfied	joyous	peaceful
gleeful	content	appreciate	attractive
beneficial	jovial	delighted	exhilarated

Document B — Three-Column Table/Proofreading Reinforcement

1. At a clear WordPerfect document window, create a table with 3 columns and 8 rows.
2. Join cells A1 through C1.
3. Change the Justification of cell A1 to Center, change the Appearance to Bold and Small Cap, and change the Size to Very Large.
4. Select cells A2 through C2, then add 10% shaded fill.
5. Select cells A4 through C4, then add 10% shaded fill.

ENDING THE SESSION

Now you may choose among the Print, Continue, and Exit options available at the end of sessions:

PRINT

If the document is on the screen:

1. Click on the Print button in the Toolbar or choose **File** → **Print**.
2. At the *Print* dialog box, click on **Print**.
3. Close the document (**File** → **Close**).

If you want to print previously saved files:

1. At a clear editing window, choose **File** → **Open**.
2. With the mouse, click on the name of the file to be printed.
   Note: You can use the mouse pointer and the Ctrl key together to highlight more than one filename. Press the ***Ctrl*** key as you click on each filename to be printed.
3. Choose File **Options** → **Print**.
4. At the *Print File* dialog box, click on **Print**.
   Note: If you had highlighted several files to be printed, you would see the question, *Do you want to print selected files?* Click on **Print** to print the whole group.
5. Click on Cancel (or press ***Esc***) to close the *Open File* dialog box.

CONTINUE

1. Print and close files.
2. If you are currently working in Freeform (WordPerfect Reinforcement), click on the KWP Next Activity button to go to the next session menu. Highlight the desired activity and click on OK to begin.

EXIT

1. Print any files, if necessary.
2. Click on the KWP Main Menu button on the Toolbar.
3. At the Main Menu, select WordPerfect Only, then click on OK.
4. Click on **File** → **Exit**.
5. Exit Windows, if necessary (**File** → **Exit**).

FIVE-MINUTE TIMINGS

Goal: 35 WAM/1 error

SI: 1.50

- Take two 5-minute timings.
- On your second attempt, try to increase speed while keeping errors at 1 per minute.

In early days of development, computers were quite large. The early computer users were quite pleased with their room-sized computer. Miles of cables were needed for the operation of the computer. By today's standards, those early computers were also very slow to process the instructions and send data. Today, computers are not only faster, but they are being produced in smaller and smaller sizes. The user of today has many sizes from which to choose.

One common model is the one known as the desktop computer. As the name implies, this machine is designed to sit on a desk. Each year, however, the amount of desk space needed grows smaller and smaller. The desktop computer is made to stay in one place, on your desk.

Portable computers are machines designed to be moved from place to place with little effort. Most machines of this type have some sort of battery power and are made to take all the small bumps and jolts to which a unit might be subjected when it is moved from place to place. Some models have strong cases in which to keep the machine while it is being moved.

Notebook computers are one type of portable computer. A notebook model is in a class that weighs less than ten pounds. The keyboard of the notebook, like the desktop keyboard, has all the keys and all the user features. The size of the notebook keyboard is somewhat smaller. Some people find it hard to type on a small keyboard and harder to read the text on the screen.

Subnotebook systems are in a class by themselves. These units are smaller than the notebook type. The weight of this class of machine is less than five pounds. One issue you might have to face when you use this model is typing on the small keyboard. The keys are quite small. Some users feel that the size of the screen is too small to get a good look at the text.

An even smaller model can be found in stores. The palm or handheld type of computer is one that can be held in the palm of your hand. These small machines can be used to make schedules, reminders, and some other limited tasks. The user should not plan to do a lot of tasks on a palm-sized unit. One reason for this limited use is that both the keyboard and the screen are quite small and are hard to use for most people.

The major value of smaller portable computers is easy to discern. You can take your small unit anywhere. However, you might be trading power, flexibility, and the ability to do a lot of tasks for the small model. Also, the smaller units sell for a higher price than the desktop models. The choice is up to you.

REINFORCEMENT: SESSIONS 1-5
SAVING AND PRINTING

SESSION GOALS

Review keys from Sessions 1-5

25 WAM/2 errors

Review saving and printing

GETTING STARTED

If you are continuing immediately from Session 5, go to step 4. If you exited the program at the end of Session 5, do the following:

1. At the Windows Program Manager screen, double-click on the WordPerfect icon.
2. At the WordPerfect editing window, click on the KWP button.
3. Go to the Main Menu, then the Keyboarding Sessions menu.
4. At the Keyboarding Sessions menu, click on Jump to return to the activity you left off with. Or, move through the program menus to access the Session 6 menu.
5. On the Session 6 menu, *Keyboarding Reinforcement Drills* should be highlighted. Click on OK to proceed.

After you finish the on-screen Reinforcement Drills, return to the text and follow the directions under "Checking Your Skill."

CHECKING YOUR SKILL: ONE MINUTE TIMING

The next activity in Session 6 is a timing to assess your keyboarding speed. You should see a message on the screen directing you to take two 1-minute timings on the paragraph that follows. The program's "clock" begins when you strike the first key. When the time is up, the keyboard will "freeze," and the program calculates your words a minute (WAM) plus errors. Your goal is to key at least 25 words a minute (25 WAM) with no more than 2 errors. Be sure to use word wrap and indent the paragraph.

> That gallant knight led the detail. A tall, thin lad assisted at the flank. The knight failed the task and feels the defeat. A sadness sifts in as his shield falls.

WORDPERFECT REINFORCEMENT

The Special Drills that follow provide additional practice on the keys that you have learned in Sessions 1-5. However, if you are already keying over 25 WAM with no more than two errors and do not hesitate when keying, click on the KWP Next Activity button **twice** to go to the Session 7 menu.

SESSION GOALS

1-Minute: 45 WAM/1 error
5-Minute: 35 WAM/1 error

Review table formatting options

GETTING STARTED

If you are continuing immediately from Session 56, go to the one-minute timings. If you exited the program at the end of Session 56, do the following:

1. Access Windows, then WordPerfect 6.1 for Windows.
2. Click on the KWP icon to access *Keyboarding with WordPerfect.*
3. Go to the Keyboarding Sessions menu and click on Jump to return to your last activity. Or, access the Session 57 menu and click on OK to begin the session.

ONE-MINUTE TIMINGS

Goal: 45 WAM/1 error

SI: 1.50

- Take two 1-minute timings.
- Use your most recent timing score to set a speed or accuracy goal.

Inkjet printers are quite popular among computer users. The cost of a printer of this type is within most buyers' budgets. Not only do users like the price, but they also like to print many of their documents in bright colors. The days of black print on white paper are almost over. The quality of the color print has been greatly enhanced through the years. Color printers are easy to use. However, printing in color is somewhat more expensive than printing in black and white. The cost per page in color is generally 20 cents per page; the cost per page in black and white is generally 3 cents per page. Sometimes people choose appearance over price. In the end, the user must be pleased with the choice, and color is almost always a winner.

If you are not at the 25 WAM level, and/or making more than two errors, proceed with the Special Drills to build speed and/or accuracy. Here are guidelines for choosing drills:

1. If you have not mastered a key reach (you hesitate before striking the key), key the speed-building lines.
2. If you are not keying at least 25 WAM, key the speed-building lines.
3. If you are making more than 2 errors per minute, key the accuracy-building lines.

Once you have completed the drills, the program directs you to take two more 1-minute timings on the paragraph on page 27. When you are finished, compare the rates with your first two attempts. Has your speed improved? Do you have fewer errors? If you are not reaching 25 WAM with fewer than three errors on at least one 1-minute timing, repeat Sessions 1-5.

Special Drills

Key each line once.

If you need more practice, key the group of lines again.

Balanced-Hand Words (Speed)

1 and the ant sit ale elf end hen she end sigh sign
2 aid fit sit did tie die dig fig and the hang then
3 halt than hand lens lake lane then than sign fish
4 idle lens lane sigh then dish disk sign half lake
5 shake snake title aisle angle fight handle island
6 angle sight digit gland eight slant height sleigh
7 signal giant tight an he if it and elf the and he

Letter Combinations (Speed)

1 de den dead deal desk denial dense deft dental de
2 di dig dish dial digest dislike dine dike disk di
3 I dislike the heat dial that fits the dental fan.

4 fi fish final fine finish fight find fig field fi
5 ga gal gas gag gale gait gallant gasket gadget ga
6 Gal, finish the gasket that the gas gadget needs.

7 ha hate hassle halt hall half hash hang handle ha
8 ki kite kiss kindle kilt kiln king kink kitten ki
9 That hanging kite tail hassles the halted kitten.

10 le lest left lead lend ledge least leaf lessen le
11 li lid lie lied lien link linking linkage like li
12 At least link the left lid and lessen the length.

Continued on next page

   b. Choose Table → **Lines/Fill**.
   c. At the *Table Lines/Fill* dialog box, click on the down-pointing arrow to the right of the **F**ill Style option (to the right of the box containing the word *Default*), then click on *10% Fill* at the drop-down menu.
   d. Choose OK to close the dialog box.

7. Change the Justification for cells B3 through B7 to Center.
8. Change the Justification for cells C3 through C7 to Right.
9. Change the right and left margin of all cells by completing the following steps:
   a. With the insertion point positioned in any cell in the table, choose T**a**ble → **F**ormat.
   b. At the *Format* dialog box, choose T**a**ble at the top of the dialog box.
   c. Change the measurement in the *Left* text box (in the Column Margins section) to **0.2**.
   d. Change the measurement in the *Right* text box (in the Column Margins section) to **0.2**.
   e. Choose OK to close the dialog box.
10. Key the text in the cells in the table. Use the ***Tab*** key to move the insertion point to the next cell or press ***Shift*** **+** ***Tab*** to move the insertion point to the previous cell.
11. Adjust the width of each column by decreasing the width so the text fits the columns as shown in Document D.
12. Add a border to the table by completing the following steps:
    a. With the insertion point positioned in any cell in the table, choose T**a**ble → **L**ines/Fill.
    b. At the *Table Lines/Fill* dialog box, choose T**a**ble at the top of the dialog box.
    c. Click on the down-pointing arrow to the right of the **B**order option (to the right of the box containing the word *<None>*, in the lower right corner of the dialog box), then click on *Thick/Thin 1*. (You will need to scroll through the list to see *Thick/Thin 1*.)
    d. Choose OK to close the dialog box.
13. Center the table vertically. (Do this at the *Center Page(s)* dialog box.)
14. Proofread and correct any errors and then complete a spell check.
15. Choose **F**ile → Save **A**s, then key **056wprd.kwp** as the filename.
16. Choose **F**ile → **C**lose to close the document.

Document D

Computer Equipment Required		
PART NO.	**DESCRIPTION**	**PRICE**
3214-Y	XGA Monitor	$399.00
12-345	101 Keyboard	79.50
XW-3454	Parallel Printer Cable	29.95
2345-45-AA	Track Ball	50.00
873-AB	Internal CD-ROM	595.00

ENDING THE SESSION

To end this session, DELETE outdated WordPerfect Reinforcement files, PRINT any files from Session 55 not printed earlier, then CONTINUE with the next session or EXIT the program.

13 sa sad sat safe sake sale said sang Sal saline sa
14 si sit site sitting signal sighted sill silken si
15 Sad Sal sang a signal as she sighted a safe site.

16 St stead still steal steadiness stateside stag st
17 ta tag talk take tall tale taste task tan tall ta
18 Steadfast Stell still talks and tells tall tales.

19 Te tea test tenth tell tend teen tennis tenant te
20 th then that than thing this theft thin thesis th
21 Then that teen tenant, Ted, did a tenth tea test.

Double-Letter Words (Accuracy)

1 see glee needs indeed feeling needless teens seed
2 egg sell sniff haggle falling eggshell stall eggs
3 eel keen sheen needle fiddles seedling sleek deed
4 add kiss stiff assist endless lifeless still hill

5 fee need sheet seeing dissent likeness steed heel
6 add fell skill allied skilled settling shell tell
7 see feel teeth indeed gallant sledding sleet knee
8 all hall shall little install knitting stall tall

9 Sadness is a feeling I assess as an alleged need.
10 Assist the skiing attendant and lessen all falls.
11 Did the sleek kitten flee the illegal attendants?
12 Haggling is a senseless dissent that is needless.
13 Flatten the stiff fiddle and install the tassels.

Longer Words (Accuracy)

1 endless athlete flatten inflated install disliked
2 lenient distant delighted heading inkling digital
3 A lenient athlete has inflated the flattened keg.

4 Hesitating likeness indefinite alkaline initiated
5 heightened stealing gaslight lengthened delegates
6 The hesitating delegate is stealing the gaslight.

7 Landslide skinflint stateside essential legislate
8 negligent lightness sightless delighted attendant
9 tasteless steadfast defendant thankless seashells
10 Seashells in the landslide delighted a skinflint.

11 Remove the table lines and add a thick top and bottom border by completing the following steps:
   a With the insertion point positioned in any cell in the table, choose **Ta**ble → **L**ines/Fill.
   b At the *Table Lines/Fill* dialog box, choose **Ta**ble at the top of the dialog box.
   c Click on the down-pointing arrow to the right of the **L**ine Style option (to the right of the box containing the word *Single*, in the upper left corner of the dialog box), then click on *<None>*.
   d Click on the down-pointing arrow to the right of the **B**order option (to the right of the box containing the word *<None>*, in the lower right corner of the dialog box), then click on *Thick Top/Bottom*. (You will need to scroll through the list to see *Thick Top/Bottom*.)
   e Choose OK to close the dialog box.

12 Center the table vertically. (Do this at the *Center Page(s)* dialog box.)

13 Proofread and correct any errors and then complete a spell check.

14 Choose **F**ile → Save **A**s, then key **056wprc.kwp** as the filename.

15 Choose **F**ile → **C**lose to close the document.

Document C

A Sampling of Cities with over 10,000 Telephones			
Akron	**Albuquerque**	**Amarillo**	**Atlanta**
Austin	**Baltimore**	**Boston**	**Calgary**
Canton	**Charlotte**	**Chicago**	**Cleveland**
Dallas	**Dayton**	**Detroit**	**El Paso**
Flint	**Gary**	**Halifax**	**Houston**
Indianapolis	**Las Vegas**	**London**	**New York**
Omaha	**St. Louis**	**Seattle**	**Tampa**

Document D — *Table with Shaded Fill and Thick Border*

1 At a clear WordPerfect document window, create a table with 3 columns and 7 rows.

2 Join cells A1 through C1.

3 With the insertion point positioned in cell A1, apply the following formatting at the *Format* dialog box:
   a Display the *Format* dialog box (with Ce**l**l selected at the top).
   b Change the Justification to Center.
   c Choose **B**old and Outli**n**e in the Appearance section.
   d Change the Size to Very Large.
   e Choose OK to close the *Format* dialog box.

4 Select cells A2 through C2, display the *Format* dialog box (with Ce**l**l selected), change the justification to Center, turn on **B**old and **S**mall Cap, then choose OK to close the dialog box.

5 Center the table horizontally on the page. (Do this at the *Format* dialog box with **Ta**ble selected at the top.)

6 Add 10% shaded fill to cells A1 through C2 by completing the following steps:
   a Select cells A1 through C2.

Saving WordPerfect Reinforcement Activities

To save the document you have just created, complete the following steps:

1. Choose **File**→**Close.**
2. At the message *Save changes to Document1?*, click on Yes
3. At the *Save As* dialog box, key the filename, **006wpr.kwp**.
4. Press ***Enter*** or click on OK.
5. Click on the KWP Next Activity button and proceed with the Timings.

ONE-MINUTE TIMING

Now that you have completed the drills, take two 1-minute timings on the paragraph on page 27. Compare the rates with your first attempt. Has your speed improved? Do you have fewer errors? If you are not reaching 25 WAM with two or fewer errors, repeat Sessions 1-5.

ENDING THE SESSION

The program automatically takes you to the next session and highlights *Warm-Up* on the Session 7 menu. However, if you need to print Session 6 activities before continuing with Session 7, read the information that follows on using a new option to print files.

Printing Files from Disk

Previously, you have used the **File** → **O**pen → **P**rint sequence to print files already saved to your data disk. WordPerfect offers another way to print files from disk, and you will use this method to print the Session 6 files:

1. Click on Back until you reach the KWP Main Menu.
2. With the mouse pointer, highlight *Freeform*, then click on OK or press ***Enter***.
3. Click on the Print button or choose **F**ile → **P**rint. This takes you to the *Print* dialog box.
4. Under *Print Selection*, select the **D**ocument on Disk option and press ***Enter*** or click on **P**rint.
5. At the *Document on Disk* dialog box, click on the list button at the right of the filename text box (which contains an image of a file folder). At the *Select File* dialog box, note that there are three documents in Session 6: *006ses.kwp, 006wpr.kwp* and *006tim.kwp*. The *006tim.kwp* file contains the timed writing(s) that you completed in Session 6.
6. Highlight the file to be printed and click on OK.
7. At the *Document on Disk* dialog box, click on **P**rint, leaving the Page(s)/Label(s) default set to *all* to print the entire document.
8. Repeat steps 3-7 to print the second and third documents. To continue with Session 7, go to the next step. To exit the program, click on the KWP Main Menu button, then select WordPerfect Only. Click on **F**ile → **E**xit. Then exit Windows, if necessary (**F**ile → **E**xit).
9. Click on the KWP Main Menu button.
10. At the Main Menu, highlight *Keyboarding Sessions* and click on OK.
11. Click on Jump to go to Session 7.

Document B ← Inserting/Deleting Rows in a Table

1. At a clear WordPerfect document window, open **056wpra.kwp**.
2. Insert a row above row 7 by completing the following steps:
   a. Position the insertion point in cell A7.
   b. Choose T**a**ble → **I**nsert.
   c. At the *Insert Columns/Rows* dialog box make sure *1* displays in the ***Rows*** text box (in the Insert section), then choose OK or press ***Enter*** to close the dialog box.
3. Key the following text in the specified cell:

   A7 = **CPU**
   B7 = **Monitor**
   C7 = **Modem**
4. Delete rows 4 and 5 by completing the following steps:
   a. Position the insertion point in cell A4.
   b. Choose T**a**ble → **D**elete.
   c. At the *Delete* dialog box, click once on the up-pointing triangle to the right of the **R**ows option (in the Delete section). (This should display *2* in the ***Rows*** text box.)
   d. Choose OK or press ***Enter*** to close the dialog box.
5. Choose **F**ile → Save **A**s, then key **056wprb.kwp** as the filename.
6. Choose **F**ile → **C**lose to close the document.

Document C ← Four-Column Table with Inside Lines Removed

1. At a clear WordPerfect document window, create a table with 4 columns and 8 rows.
2. Join cells A1 through D1.
3. With the insertion point positioned in cell A1, apply the following formatting at the *Format* dialog box:
   a. Display the *Format* dialog box (with C**e**ll selected at the top).
   b. Change the Justification to Center.
   c. Choose **B**old and **I**talic in the Appearance section.
   d. Change the Size to Large.
   e. Choose OK to close the *Format* dialog box.
4. Center the table horizontally on the page. (Do this at the *Format* dialog box with T**a**ble selected at the top.)
5. Add 10% shaded fill to cells A2 through D2 by completing the following steps:
   a. Select cells A2 through D2.
   b. Choose T**a**ble → **L**ines/Fill.
   c. At the *Table Lines/Fill* dialog box, click on the down-pointing arrow to the right of the **F**ill Style option (to the right of the box containing the word *Default*), then click on *10% Fill* at the drop-down menu.
   d. Choose OK to close the dialog box.
6. Select cells A4 through D4, then add 10% shaded fill.
7. Select cells A6 through D6, then add 10% shaded fill.
8. Select cells A8 through D8, then add 10% shaded fill.
9. Key the text in the cells in the table. Use the ***Tab*** key to move the insertion point to the next cell or press ***Shift*** + ***Tab*** to move the insertion point to the previous cell.
10. Adjust the width of each column by decreasing the width so the text fits the columns as shown in Document C.

P, R, QUESTION MARK
REVIEW OF PRINTING, OPENING, SAVING

SESSION GOALS

 **P, R, and Question Mark**

 **Practice printing and closing files**

 **25 WAM/2 errors**

 **-ed and -ing word endings**

GETTING STARTED

If you are continuing immediately from Session 6, go to step 4. If you exited the program at the end of Session 6, do the following:

1. At the Windows Program Manager screen, double-click on the WordPerfect icon.
2. At the WordPerfect editing window, click on the KWP button.
3. Go to the Main Menu, then the Keyboarding Sessions menu.
4. At the Keyboarding Sessions menu, click on Jump to return to the activity you left off with. Or, move through the program menus until you reach the Session 7 menu.
5. On the Session 7 menu, *Warm-Up* is highlighted. Click on OK to proceed. If your fingers are already warmed up, or if you have completed part of the session, highlight the desired activity and click on OK.

The program will guide you step by step through the remainder of the session. When you have completed the on-screen keyboarding instruction, you will be directed to return to the text to do the WordPerfect Reinforcement activities.

WORDPERFECT REINFORCEMENT

Some of the drills presented by the *Keyboarding with WordPerfect* program earlier in Session 7 are repeated here to give you practice using WordPerfect. After completing the WordPerfect Reinforcement activities, you will take two 1-minute timings. Watch for directions on the screen.

Reviewing the P, R, and Question Mark Keys

P Key

R Key

Question Mark Key

a Display the *Format* dialog box (with Cell selected at the top).
b Change the Justification to Center.
c Choose **B**old, Outli**n**e, and **S**mall Cap in the Appearance section.
d Change the Size to Large.
e Choose OK to close the *Format* dialog box.

4 Center the table horizontally on the page. (Do this at the *Format* dialog box with Ta**b**le selected at the top.)

5 Add a double-line border to the table by completing the following steps:
a With the insertion point positioned in any cell in the table, choose Ta**b**le → **L**ines/Fill.
b At the *Table Lines/Fill* dialog box, choose Ta**b**le at the top of the dialog box.
c Click on the down-pointing arrow to the right of the **B**order option (to the right of the box containing the word <*None*>, in the lower right corner of the dialog box), then click on *Double*. (You will need to scroll through the list to display *Double*.)
d Choose OK to close the dialog box.

6 Add 10% shaded fill to cell A1 by completing the following steps:
a Position the insertion point in cell A1.
b Choose Ta**b**le → **L**ines/Fill.
c At the *Table Lines/Fill* dialog box, click on the down-pointing arrow to the right of the **F**ill Style option (to the right of the box containing the word *Default*), then click on *10% Fill* at the drop-down menu.
d Choose OK to close the dialog box.

7 Select cells A2 through C2 then change the Justification for cells in all three columns to Center. (Do this at the *Format* dialog box with Co**l**umn selected at the top.)

8 Key the text in the cells in the table. Use the ***Tab*** key to move the insertion point to the next cell or press ***Shift* + *Tab*** to move the insertion point to the previous cell.

9 Adjust the width of each column by decreasing and/or increasing the width so the text just fits the columns as shown in Document A.

10 Center the table vertically. (Do this at the *Center Page(s)* dialog box.)

11 Proofread and correct any errors and then complete a spell check.

12 Choose **F**ile → Save **A**s, then key **056wpra.kwp** as the filename.

13 Choose **F**ile → **C**lose to close the document.

Document A

INFORMATION SYSTEMS TERMINOLOGY		
Relative	Printer	Magnetic
File	Disk	Terminal
Computer	Access	Data
Program	Symbolic	Random
Source	Object	Software
Read	Write	Sequential
Density	Flowcharting	Laser

P Drill

Key lines 1–3 once, pushing for speed.

1 ;p pan pat pea peg pen pep pet pie pig pin pit ;p
2 ;p ship tape pink skip slap taps gaps pest sap ;p
3 Peasant Pennant Pitfall Patient Pheasant Pleasant

Key lines 4–6 once, focusing on either speed or control.

4 A tall, split, peeling aspen sapling is diseased.
5 Pat speaks and pleads and defends the plaintiffs.
6 Did Jane tape that splint and dispense the pills?

R Drill

Key lines 1-3 twice: first for speed, then for control.

1 fr rain rare real rink rake rage rear ripe rip fr
2 stare there their after pride tired far her press
3 Refrain Repress Release Retreat Resident Register

Question Mark Drill

Important: Tap the space bar **once** after the question mark at the end of the sentence. This rule applies to all end-of-sentence punctuation when you are using the WordPerfect 6.1 for Windows default font, Times New Roman. When a question mark ends a line in the drill, press ***Enter*** immediately—there is no need to tap the space bar.

Key lines 1–3 once, keeping your eyes on the copy.

1 Is Jennie ahead? Is Dennis safe? Is Allen late?
2 Is Ken late? Is Dale fit? Is Neil in his teens?
3 Did she dine? Did the leaf fall? Did Jane flee?

What Is a Keyboarding Error?

Some errors affect only the appearance of a document. On the other hand, certain keyboarding errors can have a drastic effect on the message being communicated. Consider the result of transposing two numbers in a customer's invoice, for example, keying $19 instead of $91. Following is a list of some common keyboarding mistakes. You will find it helpful to review the list to ensure that you are aware of possible errors as you complete timings and later as you prepare letters and other documents.

Common Keyboarding Errors

- Keying wrong words
- Transposing numbers
- Placing extra spaces between words or numbers

Inserting Rows or Columns

With the *Insert* option from the Table drop-down menu, you can insert rows or columns in a table. By default, a row is inserted above the row where the insertion point is positioned and a column is inserted to the left of the column where the insertion point is positioned.

To insert a column or row, choose Table → Insert. At the *Insert Columns/Rows* dialog box, specify the number of rows or columns to be inserted as well as the whether the rows or columns are to be placed before or after the location of the insertion point. After making changes to the dialog box, choose OK or press ***Enter*** to close the dialog box.

Deleting Rows or Columns

Rows or columns in a document can be deleted with the ***Delete*** option from the Table drop-down menu. To delete a row(s) or column(s), choose Table → Delete. At the *Delete* dialog box, specify the number of rows or columns to be deleted then choose OK or press ***Enter*** to close the dialog box.

Changing Line Styles

A table consists of two elements—lines and a border. Lines make up the columns, rows, and cells. The border surrounds the table and masks the outer table lines. These are two distinct elements and can be customized separately.

Table lines or border lines can be customized with the Line Styles options at the *Table Lines/Fill* dialog box. To display this dialog box, position the insertion point in any cell in the table, then choose Table → Lines/Fill. At the *Table Lines/Fill* dialog box, you can customize all cell lines within a table, border lines, specific lines within a cell, all lines within selected cells, or all lines outside selected cells. To customize a line within a cell, choose one of the Line Styles options at the *Table Lines/Fill* dialog box. You can also change lines styles with the Line Styles drop-down menu.

With the Fill Style option in the Fill Options section of the *Table Lines/Fill* dialog box, you can add fill to a cell, selected cells, or all cells in a table. A wide variety of fill options are available including various shades of gray, designs, and patterns. You can also add fill with the Fill Style drop-down menu.

Changing Cell Margins

At the *Format* dialog box with Table selected at the top, the left and right margins of all cells in the table can be adjusted. By default, each cell contains a left and right margin of 0.083 inches. This can be increased or decreased. To do this, display the *Format* dialog box with Table selected at the top, change the measurements in the Left and Right text boxes in the Column Margins section, then choose OK to close the dialog box.

Document A — *Three-Column Table with Shaded Fill and a Double-Line Border*

1. At a clear WordPerfect document window, create a table with 3 columns and 8 rows using the Power Bar.
2. Join cells A1 through C1.
3. With the insertion point positioned in cell A1, apply the following formatting at the *Format* dialog box:

- Placing a space before a punctuation mark
- Not capitalizing a proper noun or the first word of a sentence
- Capitalizing a word in a sentence that should not be capitalized
- Placing too many spaces after a punctuation mark or between paragraphs
- Using improper left, right, top, or bottom margins
- Not indenting properly
- Being inconsistent in vertical spacing
- Using incorrect punctuation

Printing WordPerfect Reinforcement Activities

To save and print the WordPerfect Reinforcement activities completed in Session 7, complete steps 1-6 that follow. (***Remember:*** The work you completed up to the WordPerfect Reinforcement section has already been saved automatically.)

1. Choose **F**ile → Save **A**s (or F3).
2. At the *Save As* dialog box, key the new filename, **007wpr.kwp**. Press ***Enter*** or click on OK. Your document has been saved to disk, and it also remains on the screen.
3. To print 007wpr.kwp, choose **F**ile → **P**rint (or F5).
4. Click on **P**rint or press ***Enter***.
5. Close the file (click on **F**ile → **C**lose).
6. Click on the KWP Next Activity button.

CHECKING YOUR SKILL

In Session 6 you completed a 1-minute timing. The goals for the timing under the Timings Check that follows are based on your performance in Session 6. If you don't remember your scores, you may review them by accessing the Student Report from the Main Menu or from the Toolbar, as explained below.

Viewing the Student Report

During a session you may check your Timings and Production scores in the Student Report by completing the following steps:

1. Click on the KWP Rep (Student Report) button on the Toolbar. ***Note:*** Make sure the program is not waiting for a response to a question or a choice on a menu before you click on the Student Report buttton. If so, make the appropriate response first.
2. Your scores are listed on the Timings screen.
3. Once you have checked your scores, click on OK to return to your previous location.

ONE-MINUTE TIMINGS

Take a 1-minute timing on each paragraph; if you finish before time is up, start over.

If you did not reach at least 25 WAM on your most recent timing, push for speed. If you are keying at least 25 WAM but are making more than two errors per minute, concentrate on accuracy. If you are above 25 WAM and are making fewer than three errors, push for speed.

FIVE-MINUTE TIMINGS

Goal: 35 WAM/1 error

SI: 1.51

- Take two 5-minute timings.

When computer monitors were first sold, users had a big problem. If the monitor was turned on and sat idle for a long time, the result would be burn-in. The burn-in of a monitor could be seen the next time a user turned on the system. The user would see a faint image of the text that was on the idle screen for a long time. This faint image could never be removed, and the monitor was damaged forever. Before long, developers had solved this problem with screen savers. The screen savers were special software programs that featured some type of moving graphic that would start after a few moments of idle time. Most monitors sold today have been designed to avoid burn-in.

Screen savers are still used today, however. Users have found that some screen savers can be used for security of data. Sometimes, a person has to leave his or her desk for a few minutes or even for a few hours. Perhaps this person has to go to a meeting, to lunch, or to another office for a moment or two. While the person is gone, the screen saver keeps others from seeing the data on the screen. It is not unusual to see moving objects or words on a screen at a desk.

Some screen savers go a step further. After the screen saver has started, the user cannot access the application program without a password. The image just keeps moving on the screen. The one problem with passwords is that most people choose a word that is easily detected by others. Passwords should be unique and hard for others to guess. When the user comes back to the desk to go back to work, he or she enters the password and the computer is up and running once more.

In addition to personalized screen savers, some users have added one more personal item to their systems. This item is a cardboard frame that is placed around the outside edge of the computer. Frames come in all sizes and shapes and descriptions. Computers can be decorated with almost any motif or theme depending on the user's personal choices. Frames are also available in brilliant colors, thus adding a touch of bright color to an otherwise dull office.

You, too, can have a screen saver that fits your personality. Just take a walk through the aisles of a software dealer and you will see all the choices available today. However, you may be like many other people who prefer to keep their desk space clean and uncluttered.

FORMATTING TABLES

In this section you will continue building your skills with tables. You will learn to insert and delete rows and columns as well as add various formatting features to table cells and borders.

1 Jane prepares legal papers and letters. She prefers reading ledgers and graphs. It is tiring and drains her. If she falters at the start, Jane is risking a defeat. The stern leader sees her stress and praises her spirit.

2 Print the paragraph in large letters. Raise the title and delete the digraphs. Insert three fresh phrases at the end. It is all right if Dane deletes that first phrase. It is a danger and a threat. Perhaps the ending is right.

ENDING THE SESSION

Once you have completed the timings, the KWP program takes you to the next session menu. If you want to print the Session 7 files, however, follow the steps below. Then continue with Session 8 or exit the program.

PRINT

1. Click on Back until you reach the KWP Main Menu.
2. At the Main Menu, select *Freeform* and click on OK or press ***Enter***.
3. Click on the Print button or choose **F**ile → **P**rint.
4. At the *Print* dialog box, select the **D**ocument on Disk option under *Print Selection*. Press ***Enter*** or click on **P**rint.
5. At the *Document on Disk* dialog box, click on the list button at the right of the filename text box.
6. With the mouse pointer, highlight the file to be printed and press ***Enter*** or click on **P**rint.
7. At the *Document on Disk* dialog box, click on **P**rint.

Repeat steps 3-7 to print additional documents on disk.

CONTINUE

1. Print and close files.
2. If you are working in Freeform, click on the KWP Main Menu button.
3. Highlight *Keyboarding Sessions*, then click on OK.
4. Click on Jump to go to the next session.

EXIT

1. Print any files, if necessary.
2. Click on the KWP Main Menu button on the Toolbar.
3. At the Main Menu, select WordPerfect Only, then click on OK.
4. Click on **F**ile → E**x**it.
5. Exit Windows, if necessary (**F**ile → E**x**it).

SESSION GOALS

1-Minute: 45 WAM/1 error
5-Minute: 35 WAM/1 error

Formatting tables

GETTING STARTED

If you are continuing immediately from Session 55, go to the one-minute timings. If you exited the program at the end of Session 55, do the following:

1. Access Windows, then WordPerfect 6.1 for Windows.
2. Click on the KWP icon to access *Keyboarding with WordPerfect.*
3. Go to the Keyboarding Sessions menu and click on Jump to return to your last activity. Or, access the Session 56 menu and click on OK to begin the session.

ONE-MINUTE TIMINGS

Goal: 45 WAM/1 error

SI: 1.49

- Take two 1-minute timings.
- Use your most recent timing speed to set a speed or accuracy goal.

In Australia's North Territory, it may appear that an 18-foot-long snake is undulating across the desert. In reality it may be a trail of more than 100 caterpillars lined up head to tail, marching endlessly over the sand. When the food supply runs low, the insects strike out in single file to find another source of food. Traveling mostly at night, the insects march in a straight line seeming never to stop. They have little to fear.

SESSION 8

M, V
REVIEW: WORDPERFECT DEFAULT TABS AND WORD WRAP

SESSION GOALS

M and V

25 WAM/2 errors

Practice saving, printing, and closing documents

Words with double letters

GETTING STARTED

If you are continuing immediately from Session 7, go to step 4. If you exited the program at the end of Session 7, do the following:

1. At the Windows Program Manager screen, double-click on the WordPerfect icon.
2. At the WordPerfect editing window, click on the KWP button.
3. Go to the Main Menu, then the Keyboarding Sessions menu.
4. At the Keyboarding Sessions menu, click on Jump to return to the activity you left off with. Or, move through the program menus until you reach the Session 8 menu.
5. On the Session 8 menu, *Warm-Up* is highlighted. Click on OK to proceed. If your fingers are already warmed up, or if you have completed part of the session, highlight the desired activity and click on OK .

The program will guide you step by step through the remainder of the session. When you have completed the on-screen keyboarding instruction, you will be directed to return to the text to complete the WordPerfect Reinforcement activities. Finally, you will take six 1-minute timings. Watch for specific instructions on your screen.

WORDPERFECT REINFORCEMENT

Some of the drills you completed during the first portion of Session 8 are presented here to reinforce your skills with the new key reaches. You will create and print a document in WordPerfect.

Reviewing the M and V Keys

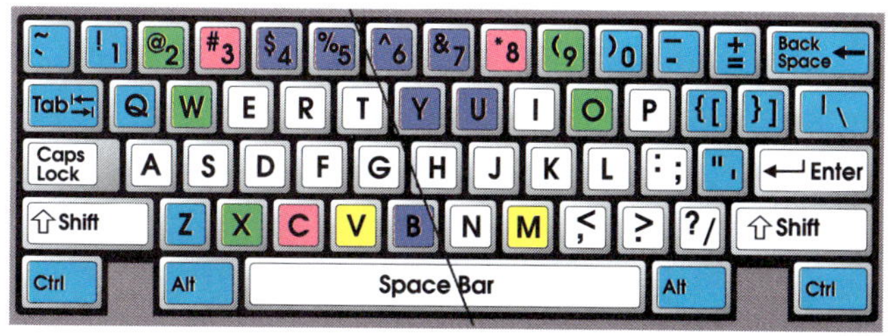

M Key

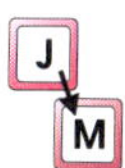

V Key

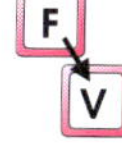

Document D

CIS 562	Desktop Publishing	Marilyn Dahl
CIS 620	LAN Design	Ray Heath
CIS 530	Telecommunications	Elaine Wilson
CIS 510	Disk Operating System	Ray Heath
CIS 610	Network System	Chris Nealy

ENDING THE SESSION

To end this session, DELETE outdated WordPerfect Reinforcement files, PRINT any files from Session 55 not printed earlier, then CONTINUE with the next session or EXIT the program.

M Drill

Key lines 1–3 once, pushing for speed.

1 jm am am him him man man mad mad jam jam me me jm
2 might might metal metal dream dream ram ram small
3 Mashed Mean Mailed Minted Melted Makes Melt Might

Key lines 4–6 twice, concentrating on control.

4 Mike is making a frame; he needs ample sandpaper.
5 Did Mamie transmit the message after amending it?
6 Did Sammie eliminate all mistakes in the message?

V Drill

Key lines 1–3 once, focusing on speed.

1 fv dive dive five five give give grieve grieve fv
2 private private deliver deliver veteran even even
3 Negative Negative Seventeen Seventeen Advertising

Key lines 4–6 twice; concentrate on control.

4 Did Van ever deliver the varnish and the shelves?
5 It is evident; the vital lever reverses the vent.
6 Marvia served vanilla malts at the private event.

Printing WordPerfect Reinforcement Activities

To save and print the WordPerfect Reinforcement activities completed in Session 8, complete steps 1-6 that follow. (***Remember:*** The work you completed up to the WordPerfect Reinforcement section has already been saved automatically.)

1. Choose **F**ile → Save **A**s (or F3).
2. At the *Save As* dialog box, key the new filename, **008wpr.kwp**. Press ***Enter*** or click on OK. Your document has been saved to disk, and it also remains on the screen.
3. To print 008wpr.kwp, choose **F**ile → **P**rint (or F5).
4. Click on **P**rint or press ***Enter***.
5. Close the file (click on **F**ile → **C**lose).
6. Click on the KWP Next Activity button.

ONE-MINUTE TIMINGS

Goal: 25 WAM with no more than 2 errors

- Take a 1-minute timing on each paragraph.
- Press ***Tab*** to indent the first line.

10 Choose **File** → Save **A**s, then key **055wprc.kwp** as the filename.

11 Choose **File** → **C**lose to close the document.

Document C

Summary of Costs	
Hardware	$48,489.25
Software	37,550.00
Installation and cabling estimate	1,800.00
Software implementation estimate	3,800.00
Education and training (24 hours)	5,525.95
Maintenance	12,000.00

Document D — *Table with Center and Right Justification*

1 At a clear WordPerfect document window, create a table with 3 columns and 5 rows using the Power Bar.

2 Center the table horizontally on the page. (Do this at the *Format* dialog box with Ta**b**le selected at the top.)

3 Change the Justification for cells in column B to Center. (Do this at the *Format* dialog box with Col**u**mn selected at the top.)

4 Change the Justification for cells in column C to Right. (Do this at the *Format* dialog box with Col**u**mn selected at the top.)

5 Key the text in the cells in the table. Use the ***Tab*** key to move the insertion point to the next cell or press ***Shift*** + ***Tab*** to move the insertion point to the previous cell.

6 Adjust the width of column A by positioning the insertion point in any cell in column A, then pressing ***Ctrl*** + ***Shift*** + < enough times so the text just fits in the cells in the column.

7 Adjust the width of column B by positioning the insertion point in any cell in column B, then pressing ***Ctrl*** + ***Shift*** + < enough times so the text just fits in the cells in the column.

8 Adjust the width of column C by positioning the insertion point in any cell in column C, then pressing ***Ctrl*** + ***Shift*** + < enough times so the text just fits in the cells in the column.

9 Press ***Ctrl*** + ***Home*** twice to position the insertion point at the beginning of the document, then center the table vertically. (Do this at the *Center Page(s)* dialog box.)

10 Proofread and correct any errors and then complete a spell check.

11 Choose **File** → Save **A**s, then key **055wprd.kwp** as the filename.

12 Choose **File** → **C**lose to close the document.

- Press ***Enter*** only at the end of a paragraph. Word wrap will end the other lines automatically.
- If you finish a paragraph before time is up, start over.

1 Marna smelled the simmering meat. The steam permeated the air. She managed a small taste and smiled. The meat and milk might help that little girl and ease her pain.

2 As he firmed the damp earth at the tree, the miser imagined he heard a small sigh. Mirages in the misted marsh alarmed him. Grim fears emerged as his mindless tramping faltered.

3 Make that simple diagram first. Then send a message in the mail. Tell that salesman that his latest remarks made the manager mad. The meeting impaired the imminent merger.

4 Traveling in this vast native land is a near marvel. The savage rivers and varied paved miles are impressive. Vivid sights revive the mind and lift spirits. Villages reveal veiled vestiges; a dividend is derived.

5 Even if Gavin is vain, she has avid fans and attentive friends. Her singing is sensitive; she reveals her vast talent. She deserves lavish and vivid praise. Her versatile verses are a massive advantage and elevate her fevered fans.

6 Navigate the even trail in life. Derive all things that are pleasant and reap the advantages. Preserve the vital past and evade vile evils. An avid, aggressive striving is needed in all lives. A varied and diverse path prevents grief.

ENDING THE SESSION

Once you have completed the timings, the KWP program takes you to the next session menu. If you want to print the Session 8 files, however, follow the steps below. Then continue with Session 9 or exit the progam.

PRINT

1. Click on Back until you reach the KWP Main Menu.
2. At the Main Menu, select *Freeform* and click on OK or press ***Enter***.
3. Click on the Print button or choose **F**ile→**P**rint.
4. At the *Print* dialog box, select the **D**ocument on Disk option under *Print Selection*. Press ***Enter*** or click on **P**rint.
5. At the *Document on Disk* dialog box, click on the list button at the right of the filename text box.
6. With the mouse pointer, highlight the file to be printed and press ***Enter*** or click on **P**rint.
7. At the *Document on Disk* dialog box, click on **P**rint.

Repeat steps 3-7 to print additional documents on disk.

Document B

Costs of Maintaining an Office	
Facilities rental	$2,400
Lighting	210
Heat	240
Water	28
Janitorial services	900

Document C Table with Decimal Align Justification

1 At a clear WordPerfect document window, create a table with 2 columns and 7 rows using the Power Bar by doing the following:
   a Position the arrow pointer on the Tables button on the Power Bar.
   b Hold down the left mouse button, drag the arrow pointer down and to the right until *2x7* appears at the top of the grid, then release the mouse button.
2 Join cells A1 and B1.
3 Center the table horizontally on the page. (Do this at the *Format* dialog box with Table selected at the top.)
4 Format cell A1 by doing the following:
   a With the insertion point positioned in cell A1, choose Table → Format.
   b At the *Format* dialog box, make sure Cell is selected at the top of the dialog box.
   c Change the Justification option to Center.
   d Choose Bold, Italic, then Shadow in the Appearance section. (This will insert an X in the Bold and Italic and Shadow check boxes.)
   e Change the Size option (located in the Text Size section) to Large.
   f Choose OK to close the dialog box.
5 Decimal align the numbers to be keyed in cells B2 through B7 by doing the following:
   a Select cells B2 through B7.
   b Choose Table → Format.
   c At the *Format* dialog box, change the Justification to Decimal Align.
   d Choose OK to close the dialog box.
6 Key the text in the cells in the table. Use the ***Tab*** key to move the insertion point to the next cell or press ***Shift* + *Tab*** to move the insertion point to the previous cell. (***Remember***: Do not press ***Tab*** after keying the text in the last cell.)
7 Adjust the width of the columns by doing the following:
   a Position the insertion point in any cell in column A (except cell A1).
   b Press ***Ctrl* + *Shift* + <** 10 times. (This decreases the size of the column.)
   c Position the insertion point in any cell in column B.
   d Press ***Ctrl* + *Shift* + <** 30 times. (This decreases the size of the column.)
8 Press ***Ctrl* + *Home*** twice to position the insertion point at the beginning of the document, then center the table vertically. (Do this at the *Center Page(s)* dialog box.)
9 Proofread and correct any errors and then complete a spell check.

CONTINUE

1. Print and close files..
2. If you are working in Freeform, click on the KWP Main Menu button.
3. Highlight *Keyboarding Sessions*, then click on OK.
4. Click on Jump to go to the next session.

EXIT

1. Print any files, if necessary.
2. Click on the KWP Main Menu button on the Toolbar.
3. At the Main Menu, select WordPerfect Only, then click on OK.
4. Click on **F**ile → E**x**it.
5. Exit Windows, if necessary (**F**ile → E**x**it).

Document B Two-Column Table with Left and Right Column Justification

1. At a clear WordPerfect document window, create a table with 2 columns and 6 rows by doing the following:
   a. Choose Table → Create.
   b. At the *Create Table* dialog box, key **2** in the Columns text box, then press ***Tab***.
   c. Key **6** in the ***Rows*** text box.
   d. Choose OK to close the dialog box.
2. Change the column width for both columns by doing the following:
   a. Select cells A1 and B1.
   b. Choose Table → Format.
   c. At the *Format* dialog box, choose Column at the top of the dialog box.
   d. Change the Width measurement (located in the Column Width section in the lower left corner of the dialog box) to **1.5**.
   e. Choose OK to close the dialog box.
3. Join the cells in the first row by doing the following:
   a. Select cells A1 and B1. (These cells may already be selected.)
   b. Choose Table → Join → Cell.
4. Center the table horizontally by doing the following:
   a. Choose Table → Format.
   b. At the *Format* dialog box, choose Table at the top of the dialog box.
   c. Position the arrow pointer in the Table Position option (located in the lower left corner, containing the word *Left*), hold down the left mouse button, drag the arrow pointer to *Center*, then release the mouse button.
   d. Choose OK to close the dialog box.
5. Before keying text in cells, format cell A1 by doing the following:
   a. Position the insertion point in cell A1.
   b. Choose Table → Format.
   c. At the *Format* dialog box, make sure Cell is selected at the top of the dialog box.
   d. Change the Justification option to Center.
   e. Choose Bold and Small Cap in the Appearance section. (This will insert an X in the Bold and Small Cap check boxes.)
   f. Change the Size option (located in the Text Size section) to Very Large.
   g. Choose OK to close the dialog box.
6. Align the numbers to be keyed in cells B2 through B6 at the right by doing the following:
   a. Select cells B2 through B6.
   b. Choose Table → Format.
   c. At the *Format* dialog box, change the Justification to Right.
   d. Choose OK to close the dialog box.
7. Key the text in the cells in the table. Use the ***Tab*** key to move the insertion point to the next cell or press ***Shift + Tab*** to move the insertion point to the previous cell. (***Remember:*** Do not press ***Tab*** after keying the text in the last cell.)
8. Press ***Ctrl + Home*** twice to position the insertion point at the beginning of the document, then center the table vertically. (Do this at the *Center Page(s)* dialog box.)
9. Proofread and correct any errors and then complete a spell check.
10. Choose File → Save As, then key **055wprb.kwp** as the filename.
11. Choose File → Close to close the document.

O, B, W

SESSION GOALS

O, B, W

25 WAM/2 errors

Practice saving, printing, and closing documents

"W" and "B" Compound words

GETTING STARTED

If you are continuing immediately from Session 8, go to step 4. If you exited the program at the end of Session 8, do the following:

1. At the Windows Program Manager screen, double-click on the WordPerfect icon.
2. At the WordPerfect editing window, click on the KWP button.
3. Go to the Main Menu, then the Keyboarding Sessions menu.
4. At the Keyboarding Sessions menu, click on Jump to return to the activity you left off with. Or, move through the program menus until you reach the Session 9 menu.
5. On the Session 9 menu, *Warm-Up* is highlighted. Click on OK to proceed.

If you are already warmed up or have completed part of the session, move the mouse pointer to the desired activity and click on OK. When you have completed the on-screen activities for Session 9, you will return to the text to complete the WordPerfect Reinforcement activities. For the final activity, you will take six 1-minute timings. Watch your screen for instructions.

WORDPERFECT REINFORCEMENT

Some of the software drills you completed during the first portion of Session 9 are repeated here to reinforce your learning of the O, B, and W keys.

Reviewing the O, B, and W Keys

O Key

B Key

W Key

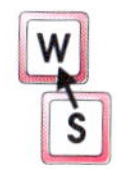

- e Choose OK to close the dialog box.

3 Join the cells in the first row by doing the following:
   - a Select cells A1 and B1. (These cells may already be selected.)
   - b Choose **T**able → **J**oin → **C**ell.

4 Center the table horizontally by doing the following:
   - a Choose **T**able → **F**ormat.
   - b At the *Format* dialog box, choose **T**able at the top of the dialog box.
   - c Position the arrow pointer in the Table Position option (located in the lower left corner, containing the word *Left*), hold down the left mouse button, drag the arrow pointer to *Center*, then release the mouse button.
   - d Choose OK to close the dialog box.

5 Before keying text in cells, format cell A1 by doing the following:
   - a Position the insertion point in cell A1.
   - b Choose **T**able → **F**ormat.
   - c At the *Format* dialog box, make sure **C**ell is selected at the top of the dialog box.
   - d Change the Justification option to Center.
   - e Choose **B**old in the Appearance section. (This will insert an X in the **B**old check box.)
   - f Change the Size option (located in the Text Size section) to Very Large.
   - g Choose OK to close the dialog box.

6 Key the text in the cells in the table. Use the ***Tab*** key to move the insertion point to the next cell or press ***Shift*** + ***Tab*** to move the insertion point to the previous cell. (***Remember:*** Do not press ***Tab*** after keying the text in the last cell.)

7 Press ***Ctrl*** + ***Home*** twice to position the insertion point at the beginning of the document, then center the table vertically. (Do this at the *Center Page(s)* dialog box.)

8 Proofread and correct any errors and then complete a spell check.

9 Choose **F**ile → Save **A**s, then key **055wpra.kwp** as the filename.

10 Choose **F**ile → **C**lose to close the document.

Document A

Capitals of Selected States	
Montana	Helena
Arizona	Phoenix
South Dakota	Pierre
Kansas	Topeka
New Mexico	Santa Fe
Minnesota	St. Paul
Wisconsin	Madison
Tennessee	Nashville
Hawaii	Honolulu

O Drill

Key lines 1–3 once for control.

1 lo do for hop log one old not off pot son golf lo
2 along avoid drove prior other toast option oppose
3 Endorse Diamond Another Visitor Develop Insertion

Key lines 4–6 once, pushing for speed.

4 Ora ordered the onions and olives from the store.
5 The soft fog floated aloft over the lone trooper.
6 Did the florist remove the thorns from the roses?

B Drill

Key lines 1–3 once; push for speed.

1 fb bad bag ban bar bat bed bee beg Ben bet bid fb
2 barter member harbor banker ballot border benefit
3 Alphabet Basement Neighbor Remember Remarkable Be

Key lines 4–6 twice: first for speed, then for control.

4 I grabbed a dab of bread and biked to the harbor.
5 Babe is baffled; the beverage bottles are broken.
6 Barni, the beagle, barks and begs for a big bone.

W Drill

Key lines 1–3 once for control.

1 sw jaw wag raw two war wet saw hew how new sew sw
2 review warmer bowler wiring inward wisdom preview
3 Hardware Workable Followed Weakness Endowment Two

Key lines 4–6 twice: first for control, then for speed.

4 Wear a warm gown if it snows; the weather is raw.
5 The new lawn will grow when watered well at dawn.
6 It is wise to wire the news to the waiting woman.

To change the justification for an entire column of cells, you would choose Column from the *Format* dialog box and then change the Justification as desired. By default, WordPerfect applies the current column's justification settings to a cell if there is no justification specified for an individual cell. If you do not want this to occur, remove the X from the Use Column Justification option at the *Format* dialog box for cells, or choose another Justification option at the *Format* dialog box.

Changing Appearance

The Appearance section of the *Format* dialog box contains a variety of formatting check boxes. By choosing one or more of these check boxes, you can apply formatting within a cell or a group of selected cells. There may be occasions when gray shading appears in a check box (or check boxes) in the Appearance section of the *Format* dialog box. This shading indicates that the appearance option has been turned on for some, but not all, of the selected cells. As you make changes to the options at the *Format* dialog box, the Preview box in the lower right corner reflects the changes.

You can also format text within a cell using the formatting options on the Menu Bar or Power Bar. When using either of these, formatting codes are inserted in the cell in the table. These formatting codes can be seen in Reveal Codes. When you format text within cells with options from the *Format* dialog box, codes are not inserted in the cells.

Changing the Horizontal Position of a Table

By default, a table is positioned at the left margin. This position can be changed to right, center, full (to the left and right margins), or a specific distance from the left edge of the page. Change the horizontal position of the table at the *Format* dialog box. To do this, you would complete the following steps:

1. With the insertion point positioned in any cell in the table, choose Table → Format.
2. At the *Format* dialog box, choose Table at the top of the dialog box.
3. Position the arrow pointer in the Table Position option (located in the lower left corner, containing the word *Left*), hold down the left mouse button, drag the arrow pointer to the desired position, then release the mouse button.
4. Choose OK to close the dialog box.

Document A ← *Two-Column Table*

1. At a clear WordPerfect document window, create a table with 2 columns and 10 rows by doing the following:
   a. Choose Table → Create.
   b. At the *Create Table* dialog box, key **2** in the ***Columns*** text box, then press ***Tab***.
   c. Key **10** in the ***Rows*** text box.
   d. Choose OK to close the dialog box.
2. Change the column width for both columns by doing the following:
   a. Select cells A1 and B1.
   b. Choose Table → Format.
   c. At the *Format* dialog box, choose Column at the top of the dialog box.
   d. Change the Width measurement (located in the Column Width section in the lower left corner of the dialog box) to **1.75**.

THINKING DRILL

Using the list below, key as many words as you can think of that begin with the letters given.

bo wo

bi wh

Key the words in a list. Key all the "bo" words first. Then go to the next set of letters. Try to think of at least 10. If you can think of 20 to 30 words, that's super. Correct all errors.

Printing WordPerfect Reinforcement Activities

To save and print the WordPerfect Reinforcement activities completed in Session 9, do the following. (***Remember:*** The work you completed up to the WordPerfect Reinforcement section has already been saved automatically.)

1. Choose **F**ile → Save **A**s (or F3).
2. At the *Save As* dialog box, key the new filename, **009wpr.kwp**. Press ***Enter*** or click on OK. Your document has been saved to disk, and it also remains on the screen.
3. To print 009wpr.kwp, choose **F**ile → **P**rint (or F5).
4. Click on **P**rint or press ***Enter***.
5. Close the file (click on **F**ile → **C**lose).
6. Click on the KWP Next Activity button.

ONE-MINUTE TIMINGS

Goal: 25 WAM with no more than 2 errors

- Take a 1-minute timing on each paragraph.
- Press ***Tab*** to indent the first line.
- If you finish a paragraph before time is up, start over.
- Press ***Enter*** only at the end of a paragraph.

1 It is good to have honest goals. Nothing is gained if one goes forth in pointless roaming. A major effort is needed to prosper. Isolate those foolish errors and avoid them. Hold to a strong, firm hope and move along.

2 Floss shook in terror as the tornado stormed along the shore. The radio droned on foretelling doom and gloom. The phone popped in her ear as a torrent of rain fell. Alone in the old mansion, her fear overtook her for a moment.

3 Bif booked a berth on the battered boat. As he bragged to his somber brother, the boom of the harbor bells vibrated. Beneath the boasting, Bif began to babble. A belated bolt of disbelief and brooding stabbed at him.

4 Labor to do a noble job. Bosses like brains and ambition. A blend of both brings a desirable habit that boosts a beginner. A babbling boaster absorbs a bore. The absent laborer blemishes his possible bankroll boost.

5 We will await the word of warning in the new tower. The wise, stalwart leader wants to preview the writings of men of worth. He frowns on wrong narrow views. We will follow wise wishes and win a wearisome war and bestow a renewed foothold.

Continued on next page

1. Select cells A1 and B1 using one of the methods described earlier.
2. Choose T**a**ble → **J**oin → **C**ell.

You can also use the Table *QuickMenu* to join cells by doing the following:

1. Select cells A1 and B1.
2. With the insertion point and mouse pointer positioned inside the table, click the **right** mouse button.
3. At the QuickMenu, choose **J**oin → **C**ells.

Changing the Column Width in a Table

When a table is created, the columns are the same width. The width of the columns depends on the number of columns as well as the document margins. You can change the width of columns using the mouse, the Ruler Bar, or the *Format* dialog box.

To adjust or change all columns in a table to the same width, do the following:

1. Select all cells in one row in the table.
2. With the insertion point and mouse pointer inside the table, click the **right** mouse button.
3. At the QuickMenu, choose **F**ormat.
4. At the *Format* dialog box, select Co**l**umn at the top of the dialog box.
5. Key the desired column width in the *Width* text box located in the lower left of the dialog box.
6. Click on OK. All the selected columns should now be sized to the desired width.

To change column widths at the document screen with the mouse, position the I-beam pointer on the line separating columns until it turns into a left- and right-pointing arrow with a vertical line between. Hold down the left mouse button, drag the column line to the desired location, and then release the mouse button. This moves only the column line where the I-beam pointer is positioned. If you hold down the Shift key while you drag a column line, all columns to the right are also moved.

Columns can also be sized from the keyboard by positioning the insertion point inside the column to be changed and pressing ***Crl*** + ***Shift*** + < to decrease the column width or ***Ctrl*** + ***Shift*** + > to increase the column width.

Formatting Cells

By default, text in a cell is aligned at the left margin of the cell. This justification can be changed to Right, Center, Full, All, or Decimal Align. These options operate in the same method as they do in a regular document. In addition to changing the justification for a cell or a group of selected cells, justification can also be changed using the Justification option at the *Format* dialog box. To change the justification of a cell or a group of selected cells, you would do the following:

1. Select the cells within the table.
2. With the insertion point and mouse cursor located in the table, click the right mouse button and select F**o**rmat from the QuickMenu.
3. At the *Format* dialog box, make sure **C**ell is selected. Change the Justification to the desired format by clicking and dragging the arrow pointer at the drop-down menu to the appropriate format and then releasing the mouse button.
4. Click on OK to return to the table.

6 Will reviewed the written words. He did not wish to show that witless newsman how shallow his words were. However, he wanted to warn the world of the wasted wealth in the wages of the man. He showed the network the handwriting on the wall.

ENDING THE SESSION

Once you have completed the timings, the KWP program takes you to the next session menu. If you want to print the Session 9 files, however, follow the steps below. Then continue with Session 10 or exit the progam.

PRINT

1. Click on Back until you reach the KWP Main Menu.
2. At the Main Menu, select *Freeform* and click on OK or press ***Enter***.
3. Click on the Print button or choose **F**ile → **P**rint.
4. At the *Print* dialog box, select the **D**ocument on Disk option under *Print Selection*. Press ***Enter*** or click on **P**rint.
5. At the *Document on Disk* dialog box, click on the list button at the right of the filename text box.
6. With the mouse pointer, highlight the file to be printed and press ***Enter*** or click on **P**rint.
7. At the *Document on Disk* dialog box, click on **P**rint.

Repeat steps 3-7 to print additional documents on disk.

CONTINUE

1. Print and close files.
2. If you are working in Freeform, click on the KWP Main Menu button.
3. Highlight *Keyboarding Sessions*, then click on OK.
4. Click on Jump to go to the next session.

EXIT

1. Print any files, if necessary.
2. Click on the KWP Main Menu button on the Toolbar.
3. At the Main Menu, select WordPerfect Only, then click on OK.
4. Click on **F**ile → E**x**it.
5. Exit Windows, if necessary (**F**ile → E**x**it).

Entering Text in Cells

With the insertion point positioned in a cell, you can key or edit text. To move the insertion point to the right or the next cell, press ***Tab***. Pressing ***Shift + Tab*** moves the insertion point to the left or back to the previous cell. You can also use the mouse to position the insertion point in the desired cell by clicking the left mouse button inside the cell. The arrow keys can also be used to position the insertion point in the desired cell.

Text can be keyed into the cells in the table in any order desired. If text is keyed in a cell in the table and it does not fit on one line, it wraps to the next line. If you press ***Enter*** within a cell, the insertion point is moved to the next line within the **same** cell. The cell will *vertically* expand to accommodate the text and thereby extend all cells by the same vertical measurement in the row.

When the insertion point is located in the last cell in the last row of a table and you press ***Tab***, WordPerfect adds another row to the Table. If you do not want to add another row to your table, do not press ***Tab*** when the insertion point is located in the last cell of a table. Use the arrow keys or the mouse pointer to move the insertion point outside the table.

Selecting Cells

A table can be formatted in special ways. For example, the alignment or margins of text in cells or rows can be changed or character formatting can be added. To identify the cells that are to be affected by any formatting, the specific cells need to be selected.

Selecting Cells with the Mouse

The mouse pointer can be used to select a cell, row, column, or an entire table. The *table selection arrows* are used to select specific cells in a table. There is a left-pointing arrow called the *horizontal selection arrow* and an up-pointing arrow called the *vertical selection arrow*. To display the ***horizontal selection arrow***, move the I-beam pointer to the left border of any cell until it changes to a left-pointing arrow. To display the *vertical selection arrow*, move the I-beam pointer to the top border of any cell until it changes to an up-pointing arrow. Once you have either the horizontal or vertical selection arrow, select specific cells in a table with the following selections:

Using the ***horizontal*** selection arrow:

1. Click the left mouse button **once** in any cell to select that cell.
2. Double-click the left mouse button in any cell in a row to select that row.

With the ***vertical*** selection arrow selected:

1. Double-click the left mouse button in any cell in a column to select that column
2. Triple-click the left mouse button in any cell in the table to select all the cells in the table.

You can also use the click and drag technique to select cells and/or text in a table.

Joining Cells in a Table

Cells can be joined with the ***Join*** option from the T**a**ble drop-down menu. Before joining cells, you must select the cells to be joined. For example, to join cells A1 and B1, you would do the following:

REINFORCEMENT OF SESSIONS 1-9

SESSION GOALS

 Review all keys presented in sessions 1-9

 Practice saving, printing, and closing documents

 25 WAM/2 errors

GETTING STARTED

If you are continuing immediately from Session 9, go to step 4. If you exited the program at the end of Session 9, do the following:

1. At the Windows Program Manager screen, double-click on the WordPerfect icon.
2. At the WordPerfect editing window, click on the KWP button.
3. Go to the Main Menu, then the Keyboarding Sessions menu.
4. At the Keyboarding Sessions menu, click on Jump to return to the activity you left off with. Or, move through the program menus until you reach the Session 10 menu.
5. On the Session 10 menu, *Keyboarding Reinforcement Drills* is highlighted. Click on OK to proceed with the drills.

CHECKING YOUR SKILL—TIMING

In Sessions 7-9 you completed a series of 1-minute timings. Before you take the 1-minute timing that follows, check your scores on the Student Report by completing the following steps:

1. Click on the KWP Rep button. (Remember that you must respond to any program questions or choices on the screen first.)
2. Your timing scores are listed on the screen.
3. Click on OK to return to your previous location.

Goal: 25 WAM with 2 or fewer errors.

1 When the winter snow thaws, warm rain washes the world. Wild flowers begin to weave in a slow swing with the wind. Whiffs of a meadow awakened swirl down at the dawn. The dew is a rainbow and twinkles as a jewel. Winter has blown onward.

The **Table** feature can be used to create vertical columns and horizontal rows of information. The intersection of a row and a column is called a *cell*. These columns and rows may or may not be surrounded by horizontal and vertical lines. The formatting choices available with the Table feature are quite extensive and allow flexibility in creating a variety of tables.

There are several ways to create a table using WordPerfect's Table feature. You can access the Tables button on the Power Bar or use the Table option from the Menu Bar. To create a table using the Power Bar, you would complete the following steps:

1 Position the arrow pointer on the Tables button.
2 Hold down the left mouse button. This causes a grid to appear.
3 Drag the arrow pointer down and to the right or left until the correct number of rows and columns are displayed in black above the grid, then release the mouse button. A table with the designated number of columns and rows appears at the location of the insertion point.

You can also create a Table using the Table option from the Menu Bar by completing the following steps:

1 Choose T**a**ble → **C**reate.
2 At the *Create Table* dialog box, make certain Table is selected.
3 In the *Table Size* text boxes, key the number of Columns in your table, press ***Tab,*** then key the number of Rows.
4 Choose OK to close the *Create Table* dialog box. A table with the designated number of columns and rows appears at the location of the insertion point. The table in figure 55.1 is a two-column table created with the Table option.

Major Automobiles	
Chevelle	Prelude
Nova	Mustang
Firebird	Sunbird
Seville	Continental
Integra	Camaro
Probe	Celica
LTD Landau	Impala
Civic	Accord
Taurus	Audi Fox
Maxima	Cavalier

Figure 55.1 Two-Column Table

When a table is created, columns are lettered from left to right, beginning with A. The rows in a table are numbered from top to bottom, beginning with 1. Every cell (the intersection of a column and a row) has a letter and a number (A1, B1, A2, B2) to identify it. When the insertion point is located in a cell in the table, the name of the cell is displayed at the left side of the Status Bar.

WORDPERFECT REINFORCEMENT

The Special Drills that follow provide additional practice on the keys that you have learned in Sessions 1-9. However, if you are already keying over 25 WAM with no more than two errors and do not hesitate when keying, click on the KWP Next Activity button twice to go to the next session. If you are not at the 25 WAM with fewer than 3 errors level, proceed with the Special Drills to build speed and/or accuracy. Here are guidelines for choosing drills:

1. If you have not mastered a key reach (you hesitate before striking the key), key the speed-building lines.
2. If you are making more than 2 errors per minute, key the accuracy-building lines.
3. If you are not keying at least 25 WAM and/or are making more than two errors, key the speed-building lines.

Special Drills

- Key each line once.
- If you need more work on speed or accuracy, key the appropriate group of lines again.

Keys Review (Speed)

1 asdf jkl; ;p; frf jmj fvf lol fbf sws pr mv db wm
2 p pad pan peg pen pin pit pie plan phase pledge p
3 r rap ran red rip rent rests real repels refers r
4 m ham hem men him mate mind mesh manage mandate m
5 v vat vim vet vise vent vane vigil valid veneer v
6 o oh or odd old one oaf opens omit ogle oval of o
7 b bad beg bid bop brag blend board brake better b
8 w was wed who win woe were when went where with w
9 Janell Kenneth Morris William Shanon Olan Bronson

Balanced-Hand Words (Speed)

1 lamb blend bland blame amble emblem problem bible
2 lap nap pen paid pane flap span pale spent dispel
3 air pan sir risks lair heir pair hair flair widow
4 map maid mane melt sham lame mend firm make flame
5 vie via pair vivid pelvis disown pens laps disown
6 fog sod oak rod foam fork form foam odor soak rod
7 bow wig wow vow down gown wisp with wish when wit
8 Did the lame lamb amble down to the big pale oak?
9 The pale widow paid for the vivid gown and a wig.
10 When did Vivian mend the pair of problem emblems?

FIVE-MINUTE TIMINGS

Goal: 35 WAM/1 error

SI: 1.49

- Take two 5-minute timings.

All machines are made up of parts that work together to perform functions or accomplish tasks for the user. If a machine is to work correctly, all those parts must be in top working condition. One way to make sure that the parts all work correctly is to maintain a regular schedule of cleaning the parts.

A computer is a machine. Therefore, if you want your computer system to work efficiently and have a long life, you need to pay close attention to keeping its parts clean. The parts of a computer system are the mouse, the mouse pad, the monitor, the keyboard, and the central processing unit.

Always turn off the computer before you begin your cleaning routine. The first step in computer cleaning is to use a soft brush or a soft brush attachment for the vacuum cleaner. Carefully brush or vacuum all the cracks and crevices on your monitor, keyboard, and central processing unit. Be sure to brush between the keys on your keyboard and any other hard-to-reach places. While you are brushing, don't forget to brush your mouse pad. In fact, you should brush your mouse pad once a day.

When you have brushed the surface dust and particles away, you can then use liquid cleaners to get rid of the grime that is in the air. Isopropyl alcohol (70%) is one of the most often recommended cleaning agents. You can also use a commercial window cleaner diluted. If you use the alcohol solution, be very careful not to use it directly on the keys, logos, or printed labels, as alcohol will remove some printing. Never pour alcohol directly onto your computer's parts.

Monitors, like windows, pick up particles from the air. The dust and grime that adhere to windows and mirrors also stick to monitor screens. You may even find the words on your screen hard to read through all the dust and fingerprints. Each week, you should clean your screen. You will need a soft brush (or soft vacuum brush), a soft, lint-free cloth or tissue, and a commercial window cleaner or isopropyl alcohol. When you are ready to clean the screen or other external parts, pour a little alcohol or window cleaner onto a lint-free cloth or tissue. Wipe the screen or other part and discard the cloth or tissue. Then, pour a little more cleaning solution onto the tissue and wipe the same area again. Be sure to get the corners clean. You can use small cotton swabs for the corners. Once your computer is clean and working well, set aside a day each week for routine cleaning.

CREATING TABLES

A large amount of the information processed in business consists of numerical data. Because of the very nature of this type of data, it is often difficult and impractical to present it in sentence and paragraph form. An attractive and readable table is usually centered vertically as well as horizontally on a sheet of paper. WordPerfect's **Table** feature makes creating tables a breeze!

Two-Letter Combinations (Speed)

1 pe peg pen pest peeps peddles pellet pets peep pe
2 pi pin pie piles pills pitfall pipes pink pine pi
3 That pill peddler peddled piles of pinkish pills.

4 ra ran rap ranks rake rates raised range rapid ra
5 ri rid rip rises ripe right ridges rigid rinse ri
6 Rapid Red ran to the raised ridges on that range.

7 ma man mat math make mail marsh manager margin ma
8 mi mid mild mind mint midst might misting mire mi
9 The manager might mail the mild mints to the man.

10 va van vat vane vases vast valid varied vanish va
11 vi vie vim vise vile vine visits vital vintage vi
12 The vital vintage vases vanished from a vast van.

13 oa oak oats oath oatmeal load toad roast float oa
14 of off offers offends offset offense offensive of
15 Those offensive oats floated off that old oatmeal.

16 ba bad bag bail balk bath badge barks bandages ba
17 bl blade bleak blast blank blight blind blinks bl
18 The bat blinked at a baboon blinded in bandages.

19 wa was war wag wade wait wane wash waste waves wa
20 wi win wit wig wide wipe will wise wield wiper wi
21 Winna washed and wiped her wig; she wasted water.

Double-Letter Words (Accuracy)

1 slipping sipping happen flipping appease shipping
2 terriers irritates terrains follow all narratives
3 dimmer dinners hammering manners immense immerges
4 moon roof pool hood hook loot took mood root door
5 gobble rabble hobble babble pebble nibbles rabbit
6 Janell slipped the irritated terrier in the door.
7 That immense rabbit emerged and nibbled a bottle.
8 She will be shipping the poor winter winner soon.

SESSION 55

SESSION GOALS

1-Minute: 45 WAM/1 error
5-Minute: 35 WAM/1 error

Using the Table feature

GETTING STARTED

If you are continuing immediately from Session 54, go to the one-minute timings. If you exited the program at the end of Session 54, do the following:

1. Access Windows, then WordPerfect 6.1 for Windows.
2. Click on the KWP icon to access *Keyboarding with WordPerfect*.
3. Go to the Keyboarding Sessions menu and click on Jump to return to your last activity. Or, access the Session 55 menu and click on OK to begin the session.

ONE-MINUTE TIMINGS

Goal: 45 WAM/1 error

SI: 1.47

- Take two 1-minute timings on the following material.
- Use your most recent timing speed to set a speed or accuracy goal.

The hard times and severe economic problems that were a part of the early Thirties affected all circuses. More circuses had to close their doors than ever before. The yearning and the need for exciting entertainment, however, still lingered in the hearts and minds of the people. It is true that the modern circus is usually held in a large arena or building and some of the old atmosphere is missing. But, an element of excitement and fun lives on. The music, the cotton candy, the animals, and the performers carry on a fine tradition.

Longer Words (Accuracy)

1 elephant dependent safekeeping plaintiff pipeline
2 standard registrar parenthesis telegrams resident
3 That resident registrar sends standard telegrams.

4 familiar eliminate sentimental dependent estimate
5 retrieve primitive advertising privilege negative
6 Eliminate that sentimental, familiar advertising.

7 rational tradition imagination negotiate renovate
8 ambition elaborate observation establish possible
9 stalwart knowledge handwriting wholesale whenever
10 Establish rational imagination whenever possible.

Saving and Printing WordPerfect Reinforcement Activities

To save and print the WordPerfect Reinforcement activities completed in Session 10, do the following. (***Remember:*** The work you completed up to the WordPerfect Reinforcement section has already been saved automatically.)

1 Choose **F**ile → Save **A**s (or F3).
2 At the *Save As* dialog box, key the new filename, **010wpr.kwp**. Press ***Enter*** or click on OK. Your document has been saved to disk, and it also remains on the screen.
3 To print 010wpr.kwp, choose **F**ile → **P**rint or (F5).
4 Click on **P**rint or press ***Enter***.
5 Close the file (click on **F**ile → **C**lose).
6 Click on the KWP Next Activity button to bring up the Timing screen.

ONE-MINUTE TIMING

Now that you have completed the drills, you are to take two 1-minute timings on the timing paragraph at the beginning of the session. Compare the rates with your first attempt. Has your speed improved? Do you have fewer errors? If you are not reaching 25 WAM with two or fewer errors on the 1-minute timing, repeat Sessions 7-9.

ENDING THE SESSION

Once you have completed the timings, the KWP program takes you to the next session menu. If you want to print the Session 10 files, however, follow the steps below. Then continue with Session 11 or exit the progam.

PRINT

1 Click on Back until you reach the KWP Main Menu.
2 At the Main Menu, select *Freeform* and click on OK or press ***Enter***.
3 Click on the Print button or choose **F**ile → **P**rint.
4 At the *Print* dialog box, select the **D**ocument on Disk option under *Print Selection*. Press ***Enter*** or click on **P**rint.

UNIT

10

TABLES

5 At the *Document on Disk* dialog box, click on the list button at the right of the filename text box.
6 With the mouse pointer, highlight the file to be printed and press ***Enter*** or click on **P**rint.
7 At the *Document on Disk* dialog box, click on **P**rint.

Repeat steps 3-7 to print additional documents on disk.

CONTINUE

1 Print and close files.
2 If you are working in Freeform, click on the KWP Main Menu button.
3 Highlight *Keyboarding Sessions*, then click on OK.
4 Click on Jump to go to the next session.

EXIT

1 Print any files, if necessary.
2 Click on the KWP Main Menu button on the Toolbar.
3 At the Main Menu, select WordPerfect Only, then click on OK.
4 Click on **F**ile → E**x**it.
5 Exit Windows, if necessary (**F**ile → E**x**it).

Document C ◄-- *Composing a Memo Report*

At a clear WordPerfect editing window, compose a memo report to your instructor comparing two products (for example, two different makes of cars); two services (for example, two different fast-food restaurants); or two concepts/ideas (for example, is it easier to learn by presenting the parts that eventually lead to the whole or by presenting the whole and then the parts?). In developing your memo report be sure to provide an introduction, the features/characteristics of the items being compared, and a conclusion (which of the two is best and why).

In preparing this document, apply the appropriate document formatting guidelines, WordPerfect features, and writing guidelines that you have learned throughout the sessions.

When you are ready to key the document, click on WAM Only to have the KWP program calculate your WAM rate. When you are finished, click on Stop WAM. Be sure to proofread the document and check the spelling. Save the file as **054wprc.kwp**. Then print and close the file.

ENDING THE SESSION

To end this session, DELETE outdated WordPerfect Reinforcement files, PRINT any files from Session 54 not printed earlier, then CONTINUE with the next session or EXIT the program.

DELETING FILES

SESSION GOALS

U, Z, C

Deleting files
Review cursor movement

-ed and -ing endings

GETTING STARTED

If you are continuing immediately from Session 10, go to step 4. If you exited the program at the end of Session 10, do the following:

1. Access Windows, then WordPerfect 6.1 for Windows.
2. At the WordPerfect editing window, click on the KWP icon.
3. Go to the Main Menu, then the Keyboarding Sessions menu.
4. At the Keyboarding Sessions menu, click on Jump to return to the activity you left off with. Or, move through the program menus until you reach the Session 11 menu.
5. On the Session 11 menu, *Warm-Up* is highlighted. Click on OK to proceed with the Warm-Up activities.

If you are already warmed up or have completed a portion of the session, position the mouse pointer on the desired activity and click on OK or press ***Enter***. When you have completed the new-key drills, Thinking Drill, and WordPerfect Reinforcement activities, you will take several 1-minute timings on short paragraphs of text.

WORDPERFECT REINFORCEMENT

Some of the drills presented earlier on the computer screen are repeated here to reinforce your keyboarding skills. In addition, you will review the WordPerfect options for insertion point movement and learn to delete outdated files.

Reviewing the U, Z, and C Keys

U Key

Z Key

C Key

D
C

is expected to increase about 22 percent by the year 2000. Golfing demand in the year 2010 has been projected to be 58 percent greater than it was in 1990. Estimates for our state indicate a need for an additional 488 nine-hole courses by the year 2010.

Current Status. At the present time, our city has four golf courses: two country clubs and two privately owned courses. Each of the four courses has undesirable features for our citizens and for visitors. One country club is private and not open to the public; another country club is open only one day a week to the general public. One of the privately owned courses is located between two cities, and thus it is used by golfers from both areas. In addition, it is only a nine-hole course. The other course open to the public is only a par-three course.

Supply vs. Demand. To compare the supply and demand in golf, it is necessary to base all projections on the amount of play a course can handle. The National Golf Foundation has created a means of determining maximum potential. Using statistics provided by the four courses, the foundation has determined that there are about 550 golfers per day (six months only) who wish to play but are unable to secure reservations.

Costs. A survey was conducted to determine the average construction costs for our state and the four surrounding states. Actual construction costs will vary from the estimate depending on the site of the proposed golf course, the amount of earth-moving necessary, the type of watering system used, and the size of the clubhouse. For a golf course in our city, the site should be approximately 225 acres or larger. Of these 225 acres, 175 would be used for an 18-hole course, clubhouse, and parking lot. The remaining 50 acres should be used for an additional nine-hole course when demand exceeds supply.

Recommendation. It is recommended by the committee that the board seriously consider the development of a course in our city. Board members may wish to obtain additional data on the following items:

1. Availability of 225 acres of unimproved land in a suitable location.
2. Availability of experienced personnel.
3. Amount of capital available.

(Send copies to S. Harder, W. Simmonson, and J. Cotton.)

U Drills

Key lines 1–3 once, pushing for speed.

1 ju put put sun sun fun fun mud mud gum gum sum ju
2 vault audit rumor truth about nurse sprung refund
3 Fusion Lawful Nature Urgent Plural Module Suppose

Key lines 4–6 twice: first for speed, then for accuracy.

4 Just be sure to return that blouse to the bureau.
5 That auto bumper is a hunk of junk; it is ruined.
6 A stout runner shouted and slumped to the ground.

Z Drills

Key lines 1–3 once, pushing for speed. Don't stop to correct errors unless directed by your instructor.

1 az jazz jazz maze maze doze doze raze raze zip az
2 seize breeze amaze razor pizza hazel zombi wizard
3 Trapeze Zealous Pretzel Drizzle Horizon Embezzler

Key lines 4–6 twice: first for speed, then for control.

4 Liz seized that sizzling pizza and ate with zeal.
5 Minimize the hazard and stabilize that bulldozer.
6 Zeb baked a dozen pretzels in the sizzling blaze.

C Drills

Key lines 1–3 once, pushing for speed.

1 dc calk cane case calf camp carp cave cede cad dc
2 camera notice commit impact circle decide attract
3 Compare Produce Consult Service Council Enclosure

Key lines 4–6 twice: first for speed, then for control.

4 Carlton, the cat, curled in comfort in the chair.
5 Chris decided to purchase a record and a picture.
6 Cecelia consumed a rich chocolate ice cream cone.

third-level head

Disadvantages ← second-level head

→ Costly to produce. In some cases, the manual can be quite costly to produce. A major expense to consider is the time spent in the development of the manual. Can you afford to assign the project to several staff members, or should you hire an outside consultant and allow your employees to focus on their areas of expertise? The cost of regularly updating and revising the manual is another major expense.

Document B ← Memo Report

1 At the *Production–Session 54 Document B* screen, key Document B as a memo report. Include the following formatting changes:
   - a Insert the date automatically.
   - b Set a tab at 1.25" on the Ruler Bar for the numbered items (the text that is indented after each number under "Recommendation" and the copy notation).
   - c Create a header for the second-page heading. (See Session 48.)
   - d Turn on Widow/Orphan to prevent any undesirable page breaks.

2 Proofread and correct any errors and complete a spell check.

3 Click on Check to automatically name (**054prob.kwp**), save, and check the document.

4 To print with errors highlighted, click on the Print button.

5 To correct errors, click on View Original. Make changes, then recheck the document.

6 Close the document and click on the KWP Next Activity button to bring up a clear WordPerfect editing window.

Document B

To: Esther Ramell, Chair, Board of Directors/From: Proposal Development Committee (Berra, Kottke, Lanzel, Oberg, and Risgaard)/Subject: Recommendations for the Development of a Public Golf Course/This committee was charged at the last board meeting with creating a basic proposal regarding the need and cost for constructing a new public golf course in our city. Accordingly, the committee has gathered the data and prepared this report. Summary. The city presently has four golf courses. Two courses are open entirely to the general public; one course is open to the public only one day per week; and one course is private and not open to the public. User statistics show that this area could profitably support another 18-hole golf course. Construction costs could be returned within five or six years after the operation begins. Background. The remarkable growth in the number of golf courses has been due primarily to the promotion of the game on a national basis. Golfers' demands for additional facilities and the possibility that these would prove self-sustaining have prompted many cities and private organizations such as ours to make adequate provisions for golf. Studies have revealed that income has exceeded operating expenses by a considerable margin at every course that has been opened in the past 15 years./In our state, golfing demand

Continued on next page

WordPerfect Insertion Point Movement: A Review

For the final WordPerfect Reinforcement activity in Session 11, practice the following insertion point movements:

Ctrl + Home	Moves insertion point to the beginning of the document
Alt + Page Down	Moves insertion point to the top of the next page
End	Moves insertion point to the end of the line
Ctrl + ←	Moves insertion point to the beginning of previous word
Ctrl + →	Moves insertion point to the beginning of next word
Ctrl + End	Moves insertion point to the end of the document
Alt + Page Up	Moves insertion point to the top of the previous page
Home	Moves insertion point to the beginning of the line
Page Down	Moves insertion point to the bottom of the screen
Page Up	Moves insertion point to the top of the screen

Do this exercise two more times to help reinforce your learning of insertion point movements.

Printing WordPerfect Reinforcement Activities

To save and print the WordPerfect for Windows document you have created, complete steps 1-5 that follow. (***Remember:*** The work you completed up to the WordPerfect Reinforcement section has already been saved automatically.)

1. Choose **F**ile→Save **A**s (or F3).
2. At the *Save As* dialog box, key the new filename, **011wpr.kwp**. Press ***Enter*** or click on the OK button. Your document has been saved to disk, and it also remains on the screen.
3. To print 011wpr.kwp, choose **F**ile→**P**rint (or F5).
4. Click on the Print button or press ***Enter***.
5. Close the file (click on **F**ile→**C**lose).

Deleting Files

Throughout the first ten sessions, the activities and timed writings you completed in the *Keyboarding with WordPerfect* software were saved automatically. You were responsible for saving the activities completed in the WordPerfect Reinforcement part of each session.

A good habit to develop is to delete documents from your floppy disk or hard drive regularly. The disk you use to store the sessions for this program provides an excellent opportunity to develop this habit.

The *Keyboarding with WordPerfect* program automatically deletes the Session and Timings files that were done ten sessions earlier. Thus, only the ten most recent Session and Timing files are retained on your data disk. It will be your job to delete selected **wpr** (WordPerfect Reinforcement) files on a regular basis.

From now on, unless instructed otherwise, keep only the ten most recently completed **wpr** files on your disk. This eliminates the need to keep multiple disks (and saves money), and you will not find yourself in situations where there is insufficient space on your disk to store work you have completed.

Your goal is to key each document in mailable form at 25 words a minute (2.5 lines a minute) or higher. The timing starts as you begin keying the first line of the manuscript or business report and ends when the document is saved (corrections have been made and the spelling check has been completed). It is your responsibility to review each document before it is keyed. **The document may be formatted improperly or it may be missing required features such as the filename.**

If you key any documents at a rate below 25 WAM and/or are missing errors that should have been corrected, your instructor may ask you to repeat those specific documents.

Document A — *Bound Manuscript*

1 At the *Production–Session 54 Document A* screen, key Document A as a multiple-page bound manuscript with headings. Use double line spacing, page numbering (upper right corner, beginning on page 2), and Widow/Orphan protection.
2 Proofread and correct any errors and complete a spell check.
3 Click on Check to automatically name **(054proa.kwp)**, save, and check the document.
4 To print with errors highlighted, click on the Print button.
5 To correct errors, click on View Original. Make changes, then recheck the document.
6 Close the document.

Document A

] Office MANUALS [bf and all caps
Electronic

bf
Purpose

More and more offices are preparing and utilizing electronic office manuals. There are many reasons for developing electronic procedure guides.

Information second-level head

The manual usually is developed to share pertinent facts and basic information with all employees. Valuable supervisory time is saved because initial instructions to new employees need not be repeated. The new worker can read the manual carefully from the screen and refer back to it if necessary.

The electronic manual is available to all employees at any time. This allows the employees to know exactly the areas of his or her responsibilities and duties.

Advantages and Disadvantages ← first-level head

As with any on-line data, the use of electronic manuals has both advantages and disadvantages.

Advantages ← second-level head

Publicizing the advantages of an electronic office manual will make it much easier to gain employee acceptance.

an electronic

Saves money. Using a printed office manual saves money because supervisory time is not taken up with endless repetitions of instructions. and updates can be made at any time

Eliminates errors. If an employee has a question about procedure and the supervisor isn't available, he or she can refer to the manual promptly before a costly error is made.

Continued on next page

For your first deleting activity, delete the **wpr** file for Session 1. To delete this file, do the following:

1. Choose **F**ile → **O**pen.
2. At the *Open File* dialog box, select the file *001wpr.kwp* (click on it with the left mouse button).
3. Choose File **O**ptions → **D**elete.
4. At the *Delete File* dialog box, click on **D**elete.
5. To close the *Open File* dialog box, click on Cancel or press ***Esc***.
6. Click on the KWP Next Activity button.

Note: Once the file to be deleted has been selected (highlighted) in the *Open File* dialog box, you can press the ***Delete*** key on the keyboard to delete the file rather than using File **O**ptions → **D**elete.

ONE-MINUTE TIMINGS

Goal: 25 WAM with no more than 2 errors

- Take a 1-minute timing on each paragraph.
- Press ***Tab*** to indent the first line.
- If you finish a paragraph before time is up, start over.
- Let word wrap control line endings.

1 The blunt auditor suggested to Duke that the business returns were a fraud. The usual routine of minimum turnovers of funds had been sound, but that fortune of thousands paid to a juror had not been inserted in the annual input. Duke presumed he was ruined and flushed with guilt.

2 Ruth sulked as her aunt poured a dose of the awful blue fluid. The sour stuff was supposed to be used for fatigue from the flu. She paused for a minute and gulped it down. Her aunt found four lumps of sugar for a bonus. Sullen disgust would turn into a laugh as a result.

3 Zeb zipped to that zoo with zest and nuzzled the zebras. He sneezed in the breeze and went to see the lizards. He wants to be a zoologist when he gets older. He knows a zillion things and his dazed and puzzled parents are amazed.

4 Zelda gazed in amazement as Zip, the wizard, seized a wand. It was ablaze with a maze of fire and lights. He did dozens of hazardous feats and puzzled all at the bazaar. He also was a trapeze whiz and dazzled folks.

5 A cookout on the beach could include cheese, carrots, meat sandwiches, and cold juice. If the chill of the ocean is too much, hot chocolate and hot coffee can chase the cold chills. The decent lunch and a chat with chums can enrich affection.

6 An office clerk who lacks basic ethics could become the subject of scorn. Those persisting in cruel and careless attacks on certain new workers can cause havoc. It is logical to follow strict, concise rules concerning office tact. Choose the right track and be sincere.

FIVE-MINUTE TIMINGS

Goal: 35 WAM/1 error

SI: 1.49

- Take one 5-minute timing.

Each day, many people move all of their belongings from one place to another place. The move may be a short one, just across the street. Or, the move may be a long one, all the way across the country.

One item many people forget until the last minute is the personal computer. Most of us do not know how to pack and move a computer safely. As with all items being moved, a computer is prone to damage if it is not packed and handled properly. There are a few well known tips for you to follow when you are planning a move.

The first thing you should do is to make a backup of your hard disk before you turn off the machine prior to the move. You can back up your files to external diskettes or to a tape backup system. Because the backup will take many external disks, you may want to invest in a tape backup system. This purchase will be of great help to you and is also quite inexpensive. While you are backing up your files, now would be a good time to write down the model and serial numbers. You will have proof and identification of each item if damage or loss should occur en route.

After you have made a complete backup of all your files and system, the next step is to begin taking your computer apart. Before you start this step, be sure to unplug your system. Then you can detach the cables from the peripheral devices such as your mouse, your printer, your keyboard, and any other devices you may be using. It is a good idea to label each cable with a small tag. That way, when you reach your destination, you can attach each cable in exactly the right place. As you unplug each cable or plug, it is also a good idea to put a small tag on each plug or port from which you removed a plug or a cable.

When you have completely detached every cable and plug, you can then begin packing your computer parts for the move. The best packing container is, of course, the original box in which your computer came. However, most of us have either misplaced this box or thrown it away. The next best container is a box that is about two inches larger than your system. Line the bottom of the box with newspapers or several inches of packing material. Foam packing materials work well; popcorn works just as well. Next, place your computer in the box and line the edges with the packing materials. Then, put the mouse and keyboard (each in a plastic bag) in the box with the computer. It would be a good idea to put layers of newspaper around these items. You can then fill the box to the top with more packing material. Seal the box and label it, and you are done.

PROGRESS CHECK

Now that you have completed the reports and manuscripts unit, it is time to determine how quickly you can key new examples of these types of documents.

Key the following documents as quickly as possible, correcting all errors. You want the document to be "mailable." In other words, when you finish the document, it will be completely correct, with no errors.

ENDING THE SESSION

Once you have completed the timings, the KWP program takes you to the next session menu. If you want to print the Session 11 files, however, follow the steps below. Then continue with Session 12 or exit the program.

PRINT

1. Click on Back until you reach the KWP Main Menu.
2. Highlight *Freeform*, then click on OK.
3. Click on the Print button or choose **F**ile → **P**rint.
4. At the *Print* dialog box, select the **D**ocument on Disk option under *Print Selection*. Press ***Enter*** or click on OK.
5. At the *Document on Disk* dialog box, click on the list button at the right of the filename text box.
6. With the mouse pointer, highlight the file to be printed and press ***Enter*** or click on **P**rint.
7. At the *Document on Disk* dialog box, click on **P**rint.

Repeat steps 3-7 to print additional documents on disk.

CONTINUE

1. Print and close files.
2. If you are working in Freeform, click on the KWP Main Menu button.
3. Highlight *Keyboarding Sessions*, then click on OK.
4. Click on Jump to go to the next session.

EXIT

1. Print any files, if necessary.
2. Click on the KWP Main Menu button on the Toolbar.
3. At the Main Menu, select WordPerfect Only, then click on OK.
4. Click on **F**ile → E**x**it.
5. Exit Windows, if necessary (**F**ile → E**x**it).

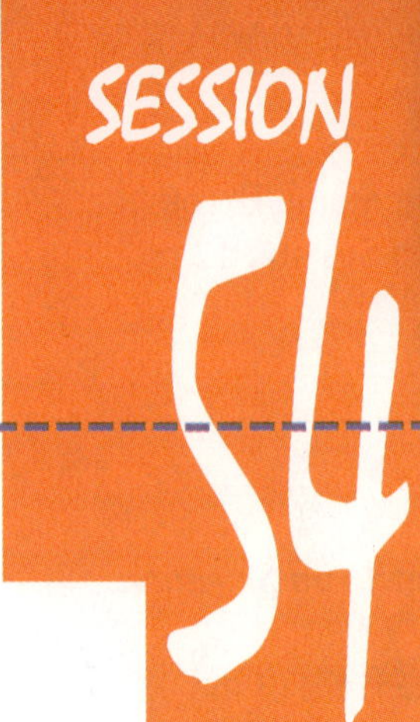

PRODUCTION PROGRESS CHECK
MANUSCRIPTS AND REPORTS

SESSION GOALS

1-Minute: 45 WAM/1 error
5-Minute: 35 WAM/1 error

Review of selected features presented in Sessions 34-53

GETTING STARTED

If you are continuing immediately from Session 53, go to the one-minute timing. If you exited the program at the end of Session 53, do the following:

1. Access Windows, then WordPerfect 6.1 for Windows.
2. Click on the KWP icon to access *Keyboarding with WordPerfect.*
3. Go to the Keyboarding Sessions menu and click on Jump to return to your last activity. Or, access the Session 54 menu and click on OK to begin the session.

ONE-MINUTE TIMING

Goal: 45 WAM/1 error

SI: 1.48

- Take a 1-minute timing on the following material.
- Use your most recent timing speed to set a speed or accuracy goal.

Planning flower displays is a time-consuming, but rewarding, task. For example, a mass of brilliant colors and textures could brighten a dark corner or highlight darker foliage and shrubs. Some annuals are better suited for border planting or edging. Others that grow quite tall can be used for unique backgrounds or screening. There are many annuals that make gorgeous bouquets of cut flowers. The gardener can enjoy the fruits of his or her labor with vases of beautiful blossoms placed all around the house. Having your own garden is a benefit you will appreciate time and again. Your friends and relatives will thank you for having a green thumb.

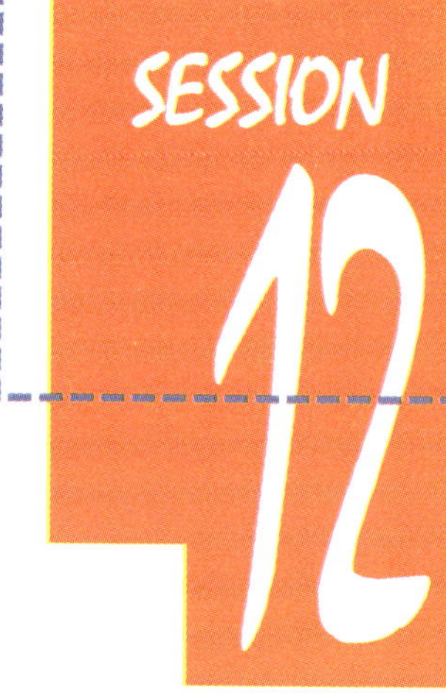

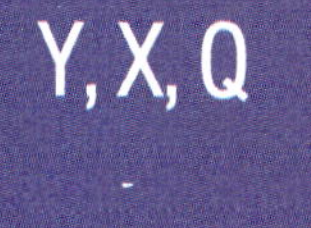

SESSION GOALS

Y, X, Q

Review saving, printing, closing, deleting

1-Minute: 25 WAM/2 errors

Y and Q words

GETTING STARTED

If you are continuing immediately from Session 11, go to step 4. If you exited the program at the end of Session 11, do the following:

1. Access Windows, then WordPerfect 6.1 for Windows.
2. At the WordPerfect editing window, click on the KWP icon.
3. Go to the Main Menu, then the Keyboarding Sessions menu.
4. At the Keyboarding Sessions menu, click on Jump to return to the activity you left off with. Or, move through the program menus until you reach the Session 12 menu.
5. On the Session 12 menu, *Warm-Up* is highlighted. Click on OK to proceed with the Warm-Up activities.

If you are already warmed up or have completed a portion of the session, move the mouse pointer to the desired activity and click on OK. When you have completed the new-key drills, the Thinking Drill, and WordPerfect Reinforcement activities, you will take several 1-minute timings on short paragraphs of text.

WORDPERFECT REINFORCEMENT

Earlier in the session you completed new-key drills presented on the screen. Now you will repeat some of those drills to reinforce your keyboarding skills and to practice working in WordPerfect.

Reviewing the Y, X, and Q Keys

Y Key

X Key

Q Key

REINFORCING WRITING SKILLS

There are a variety of ways to help individuals better understand and retain written information. Charts and graphs, for example, are an excellent choice because they display numerical data and illustrate numerical relationships almost instantly.

As you read earlier, the three most common types of graphs are line, bar, and pie. Line graphs show the relationship between two sets of information. One set of data is plotted horizontally; the other set is plotted vertically. A line connects the points where the two sets of data intersect.

Bar graphs also show relationships between sets of data. Instead of a line connecting the points where data sets intersect, however, bars are drawn either vertically or horizontally. An example of data that could be charted in a bar graph is the occupany rate for a hotel during its first six months of operation, as shown below:

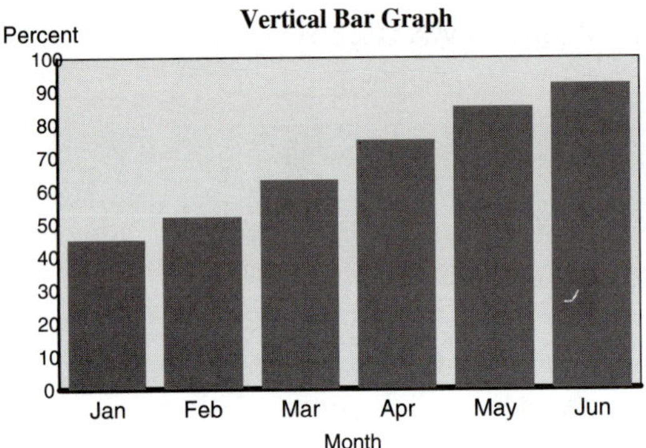

Occupancy Rate for Midland Hotel First Six Months of Operation

Pie graphs represent simple data such as percentages of a total amount. The federal budget, for example, is often represented in newspapers via a pie chart. The total pie represents 100 percent. The expenditures for defense, education, and other items are shown as a slice of the pie. The area in which our government spends the most money is shown as the largest piece of the pie.

Document D — Choosing Information to Graph

To practice deciding what information in a report to chart, review the report completed as Document A. Select areas of information that could be represented in a graph of some kind. Then write a memo (you choose the style) to your instructor explaining what information you would graph, the kind of graph you would use, and why this information should be charted. If you can think of other visuals or displays that would help explain the report data, mention those in your memo as well.

Check that your memo is written in complete, clear sentences and that you have used correct punctuation, sentence structure, word choices, and capitalization. Save the memo as **053wprd.kwp**. Then print and close the file.

ENDING THE SESSION

To end this session, DELETE outdated WordPerfect Reinforcement files, PRINT any files from Session 53 not printed earlier, then CONTINUE with the next session or exit the program.

Y Drills

Key lines 1–3 once, pushing for speed.

1 jy yard play yowl very yolk away yell lazy sly jy
2 allay spray dairy entry foggy handy lucky staying
3 Alloy Yearn Decay Empty Forty Hurry Lousy Playing

Key lines 4–6 twice: first for speed, then for control.

4 The kitty and the puppy may not enjoy happy play.
5 It is only your duty to obey every law of safety.
6 Billy is ready to carry the heavy load Wednesday.

X Drills

Key lines 1-3 once, pushing for speed.

1 sx axle next exam flex text hoax apex expedite sx
2 deluxe excise expand export prefix excite example
3 Explode Exhaust Toolbox Examine Anxiety Exporting

Key lines 4-6 twice: first for speed, then for control.

4 Did excess oxygen explode during that experiment?
5 Explain the context and expedite that experiment.
6 Fix the exhaust and examine the axle of the taxi.

Q Drills

Key lines 1-3, pushing for speed.

1 aq quote quire squid quiet squaw query qualify aq
2 quench equate squeak equity squelching quarreling
3 Squire Quarry Quaver Quorum Quartering Requesting

Key lines 4-6 twice: first for speed, then for control.

4 Do that quotient; it is a frequent quiz question.
5 Ducks squirmed and quacked in the squalid quarry.
6 Does the quitter frequently squabble and quibble?

Printing WordPerfect Reinforcement Activities

To save and print the WordPerfect for Windows document you have created, complete steps 1-5 that follow. (***Remember:*** The work you completed up to the WordPerfect Reinforcement section has already been saved automatically.)

Document C ◄-- Title Page

1. At the *Production–Session 53 Document C* screen, key Document C as a title page for the proposal on a telephone system for the Dynacare Health Clinic. Change the left margin to 1.5". Make the handwritten changes.
2. Proofread and correct any errors, then complete a spell check.
3. Click on Check to automatically name (**053proc.kwp**), save, and check the document.
4. To print with errors highlighted, click on the Print button.
5. To correct errors, click on View Original. Make changes, then recheck the document.
6. Choose **F**ile → **C**lose. This closes Document C and brings up a clear WordPerfect editing window.

Document C

(bf) A PROPOSAL FOR REPLACING
DYNACARE HEALTH CLINIC'S
TELEPHONE SYSTEM ← start on approximately line 2.0"

press Enter 12 times

Submitted to ← ds
Dr. Lawrence Isenburg
Executive Director
Dynacare Health Clinic
Dalton, Georgia

press Enter 11 times

Prepared by

Teresa Adelson
Ted Obletz
Catherine Swenson
Brent Willi
JBK Telecommunications of Atlanta
Joann^e Cooper, President

current date ← insert the current date

1. Choose **F**ile → Save **A**s (or F3).
2. At the *Save As* dialog box, key the new filename, **012wpr.kwp**. Press ***Enter*** or click on the OK button. Your document has been saved to disk, and it also remains on the screen.
3. To print 012wpr.kwp, choose **F**ile → **P**rint (or F5).
4. Click on the **P**rint button or press ***Enter***.
5. Close the file (click on **F**ile → **C**lose).

Deleting Files

In Session 11, you learned to delete documents to conserve space on your data disk. You will recall that the *Keyboarding with WordPerfect* software automatically deletes session files that are more than ten sessions old. However, it is up to you to delete your outdated WordPerfect files so that your data disk contains only the ten most current **wpr** files.

To delete the **wpr** document you completed in Session 2, follow these steps:

1. Choose **F**ile → **O**pen.
2. Select the file *002wpr.kwp* by clicking on the filename with the left mouse button.
3. With the filename highlighted, choose File **O**ptions → **D**elete.
4. At the *Delete File* dialog box, click on **D**elete.
5. To close the *Open File* dialog box, click on Cancel or press ***Esc***.

Note: Once the file to be deleted has been selected (highlighted) in the *Open File* dialog box, you can press the ***Delete*** key on the keyboard to delete the file.

Now that you have completed the WordPerfect Reinforcement activities, you are to take several 1-minute timings. Click on the KWP Next Activity button to move to the Timings. Check your screen for specific directions.

ONE-MINUTE TIMINGS

Goal: 25 WAM with no more than 2 errors

- Take a 1-minute timing on each paragraph.
- Press ***Tab*** to indent the first line of the paragraph. If you finish a paragraph before time is up, start over.

1 Basically, employers like a loyal employee. Honesty and courtesy always pay off in any job or duty. Apathy and sloppy typing are always likely to be very costly to a company. Any employee who displays a steady style will be properly rewarded and enjoy a fairly large salary.

2 There is simply no key to easy money. A bad agency may say that you are lucky and a legacy of wealthy glory is yours. Yet, if you try fancy or phony schemes, you will be mighty sorry. Steady, weekly saving is the thrifty means to easy money. Lay a penny away a day and be happy.

3 An extra exercise to help your mind relax is inhaling and exhaling deeply. It extends all the oxygen capacity before it is expelled. Choose an exact time each day to expedite an extra relaxing exertion. Your anxieties and vexations disappear and you relax. Try this exciting experience.

Document B

current date

Dr. Lawrence Isenburg
Executive Director
Dynacare Health Clinic
214 College Drive
Dalton, GA 30721-9883

Dear Dr Isenburg:

Here is the proposal prepared by the JBK Telecommunications Consulting Team with recommendations for replacing the telephone system currently being used by the Dynacare Health Clinic. Under separate cover we are sending you an addendum to this report that includes the justifications and benefits of the recommendations.

The proposal contains two alternatives in terms of a replacement telephone system. The basis for the choices is whether Dynacare wants to lease or purchase a telephone system. The addendum to this report outlines in detail the advantages of each system. Implementing either system provides numerous features to improve the quality of health care for Dynacare patients, including a feature called *Automatic Call Distribution* to prevent long waiting periods when patients call a Medical Unit within the clinic.

Please review the proposal and addendum. I will call you next Monday between 10 a.m. and noon to set up an appointment to discuss any questions you may have regarding the proposal. With your approval, we can prepare the Request for Proposal to submit to potential bidders. Dynacare will have a state-of-the-art voice communications system.

Sincerely,

Joann Cooper
President

xx/053prob.kwp

Attachment

4 Exercise an extreme caution before investing in an old duplex. Have an expert examine all the existing details and explain them to you. It may be easier to buy a luxurious and deluxe apartment house. An experienced land expert knows if it is an expensive venture.

5 The quick squad conquered the unique quintet without question. The quarterback squelched most questions about technique or quality of the team. If they qualify for the trophy, will they quietly squash the next team or will the coach require an extra practice session?

6 Angelique might request a price quotation on an exquisite antique quilt. She acquired it from a queen in a quaint town near the equator. Quiet inquiries have arisen from qualified buyers. The question is, should she keep the quality quilt or sell it quickly as requested?

ENDING THE SESSION

Once you have completed the timings, the KWP program takes you to the next session menu. If you want to print the Session 12 files, however, follow the steps below. Then continue with Session 13 or exit the program.

PRINT

1. Click on Back until you reach the KWP Main Menu.
2. Highlight *Freeform*, then click on OK.
3. Click on the Print button or choose **F**ile → **P**rint.
4. At the *Print* dialog box, select the **D**ocument on Disk option under *Print Selection*. Press ***Enter*** or click on OK.
5. At the *Document on Disk* dialog box, click on the list button at the right of the filename text box.
6. With the mouse pointer, highlight the file to be printed and press ***Enter*** or click on **P**rint.
7. At the *Document on Disk* dialog box, click on **P**rint.

Repeat steps 3-7 to print additional documents on disk.

CONTINUE

1. Print and close files.
2. Click on the KWP Main Menu button.
3. Highlight *Keyboarding Sessions*, then click on OK.
4. Click on Jump to go to the next session.

EXIT

1. Print any files, if necessary.
2. Click on the KWP Main Menu button on the Toolbar.
3. At the Main Menu, select WordPerfect Only, then click on OK.
4. Click on **F**ile → E**x**it.
5. Exit Windows, if necessary (**F**ile → E**x**it).

system change and growth requirements. Another future consideration is saving costs by expanding the telephone system to include the hospital.

Needs Analysis

Based on the findings, the JB Consultants Team proposes the following scenario to update and automate the voice communications system for the Dynacare Clinic, its remote sites, the Tidewater HMO, and Dalton Memorial Hospital.

1. Upgrade/replace the current telephone system with a system that has sufficient growth capacity and application features that address cost-effectively both internal and external voice communications.

2. Research the cost efficiencies of having a system that encompasses the Clinic, its remote sites, the HMO and the Hospital.

3. Provide a means of automatically distributing calls to the first available operator to minimize delays in contacting medical units.

4. Implement a system for reminding patients of forthcoming appointments.

5. Establish a more efficient system for recording messages.

6. Incorporate an efficient process for tracking telephone usage.

The executive summary contains the recommendations that address the findings established by the JB Consulting Team and approved by Dr. Lawrence Isenburg, the Executive Director of the Dynacare Clinic.

Document B — *Letter of Transmittal*

1. At the *Production–Session 53 Document B* screen, key Document B in the block-style format. Since this letter will accompany a report, use the same 1.5" left margin used in the report. Insert the date, make the corrections as indicated, and center the letter vertically on the page.
2. Proofread and correct any errors, then complete a spell check with Speller.
3. Click on Check to automatically name (**053prob.kwp**), save, and check the document.
4. To print with errors highlighted, click on the Print button.
5. To correct errors, click on View Original. Make changes, then recheck the document.
6. Choose **File** → **Close**. This closes Document B and brings up the Document C screen.

SESSION 13

REINFORCEMENT: SESSIONS 1-12

SESSION GOALS

Review keys from Sessions 1-12

Review saving, printing, closing, deleting

1-Minute: 25 WAM/2 errors

GETTING STARTED

If you are continuing immediately from Session 12, go to step 4. If you exited the program at the end of Session 12, do the following:

1 Access Windows, then WordPerfect 6.1 for Windows.
2 At the WordPerfect editing window, click on the KWP icon.
3 Go to the Main Menu, then the Keyboarding Sessions menu.
4 At the Keyboarding Sessions menu, click on Jump to return to the activity you left off with. Or, move through the program menus until you reach the Session 13 menu.
5 On the Session 13 menu, *Reinforcement Drills* is highlighted. Click on OK to proceed with the Reinforcement Drills activities. If you have already completed these drills, you may click on the KWP Next Activity button to go to the next activity, which is a 1-minute timing.

CHECKING YOUR SKILL: TIMING

In Sessions 7-9 and 11-12 you completed a series of 1-minute timings. The speed and accuracy goals were presented at the beginning of each set of timings. Check your scores now by accessing the Student Report (click on the KWP Rep button). Click on OK to exit the Student Report screen.

Now take a 1-minute timing on the paragraph that follows, using your scores for the timings in Sessions 7-9 and 11-12 as benchmarks. If you didn't reach at least 25 WAM in those previous timings, push for speed. If you reached the 25 WAM goal but had more than two errors, work for accuracy. If you achieved both the speed and accuracy goals, push for even greater speed. You will repeat this timing at the end of the session to see how you have improved.

1 It is good to have honest goals. Nothing is gained if one goes forth in pointless roaming. A major effort is needed to prosper. Isolate those foolish errors and avoid them. Hold to a strong, firm hope and move along.

WORDPERFECT REINFORCEMENT

The Special Drills that follow provide additional practice on the keys that you have learned in Sessions 1-12. You will save and print the drills in WordPerfect for Windows.

(Dalton Memorial Hospital has its own PBX telephone system.)

The combination of Centrex service and key telephone systems has functioned fairly well for its original purpose. However, these systems are not being used to perform at a level of communications beyond their intended design in the current configuration.

Dynacare Clinic Console Observations. Here are facts and figures regarding the use of the Clinic Console.

- Sixty percent of all callers ask for departments by name and these calls required 6.5 seconds of operator time.
- Callers requiring direction or assistance amounted to 31 percent of the total calls and averaged 19.1 seconds in operator time.
- Nine percent of the calls transferred inward received a busy signal thereby resulting in a double attempt by the operator to connect the call. In addition to the busy signals created by the "held" calls, the operator handling time to complete the call exceeded 30 seconds.
- The console operator does not have access to private departmental numbers, and when all lines are busy, the operator has to wait to connect emergency numbers.

Incoming Calls. Here are complaints from those calling the Dynacare Clinic.

- Callers have waited up to 25 rings before their call is answered, and they are often put on hold for 10 to 15 minutes.
- Caller volume is overwhelming the appointment desks in most medical units with Monday being the worst day of the week.
- Many physicians will not take incoming calls. This requires that staff members provide excuses, take messages, and/or find an alternate who will take the call.
- Many messages result in telephone tag because they lack the necessary information desired by the original caller. This results in wasted calls and lost productivity.

Internal Use of the Telephone System. Internally within the Clinic the complaints most often expressed by doctors and support staff were as follows:

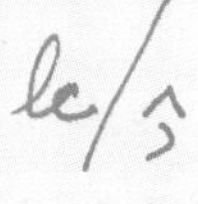

- The doctors indicated that the telephone answering service did not screen non-emergency calls.
- The current telephone system doesn't provide for an automatic patient reminder system related to forthcoming appointments. Patient no-shows reduces doctor/staff productivity.
- Personnel are unaware that incoming calls are often stacked up and waiting to be answered.
- There is an inability to share and/or cover appointed call volumes during peak periods.
- Telephone tag is a common occurrence when calling other staff members. Often times messages received are incorrect or delayed.

The above represent a reliable sampling of the concerns and complaints related to Dynacare Clinic's current telephone system. Most of these concerns and complaints are to be expected with a communications system of its vintage and design. However, all the problems can be corrected.

In addition to addressing the present system's inefficiencies, there is a need to predict

Continued on next page

Reinforcing the Keying of Alphabetic Characters

At a clear screen, try these drills to improve your general keyboarding skills:

1. For locational security, key the entire alphabet, keying each letter twice (aa bb cc dd ee ff...). Repeat this process once or twice.
2. To develop your thinking-and-keying skills, key the alphabet backwards (z y x...).
3. Key the following sentence two or three times to practice all the letters of the alphabet:

   The quick brown fox jumped over the lazy dogs.

Repeat these drills whenever you can. They will help you master the alphabetic keys.

Assessing Your Skills

The drills that follow provide additional practice on the keys that you have learned. However, if you are keying over 25 WAM with no more than two errors and do not hesitate when keying, you may skip the drills and go to the next session by clicking on the KWP Next Activity button twice. If you have not achieved the 25 WAM or less than 2 errors level, use the following guidelines to choose drills that will help you progress toward the 25 WAM/2 error keyboarding level:

Guidelines for Choosing Drills

1. If you cannot key as rapidly as you would like (at least 25 WAM), key each line once of the Balanced-Hand Words.
2. If you have not mastered the reach to a key(s) (you hesitate before striking the key), key each line once of the Balanced-Hand Words and Letter Combinations drills.
3. If you are making more than 2 errors per minute, key each line once of the Double-Letter Words and the Longer Words drills.

Balanced-Hand Words (Speed and Mastering Key Reaches)

1 sign and the sigh ant sit ale elf hen end she and
2 then hang the and fig dig die tie did sit fit aid
3 fish sign than then lane lake lens hand than halt
4 lake idle half lens lane sign dish sign then disk
5 aisle island handle fight angle title shake snake
6 gland sleigh height fight slant digit angle eight
7 he and the elf and it if he an tight giant signal
8 amble bible problem blame bland blend lamb emblem
9 gown wig bow wow vow down wit when wish with wisp
10 flap pane paid pale spent dispel lap nap pen paid
11 foam fork form foal odor soak rod fog sod oak rod
12 heir lair risks sir pan air widow flair hair pair
13 pelvis disown pens laps vie via pair vivid flames
14 map mane maid melt sham lame mend firm make disks
15 The pale maid paid for the vivid title and a wig.
16 Did the lank lamb amble down to the big dark pen?
17 When did Victor sign the pair of problem emblems?

Justification/Benefits

An addendum to this proposal outlines the justification and additional benefits of the recommendations. This portion of the proposal is being provided under separate cover and includes an extensive discussion on the merits of a PBX and the Centrex. This information will be extremely helpful to the Dynacare Board of Directors in the final selection process.

Introduction ← start a new page here

The Dynacare Clinic Association has contracted with JB Telecommunications of Atlanta, Georgia, to assess the voice communication needs of the Clinic and identify the two best alternatives for replacing the current system. Joanne Cooper, President of JB, has coordinated the development of this report with Dr. Lawrence Isenburg, the Executive Director of the Dynacare Clinic.

A consulting team consisting of four JB Associates spent two weeks at the Dynacare sites included in this study. In addition to interviews, observations, and inventories of the current telephone system, face-to-face meetings and telephone conversations were held with individuals representing telephone companies and providers of hardware and software for telephone systems and services. The on-site visits included interviews with individuals representing all levels of personnel in the Clinic to include those working the laboratory, the pharmacy, the administrative office facility, the HMO complex, the remote Clinic sites and the Hospital.

The information that is included in this report includes:

- An Executive Summary
- Introduction
- Findings
- A Needs Analysis

Findings ← start a new page here

Telephone System

Dynacare Clinic utilizes a combination of leased Bell Atlantic Centrex lines and Clinic-owned key telephone systems to serve its telephone communication needs. As the Clinic grew through the years and expanded to locations outside the main Clinic location, these two services were expected to meet the existing needs.

The Centrex service, which is leased from Bell Atlantic provides the communication links that allow all sites in the Dalton area to communicate with each other. The number of lines and costs to Dynacare are as follows:

Dynacare Clinic	121
Tidewater HMO	246
Remote clinic sites	132 ← check this total
TOTAL	499 (average cost $12 per month)

Continued on next page

Letter Combinations (Mastering Key Reaches)

1 ta tall tan task taste tale tall take talk tag ta
2 th thesis thin theft this think than that then th
3 te tenant tennis teen tend tell tenth test tea te
4 st stead still steal steadiness stateside stag st
5 sa sad saline Sal sang said sale sake safe sat sa
6 si since simple sinker sit single sift sip sin si
7 pe peep pets pellet peddles peeps pest pen peg pe
8 pi pine pink pipes pitfall pills piles pie pin pi
9 li like linkage linking link lien lied lie lid li
10 le lessen leaf least ledge lend lead left lest le
11 bl blade bleak blast blank blinds blind blight bl
12 ba bandages barks badge bath balk bail bag bad ba
13 mi mire misting might midst mint mind milk mid mi
14 ma margin manager marsh mail make math mat man ma
15 oa float roast toad load oatmeal oath oats oak oa
16 of offensive offense offset offends offers off of
17 ri rinse rigid ridges right ripe rises rip rid ri
18 ra rapid range raised rates rake ranks rap ran ra
19 vi vintage vital visits vine vile vise vim vie vi
20 va vanish varied valid vast vases vane vat van va
21 wa waves waste wane wait wade wag war was wash wa
22 wi wiper wield wise will wipe wide wig wit win wi

Sentences with Letter Combinations (Mastering Key Reaches)

1 Janie washed and wiped her wig; she wasted water.
2 The babe blinked at a baboon blinded in bandages.
3 Those offensive oats floated off of that oatmeal.
4 The vital vintage vases vanished from a vast van.
5 The manager might mail the mild mints to the man.
6 Rapid Red ran to the raised ridges on that range.
7 That pill peddler peddled piles of pinkish pills.
8 Then that teen tenant, Ted, did a tenth tea test.
9 Steadfast Stella still talks a lot and tells tall tales.
10 Sad Sal sang a signal as she sighted a safe date.
11 At least lower the left lid and lessen the length.
12 That hanging kite tail hassles the horrified kitten.
13 Gal, finish the gasket that the gas gadget needs.
14 I dislike the heat dial that fits the dental fan.

additional personnel, patient complaints of not being handled efficiently, and potentially lost patients and revenues if a frustrated patient cannot be handled in an expedient fashion.

a feature that

Competing clinics have call management systems, which is not being used with Dynacare's current telephone system. Information such as the number of calls coming into the Clinic, the number of rings before a call is answered, and the number of abandoned calls would be extremely helpful in providing appropriate staffing levels. As this information is not available in Dynacare's telephone system, one must operate from general observations and customer complaints. lc

Recommendation s

It is recommended that Dynacare replace their current telephone system with one of the following:

Dalton Memorial

- Purchase a digital PBX and network it with the hospital, the Tidewater HMO, and the remote clinic sites.
- Lease a digital CENTREX service to support the Clinic, the hospital, the HMO, and the remote clinic sites.

The following features are to be included with the selection of either alternative:

Direct Inward Dialing. This allows patients to call directly to a Medical Unit without having to go through a central operator. lc

Automatic Call Distribution. Management is able to determine call volumes, calls in queue waiting to be answered, appointment desk availability to take calls, etc. Adjustments in the number of personnel available at the appointment desk can be made on a real-time basis so as to serve the client s in an efficient manner.

Automatic Appointment Reminder System. This system is used in conjunction with your computer system and digitized and synthesized voice technology to call patients to remind them of forthcoming appoints. up

ment

Voice Mail. A voice mail system would enable staff to improve client relations by offering choices. A vast improvement in communications along with a reduction in workloads as receptionists do not have to take lengthy notes and the service is available 24 hours a day. s the

This results in

Station Message Detail Recording. This allows for the tracking of outgoing calls, including local, for each extension number. Cost allocations and policing of unauthorized calling is automatically accomplished. are

With the implementation of either alternative, Dynacare Clinic will have addressed the needs identified for establishing a state-of-the-art communication system. The Clinic Administration has to decide whether it is best to lease or purchase the telephone system.

Continued on next page

Double-Letter Words (Accuracy)

1 seed teens needless feeling indeed needs glee see
2 tall stall knitting install little shall hall all
3 heel steed likeness dissent seeing sheet need fee
4 see feel teeth indeed gallant sledding sleet knee
5 hill still lifeless endless assist stiff kiss add
6 eggs stall eggshell falling haggle sniff sell egg
7 tell shell settling skilled allied skill fell add
8 deed sleek seedling fiddles needle sheen keen eel
9 rabble rabbit gobble nibbles pebble babble hobble
10 narratives all follow terrains irritates terriers
11 door root mood took loot hook hood pool roof moon
12 immerges immense manners hammering dinners dimmer
13 shipping appease flipping happen sipping slipping
14 She will be stalling the nice contest winner now.
15 That immense rabbit emerged and nibbled a carrot.
16 Tu Wee slipped the irritated kitten into the house.

Longer Words (Accuracy)

1 negative retrieve primitive privilege advertising
2 estimate familiar eliminate dependent sentimental
3 eliminate that sentimental, familiar advertising.
4 resident standard telegrams registrar parenthesis
5 pipeline elephant dependent plaintiff safekeeping
6 That resident registrar sends standard telegrams.
7 initiated hesitating alkaline likeness indefinite
8 delegates heightened lengthened stealing gaslight
9 The hesitating delegate is stealing the gaslight.
10 digital lenient distant inkling heading delighted
11 disliked endless athlete install flatten inflated
12 A lenient athlete has inflated the flattened keg.
13 Whenever stalwart wholesale handwriting knowledge
14 renovate negotiate imagination tradition rational
15 possible establish observation elaborate ambition
16 Establish rational imagination whenever possible.
17 seashells tasteless steadfast thankless defendant
18 attendant delighted sightless lightness negligent
19 legislate essential stateside skinflint landslide
20 Seashells in the landslide delighted a skinflint.

Changing Top and Bottom Margins

Just as WordPerfect allows you to change left and right margins, top and bottom margins can be changed as well. There are a number of reasons for changing the vertical margins. Some reports will be bound at the top, so additional room must be provided for the binding. In other cases, you may need to fit all the information on a predetermined number of pages and therefore will have to adjust top, bottom, and side margins accordingly.

To change the top and/or bottom margin of a document, you would complete the following steps:

1. Click on Format → **M**argins.
2. At the *Margins* dialog box, click on the box to the right of *Top* (or *Bottom*), then key the desired margin. Or, click on the up- or down-pointing arrow and hold down the left mouse button until the desired margin setting displays.
3. Click on OK.

Document A ← Bound Business Report

1. At the *Production–Session 53 Document A* screen, key Document A as a bound business report. Before you begin, make the following formatting changes:
   - a. Change the left margin to 1.5" and the top and bottom margins to 1.25".
   - b. Turn on the Widow/Orphan feature.
   - c. Turn on page numbering (beginning with page 2) and position the numbers in the upper-right corner.
   - d. Set a tab at 1.75" on the Ruler Bar for the indent within bulleted and numbered items.
2. Center the heading on the first page on approximately Line 1.5", then key the document.
3. Proofread and correct any errors, then complete a spell check.
4. Click on Check to automatically name (**053proa.kwp**), save, and check the report.
5. To print with errors highlighted, click on the Print button.
6. To correct errors, click on View Original. Make changes, then recheck the document.
7. Choose **F**ile → **C**lose. This closes Document A and brings up a clear WordPerfect editing window.

Document A

A PROPOSAL FOR REPLACING DYNACARE CLINIC'S
TELEPHONE SYSTEM

Executive Summary

Background

Dynacare Clinic, ~~as~~ like all ~~other~~ health care facilities, is faced with renewed demands for cost control. This means lowering costs by increasing efficiencies of both human and plant resources. Health care systems across the country ~~is~~ are using advanced technology to improve the bottom line.

Dynacare Clinic has not implemented office automation technology associated with state-of-the-art telephone systems. This has ~~resulted in~~ produced a duplication of effort resulting in

Continued on next page

Printing WordPerfect Reinforcement Activities

To save and print the WordPerfect for Windows document you have created, complete steps 1-5 that follow. (***Remember:*** The work you completed up to the WordPerfect Reinforcement section has already been saved automatically.)

1 Choose **F**ile → Save **A**s (or F3).
2 At the *Save As* dialog box, key the new filename, **013wpr.kwp**. Press ***Enter*** or click on the OK button. Your document has been saved to disk, and it also remains on the screen.
3 To print 013wpr.kwp, choose **F**ile → **P**rint or (F5).
4 Click on the **P**rint button or press ***Enter***.
5 Close the file (click on **F**ile → **C**lose).

Deleting Files

In Session 11, you learned to delete documents to conserve space on your data disk. You will recall that the *Keyboarding with WordPerfect* software automatically deletes session files that are more than ten sessions old. However, it is up to you to delete your outdated WordPerfect files so that your data disk contains only the ten most current WPR files.

To delete the **wpr** document you completed in Session 3, follow these steps:

1 Choose **F**ile → **O**pen.
2 Select the file *003wpr.kwp* by clicking on the filename with the left mouse button.
3 With the filename highlighted, choose File **O**ptions → **D**elete.
4 At the *Delete File* dialog box, click on **D**elete.
5 To close the *Open File* dialog box, click on Cancel or press ***Esc***.

Note: Once the file to be deleted has been selected (highlighted) in the *Open File* dialog box, you can press the ***Delete*** key on the keyboard to delete the file.

Now that you have completed the WordPerfect Reinforcement activities, you are to take several 1-minute timings. Click on the KWP Next Activity button to access the Timing.

REPEATING THE ONE-MINUTE TIMING

Now that you have finished the WordPerfect Reinforcement section, the next activity is to take two timings on the paragraph offered at the beginning of this session. (Check your screen for specific information.) Compare the results with your earlier attempt. Has your speed improved? Do you have fewer errors? If you are not reaching 25 WAM with two or fewer errors on the 1-minute timings, repeat Sessions 11-12.

ENDING THE SESSION

Once you have completed the timings, the KWP program takes you to the next session menu. If you want to print the Session 13 files, however, follow the steps below. Then continue with Session 14 or exit the program.

PRINT

1 Click on Back until you reach the KWP Main Menu.
2 Highlight *Freeform*, then click on OK.
3 Click on the Print button or choose **F**ile → **P**rint.

RECOMMENDATIONS FOR THE MADISON STREET CROSSING

This report contains the basic data gathered and analyzed to make recommendations regarding the Madison Street crossing. The recommendation made by this committee strongly supports the rebuilding of the crossing as soon as possible.

Purpose

The purpose of this committee was to study possible alternatives to the traffic problem as it now exists at the Madison Street crossing. This includes recommendations for an arterial street improvement, which would serve the central part of the city, provide access to the downtown area and the major industrial complex, link U.S. Highway 73 with the east/west arterial street system across the Chippewa River, and eliminate the serious and chronic problem with the Chicago and Eastern Railroad traffic.

The objective of the recommendation is to relieve traffic congestion that affects the business and industrial portions of the city, while also providing for safe and more efficient travel.

The Problem

Existing conditions. Topography and the location of commercial business has primarily determined the character and location of the street network in the immediate area. Because of the steep grades in certain areas, several industries are located on the plateau of the river. As a result, access roads have tended to be located in valleys, where lesser slopes are available. Such locations, however, limit the continuity, which results in many jogs and offsets in the street system.

For instance, when traveling up the hill on Madison Street, motorists must travel in the northeast direction (See Exhibit A). Immediately after crossing the railroad tracks which cannot be seen until the motorist is directly upon them a seven-degree jog to the right must be made. Right turns onto Dewey Street are permitted, but the effort involved to make such a turn is such that many motorists make it improperly and dangerously. The net result is often confusion, danger to both motorists and pedestrian traffic, and generally bad feelings.

Train traffic, which at this point is the main double track line (mainline) of the Chicago and Eastern Railroad Line with several side tracks south of Madison Street, is a serious barrier to automobile traffic and has long been recognized as too heavy for this highly congested area. A
separation of grades was planned by the railroad more than 30 years ago, but the expense involved was so great that no steps have ever been taken to carry out the needed construction.

2

Traffic. The route including Birch Street, Germania Street, and East Madison Street is the only east/west arterial serving the northern half of the city. The use of this particular route has developed due to the industry in the northern part of the city and highway traffic to and from the principally rural areas to the north and east.

Studies have shown travel patterns in the city to be of three basic types: local traffic within the city, travel from outlying regions into the city and returning, and external traffic passing through the city. Industry located in the northern part of the city probably is responsible for the largest part of the traffic. The greatest proportion of traffic to and from these industries originates to the north and east. There are three routes serving the northeast section of the city from Starr Avenue/Birch Street, U.S. Highway 73/Birch Street, and C.T. Highway Q/Birch Street. Of these, because of the construction of a major interchange and viaduct now in progress, the majority of the traffic naturally travels west on Birch Street from U.S. Highway 73. A good arterial street connection between this route and the downtown area is therefore vitally important.

Traffic studies conducted have revealed the overall average daily traffic using this route is one automobile every 4.5 seconds during the daytime hours, making it one of the highest volume routes serving the central city (see Exhibit B). Only short segments of two other city streets approach this volume. Traffic volume is fairly well distributed, however, with the largest volumes being recorded early in the morning and later in the afternoon, corresponding to local industrial shift changes.

Congestion. In addition to peak hour capacities, congestion is caused by four existing conditions:

1. A major delay is created by the at-grade level crossing of the railroad. Heavy vehicular traffic and 15 regular trains and several locals and switching movements each day make it quite evident that the railroad represents a significant disruption to traffic flow.

2. Due to reasons previously mentioned, sharp turns at the Birch Street/Germania and Germania/East Madison intersections cause a general slowdown of traffic, which often affects traffic flow at the crossing.

3. The combination of steep grades and the at-grade roadway causes congestion, as normal traffic is not able to pass slow-moving traffic. This problem is compounded on East Madison Street where a steep grade is encountered (see Exhibit C).

Figure 53.1 Example of a formal, left-bound report

Guidelines for Preparing Formal Business Reports

- **Structure:** The sequence of the parts of a business report usually differs somewhat from educational reports. For example, the executive summary often is the first section of a business report but the last section of an educational report. Most business reports place all reference information at the end of the report. One important addition to the business report is the preparation and distribution information, which includes the name(s) of the individual(s) who prepared the report and the names of the individuals who will receive it. This information is sometimes placed on the cover sheet or on a separate page immediately following the cover sheet.
- **Format:** Business reports are usually single-spaced with a double space between paragraphs and no paragraph indent. Pages are numbered, beginning with page 2.
- **Displays:** Business reports often contain visual displays such as photographs, tables, graphs, inked drawings, illustrations, and so on. With microcomputer peripherals such as laser scanners, laser printers, and various software packages, the keyboarder can create most, if not all, of the visual displays needed. Always place a display **after** it has been referred to in the text, not before. When displays are too long and/or too large to illustrate within the body of a report, they are usually placed at the back and identified as "exhibits."

  With WordPerfect, you can create a variety of graphs, including line graphs, bar graphs, and pie charts. However, charting (graphing) is an advanced feature and as such, is not covered in this text.

4 At the *Print* dialog box, select the **D**ocument on Disk option under *Print Selection*. Press ***Enter*** or click on OK.
5 At the *Document on Disk* dialog box, click on the list button at the right of the filename text box.
6 With the mouse pointer, highlight the file to be printed and press ***Enter*** or click on **P**rint.
7 At the *Document on Disk* dialog box, click on **P**rint.

Repeat steps 3-7 to print additional documents on disk.

CONTINUE

1 Print and close files.
2 If you are working in Freeform, click on the KWP Main Menu button.
3 Highlight *Keyboarding Sessions*, then click on OK.
4 Click on Jump to go to the next session.

EXIT

1 Print any files, if necessary.
2 Click on the KWP Main Menu button on the Toolbar.
3 At the Main Menu, select WordPerfect Only, then click on OK.
4 Click on **F**ile → E**x**it.
5 Exit Windows, if necessary (**F**ile → E**x**it).

FIVE-MINUTE TIMINGS

Goal: 35 WAM/1 error

SI: 1.47

- Take two 5-minute timings.

One of the finest fruits on the market today is the mango, which is a fruit found in the tropics. The mango has become more popular all over the nation. The papaya is also a very good tropical fruit that has lots of vitamins and is good to eat. A carambola is quite a strange looking fruit. It has a waxy appearance and contains a solid meat. The cherimoya, or custard apple, is shaped like the strawberry and is green in color and oval in shape. The fruit is not very attractive, but has a delicious and delicate flavor. Kiwi fruit, the Chinese gooseberry, is grown in New Zealand; thus the name "kiwi" has been given to this fruit in honor of the native kiwi bird. The taste is mild and quite enjoyable.

The celery root has an ugly appearance. The outside of the root is deceiving, for inside the ugly wrapping lies a great surprising flavor treat for vegetable lovers. Fine Jerusalem artichokes, also known as sunchokes, have lots of uses. The crispy, crunchy food has a nutlike flavor and makes a great finger food. A jicama is sometimes known as a Mexican or Chinese potato. The brownish vegetable looks like a raw turnip. The crispy and crunchy taste treat is quite good when served with a dip of some sort.

Although all of us seem to be creatures of habit, there is a new world of eating delights right in the produce bins, waiting for us to discover new taste treats. All it takes is some searching and a very sincere desire to try something new. Maybe a recipe or two would add to the variety of these exotic vegetables and fruits. Many cookbooks contain delightful recipes with which to vary our menus.

PREPARING FORMAL BUSINESS REPORTS

Formal business reports are similar in style and format to educational reports or manuscripts. Both use levels of headings to help the reader categorize the information, and the left-bound business report follows the same margin guidelines (1.5" left margin) as the left-bound educational report. The differences between formal business reports and formal educational reports primarily involve the structure and the amount of illustrations and exhibits included. Study figure 53.1 and note the differences as you review the preparation guidelines.

UNIT 2

NUMERIC KEYS

SESSION GOALS

1-Minute: 45 WAM/1 error
5-Minute: 35 WAM/1 error

Review changing top and bottom margins

Enhancing text with visuals

GETTING STARTED

If you are continuing immediately from Session 52, go to the one-minute timings. If you exited the program at the end of session 52, do the following:

1. Access Windows, then WordPerfect 6.1 for Windows.
2. Click on the KWP icon to access *Keyboarding with WordPerfect.*
3. Go to the Keyboarding Sessions menu and click on Jump to return to your last activity. Or, access the Session 53 menu and click on OK to begin the session.

ONE-MINUTE TIMINGS

Goal: 45 WAM/1 error

SI: 1.48

- Take two 1-minute timings on the following material.

There are many sources to tap when searching for that first job. Schools usually employ guidance counselors who will assist you with a search for your first job. Some large schools also have a job referral service, which brings an employer and an employee together. Frequently, the local employment service is an excellent source for employment opportunities. If you are out of school, the Civil Service Office will also make information available to you. The student who is determined to find that first job will learn quite rapidly that there are many kinds of new career choices in the marketplace.

1, 2, 3

SESSION GOALS

 **1, 2, 3**

 **1-Minute: 30 WAM/2 errors**

 **Review saving, printing, closing, deleting**

Session 14 is the first session on mastering the number row, located just above the alphabetic keys on your keyboard. Since numbers are used so frequently with the alphabetic keys and with many of the symbols (for example, the percent sign), it is important that you develop equal skills with numbers and letters.

If your instructor has directed you to master the number keys in Sessions 14-17 before completing the alphabetic keys, be sure to skip any activities that require mastery of the alphabetic keyboard. Some instructors prefer this approach since there are only 10 numbers compared to 26 letters, and the letters are mixed on the keyboard while the numbers are in order.

GETTING STARTED

If you are continuing immediately from Session 13, go to step 4. If you exited the program at the end of Session 13, do the following:

1. Access Windows, then WordPerfect 6.1 for Windows.
2. At the WordPerfect editing window, click on the KWP icon.
3. Go to the Keyboarding Sessions menu, then click on Jump to return to the activity you left off with. Or, move through the program menus until you reach the Session 14 menu.
4. On the Session 14 menu, *Space Bar* is highlighted. Click on OK to proceed with the Space Bar activities.

If you have completed part of the session, move the mouse pointer to the desired activity and click on OK or press ***Enter***. When you have completed the new-key drills and the WordPerfect Reinforcement activities, you will take several 1-minute timings.

 WORDPERFECT REINFORCEMENT

Some of the drills presented earlier on the screen are repeated here to strengthen your keyboarding skills while you also practice using WordPerfect for Windows.

Document E

BIBLIOGRAPHY

Armes, Jane, E. J. James, and Betty Jane Onis. *End-Users Information Systems*. Cincinnati, Ohio: Poston, Inc., 1995, pp. 286-288.

Dane, Deborah. "The Rising Cost of Record Storage," *Management and Money*. April, 1995, p. 52.

Holbreck, Judy L. and Vincent T. Marcus. *Problems in Record Storage*. Dayton, Ohio: Western Publishing Company, 1994, p. 2.

Onis, George. *Control in the Office*. Chicago, Illinois: A-Z Publishing Company, 1996, p. 194.

Prentis, Richard A. and James E. Johnson. *Information Systems*. Dallas, Texas: Weston Publishers, 1993, pp. 134-136.

"Speed and Quality in Handling Workflow," *Office Systems*. Vol. 29, No. 3, January, 1995, p. 4.

White, Ben and Vera Riles. *Filing, Retrieving, and Safekeeping*. Denver, Colorado: Mountain Air Printing Company, 1994, pp. 1-3.

Wilson, James. *Using Your Skills*. New York: Creative Enterprises, 1995, p. 4.

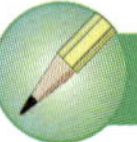

REINFORCING WRITING SKILLS

Quoting directly or indirectly from sources referenced in your manuscript lends credence to the thesis (main point) of your manuscript or research paper. These references to your sources also indicate the extent of your research.

Quotations, especially direct quotations, can be over-used. Including more than five or six per page may give the impression that you have merely gathered information and have not analyzed it or presented any new ideas. Instead, use direct quotations occasionally for effect or when the direct quote is a powerfully written statement that would lose its impact if summarized.

Paraphrased or summarized statements (quotations or statements of others expressed in your own words) help maintain a consistency of tone and writing style and also give the impression that you have understood the material and can combine the various pieces of information to produce perhaps new or different ideas.

Document F — *Summarizing*

To practice your summarizing (paraphrasing) skills, open document **051proc.kwp** and read the information carefully. Then key a one-page summary of the main ideas. Title the document **Summary of the Multimedia PCs Article** (center and bold the title). Then save the summary as **052wprf.kwp**. Print and close the file.

ENDING THE SESSION

To end this session DELETE outdated WordPerfect Reinforcement files, PRINT any files from Session 52 not printed earlier, then CONTINUE with the next session or EXIT the program. (If necessary, review the specific steps from a previous session.)

Keying Numbers

Whether you keyboard for personal or for business use, you will frequently key numbers. Some of the numbers that occur regularly in textual material include social security, telephone, address/ZIP Code/postal zone, age, weight, height, credit card, and driver's license numbers.

Reviewing the 1, 2, and 3 Keys

- Use the home-row method (anchor the left hand on asdf, the right hand on jkl;).
- Whenever possible, think of numbers in units of two and three digits (as you key 11, think eleven).
- When letters and numbers are combined, think of the letter(s) plus a two- or three-digit number (for a111, think a/one-eleven).

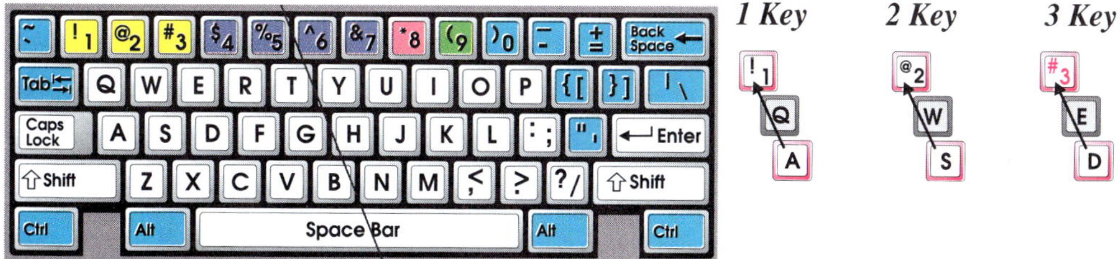

1 Key Drill

Key line 1 for control; key line 2 for speed. Note that the lines contain the number 1, not the letter l.

1 al lal alll al al all alll al llall al lal all al
2 all alll lla al lal all llla 111 lla 11 al lla la

2 Key Drill

Key line 1 twice for control; key line 2 for speed.

1 1 2 1 21 221 122 121 221 2 1 212 112 1 12 21 21 2
2 al2 2al 112a 12al2 21al 122a all a2a 12a la2a 122

Note: Did you think of 221 as ***two-twenty-one***? Did you think of 112a as ***one-twelve/ay***?

Keying Numbers with Four Digits

When working with groups of numbers having four digits and no natural break, think of the numbers as two pairs.

Key lines 1 and 2; read the numbers in pairs to gain speed.

1 1221 1112 1221 1112 2112 2112 1122 1122 1221 2221
2 a1122 a1221 1112a 1212a a1112 a2112 a1212 a1221a2

Joynter, Louise R. *Living Values*. Denver, Colorado: Marchant Press, 1994, pp. 64-67.

Formatting Considerations

- List author's last name first followed by a comma, then first name followed by a period.
- Space only once after periods, question marks, and colons.
- Indent the second and succeeding lines with one Tab space (a hanging indent).
- Separate the place of publication from publisher's name with a colon (:).
- Include page numbers in the footnote bibliography entry.
- End all entries with a period.
- Single-space each entry. Double-space between entries.

The format for bibliographical entries used in this text is one of the more common styles. Other authors, institutions, and individuals may require a slightly different format. Consult your instructor or a style reference manual for further details.

Guidelines for Preparing a Bibliography

1. The title "Bibliography" is centered on Line 2". Double-space after the title.
2. Entries in the bibliography are listed alphabetically, according to the author's last name. If there is no author information (such as for a magazine article or newspaper article), key the entry as follows:

   "Time Marches On." *The Los Angeles Flyer*. March 10, 1995, p. 38.

   Use the word *Time* in alphabetizing.

Document E ← *Bibliography*

1. At a clear WordPerfect editing window, press ***Enter*** enough times to move the insertion point to approximately *Line 2"*.
2. Center and bold the title, **BIBLIOGRAPHY.**
3. Press ***Enter*** three times. Then key the remainder of the bibliography, adding a line space between each entry. Create hanging indented paragraphs by doing the following:
   a. With the insertion point located at the left margin where the first bibliography entry is to be keyed, press **Ctrl + F7**.
   b. Key the bibliography entry.
   c. Press **Ctrl + F7** before keying the next bibliography source.
4. Choose **File** → **S**ave As and key **052wpre.kwp** as the filename.
5. Choose **File** → **C**lose to close Document E and clear the editing window.

Keying Numbers with Five or More Digits

When keying number groups that have more than four digits and no natural breaks such as spaces, commas, or decimals, use a 2-3-2 reading pattern. For the number 21221, think ***twenty-one/two twenty-one***. For the number 2121221, think ***twenty-one/two-twelve/twenty-one***.

Key lines 1–5 once; mentally pronounce the number combinations as they are keyed.

1 21 221 21 221 21 221 a21 212a 12 11a 2121 a121 a2

2 21221 21121 21221 a21112 a12212 a12121 21212 a122

3 a2112121 22 1 21a 2122121 12221 a212a 1221a 12221

4 12 12 12 12 121 121 121 121 a2a a221 a221 2a211 1

5 212a1 121221a 12122a1 22221a 12212a 221221a 21a22

Remember: Keep your fingers on the home row and reach from that position to key a particular number or several numbers. Return your finger to the home-row position after striking a number.

3 Key Drill

Key lines 1–3. Repeat the lines, keeping your eyes on the copy while mentally reading the numbers as combinations.

1 332 32 213 231 12 1321 231 32 231 2312 232 1213 3

2 a33 a3 a32 a321 a233 a3232 a132 13232 3223212 a23

3 a323 a3212321 a13231a a1 231a a123 232 32 332 a13

Important: If you have not completed Sessions 1–13 (the alphabetic keys), go to Ending the Session. Otherwise proceed to the Sentences practice that follows:

Sentences

Key lines 1–3 once for speed.

1 Jean shall sell the 321 seashells and 212 stones.

2 Taste the lean tea; handle the kettle that leaks.

3 The 11 attendants halted a ring of thieves. They felt proud.

Key lines 4–6 once for control. Key lines 4–6 again. If you make a mistake on a line, start over until you can complete the line without error. Then go to the next line.

4 See, he is ill; his skin is flushed; he feels faint.

5 Enlist the 14 students to help with the many tasks.

6 She is a skilled athlete who strives for perfection.

Printing WordPerfect Reinforcement Activities

To save and print the WordPerfect for Windows document you have created, complete steps 1-5 that follow. (***Remember:*** The work you completed up to the WordPerfect Reinforcement section has already been saved automatically.)

Document C ◄-- *Footnotes*

1 At a clear WordPerfect editing window, open **050prob.kwp**.

2 Move the insertion point to the space after the period at the end of the second paragraph and insert a footnote by doing the following:

   a Choose **I**nsert → **F**ootnote → **C**reate.

   b At the *footnote* window, key the following footnote reference. (***Note:*** Do not press ***Tab*** before keying the footnote and do not press **Enter** at the end of the footnote text.)

   Arthur J. Strage, *Health Care in the '90s* (Dallas, Texas: Marston Printing Company, 1994), p. 145.

   c Click on Close to exit the *footnote* window and return to your document. The footnote reference number is inserted in your document at the insertion point location.

3 Move the insertion point to the space after the period at the end of the fourth paragraph and insert the following footnote reference (follow the directions in step 2):

   Nathan E. Tyler and Jeannie Schwartz, *At-Home Care* (Sacramento, California: AB Publishers, 1994), p. 26.

4 Move the insertion point to the space after the period at the end of the last paragraph and insert the following footnote reference:

   Rita N. Collier, "Cutting the Costs of Health Care," *Health Care Manager* (April 14, 1992), p. 5.

5 Choose **F**ile → **S**ave As and key **052wprc.kwp** as the filename.

6 Choose **F**ile → **C**lose. This closes Document C and brings up a clear editing window.

Document D ◄-- *Footnotes*

1 At a clear WordPerfect editing window, open **052wprc.kwp**.

2 Delete the footnote at the end of the fourth paragraph by doing the following:

   a Position the insertion point directly on the footnote number at the end of the fourth paragraph.

   b Press the ***Delete*** key.

3 Move the insertion point to the space after the period at the end of the first paragraph and insert the following footnote reference:

   Sylvia A. French, *Health Care Problems* (Portland, Oregon: Douglas Publishing, 1991), p. 35.

4 Choose **F**ile → **S**ave As and key **052wprd.kwp** as the filename.

5 Choose **F**ile → **C**lose. This closes Document D and clears the window for Document E.

WP PREPARING A BIBLIOGRAPHY

A bibliography is a formalized listing of all the books, magazines, and other sources used in your report. The listing is placed at the end of the paper. Each bibliographical entry contains the author's name, title, publication facts, and specific page numbers (if appropriate), as follows:

1 Choose **F**ile → Save **A**s (or F3).
2 At the *Save As* dialog box, key the new filename, **014wpr.kwp**. Press ***Enter*** or click on the OK button. Your document has been saved to disk, and it also remains on the screen.
3 To print 014wpr.kwp, choose **F**ile → **P**rint (or F5).
4 Click on the **P**rint button or press ***Enter***.
5 Close the file (click on **F**ile → **C**lose).

Deleting Files

In Session 11, you learned to delete documents to conserve space on your data disk. You will recall that the *Keyboarding with WordPerfect* software automatically deletes session files that are more than ten sessions old. However, it is up to you to delete your outdated WordPerfect files so that your data disk contains only the ten most current WPR files.

To delete the **wpr** document you completed in Session 4, follow these steps:

1 Choose **F**ile→**O**pen.
2 Select the file *004wpr.kwp* by clicking on the filename with the left mouse button.
3 With the filename highlighted, choose File **O**ptions→**D**elete.
4 At the *Delete File* dialog box, click on **D**elete.
5 To close the *Open File* dialog box, click on Cancel or press ***Esc***.

Note: Once the file to be deleted has been selected (highlighted) in the *Open File* dialog box, you can press the ***Delete*** key on the keyboard to delete the file.

Now that you have completed the WordPerfect Reinforcement activities, you are to take several 1-minute timings. Click on the KWP Next Activity button to bring up the Timings screen.

ONE-MINUTE TIMINGS

Goal: 30 WAM with no more than 2 errors

- Take a 1-minute timing on each paragraph.
- Press ***Tab*** to indent the first line.
- If you finish a paragraph before time is up, start over.

1 When business is weak, there is not a lot of demand for money. So savings are invested in the stock market. The prices of stocks and bonds go up and interest rates go down. When business is strong, the demand for loans goes up to expand production, and consumers buy cars and homes. This pushes interest rates up.

2 The blunt auditor suggested to Duke that the business returns were a fraud. The usual routine of minimum turnovers of funds had been sound, but that fortune of thousands paid to the 12 jurors had not been inserted in the annual input. Duke presumed he was ruined and flushed with guilt.

ENDING THE SESSION

Once you have completed the timings, the KWP program takes you to the next session menu. If you want to print the Session 14 files, however, follow the steps below. Then continue with Session 15 or exit the program.

4 Click on Close to exit the *footnote* window and return to your document.

A footnote can be up to 16,000 lines long, and you can use many WordPerfect features in the special editing window including Block, Move, and Spell Check.

Editing a Footnote

Changes can be made to footnotes that have previously been entered in a document. To edit an existing footnote, do the following:

1. Choose **I**nsert → **F**ootnote → **E**dit.
2. At the *Edit Footnote* dialog box, key the number of the footnote you wish to edit and click on OK.
3. The footnote text is displayed in the *footnote* window. Make any necessary changes.
4. Click on Close to exit the *footnote* window and return to your document.

Deleting a Footnote

A footnote can be removed from a document by moving the insertion point to the footnote number and pressing either the ***Delete*** or the ***Backspace*** key. To use the ***Delete*** key, position the insertion point directly on the footnote number. To use the ***Backspace*** key, position the insertion point to the right of the number. WordPerfect deletes the footnote number as well as the footnote reference from the document. In addition, WordPerfect automatically renumbers the remaining footnotes.

Printing a Footnote

When a document containing footnotes is printed, WordPerfect automatically reduces the number of text lines on a page by the number of lines in the footnote along with two lines for spacing between the text and the footnote. If there is not enough room on the page, the footnote number and footnote are taken to the next page. WordPerfect separates the footnotes from the text with a 2-inch line beginning at the left margin.

The footnote number in the document and the footnote number before the reference information print as superscript numbers above the line.

Footnote Considerations

Footnotes assume the default one-inch left and right margins regardless of the margins set in the document. If you want the footnote margins to match the document margins, you must set the document margins with the Initial Codes Style option, as follows:

1. Choose Fo**r**mat → **D**ocument → Initial Codes **S**tyle.
2. At the *Styles Editor* dialog box, set the desired margins by doing the following:
   a. Choose Fo**r**mat → **M**argins.
   b. Key the new margin settings in the *Left* and *Right* text boxes.
   c. Click on OK to exit the *Margins* dialog box.
   d. Click on OK to exit the *Styles Editor* dialog box and return to your document.

If line spacing is changed in a document containing footnotes, the footnotes do not assume the new line spacing. Line spacing in footnotes (or endnotes) is separate from the main document.

PRINT

1. Click on Back until you reach the KWP Main Menu.
2. Highlight *Freeform*, then click on OK.
3. Click on the Print button or choose **F**ile → **P**rint.
4. At the *Print* dialog box, select the **D**ocument on Disk option under *Print Selection*. Press ***Enter*** or click on OK.
5. At the *Document on Disk* dialog box, click on the list button at the right of the filename text box.
6. With the mouse pointer, highlight the file to be printed and press ***Enter*** or click on **P**rint.
7. At the *Document on Disk* dialog box, click on **P**rint.

Repeat steps 3-7 to print additional documents on disk.

CONTINUE

1. Print any files, if necessary.
2. If you are working in Freeform, click on the KWP Main Menu button.
3. Highlight *Keyboarding Sessions*, then click on OK.
4. Click on Jump to go to the next session.

EXIT

1. Print any files, if necessary.
2. Click on the KWP Main Menu button on the Toolbar.
3. At the Main Menu, select WordPerfect Only, then click on OK.
4. Click on **F**ile → E**x**it.
5. Exit Windows, if necessary (**F**ile → E**x**it).

5. Office Equipment (book)—edited by Mark Nelson, published by Ralsten Publishers, Inc., in 1996—location, Des Moines, Iowa. Material quoted from p. 397.

6. Used quote from p. 86 in March 1995 issue of Times & Trends magazine in article entitled Dynamic Decorating—no author given.

7. Report by Jane Green, Office Issues & Trends, put out by New York Office Managers Association, New York City, in 1995, page 46.

The Footnote System

Footnotes are used to tell your reader the exact source of your quoted material and where additional information can be found. The formats for keying footnotes can differ slightly, depending on which reference book is used. Choose one method and be consistent throughout the entire manuscript. One of the most accepted formats is used in this text. Generally, a footnote must include the following: author, title, facts of publication within parentheses (place, publisher, date), and page on which you found the information. Look at this example:

> [1]James L. Johnson, *All You Wanted to Know About the Moon* (Tucson, Arizona: Minute Publishing Company, 1993), p. 117.

Footnotes are numbered to prevent confusion about sources. Notice that the number is raised from the rest of the line as a **superior** or **superscript** number. WordPerfect has both superscript and subscript capabilities. Also note that there is only one space after the colon following the publisher's city and state.

Remember: Titles of poems, short stories, chapters, essays, and articles in magazines are enclosed in quotation marks. Titles of books, newspapers, and magazines are keyed in italics (underlining is also acceptable, but only as a second alternative).

CREATING FOOTNOTES WITH WORDPERFECT

When using WordPerfect to create a research paper or report, a footnote can be included as the document is being keyed or it can be inserted after the entire document is completed. WordPerfect simplifies the task of spacing for footnotes. The writer simply identifies the location of the footnote notation, accesses the Footnote feature, and keys the footnote reference. WordPerfect determines the number of lines needed at the bottom of the page and adjusts the page endings accordingly.

In WordPerfect, endnotes and footnotes have the same format. Endnotes are printed at the end of the document, however, as opposed to the foot of the page. Do not let this atypical use of terminology confuse you. Your basic choice of source note style is still the text note or the footnote.

To create a footnote, do the following:

1 Move the insertion point to the location in the document where the notation is to appear.
2 Choose **I**nsert → **F**ootnote → **C**reate.
3 At the *footnote* window, key the footnote reference information.
Note: Do not press ***Enter*** at the end of the footnote text.

4, 5, 6

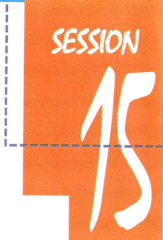

SESSION GOALS

4, 5, 6

Review saving, printing, closing, deleting

Numbers (1-Minute): 25 WAM/2 errors
Letters (1-Minute): 30 WAM/2 errors

GETTING STARTED

If you are continuing immediately from Session 14, go to step 4. If you exited the program at the end of Session 14, do the following:

1. Access Windows, then WordPerfect 6.1 for Windows.
2. At the WordPerfect editing window, click on the KWP icon.
3. Go to the Keyboarding Sessions menu, then click on Jump to return to the activity you left off with. Or, move through the program menus until you reach the Session 15 menu.
4. On the Session 15 menu, *Warm-Up* is highlighted. Click on OK to proceed with the Warm-Up activities.

If you are already warmed up or have completed a portion of the session, move the mouse pointer to the desired activity and click on OK or press ***Enter***. When you have completed the new-key drills and WordPerfect Reinforcement activities, you will take several 1-minute timings on lines of numbers and then on regular text.

WORDPERFECT REINFORCEMENT

Some of the Session 15 drills that were presented on-screen are repeated here to reinforce your sense of where keys are located. You will also practice creating, saving, printing, and deleting files.

Reviewing the 4, 5, and 6 Keys

4 Key

5 Key

6 Key

The Text Note System

The text note system for referencing notes places the complete source information in a bibliography or works-cited list at the back of the paper. The abbreviated note that is placed in the text refers the reader to the bibliography or works-cited list if more information is desired. This system is easy to key. ***Remember:*** Before keying a paper, always determine which style of referencing is required.

Use the following procedure to key the text note method of referencing:

1. Space once following the quoted material and key the author's last name and page number enclosed in parentheses.
   Example:
   . . . and equipment" (Holbreck 2).
2. Do not put any source note information at the bottom of the page; continue keying the text material down to the point where there is 1 to 1.5 inches at the bottom of the page.
3. If you have more than one publication by the same author(s) with the same publication date, use **a**, **b**, **c**, and so on to let the reader know which publication in the bibliography is being referenced.
   Example:
   (Holbreck and Marcus a 2) (listed first in bibliography)
   (Holbreck and Marcus b 16) (listed second in bibliography)
   (Holbreck and Marcus c 118) (listed third in bibliography)
4. If a publication has no author, use the title instead for the text note reference and bibliography.

Document B ← *Text Notes*

1. At the *Production–Session 52 Document B* screen, key a correct text note entry for each information source listed in Document B. Key the number of the reference plus a period (1., 2., etc.), press ***Tab***, then key the text note entry.
2. Click on Check to automatically name (**052prob.kwp**), save, and check the document.
3. To print the document with errors highlighted, click on the Print button.
4. To correct errors, click on View Original. Make changes, then recheck the document.
5. Choose **File** → **Close** to close Document B and bring up the Document C screen.

Document B

1. Twenty-Nine Ways to Please Customers—Barker Review (magazine) by Ms. Gladys Fox. Appeared in the March, 1995, issue on page 29.

2. Book—Exciting Sales Techniques by J. R. Scott. Published by Winston Royal Pub. Co. in Havertown, New Jersey in 1995. Taken from page 14.

3. Book by Joanne Dowl and Kenneth Eden. Title: Will Friday Never Come? Published in 1994 by the Fridley Pub. Co. in Dallas, Texas. Quoted information on pp. 196-200.

4. Quoted from the Sept. 19, 1995, issue of the San Jose Independent newspaper, page 17, column 3.

Continued on next page

4 Key Drill

Key lines 1–3 twice: first for speed, then for control. You will key faster if you think of the numbers in groups.

1 14 134 1431 2343 343123 43 334 3 3421 23214 432442

2 al4 a4231 24 4a24 1432a 34 a4321 a4323 a431 a342 a

3 4343213413 34343213311 4323412341 3431233 44342 43

5 Key Drill

Key lines 1–3 twice: first for control, then for speed. Anchor the "a" or "f" finger on the home row, and read the numbers in groups.

1 11 55 a55 11 55 a55 11 55 55 11 51 a51 15 15 15 5

2 55 44 a45 54 14 15 24 25 34 35 53 43 52 42 51 41a

3 15115 15115 a55151 a55151 15 5151 151 al55 a51151

6 Key Drill

Key lines 1–3 twice: first for control, then for speed. Anchor the ";" finger on the home row.

1 11 a66 11 66 11 66 11 66 11 66 a66 11 66 11 66 61

2 166 166 a661 661 161 161 a611 661 661 116 11 a666

3 11666 16661 61 66 66 111 666 661 1166 16661 61 61

Important: If you have not completed Sessions 1-13 (the alphabetic keys), go to Ending the Session. Otherwise proceed to the Sentences practice that follows.

Sentences

Key lines 1–10 twice: first for speed, then for control.

1 Dennis and Gene nailed 16 boards onto the old gate.

2 Helen had seen the 12 lighted signs shining at night.

3 Anne and Bill ate a salad and 15 figs and a big steak.

4 Leslie sang a tiny jingle as she dashed ahead in glee.

5 When Tom tested his stiff ankle, he gnashed his teeth.

6 Please appease that helpless, pleading, pious plaintiff.

7 A tall, split, peeling aspen sapling is plainly diseased.

8 Pat speaks and pleads and defends the three plaintiffs.

9 Did Tim tape that splint and dispense the correct pills?

10 The spaniel has 134 bites and needs some skilled help.

Dr. Davis has emphasized the importance of early training of the young puppy. . . .

It is clear that there continues to be an overwhelming need for control of our animal population, according to recent sources.

The *Otis Flyer* has reported that only 20 percent of the animal population is really neglected.

"Although you may find this strange to believe, there are no cures for the deadly bacteria found in dogs' ears during the month of August."

Source Note Style—Text Notes or Footnotes?

In recent years, there has been a growing trend to use **text notes** rather than **footnotes** to cite information sources. Text notes are easier and faster to key, and they provide immediate identification. Readers do not need to switch their attention to the bottom of the page to find the publication name and author. Since both footnotes and text notes may be used to cite sources, be sure to find out which style your organization prefers and use that style consistently throughout your document.

In the following examples of the sample manuscript "Our Paper Highway," the writer quotes material from an article written by Deborah Dane entitled "The Rising Cost of Record Storage" from the April 1995 edition of the magazine *Management and Money*, page 52, and from a book written by Judy L. Holbreck and Vincent T. Marcus, *Problems in Record Storage*, published in Dayton, Ohio, by the Western Publishing Company in 1994. The first example shows the text note style. The second example shows the traditional footnote style.

OUR PAPER HIGHWAY

The storing of valuable documents and records has had a place in history almost from the beginning of time. Even then, people tried to find a way to preserve and keep important records of their existence. As buying and selling evolved, the need to keep important records of major business transactions also grew. Throughout history, records storage and retrieval has always been an exciting and interesting career field.

Importance of Records Storage

Because of added productivity and correspondence of businesses of today, the sheer volume of paperwork has increased beyond human expectations or imagination. Business records, in spite of computerized data storage, take up more space than any other single item (Holbreck and Marcus 2). Not only has the need for additional space become critical, but the added expense of maintaining the records storage has also risen.

One expert indicated that if trends continue, the cost of storing just one document could rise to thirty cents (Dane 57). The storage problem will continue to increase, as one file drawer can hold only a certain number of items. Not only do the records take up precious space, but the need for higher salaries and equipment soars. Quite obviously, any time or effort spent by office workers or any money spent by a business firm is totally wasted if the records are not really needed, or if those records cannot be easily located and retrieved

Figure 52.1 Manuscript with source notes in Simplified Format (text note style)

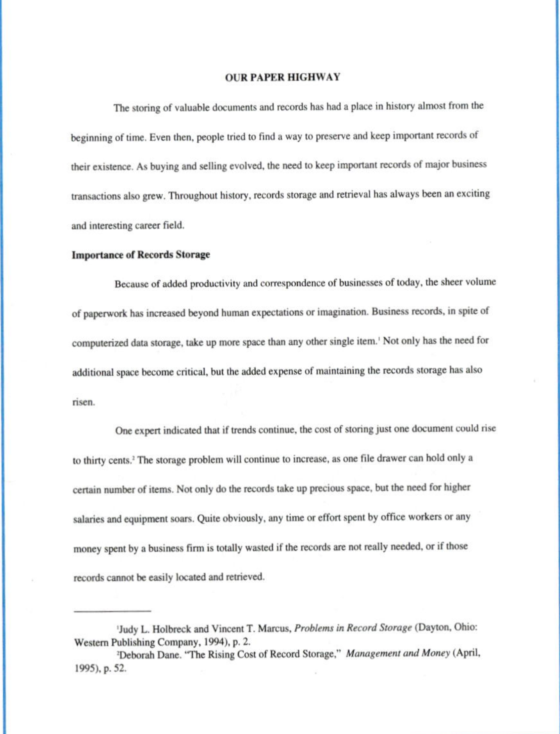

OUR PAPER HIGHWAY

The storing of valuable documents and records has had a place in history almost from the beginning of time. Even then, people tried to find a way to preserve and keep important records of their existence. As buying and selling evolved, the need to keep important records of major business transactions also grew. Throughout history, records storage and retrieval has always been an exciting and interesting career field.

Importance of Records Storage

Because of added productivity and correspondence of businesses of today, the sheer volume of paperwork has increased beyond human expectations or imagination. Business records, in spite of computerized data storage, take up more space than any other single item.[1] Not only has the need for additional space become critical, but the added expense of maintaining the records storage has also risen.

One expert indicated that if trends continue, the cost of storing just one document could rise to thirty cents.[2] The storage problem will continue to increase, as one file drawer can hold only a certain number of items. Not only do the records take up precious space, but the need for higher salaries and equipment soars. Quite obviously, any time or effort spent by office workers or any money spent by a business firm is totally wasted if the records are not really needed, or if those records cannot be easily located and retrieved.

---

[1]Judy L. Holbreck and Vincent T. Marcus, *Problems in Record Storage* (Dayton, Ohio: Western Publishing Company, 1994), p. 2.

[2]Deborah Dane. "The Rising Cost of Record Storage," *Management and Money* (April, 1995), p. 52.

Figure 52.2 Manuscript with source notes in Traditional Format (footnote style)

Printing WordPerfect Reinforcement Activities

To save and print the WordPerfect for Windows document you have created, complete steps 1-5 that follow. (***Remember:*** The work you completed up to the WordPerfect Reinforcement section has already been saved automatically.)

1 Choose **F**ile → Save **A**s (or F3).
2 At the *Save As* dialog box, key the new filename, **015wpr.kwp**. Press ***Enter*** or click on the OK button. Your document has been saved to disk, and it also remains on the screen.
3 To print 015wpr.kwp, choose **F**ile → **P**rint (or F5).
4 Click on the **P**rint button or press ***Enter***.
5 Close the file (click on **F**ile → **C**lose).

Deleting Files

In Session 11, you learned to delete documents to conserve space on your data disk. You will recall that the *Keyboarding with WordPerfect* software automatically deletes session and timing files that are more than ten sessions old. However, it is up to you to delete your outdated WordPerfect files so that your data disk contains only the ten most current WPR files.

To delete the **wpr** document you completed in Session 5, follow these steps:

1 Choose **F**ile → **O**pen.
2 Select the file *005wpr.kwp* by clicking on the filename with the left mouse button.
3 With the filename highlighted, choose File **O**ptions → **D**elete.
4 At the *Delete File* dialog box, click on **D**elete.
5 To close the *Open File* dialog box, click on Cancel or press ***Esc***.

Note: Once the file to be deleted has been selected (highlighted) in the *Open File* dialog box, you can press the ***Delete*** key on the keyboard to delete the file.

Now that you have completed the WordPerfect Reinforcement activities, you are to take several 1-minute timings. Click on the KWP Next Activity button to bring up the Timings screen.

NUMBER TIMINGS

Goal: 25 WAM with no more than 2 errors

- Take a 1-minute timing on each group of numbers.
- Press ***Enter*** at the end of each line.
- Remember to start over if you finish before the time is up.

1 333 333 333 444 444 444 555 555 555 666 666 666 56
333 333 444 444 555 666 666 111 111 222 222 123 45
12223 12224 13335 13336 14442 14443 12224 12225 16
32221 42221 53331 63331 24441 34441 42221 52221 63

2 26 35 346 34 45 46 251 2346 235 325 625 463 51616 2
6242 4621 31446 51432 51431 4265 4261 5431 5421 6
16 61 61 31 31 31 3655 66 16 62 5661 6546 665 566 2
16 661 626 365 4466 1263 4565 16 15 1615 26 62 54 3

Citing Sources

Quotations Direct or Paraphrased

1 ***Direct Quotation:*** Use quotation marks to enclose the exact words or ideas of another person whom you are quoting directly. ***Note:*** The source note information in the following examples is shown in the **text note format**.

Dane stated, "If current trends continue, the cost of filing just one document could rise to thirty cents" (Dane 57).

"If current trends continue," stated Dane, "the cost of filing just one document could rise to thirty cents" (Dane 57).

2 ***Paraphrased Quotation:*** In formal writing, material that has been directly quoted is enclosed in quotation marks as shown. If you paraphrased (did not quote the words exactly), you would not need the quotation marks, but you must still give credit for the idea by using a source note. ***Note:*** The source note information in the following example is shown in the **footnote format**. A superscript number is placed after the quote in the text of your written report; this same number is also placed at the beginning of the corresponding footnote at the bottom of the page.

One expert indicated that if trends continue, the cost of storing just one document could rise to thirty cents.[1]

3 ***Ellipsis:*** In some printed materials, you will notice a series of three evenly spaced periods (. . .), called an **ellipsis**. The ellipsis indicates that some words have been omitted from quoted material. When an ellipsis appears at the end of a statement, four periods are used.

Document A ← *Quotation Marks*

1 At a clear WordPerfect editing window, key each of the statements shown in Document A. Concentrate on keying the quotation marks and other punctuation marks in the proper position.
2 Choose **F**ile → **S**ave As and name the document **052wpra.kwp**.
3 Choose **F**ile → **C**lose. This closes Document A and brings up the Document B screen.

Document A

In his latest book, Strage states, "Dogs should never be given more food than they can eat in one sitting."

Star and Smith have said, "The coat of a healthy dog is shining and glowing at all times."

Hearthic has stated clearly, "There is no excuse for an unhealthy dog in this day and age."

According to the latest information, the one leading cause of animal neglect is human indifference.

Zich has declared that, "Nine million dogs are suffering each day in our country."

Continued on next page

LETTER TIMINGS

Goal: 30 WAM with no more than 2 errors

- Take a 1-minute timing on each paragraph.
- Press ***Tab*** to indent the first line.
- Start over if you finish before time is up.

1 Over 25 million pagers have been sold. More than half of all pagers sold are for personal use. Parents have beepers so babysitters can reach them when they go out. Adults give their elderly parents and teenagers their beeper number so they can be reached easily. Construction and factory workers use pagers because they do not have easy access to a telephone.

2 Muffin is a genuine bulldog. Although he weighs 64 pounds, he bounds about with a flourish. It is fun to see him plunge around, indulging in the pure pleasure of running. He huffs and puffs and slumps to the ground. No doubt, he will jump and lunge again after a pause and find trouble.

3 Thomas bought a used car from a dealer at 16532 Halsted Street. Although the bumper and the trunk were ruined, he assumed that it would run. If he would flush the rust from the lumbering hulk of junk, he might be able to use it. His woeful anguish spurred a new thought; perhaps it was useless.

ENDING THE SESSION

Once you have completed the timings, the KWP program takes you to the next session menu. If you want to print the Session 15 files, however, follow the steps below. Then continue with Session 16 or exit the program.

PRINT

1. Click on Back until you reach the KWP Main Menu.
2. Highlight *Freeform*, then click on OK.
3. Click on the Print button or choose **F**ile → **P**rint.
4. At the *Print* dialog box, select the **D**ocument on Disk option under *Print Selection*. Press ***Enter*** or click on OK.
5. At the *Document on Disk* dialog box, click on the list button at the right of the filename text box.
6. With the mouse pointer, highlight the file to be printed and press ***Enter*** or click on **P**rint.
7. At the *Document on Disk* dialog box, click on **P**rint.

Repeat steps 3-7 to print additional documents on disk.

CONTINUE

1. Print any files, if necessary.
2. If you are working in Freeform, click on the KWP Main Menu button.
3. Highlight *Keyboarding Sessions*, then click on OK.
4. Click on Jump to go to the next session.

EXIT

1. Print any files, if necessary.
2. Click on the KWP Main Menu button on the Toolbar.
3. At the Main Menu, select WordPerfect Only, then click on OK.
4. Click on **F**ile → E**x**it.
5. Exit Windows, if necessary (**F**ile → E**x**it).

THREE-MINUTE TIMINGS

Goal: 35 WAM/1 error

SI: 1.49

- Take two 3-minute timings.

When guests visit our homes, most of us enjoy the experience. The preparation period preceding a visit is not so enjoyable. Usually, a thorough cleaning and polishing is in order, along with planning good meals for the guests. The entire family labors to prepare their home for the expected guests. Excitement mounts as the magic time for the arrival of the guests draws nearer. Sometimes, the waiting will seem like an eternity. After the guests have arrived, there is usually an excited hustle and bustle as the unpacking chores are done. Everyone can then settle down for a friendly chat to catch up on all events at a leisurely pace.

A welcome guest is one who tries not to intrude in established family routines. Guests might assist, whenever possible, with the burden of routine chores such as cooking, cleaning, or other duties. If a visit is lengthy, it is traditional to send a gift or a small token of thanks to the host family after the visit is over. An accompanying personal note is needed to thank the host family.

PREPARING RESEARCH SOURCE NOTES

An important part of the manuscript writing process is creating the research source notes, which are a means for crediting the source of ideas or information you have used in your manuscript. To use another writer's words or ideas without giving credit is called *plagiarism*, which in some cases is against the law and in all cases is unethical. You **must** give credit to another author if you use his or her ideas.

If you quote directly or indirectly from another source, you can identify the quote by using source notes in the form of text notes, footnotes, or endnotes.

Text notes are brief parenthetical references to the source of an indirect or direct quotation. A text note includes the author's last name and a page number from the work cited, for example, (Updike 25). The works cited are then listed in a more complete form at the end of the report as a *works cited list* or a *bibliography*.

Footnotes are numbered references that appear at the foot (bottom) of the page. A footnote includes the author's last name, publication title, place of publication, publisher, date of publication, and the page number of the information cited. The information cited is coded with a superscript number (a small-size number that appears at the upper-right of a word in the text), and the information source, identified with the same number, is listed at the foot of the page.

Another kind of note that is often confused with a footnote is the **endnote**. Endnotes offer additional explanation of material cited in the text of a report. Endnotes are numbered with superscripts. Unlike footnotes, however, endnotes all appear at the end of a report and offer additional information rather than the source of a direct or indirect quotation.

7, 8, 9, 0, COMMA, DECIMAL

SESSION GOALS

7, 8, 9, 0, Comma, Decimal

Review saving, printing, closing, deleting

Numbers (1-Minute): 25 WAM/2 errors
Letters (1-Minute): 30 WAM/2 errors

GETTING STARTED

If you are continuing immediately from Session 15, go to step 4. If you exited the program at the end of Session 15, do the following:

1. Access Windows, then WordPerfect 6.1 for Windows.
2. At the WordPerfect editing window, click on the KWP icon.
3. Go to the Keyboarding Sessions menu, then click on Jump to return to the activity you left off with. Or, move through the program menus until you reach the Session 16 menu.
4. On the Session 16 menu, *Warm-Up* is highlighted. Click on OK to proceed with the Warm-Up activities.

If you are already warmed up or have completed a portion of the session, move the mouse pointer to the desired activity and click on OK or press ***Enter***. When you have completed the new-key drills and the WordPerfect Reinforcement activities, you will take several 1-minute number and letter timings.

WORDPERFECT REINFORCEMENT

Earlier in the session you completed new-key drills presented on the screen. Now you will repeat some of those drills to reinforce your keyboarding skills and to practice working in WordPerfect.

Reviewing the 7, 8, 9, and 0 Keys

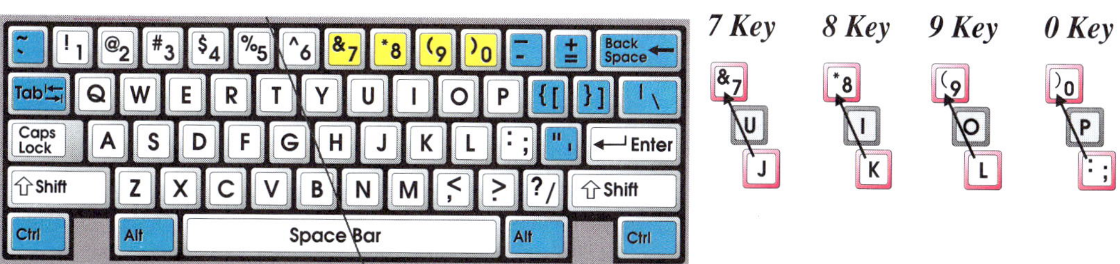

SESSION GOALS

1-Minute: 40 WAM/1 error
3-Minute: 35 WAM/1 error

Footnotes
Hanging indents

Using direct quotations

GETTING STARTED

If you are continuing immediately from Session 51, go to the one-minute timings. If you exited the program at the end of session 51, do the following:

1. Access Windows, then WordPerfect 6.1 for Windows.
2. Click on the KWP icon to access *Keyboarding with* WordPerfect.
3. Go to the *Keyboarding Sessions* menu and click on Jump to return to your last activity. Or, access the Session 52 menu and click on OK to begin the session.

ONE-MINUTE TIMINGS

Goal: 40 WAM/1 error

SI: 1.49

- Take two 1-minute timings.

How fast should you exercise? It may surprise you to know that experts say slow and easy may be better for you than fast and hard, especially if you are out of shape. The body burns two types of fuel: glycogen (high-grade) and fat (low-grade). It stands to reason that if you are driving your body as if it were a race car, you are going to consume high-grade fuel. But if you are rolling smoothly along, your body can eat up more of the low-grade stuff, which is the fat.

7 Key Drills

Key lines 1–3 twice: first for control, then for speed. Anchor the ";" finger on the home row.

1 a55 77 66 76 57 57 a76 77 777 677 a555 76 6 a755a a755a

2 767 767 5767 5757 a576 7675a 7675a 77 777 666 555 a75a

3 a576a 76a5a 6675a 6675 5667 777 a65a7 5672 a7765 a575a

See how quickly you can complete the following:

1. Key the numbers 1 through 7 three times. Space once after each number.
2. Reverse the order; key from 7 down to 1. Space once after each number.

8 Key Drills

Key lines 1–3 twice: first for control, then for speed. Anchor either the "j" or the ";" finger on the home row.

1 88 11 588 11 88 11 88 11 88 11 688 11 88 11 8 8823 1482

2 8182 81828 2845 6817 71882 6818 2238 885 888 288 388

3 557 8283 38482 78681 11812 8823 28 28 888 321 854 488

Now complete the following drill to develop speed and concentration:

1. Key the numbers 1 through 8 three times. Space once between numbers.
2. Reverse the order; key from 8 back to 1 three times. Space once between numbers.

9 Key Drills

Key lines 1–3 twice for control. Anchor the "j" finger at home as the "l" finger keys 9. Remember to read the numbers as groups.

1 8489 19891 1919 1891 9981 19867 183218 189 19 698 98

2 99 88 589 998 998 888 991 999 498 98 99 88 94 32989 29

3 23 1989 2239 39823 59891 123 698 92919 9812 375 688 9

Here's another drill to develop speed with the 9 key:

1. Key the numbers 1 through 9 three times. Space once between numbers.
2. Reverse the order; key from 9 back to 1 three times. Again, space once between numbers.

0 (Zero) Key Drills

Key the following line three times for control. Anchor the "j" finger at home as the ";" finger strikes 0.

Note: Be sure to use the zero key, not the capital O.

10 20 30 40 50 60 70 80 90 a10 a20 a30 240 250 10 115 619 057

functions of the codec are twofold. They digitize the video signal and compress it to reduce the amount of storage required on the hard drive. Full motion video, the kind you watch when watching a TV program, displays 30 frames (screens) per second. Full motion video signals are transmitted at 90 million bits per second. With Codecs, video signals can be compressed to less than 1 million bits per second. lc

- Additional components are necessary depending on how you are using the multimedia PC: a 3.5-inch, high-density floppy drive, 256K of cache memory, a 17-inch SVGA monitor, controller cards, a 28.8 Kbps fax/data modem, two serial and one parallel port, a mouse, a 6-speed internal CD-ROM drive, a MIDI (Musical Instrument Digital Interface) card, a flatbed scanner, and color inkjet printer. ports a

Conclusion

The best approach to follow before investing in a multimedia PC is to identify the planned uses, the software needed for these applications, and the hardware that can has the capacity to support these applications. It is a good idea to have one or more "multimedia experts" review your intended uses, the software, and the hardware before investing. Frequently, they can save you money and/or identify missing components.

Document D — *Bound Manuscript*

1. At a clear WordPerfect editing window, open Document **051proc.kwp**. Using the Find and Replace feature, make the following changes.
   a. Wherever the term *multimedia PC* occurs in the manuscript, change it to *MPC*, except in the first paragraph. In the last paragraph, changing to *MPC* requires that *a* be changed to *an*.
   b. Where the term *MB* appears in the document, change it to *megabytes*.
2. Choose **F**ile → Save **A**s to save the document, then key the filename **051wprd.kwp**.
3. Choose **F**ile → **C**lose to close the document and clear the editing window.

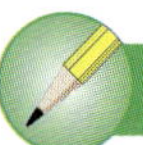

REINFORCING WRITING SKILLS

Have you noticed how headings have been used in the three bound manuscripts (Documents A-C) completed in this session? To improve the "readability" of your documents, especially those that require multiple pages, create first-, second-, and third-level headings to help the reader focus on the content. Information that can be shown in logical groups is easier to digest and will be retained for longer periods of time.

Document E — *Creating Headings within a Manuscript*

Open **050prob.kwp**, an unbound manuscript you keyed in Session 50. Read the document carefully, then think of appropriate headings (first, second, third, or combinations of them) and insert them in the proper locations. Format them according to the guidelines you used in this session. Save the new document as **051wpre.kwp**, then print and close the file.

ENDING THE SESSION

To end this session, DELETE outdated WordPerfect Reinforcement files, PRINT any files from Session 51 not printed earlier, then CONTINUE with the next session or EXIT the program.

Now try this drill to help you focus on the location of each number key:

1. Key the numbers from 1 to 100. Space once after each number. Use word wrap.
2. Key the numbers from 2 to 200 by twos. Space once after each number. Again, use word wrap.

Number Concentration Drill

Key lines 1–5 twice for control. Concentrate on reading the numbers in groups.

1 11201 1316 14037 22304 3405 4506 35607 6708 78092 1415
2 6816 62317 73218 2219 32206 8782 19222 90234 1929 3030
3 45317 7932 34332 13476 9535 87369 1370 1743 37744 7645
4 2674 65647 1674 84859 34750 25151 23270 45524 8910 573
5 91524 7853 85426 1927 52938 22304 11201 78092 7753 361

Comma and Decimal Keys

You have now been introduced to all ten digits and are ready to review other areas of the keyboard. There are two symbols used frequently with numbers—the ***comma*** and the ***decimal point*** (also used as a period at the end of a sentence). These keys were reviewed in Session 3 but because they are used frequently with numbers, more practice is offered here.

Comma Key

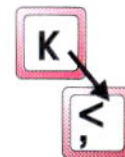

Decimal Key

Comma Key Drill

When numbers are separated by commas, decimals, spaces, letters, or other symbols, use those division points as natural breaks between groups of numbers. For example, 5,134 would be read ***five/comma/one thirty-four***.

Key lines 1–3 twice: first for control, then for speed. Concentrate on grouping the numbers by division points.

1 1,368 16,434 92,860 58,167 34,511 76,924 6,331 21,468
2 38,107 48,243 1,509 5,114 15,816 6,184,336 98,165,225
3 4,408,452 251,145 12,259 1,259 159,467 43,410 875,243

Decimal Key Drill

Key lines 1–3 for control. Concentrate on reading numbers by division points. If you make a mistake, start over until you complete the line without an error.

1 41,345.51 15,378.78 31,428.27 89,261,500.68 59.63 61.3
2 91,007.23 851,267.18 109.01 13.17 8.43 4.40 596.27 39.8
3 990.85 67,349.34 23,265.08 186.84 4.23 .87 8,582 13.455

instructional materials, presentation programs, and the general improvement of communications. They are particularly popular for home use, probably because of the fantastic games both children and adults can play on them.

Purchasing Considerations

When purchasing a microcomputer for multimedia applications, be sure to address the following three areas:

- What applications are you going to pursue?
- What hardware is needed to address these applications?
- What software is required?

Applications. Will you use your multimedia PC to take advantage of programs that are already on the market, or will you be developing your own materials? Once you have identified how your multimedia PC will be used, determine whether your applications will involve integrating text, image, voice, video, and animation or only combinations of these communication alternatives. Once a commitment has been made to the anticipated applications, the next step is to address the software and hardware needed.

Applications Software. Depending on the ultimate uses you have planned for your multimedia PC, there are a wide variety of software packages on the market. For example, if your needs call for integrating text and images, an office suites package that contains word processing, database, spreadsheet, and graphics modules is a must. In addition, there are software packages for sound applications, including music, voice, video effects, and animation. Also available are software packages used for planning/developing integrated presentations based on the storyboard approach.

Operating/Communication System Software. Once application software is selected, the next step is to identify the operating system that supports that software. The workstation operating system software will probably GUI (graphical user interface) based. Other software considerations in this category include communications software for local area network and wide area network activities. For example, if it is important to be able to access the Internet to search for information, request information, or send messages to others, special software is required.

Hardware. The hardware necessary to operate multimedia applications includes several components:

- A microprocessor that addresses at least 32 bits at a cycle speed of at least 133 MHz is a must. The microprocessor is the key to the speed and power of your Multimedia PC.
- Random Access Memory (RAM) of at least 16 MB expandable to 64 MB is critical when integrating functions. The more RAM memory available, the faster the processing of information. Remember that during applications processing, RAM is holding the operating system software, the applications software, and the files that you are generating.
- Multimedia PCs require hard drive storage capacities of several gigabytes (billions of bytes). For example, one second of quality stereo sound takes up to 150,000 bytes of memory. This is a drop in the bucket when compared to video storage.
- If you plan to use music, voice, or other forms of sound, your system must have a sound card, stereo speakers, a microphone for input, and headphones so that only the user hears the sounds.
- Codecs are necessary if you plan to use video in your multimedia PC. The codec is a card that takes up one of the slots in your multimedia PC. The

Continued on next page

Important: If you have not completed Sessions 1-13 (the alphabetic keys), go to Ending the Session. Otherwise proceed to the Sentences practice that follows:

Sentences

Key lines 1–10 twice: first for speed, then for control.

1 Of the 15,220 rangers, 170 sprained their ankles last year.
2 Dirk did the drills first and drank the delicious tea later.
3 Take 12 or 13 fresh, green grapes as your dessert treat.
4 He risks great danger if he departs after today's dinner.
5 The 14 interns gratefully lingered in the green garden .
6 The meat manager made a simple remark and smirked.
7 Did Mary send the 380 messages after amending them?
8 Pam had made some malts with milk, mint, and mango.
9 The firefighters attempted an immense task and missed.
10 Did Sammie eliminate the 16 mistakes in the message?

Printing WordPerfect Reinforcement Activities

To save and print the WordPerfect for Windows document you have created, complete steps 1-5 that follow. (***Remember:*** The work you completed up to the WordPerfect Reinforcement section has already been saved automatically.)

1. Choose **F**ile → Save **A**s (or F3).
2. At the *Save As* dialog box, key the new filename, **016wpr.kwp**. Press ***Enter*** or click on the OK button. Your document has been saved to disk, and it also remains on the screen.
3. To print 016wpr.kwp, choose **F**ile → **P**rint (or F5).
4. Click on the **P**rint button or press ***Enter***.
5. Close the file (click on **F**ile → **C**lose).

Deleting Files

As you recall, the *Keyboarding with WordPerfect* software automatically deletes session files that are more than ten sessions old. However, it is your responsibility to delete your outdated WordPerfect files so that your data disk contains only the ten most current WPR files.

To delete the **wpr** document you completed in Session 6, follow these steps:

1. Choose **F**ile → **O**pen.
2. Select the file *006wpr.kwp* by clicking on the filename with the left mouse button.
3. With the filename highlighted, choose File **O**ptions → **D**elete.
4. At the *Delete File* dialog box, click on **D**elete.
5. To close the *Open File* dialog box, click on Cancel or press ***Esc***.

Note: Once the file to be deleted has been selected (highlighted) in the *Open File* dialog box, you can press the ***Delete*** key on the keyboard to delete the file.

Now that you have completed the WordPerfect Reinforcement activities, you are to take several 1-minute timings. Click on the KWP Next Activity button to bring up the Timing screen.

Inflationary times. During the past ten years, the pattern of constantly rising costs has been consistent. In response, businesses are forced to cut costs in every conceivable manner. It is the responsibility of the office systems manager to continually analyze costs and determine new methods for efficient production.

Change in Employees

There also has been a dramatic change in the characteristics of office personnel throughout the years.

Retiring workers. Many employers feel that there just aren't enough employees to replace older, experienced workers who have retired. New workers are costly to train and sometimes just cannot do the job.

Lack of skills. Until a few years ago, office workers could usually obtain employment directly after high school. Many of today's office positions, however, require more specialized training.

Automated equipment. Because of the development of highly automated equipment, many offices require employees with a background in electronic office systems. The new employee must be skilled in software-driven electronic systems and thoroughly understand the impact of office automation and telecommunications.

Career as Office Systems Manager

Because of the changes that have taken place, there is a definite need for offices to use modern techniques and scientific methods. This, in turn, increases the need for efficient office systems managers. The area of office management as a career can be profitable and productive. Training is available at most post-secondary schools that offer specialized courses in "office systems management."

Document C — *Bound Manuscript*

1. At the *Production–Session 51 Document C* screen, key Document C as a bound manuscript with a 1.5" left margin and 1-inch right margin. Before keying the document, make the following formatting changes: change the line spacing to double, turn on Widow/Orphan, turn on page numbering (beginning on page 2) with page numbers at the bottom center.
2. Proofread and correct any errors, then complete a spell check with Speller.
3. Click on Check to automatically name **(051proc.kwp)**, save, and check the document.
4. To print with errors highlighted, click on the Print button.
5. To correct errors, click on View Original. Make changes, then recheck the document.
6. Choose **F**ile → **C**lose. This closes Document C and brings up a clear WordPerfect screen.

Document C

MULTIMEDIA PCS

Introduction (bf)

The microcomputer is only in its second decade. During its short life, the number of microcomputers in home and business use has grown beyond all expectations. Concurrently, the applications for the microcomputer have expanded beyond imagination. One of the applications that generates a great deal of press is the integration of text, image, voice, video, and animation. Microcomputers that have the capacity to integrate these functions are called Multimedia PCs. (MPCs)

Multimedia PCs are used in a variety of ways, including the development of

Continued on next page

NUMBER TIMINGS

Goal: 25 WAM with no more than 2 errors

- Take a 1-minute timing on each paragraph.
- Press ***Enter*** at the end of each line.
- Start over if you finish a paragraph before time is up.

1 81 85 823 8466 8877 7868 58 45 238 845 866 8143 8 8123
5671 82345 3458 8612348 3467 1238 886 81387 5834278
58743218 11386518 2251386 87 88 8811318 8 5481 8375
18 2368 8 7628 81 61842 8811318 18 8788 5792 6139 144

2 91 95 923 8466 9977 7898 69 45 239 945 966 9143 9 9123
5671 92345 3458 9612349 3467 12392 996 81389 5934278
59743219 11386519 2251396 973 99 9911319 9 5491 9375
19 2368 9 7629 947 61942 99111319 19 979 7426 5187 239

3 27 821 59361 40352 89734 92035 64019 9356 693 958 3177
501 6512 96 8742 56034 56832 85923 780 847 91 6409 7483
9467 3520 5945 2635 5705 8932 6485 1956 23670 81251800
165 208125635 69312 9871 6017340 2 716941 8320193 5163
8613 5113818 8542001 88490 6 2361 15432 11621618 11234
19051 3399 668 45441 4091 25937 68465 21893 492 591 783

LETTER TIMINGS

Goal: 30 WAM with no more than 2 errors

- Take a 1-minute timing on each paragraph.
- Press ***Tab*** to indent the first line of each paragraph.
- If you finish a paragraph before time is up, start over.

1 Zeb went to the zoo to see the 179 new animals. He went especially to see the 18 species of lizards. He wants to be a zoologist when he gets older. He knows many things about animals, and his parents are really amazed.

2 A cookout on the beach could include 6 kinds of cheese, carrots, 3 types of meat sandwiches, and 14 cans of cold juice. If the chill of the ocean is too much, hot chocolate and hot coffee can chase the cold chills. The decent lunch and a chat with friends can enrich affection.

3 An office clerk who lacks basic ethics could become the subject of scorn. Those who gossip about or verbally abuse new workers can cause problems. It is smart to follow the 13 rules that are printed on the bulletin board about getting along with fellow workers. Do the right thing and be sincere.

Characteristics

Good bakers are aware of several differences between regular yeast and the fast-rising varieties that make a difference in the baked bread.

Odor. The fast-rising product gives off more yeasty odor while proofing or rising.

Rising time. Fast-rising yeast rises more quickly in warmer temperatures but also is more sensitive to temperature extremes.

Texture. Breads made with fast-rising yeast have a slightly more open texture than those made with regular yeast. The resulting breads and rolls, however, don't appear to differ significantly.

Document B — *Bound Manuscript*

1. At the *Production–Session 51 Document B* screen, make the following formatting changes before keying the document: change the left margin to 1.5 inches, change line spacing to 2.0, turn on Widow/Orphan, turn on page numbering to number pages in the top right corner, and suppress page numbering on page 1.
2. Press ***Enter*** enough times to move the cursor to approximately *Line 2"*.
3. Center and bold the title, **THE OFFICE SYSTEMS MANAGER**.
4. Press ***Enter*** once, then key the remainder of the manuscript. To create the dash, choose **I**nsert → **C**haracter, then key **4,34** in the **N**umber box.
5. Proofread and correct any errors. Complete a spell check.
6. Click on Check to automatically name **(051prob.kwp)**, save, and check the document
7. To print with errors highlighted, click on the Print button.
8. To correct errors, click on View Original. Make changes, then recheck the document.
9. Choose **F**ile → **C**lose. This closes Document B and brings up the Document C screen.

Document B

THE OFFICE SYSTEMS MANAGER

Occupational Need

The office scene has changed considerably over the past few years. Businesses have grown, more transactions are taking place, and certain incidents have occurred that require most offices of today to hire a new type of employee—the office systems manager. His or her main duties are to ensure that the office is run as efficiently as possible.

Changes in the Workplace

There are many exciting and new changes that have taken place in the office world. Some of them are inevitable and others represent an attempt to improve older methods.

Financial Costs

Many businesses have tended to view the cost of operating an office as a necessary, but unproductive, evil. Business owners have seen the cost of operating an office rise rapidly.

Increased paperwork. One reason costs have increased is the fact that paperwork in an office has increased dramatically. Unless the flow of paperwork is carefully controlled, costs will skyrocket.

Continued on next page

ENDING THE SESSION

Once you have completed the timings, the KWP program takes you to the next session menu. If you want to print the Session 16 files, however, follow the steps below. Then continue with Session 17 or exit the program.

PRINT

1. Click on Back until you reach the KWP Main Menu.
2. Highlight *Freeform*, then click on OK.
3. Click on the Print button or choose **F**ile → **P**rint.
4. At the *Print* dialog box, select the **D**ocument on Disk option under *Print Selection*. Press ***Enter*** or click on OK.
5. At the *Document on Disk* dialog box, click on the list button at the right of the filename text box.
6. With the mouse pointer, highlight the file to be printed and press ***Enter*** or click on **P**rint.
7. At the *Document on Disk* dialog box, click on **P**rint.

Repeat steps 3-7 to print additional documents on disk.

CONTINUE

1. Print any files, if necessary.
2. If you are working in Freeform, click on the KWP Main Menu button.
3. Highlight *Keyboarding Sessions*, then click on OK.
4. Click on Jump to go to the next session.

EXIT

1. Print any files, if necessary.
2. Click on the KWP Main Menu button on the Toolbar.
3. At the Main Menu, select WordPerfect Only, then click on OK.
4. Click on **F**ile → E**x**it.
5. Exit Windows, if necessary (**F**ile → E**x**it).

Document A ◂-- *Bound Manuscript*

1. At the *Production–Session 51 Document A* screen, make the following formatting changes before you begin keying: change the left margin to 1.5 inches; change line spacing to 2.0; turn on Widow/Orphan; turn on page numbering to number pages at the top right; and suppress the page numbering on page 1.
2. Press ***Enter*** enough times to move the insertion point to approximately *Line 2"*.
3. Center and key the title, **RISING TO THE OCCASION.**
4. Press ***Enter*** once, then key the remainder of the manuscript in Document A.
5. Proofread and correct any errors. Complete a spell check.
6. Click on Check to automatically name **(051proa.kwp)**, save, and check the document.
7. To print with errors highlighted, click on the Print button.
8. To correct errors, click on View Original. Make changes, then recheck the document.
9. Choose **File** → **Close**. This closes Document A and brings up the Document B screen.

Document A

RISING TO THE OCCASION

Yeast Breads

Most people bake breads for the process as much as for the product. Mixing the ingredients and kneading the warm dough by the centuries-old rhythm of push-and-pull, then fold-and-press are the first two steps. Watching the bread rise in a warm oven almost gives one the feeling of creating a living thing more than making something to eat.

Nearly one-third of all people who cook bake yeast breads. Of those people, nearly half are workers with jobs outside the home, according to Syndicated Research Data. And most of that baking takes place on weekdays.

Saving Time

The nation's leading yeast producers say there's one aspect of the bread baking process that home cooks would rather do without. That's the time it takes to let yeast dough rise. Most recipes require at least one rising of an hour or longer; many recipes require a second rising.

Both the major yeast companies, Fleischmann's and Red Star, have come out with fast-rising yeasts that can cut in half the amount of time a home cook spends waiting for breads to rise.

The fast-rising yeasts have finer grain than regular dry yeast. The firms say the finer grain adapts well to a quick-mixing technique that allows cooks to save additional time.

Procedure

According to industry literature, the technique involves setting aside one cup of flour and then mixing the yeast directly into the remaining dry ingredients. Then the dry ingredients are combined with the liquid and fat, heated to 125 to 130 degrees, and kneaded with the remaining flour.

Both firms say the fast-rising yeasts also may be rehydrated like regular yeast by dissolving them directly in water heated to 105 to 115 degrees before mixing with the remaining ingredients.

Continued on next page

SESSION 17

NUMBER PATTERNS USING PRESET TABS

SESSION GOALS

 **Number patterns**

 **Use preset tabs**
Review saving, printing, closing, deleting

 **Letters (1-Minute): 30 WAM/2 errors**

GETTING STARTED

1 Access Windows, then WordPerfect 6.1 for Windows.
2 At the WordPerfect editing window, click on the KWP icon.
3 At the Main Menu, click on Jump to return to the activity you left off with. Or, move through the program menus until you reach the Session 17 menu.
4 On the Session 17 menu, *Number Patterns* is highlighted. Click on OK to proceed with the Number Patterns activities.

If you have completed part of the session, move the mouse pointer to the desired activity and click on OK or press ***Enter***. When you have completed the new-key drills and the WordPerfect Reinforcement activities, you will take three 1-minute timings on paragraphs of text.

WORDPERFECT REINFORCEMENT

Some of the drills that were presented on-screen during the first part of Session 17 are repeated here to reinforce your keyboarding skills. In addition, the drills offer an opportunity to create, save, and print a WordPerfect document.

Keying Numbers

At a clear screen, try these drills to reinforce your number keying skills:

1 Key this line of numbers two or more times:
11 22 33 44 55 66 77 88 99 00
2 The most frequently used number is 0, followed by 5. To build your skills with these numbers, first key to 500 by tens; then key to 200 by fives.
3 To reinforce your ability to think while keying numbers, start at 100 and key to 0 by threes.

Repeat these drills whenever you can. They will help you master numbers.

Simplified Format

Major title:	Key on Line 2" on the first page; center and bold the title; capitalize all letters; double-space to the first-level heading (if used) or to the first line of the body.
First-level heading:	Center; bold and capitalize the first letter of each major word; double-space above and below.
Second-level heading:	Place it flush with the left margin on a separate line; capitalize the first letter of each major word; bold the heading; double-space above and below.
Third-level heading:	Indent with paragraph; capitalize only first letter or first word followed by a colon or period; underscore; double-space before. Note that some manuscript sections have second-level headings only, while others may have second-level headings followed by third-level headings.
Page numbering:	Place page numbers in upper-right corner beginning with page 2 and leave a double space between the number and the body.
Spacing:	Use double spacing throughout.

PROPER TELEPHONE TECHNIQUES

(ds)

The Business Image

(ds)

It is widely accepted that proper use of the telephone as a business tool is one important quality of an outstanding employee. Most office workers spend two or more hours each day in telephone contact with clients and customers.

(ds)

Caller's Response

(ds)

A prompt answer. Answering the telephone promptly will give the caller a favorable impression of the company. Use a lively, pleasant voice that creates a welcoming atmosphere.

Figure 51.1 Simplified format for manuscripts

***Note*:** In a formal report that requires chapter headings, the format would differ slightly. Consult a reliable reference book for further details.

Traditional Format

Because it requires additional steps to switch from double to triple spacing in word processing software packages (including WordPerfect), the simplified format is used in this text. In the traditional format, there is a triple space after the major title, before first- and second-level headings, and between page numbers and the body of a document.

Reading Number Groups

Remember, when numbers are grouped naturally by commas, spaces, and decimals, read the number by those groups. For example, 1,676,352.17 is read ***one/comma/six seventy-six/comma/three fifty-two/decimal/seventeen***.

Key lines 1–3 twice: first for control, then for speed. Concentrate on reading numbers in groups.

1 1,676,352.17 3,131 2.24 436,342 101.31 166,891 89

2 236,731 831,643 534.67 4,091,867 3,587.13 501,316

3 61,301.04 .36 89,341.76 31,700.73 151,317 416,319

Creating Columns of Numbers

WordPerfect has preset tabs every 0.5 inches. To create the columns of numbers shown below, key the first four-digit number and then press ***Tab*** twice to move between columns.

4901	8702	3303	3904	7205
6106	8307	9408	2709	3710
1511	5712	2613	9114	1515
5716	9117	5618	6619	3820
2621	3122	4523	2324	3125
6726	3528	8528	3529	4130
7731	6932	8533	7434	9935
8836	2337	6138	1639	5840

Numbers Drill

Key lines 1–3 twice: first for control, then for speed. Remember to read the numbers in 2-3-2 combinations.

1 7371130 91368840 1534986003 51673455189 963310931

2 21468159 515113 6873931 438761 223026501 89340013

3 6135910 619822385 3676 1090101 3948131 1788434341

Important: If you have not completed Sessions 1-13 (the alphabetic keys), go to Ending the Session. Otherwise proceed to the General Guidelines for Expressing Numbers and read and key each of the examples.

General Guidelines for Expressing Numbers

Authorities do not agree on when to spell out numbers and when to use figures. The guidelines illustrated here are those that are widely accepted. For more detailed information, consult *The Paradigm Reference Manual.*

Key the examples for each guideline. Read what you have keyed so that you have a mental image of the applications for the guidelines.

THREE-MINUTE TIMINGS

Goal: 35 WAM/1 error

SI: 1.48

- Take two 3-minute timings.
- Note that the error goal has dropped from 2 to 1 (per minute).

If you have never had the opportunity to glide through the skies at a very high rate of speed, you might be somewhat nervous or overly concerned about the first flight. You can be sure that flying is always safer than driving your own vehicle from your garage to school, work, or on a shopping trip.

Traveling via the fantastic jet airplane is the fastest and most economical way to travel for a person if the distance traveled is at least 200 miles. If two or more individuals will be covering fewer than 500 miles, traveling by car will be considerably more economical. If the distance is more than 1,000 miles, traveling by jet airplane is the fastest way to go and is usually considered to be more economical. The time saved is valuable, especially if your time is limited.

Traveling across an entire ocean to another country can be quite an enjoyable experience, especially if traveling in one of the newest wide-bodied jet planes. All seating is quite comfortable, and all the aisles are wide. These jumbo jets have a staircase that leads to an upper cabin for the first-class passengers to enjoy. Some airplanes now have a closed-circuit television screen that enables everyone to observe the take-off and landing and the cockpit gauges and controls. On longer flights, you might enjoy a full-length movie in addition to delicious meals and snacks.

PREPARING BOUND MANUSCRIPTS

A bound manuscript normally is a longer manuscript (more than four pages). It is usually placed in some type of cover or folder or stapled along the left side. Because additional space is required for the left edge "binding," a minimum 1.5-inch left margin and a l-inch right margin are used. WordPerfect automatically adjusts the center point of the paper so that it is centered within your margin settings.

Today, electronic printing and improved binding techniques are so exact that bound manuscripts are often printed with l-inch margins on the left and right. New binding methods do not necessarily require the extra half-inch in the left margin.

Manuscript Headings

The main purpose of headings is to call the reader's attention to the important ideas and sections in the manuscript. A variety of heading formats are acceptable. Two of the popular styles are the simplified format and the traditional format. Whichever format you use, follow it consistently throughout the document. Give careful attention to the punctuation and spacing in your report.

1 Spell out numbers one through ten; use figures for numbers 11 and above.

The computer science class includes six women.
At least 40 men are enrolled in beginning keyboarding.

2 If any of the numbers in a series is above ten, use figures for all the numbers.

We have 16 Macintosh computers, 14 IBM Personal Computers, and 8 IBM compatibles.

3 When a sentence begins with a number, spell it out (or rewrite the sentence).

Three hundred students are majoring in business.
Business majors number 300.

4 If the day precedes the month, express it in words.

We will meet on the sixth of December.

5 If the day follows the month, express it in figures.

We will meet on December 6 at the restaurant.

6 If the date is in the form of month, day, and year, express the day and year in figures.
Note: Always follow the year with a comma unless it appears at the end of a sentence.

We will meet on December 6, 1998, at the restaurant.

7 Use figures for measurements, percentages, and other mathematical expressions.

We need new carpet for a room that is 11 feet x 12 feet.
The package weighs about 7 pounds.
I will ask for a 6 percent raise.

8 Generally, use figures to express fractions and mixed numbers in technical writing or in physical measurements.

They used 3.5 feet of coaxial cable.

If the fraction appears alone or does not express a direct physical measurement, spell out the fraction.

He makes only half of what she makes.

9 Use figures to express decimals.

He is 6.5 feet tall.

10 For ages, follow the general guidelines for numbers.

He is 20 years old.
She is nine months old.

11 Use figures to express clock time.

Pack your bags right away so we can make the 5:20 p.m. flight.

12 Key house numbers in figures.

His address is 3103 Eddy Lane.

BOUND MANUSCRIPTS

SESSION GOALS

1-Minute: 40 WAM/1 error
3-Minute: 35 WAM/1 error

Improving the "readability" of manuscripts and reports

Review centering titles, line spacing, page numbering, setting margins, bolding, Find and Replace, Widow/Orphan

GETTING STARTED

If you are continuing immediately from Session 50, go to the one-minute timings. If you exited the program at the end of session 50, do the following:

1. Access Windows, then WordPerfect 6.1 for Windows.
2. Click on the KWP icon to access *Keyboarding with WordPerfect.*
3. Go to the Keyboarding Sessions menu and click on Jump to return to your last activity. Or, access the Session 51 menu and click on OK to begin the session.

ONE-MINUTE TIMINGS

Goal: 40 WAM/1 error

SI: 1.47

- Take two 1-minute timings.
- Use your most recent timing score to set a speed or accuracy goal. Note that the error goal has dropped to only 1 (per minute).

Betty is going to ski the best there is. Her imagination runs rampant. The mountains, trees, and powder all come together in one great rush of joy. Betty breaks into a wide, bright grin. Her face is covered with powder-white snow, and her limbs are frozen in motion. She has skied the ultimate run and still stands. Betty is free to ski, tumble, fly, and embellish to her heart's delight. She is a fleeting traveler among these huge, snowy monuments.

13 Spell out street names that contain numbers ten or below; if the numbers are above ten, express the names in figures.

The store is located on First Avenue.
My address is 5849 18th Street.

Sentences

Key lines 1-10 twice: first for speed, then for control.

1 Did Van ever deliver the varnish and the 150 shelves?
2 Vinnie lives in their villa; he enjoys the vast veranda.
3 It is evident; the vital lever reverses the vexing vent.
4 Ron delivered the 18 leather chairs late this evening.
5 Marvel served 286 vanilla shakes at two gala events.
6 The driver developed a fever; give him 13 vitamins.
7 That starving animal evaded 103 vigilant observers.
8 She does not fool them; she is not an honest senator.
9 Opal ordered the onions and olives from the market.
10 Did the florist remove all the thorns from the roses?

Printing WordPerfect Reinforcement Activities

To save and print the WordPerfect for Windows document you have created, complete steps 1-5 that follow. (***Remember:*** The work you completed up to the WordPerfect Reinforcement section has already been saved automatically.)

1. Choose **F**ile → Save **A**s (or F3).
2. At the *Save As* dialog box, key the new filename, **017wpr.kwp**. Press ***Enter*** or click on the OK button. Your document has been saved to disk, and it also remains on the screen.
3. To print 017wpr.kwp, choose **F**ile → **P**rint (or F5).
4. Click on the **P**rint button or press ***Enter***.
5. Close the file (click on **F**ile → **C**lose).

Deleting Files

As you recall, the *Keyboarding with WordPerfect* software automatically deletes session files that are more than ten sessions old. However, it is your responsibility to delete your outdated WordPerfect files so that your data disk contains only the ten most current WPR files.

To delete the **wpr** document you completed in Session 7, follow these steps:

1. Choose **F**ile → **O**pen.
2. Select the file *007wpr.kwp* by clicking on the filename with the left mouse button.
3. With the filename highlighted, choose File **O**ptions → **D**elete.
4. At the *Delete File* dialog box, click on **D**elete.
5. To close the *Open File* dialog box, click on Cancel or press ***Esc***.

Document D ← Manuscript Introduction

Using a research subject or topic that has been assigned in another class or the thesis statement "Public tax dollars are necessary to support major sports teams," compose an introductory paragraph for a manuscript on the subject. The introduction should be a paragraph of 50 to 150 words. When you have finished, edit your document for clear sentences, effective word choices, and correct punctuation, grammar, and capitalization.

Save and name the document **050wprd.kwp**. Then print and close the file.

ENDING THE SESSION

To end this session, DELETE outdated WordPerfect Reinforcement files, PRINT any files from Session 50 not printed earlier, then CONTINUE with the next session or EXIT the program.

Now that you have completed the WordPerfect Reinforcement activities, you are to take several 1-minute timings. Click on the KWP Next Activity button to bring up thc Timing screen.

ONE-MINUTE TIMINGS

Goal: 30 WAM with no more than 2 errors

- Take a 1-minute timing on each paragraph.
- Press ***Tab*** to indent the first line.
- If you finish a paragraph before time is up, start over.

1 The United States Agency for International Development sponsors a speakers program that provides citizens with an opportunity to learn about the culture of other countries. Educators, business men and women, and school administrators with a need to have firsthand information are eligible. More than 125 countries participate in this program.

2 A career in science involves selecting a path among several options. One could choose to become a doctor in a clinic or a teacher in a medical school. An active search through more than 190 college catalogs will indicate which courses to select. Contact campus finance officers to check cost factors.

3 Mack, a black Scottie, is a champion canine. A constant companion is the yellow cat called Chicco. Crowds laugh and applaud as Mack and Chicco do their tricks to music. Mack can count 15 objects and walk on his hind legs. Chicco jumps over Mack, adding a certain clownish touch to the act.

ENDING THE SESSION

Once you have completed the timings, the KWP program takes you to the next session menu. If you want to print the Session 17 files, however, follow the steps below. Then continue with Session 18 or exit the program.

PRINT

1. Click on Back until you reach the KWP Main Menu.
2. Highlight *Freeform*, then click on OK.
3. Click on the Print button or choose **F**ile → **P**rint.
4. At the *Print* dialog box, select the **D**ocument on Disk option under *Print Selection*. Press ***Enter*** or click on OK.
5. At the *Document on Disk* dialog box, click on the list button at the right of the filename text box.
6. With the mouse pointer, highlight the file to be printed and press ***Enter*** or click on **P**rint.
7. At the *Document on Disk* dialog box, click on **P**rint.

Repeat steps 3-7 to print additional documents on disk.

CONTINUE

1. Print any files, if necessary.
2. If you are working in Freeform, click on the KWP Main Menu button.
3. Highlight *Keyboarding Sessions*, then click on OK.
4. Click on Jump to go to the next session.

Document C

THE ADMINISTRATIVE MANAGER

(ts)

I. Need

(ds)

A. Rapid growth of business
B. New type of employee

(ds)

II. Changes

(ds)

A. Rising financial costs
   1. Increased paperwork
   2. Inflation
B. Employee changes
   1. Retiring workers
   2. Lack of skills
   3. Automated systems
C. Career options
   1. Definite need
   2. Post-secondary school programs

REINFORCING WRITING SKILLS

Even with a complete outline of the ideas and information to be covered in a manuscript, many writers have a difficult time writing the first paragraph, which introduces the topic and states the main point, or *thesis*. An effective introduction opens with a few sentences that "hook" the reader's interest. It concludes with a statement of the main point of the manuscript. Above all, do not make the mistake of beginning your paper with the words "I am writing this report because..." or "The purpose of this report is to... ." Unimaginative statements such as these tend to immediately turn off the reader. Instead, use one of the following "hooks":

- A surprising statistic or unusual fact
- A colorful example
- A quotation
- A question
- A comparison
- A joke or humorous statement

If you cannot think of a good hook to use, it is acceptable to begin with the thesis statement. In fact, this straightforward approach is quite common in work-related writing.

EXIT

1. Print any files, if necessary.
2. Click on the KWP Main Menu button on the Toolbar.
3. At the Main Menu, select WordPerfect Only, then click on OK.
4. Click on **F**ile → E**x**it.
5. Exit Windows, if necessary (**F**ile → E**x**it).

If given a choice, most of us would prefer to stay at home rather than go to a hospital or nursing home. Home offers us sanctuary and privacy. Being cared for at home keeps our families together. It preserves the dignity of the individual in need of care, be that person young, old, temporarily or permanently disabled, or even dying. Home care also is less expensive than institutional care. The National Association for Home Care reports that in 1994 the average cost per Medicare beneficiary was about $2,500 for home care, $3,000 for nursing care, and $7,675 for hospital care.

Home care has grown in recent years. In 1990, there were about 4,275 home-health agencies meeting Medicare standards. Today there are more than 8,000. Only about 750,000 people were served by home-care programs ten years ago. The current figures exceed three million for the elderly alone.

Medicare and Medical Assistance expenditures for home care grew from $90 million in 1988 to nearly $4 billion in fiscal 1994. But that $4 billion is minor compared with the $70 billion spent for institutional care the same year.

Skyrocketing hospital costs and the continued graying of America will place stiffer demands on the health-care system and on the public and private agencies that help pay for that care. By the year 2050, more than 22 percent of our population is expected to be older than 65. The so-called Medicare Trust Fund could be bankrupt by then. Home care's cost-effectiveness could help reduce this fiscal pressure.

During Home-Care Week, we should applaud the work of the thousands of nurses, doctors, therapists, and aides who make home care the thoughtful, humane, and effective program that it is. But we also should use this time to look to the future and address some of the needs on the horizon. It will be up to us and to our elected officials to effect further reforms in the health-care system. Reforms must reduce costs and maintain quality care for citizens of all age groups and socio-economic backgrounds and with varying needs. Home care is now and must continue to be an important part of that education and transformation.

Document C — *Manuscript Outline*

1. At the *Production–Session 50 Document C* screen, center the outline title by pressing ***Shift* + *F7***, then keying the title, **THE ADMINISTRATIVE MANAGER**.
2. Delete the default tab settings and set new left tabs every .25".
3. Press ***Enter*** three times, then turn on the Outline feature. Change the definition to Outline.
4. Key the remainder of the outline in Document C. Press ***Shift* + *Tab*** if you need to move the insertion point left to a previous tab or to the left margin to change the outline number.
5. Proofread and correct any errors. Complete a spell check.
6. Click on Check to automatically name (**050proc.kwp**), save, and check the document.
7. To print with errors highlighted, click on the Print button.
8. To correct errors, click on View Original. Make changes, then recheck the document.
9. Choose **File** → **Close**. This closes Document C and brings up a clear WordPerfect editing window.

UNIT 3

10-KEY NUMERIC KEYPAD

When the top and/or bottom margins have been changed, a code is inserted in the document that can be seen in Reveal Codes. If you changed the top and bottom margins to 1.5 inches, the code displays as *[Top Mar:1.5"]* and *[Bot Mar: 1.5"]*.

When the top and/or bottom margins are changed, the default page break is also changed. For example, if the top margin is changed to 2 inches, 8 inches of text is printed on a page rather than 9.

Unbound Manuscripts

An unbound manuscript is usually very short (four or fewer pages). If there is more than one page, the pages may be stapled in the upper-left corner. Use a minimum one-inch left and right margin for unbound manuscripts.

Document B ← *Unbound Manuscript*

1. At the *Production–Session 50 Document B* screen, turn on Widow/Orphan.
2. Press ***Enter*** enough times to move the insertion point to approximately Line 2".
3. Turn on page numbering in the **top right corner** beginning on page 2 by doing the following:
   a. Choose Format → **P**age → **N**umbering.
   b. At the *Page Numbering* dialog box, select *Top Right* from the Position drop-down menu.
   c. Click on OK.
   d. Suppress page numbering on page 1 by choosing Fo**r**mat → **P**age → **S**uppress. At the *Suppress* dialog box, choose **P**age Numbering, then choose OK.
4. Change the line spacing to double by doing the following:
   a. Click on the Line Spacing button on the Power Bar.
   b. Select *2.0*.
5. Access the Center command by pressing ***Shift + F7***.
6. Click on the Bold button on the Toolbar to turn on bold.
7. Key the title, **HOME-CARE IMPORTANCE GROWS**.
8. Click on the Bold button to turn off bold.
9. Key the remainder of the manuscript in Document B.
10. Proofread and correct any errors. Complete a spell check.
11. Click on Check to automatically name (**050prob.kwp**), save, and check the document.
12. To print with errors highlighted, click on the Print button.
13. To correct errors, click on View Original. Make changes, then recheck the document.
14. Choose **F**ile → **C**lose. This closes Document B and brings up the Document C screen.

Document B

HOME-CARE IMPORTANCE GROWS

National Home-Care Week has been set aside to pay tribute to the many care-givers who serve not only the elderly but also the sick, disabled, and terminally ill of all ages in the comfort and security of their own homes.

It is striking how few people are aware of home care. It has been around for more than 100 years. Millions of people are given necessary health-care services at home each year by thousands of dedicated individuals.

Continued on next page

HOME ROW, 0

SESSION GOALS

KEY **Home Row, 0**

WP **Review saving, printing, closing, deleting**

TIMING **30 WAM/2 errors**

GETTING STARTED

1 Access Windows, then *WordPerfect 6.1 for Windows.*
2 Click on the KWP button to access *Keyboarding with WordPerfect.*
3 At the Keyboarding Sessions menu, click on Jump to return to the activity where you left off, or move through the program menus until you reach the Session 18 menu.

Before you begin the Home Row activity, read the information that follows on the layout of the numeric keypad. If you have already completed part of the session, highlight the desired activity and click on OK to proceed.

TYPICAL 10-KEY NUMERIC KEYPAD CONFIGURATION

Microcomputers have a 10-key numeric keypad located to the right of the alphabetic keyboard. The numeric keypad allows you to enter numeric data with one hand. This keypad may be used instead of the numeric row on the alphabetic keyboard. With a minimum amount of practice, you can enter numeric data at speeds well over 100 digits per minute. By industry standards, a rate of 250 digits per minute is considered average (equivalent to 50 WAM).

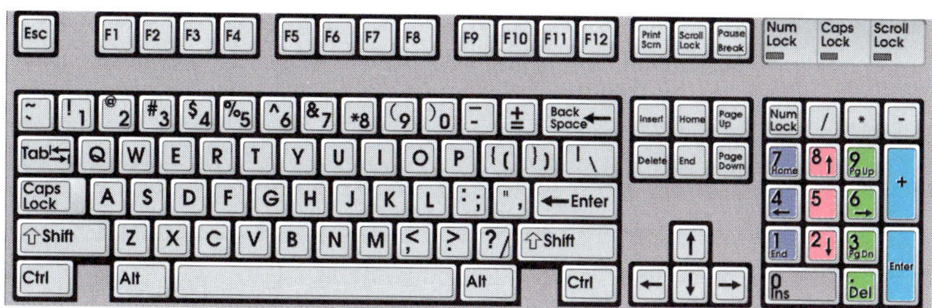

The following illustration shows the general arrangement of most 10-key numeric keypads. The top row of numbers contains the 7, 8, and 9. The middle row contains the 4, 5, and 6. This row is identified as the ***home row***. The bottom row of keys contains the 1, 2, and 3. The ***0*** (zero) key is at the very bottom. The ***Enter*** key is a larger key located to the right of the ***3*** key. The ***Enter*** key is used to enter information after keying the data.

subtracted to separate the page number from text. Page numbers do not appear on the screen in *Draft* View but do appear when the View option is set to *Page*. To see how the numbers will appear on the page, choose **V**iew → **P**age.

When page numbering is inserted in a document, a code can be seen in Reveal Codes. If page numbering is turned on at the bottom of each page, the code *[Pg Num Pos: Bottom Center]* can be seen in Reveal Codes.

The View option from the Menu bar allows you to check the appearance of **any** document before you print. You may view the document in one of three modes: Draft, Page, and Two-Page. The *Page* mode, which is the default, displays a document in what is considered WYSIWYG (What You See Is What You Get). All aspects of a document display such as headers, footers, page numbers, and watermarks. Because all elements of a document are displayed, the *Page* mode is slower than the *Draft* mode.

The *Two-Page* mode shows two pages of a document side by side. This mode is useful for viewing the position of elements on pages. You can edit in the *Two-Page* mode, but it is not practical to do this. You may want to switch to the *Two-Page* mode to see how elements are positioned, then switch back to the *Draft* or *Page* mode to make changes.

Selective Page Numbering

Page numbering can be turned off in a document where page numbering was previously turned on. To do this, do the following:

1. Move the insertion point to the beginning of the page where page numbering is to be turned off.
2. Choose Fo**r**mat → **P**age → **N**umbering.
3. At the *Page Numbering* dialog box, select *No Page Numbering* for Position.
4. Click on OK.
5. Page numbering remains off from the location of the insertion point to the end of the document or until a Page Numbering On code is encountered.

Suppressing Page Numbering

WordPerfect includes a feature that lets you supress page numbering on specific pages. This is different from turning page numbering off. When you turn page numbering off in a document, it stays off until the document ends or until numbering is turned back on. With the Suppress feature, the page number is turned off for that specific page and turned back on again for the other pages. To suppress a page number on a specific page, choose Fo**r**mat → **P**age → **S**uppress. At the *Suppress* dialog box, choose Page Numbering, then choose OK or press Enter.

Changing Top and Bottom Margins

By default, the top and bottom margins are 1 inch. For some manuscripts, these margins may need to be changed to 1.5 inches. To change the top and bottom margins to 1.5 inches, you would do the following:

1. Choose Fo**r**mat → **M**argins (or press ***Ctrl + F8***).
2. Press ***Tab*** twice to move the insertion point to the *Top* text box.
3. Key **1.5** and press ***Tab***.
4. Key **1.5** and press ***Enter*** or click on OK.

On a microcomputer the ***Num Lock*** key must be "on" (pressed) to use the 10-key numeric keypad. When ***Num Lock*** is on, a green light displays by Num Lock in the upper-right corner of the keyboard.

ALTERNATE 10-KEY PAD CONFIGURATIONS

In addition to the standard numeric keypad configuration, there are several alternate key arrangements used among computer manufacturers. Typically, the symbol keys (***plus*** (+), ***minus*** (-), ***Enter,*** and ***decimal***) are rearranged. Generally, it is more efficient to use the symbol keys next to the 10-key pad.

Study the configuration of your 10-key pad and become familiar with the arrangement of the keys. Now proceed with the on-screen activities by clicking on OK (*Home Row* is highlighted).

WP WORDPERFECT REINFORCEMENT

Earlier in the session you completed new-key drills presented on the screen. Now you will repeat some of those drills to reinforce your sense of where the keys are on the 10-key numeric keypad.

Reviewing the Home Row and 0 Keys

Drill Instructions

- Use the *f* finger of your left hand on the *space bar* to space between groups of numbers.
- Press ***Enter*** at the end of each line.
- Keep your eyes on the copy.
- Read the numbers as combinations (review page xx if necessary).

Note: If you want your numbers to appear in a single column rather than as a line, strike ***Enter*** after keying each group of numbers. However, creating a single column requires extra paper when printing.

Home Row Drill

Place right hand on home row (4, 5, 6). Use little finger for ***Enter.***

Key lines 1–6 twice for speed. Remember to think of the numbers in groups.

B. Computer storage
   1. Tape
   2. Disk

(ds)

III. Additional Problems in Records Storage

(ds)

A. Faxed documents
B. Mistrust of computer data storage

Changing Line Spacing

If you review the illustration of a bound manuscript on page 308, you will note that the text is double-spaced. Since the WordPerfect default is single spacing, you will need to change the line spacing before keying a manuscript. To change line spacing to double, you would complete the following steps:

1. Choose Format → **L**ine → **S**pacing.
2. At the *Spacing* dialog box, key **2** in the highlighted text box, then click on OK (or click on the Line Spacing button on the Power Bar and select *2.0*. Double spacing stays in effect for that document until another line spacing code is encountered.

Line spacing can be set in whole numbers or decimal numbers. Up to two decimal places can be used when setting line spacing. More than two numbers after the decimal point can be entered, but WordPerfect only counts the first two numbers after the decimal.

When changes are made to line spacing, a code is inserted in the document that can be seen in Reveal Codes. Line spacing codes can be deleted in Reveal Codes. If a line spacing code is deleted, WordPerfect reverts to the default setting of single spacing. Changes in line spacing affect text from the location of the code to the end of the document or until another line spacing code is encountered.

Numbering Pages

WordPerfect, by default, does not print numbers on pages. For documents such as memos and letters, this is usually acceptable. For manuscripts, however, page numbers may be needed.

To number all pages in a document, you would move the cursor to the first page of the document and then do the following:

1. Choose Format → **P**age → **N**umbering.
2. At the *Page Number* dialog box, position the mouse pointer on the *Position* text box and hold down the left mouse button to access the drop-down menu.
3. Select one of the page number locations.
4. Click on OK.

Page numbers can be inserted in a document at the following locations: Top Left, Top Center, Top Right, Alternating Top, Bottom Left, Bottom Center, Bottom Right, and Alternating Bottom. The Alternating Top and Bottom selections are used to print odd page numbers at the right margin and even page numbers at the left margin.

When a document includes page numbering, WordPerfect subtracts two lines from the total number of lines printed on a page. One line is subtracted for the page number and the other is

1 456 456 456 456 456 456 456 456 456 456 456 456 45

2 456 456 456 654 654 564 564 654 564 565 564 456 46

3 456 456 456 654 654 555 444 666 456 654 456 456 64

4 654 654 654 456 456 666 444 555 546 546 546 456 46

5 555 666 444 555 654 555 456 456 654 645 645 645 45

6 654 654 456 456 456 456 456 655 556 556 664 664 56

0 Drill

Place thumb of right hand on the 0 key, "f" finger on the space bar.

Key lines 1-6 twice, pushing for speed.

1 0 00 000 000 000 000 50 50 50 50 50 50 60 60 40 400

2 400 400 400 400 500 500 600 600 500 400 400 500 60

3 405 504 506 605 440 400 550 660 660 550 440 456 60

4 440 500 450 450 560 4560 4560 4560 6540 6540 56000

5 550 600 540 540 650 6540 6440 4560 6540 6054 56605

6 500 600 400 545 545 6545 4505 5460 5440 5540 50404

Printing WordPerfect Reinforcement Activities

To save and print the WordPerfect for Windows document you have created, complete steps 1-5 that follow. (***Remember:*** The work you completed up to the WordPerfect Reinforcement section has already been saved automatically.)

1. Choose **F**ile → Save **A**s (or F3).
2. At the *Save As* dialog box, key the new filename, **018wpr.kwp**. Press ***Enter*** or click on the OK button. Your document has been saved to disk, and it also remains on the screen.
3. To print 018wpr.kwp, choose **F**ile → **P**rint (or F5)
4. Click on the **P**rint button or press ***Enter***.
5. Close the file (click on **F**ile → **C**lose).

Deleting Files

As you recall, the Paradigm software automatically deletes session files that are more than ten sessions old. However, it is your responsibility to delete your outdated WordPerfect files so that your data disk contains only the ten most current WPR files.

To delete the **wpr** document you completed in Session 8, follow these steps:

1. Choose **F**ile → **O**pen.
2. At the *Open File* dialog box, select the file *008wpr.kwp* by clicking on the filename with the left mouse button.
3. With the filename highlighted, choose File **O**ptions → **D**elete.
4. At the *Delete File* dialog box, click on **D**elete.
5. To close the *Open File* dialog box, click on Cancel or press ***Esc***.

Now that you have completed the WordPerfect Reinforcement activities, you are to take several 1-minute timings. Click on the KWP Next Activity button to bring up the Timing screen.

Document A ← Manuscript Outline

1. At the *Production–Session 50 Document A* screen, choose Format → **L**ine → **C**enter (or press ***Shift + F7***).
2. Key the title, **OUR PAPER HIGHWAY**.
3. Press ***Enter*** three times, then turn on outlining by doing the following:
   a. Choose **T**ools → **O**utline.
   b. Change the style from Paragraph to Outline.
4. Key **Importance of Records Storage**.
5. Press ***Enter*** twice, press ***Tab*** once, then key **Usage today**.
6. Press ***Enter*** once, press ***Tab*** once, then key **Productivity increase**.
7. Continue keying the remainder of the outline.
   Note: Press ***Shift + Tab*** if you need to move the insertion point left to a previous tab or to the left margin to change the outline number.
8. When the outline is complete, proofread and correct any errors. Complete a spell check.
9. Click on Check to automatically name (**050proa.kwp**), save, and check the document.
10. To print with errors highlighted, click on the Print button.
11. To correct errors, click on View Original. Make changes, then recheck the document.
12. Choose **F**ile → **C**lose. This closes Document A and brings up the Document B screen.

Note: If you unintentionally delete an outline code while keying the outline, **DO NOT** enter the code from the keyboard; press ***Ctrl + H*** to reinsert the outline code that was deleted. Use ***Tab*** or ***Shift + Tab*** to adjust the level if necessary.

Document A

OUR PAPER HIGHWAY

I. Importance of Records Storage *(ts)*

    A. Usage today *(ds)*
        1. Productivity increase
        2. Correspondence volume
    B. Costs today
        1. Higher salaries
        2. Need for more equipment

II. Methods of Storage and Retrieval *(ds)*

    A. Alphabetic filing *(ds)*
        1. Characteristics
        2. Specific uses
            a. Telephone books
                (1) Uniform information presentation
                (2) Easy-to-locate format
            b. Libraries
                (1) Combination records storage
                (2) Concise retrieval system

Continued on next page

ONE-MINUTE TIMINGS

Goal: 30 WAM with no more than 2 errors

- Take a 1-minute timing on each paragraph.
- Press ***Tab*** to indent the first line.
- If you finish a paragraph before time is up, start over.

1 Current periodicals and programs are promoting the need for international business education courses. Another trend is to include international concepts in existing courses and programs. The global view of business and international protocols must be taught to students preparing for the world of work.

2 Basically, employers like a loyal employee. Honesty and courtesy always pay off in any job or assignment. Apathy and sloppy work are always very costly to a company. On the other hand, any employee who does consistently good work will be properly awarded and can expect to receive a salary increase of perhaps 8 percent.

3 There is simply no key to easy money. A bad agency may say that you are lucky and a legacy of wealthy glory is yours. Yet, if you try fancy or phony schemes, you will be mighty sorry. Steady, weekly saving is the thrifty means to easy money. Put 75 cents away each day and be happy.

ENDING THE SESSION

Once you have completed the timings, the KWP program takes you to the next session menu. If you want to print the Session 18 files, however, follow the steps below. Then continue with Session 19 or exit the program.

PRINT

1. Click on Back until you reach the KWP Main Menu.
2. Highlight *Freeform*, then click on OK.
3. Click on the Print button or choose **F**ile → **P**rint.
4. At the *Print* dialog box, select the **D**ocument on Disk option under *Print Selection*. Press ***Enter*** or click on OK.
5. At the *Document on Disk* dialog box, click on the list button at the right of the filename text box.
6. With the mouse pointer, highlight the file to be printed and press ***Enter*** or click on **P**rint.
7. At the *Document on Disk* dialog box, click on **P**rint.

Repeat steps 3-7 to print additional documents on disk.

CONTINUE

1. Print any files, if necessary.
2. If you are working in Freeform, click on the KWP Main Menu button.
3. Highlight *Keyboarding Sessions*, then click on OK.
4. Click on Jump to go to the next session.

EXIT

1. Print any files, if necessary.
2. Click on the KWP Main Menu button on the Toolbar.
3. At the Main Menu, select WordPerfect Only, then click on OK.
4. Click on **F**ile → E**x**it.
5. Exit Windows, if necessary (**F**ile → E**x**it).

preparing outlines, you may want to change the tab settings to .25" to create a more visually pleasing outline structure. (This is an example—do not key the outline.)

I. Font

A. Typeface
1. Proportional spaced
2. Monospaced
B. Type Style

1. Choose **T**ools → **O**utline.
2. Change the definition from *Paragraph* to *Outline* on the *Outline* Feature Bar.
3. Key **Font,** then press ***Enter*** twice.
4. Press ***Tab*** to move the insertion point to the first tab stop (or click on the Right Arrow) and a capital *A.* is inserted in the document.
5. Key **Typeface**.
6. Press ***Enter*** once, then press ***Tab*** (or click on the Right Arrow). This inserts the number *1.*
7. Key **Proportional spaced**.
8. Press ***Enter*** and the number *2* is inserted in the document.
9. Key **Monospaced**.
10. Press ***Enter*** and the number *3* is inserted in the document. To change this to the letter *B*, move the insertion point back to the previous tab stop by pressing ***Shift*** + ***Tab*** (or by clicking on the Left Arrow).
11. Key **Type Style**.
12. Turn off outlining by choosing **O**ptions → **E**nd Outline.
13. Choose **C**lose to turn off the display of the *Outline* Feature Bar.

Centering Manuscript Titles

Both manuscript and outline titles should be centered. Titles can be centered between the left and right margins with the Center command. To center a title, choose F**o**rmat → **L**ine → **C**enter or press ***Shift*** + ***F7***. When you press ***Shift*** + ***F7***, the insertion point moves to the center of the screen. As you key the title, text moves left one space for every two characters keyed. If you make a mistake while keying text, backspace and rekey it. This does not interfere with centering. For example, to center the heading, KEYBOARDING WITH WORDPERFECT, you would do the following:

1. Choose F**o**rmat → **L**ine → **C**enter or press ***Shift*** + ***F7***.
2. Key **KEYBOARDING WITH WORDPERFECT**.
3. Press ***Enter***.

When you press ***Enter*** at the end of the line, centering is turned off. The next line you key begins at the left margin. If you want to center the line, press ***Shift*** + ***F7*** again.

In Reveal Codes (***Alt*** + ***F3***), the code *[Hd Center on Marg]* identifies the beginning of centered text, and the code *[HRt]* identifies the end. The centered heading, KEYBOARDING WITH WORDPERFECT, looks like this in Reveal Codes:

[Hd Center on Marg]KEYBOARDING WITH WORDPERFECT[HRt]

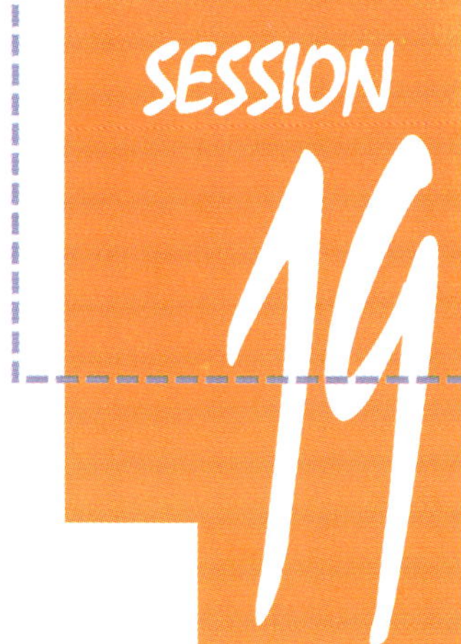

7, 8, 9

SESSION GOALS

 7, 8, and 9

 Review creating, saving, printing, and closing

 30 WAM/2 errors

GETTING STARTED

1 Access Windows, then *WordPerfect 6.1 for Windows*.
2 Click on the KWP button to access *Keyboarding with WordPerfect*.
3 At the Keyboarding Sessions menu, click on Jump to return to the activity where you left off, or move through the program menus until you reach the Session 19 menu.

If you have already completed part of the session, highlight the desired activity and click on OK to proceed. After you have completed the on-screen instructional activities for the 7, 8, and 9 keys, you will be directed to return to the text for the WordPerfect Reinforcement activities. Watch for a message on your screen.

WORDPERFECT REINFORCEMENT

Some of the drills presented on the screen earlier in the session are repeated now in the text to reinforce your sense of where the keys are located on the numeric keypad.

Reviewing the 7, 8, and 9 Keys

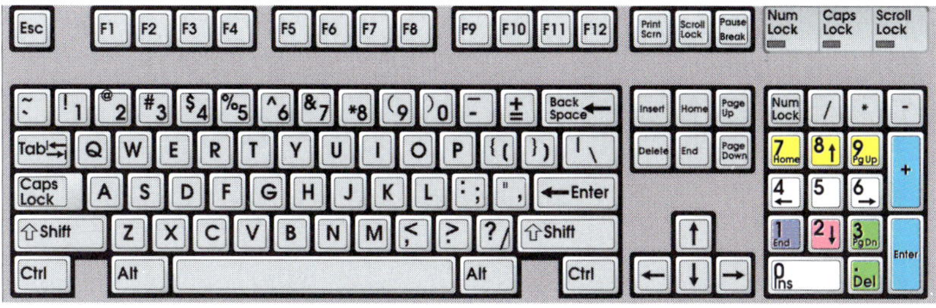

Drill Instructions

- Use your "f" finger to tap the space bar.
- Press ***Enter*** at the end of each line.

The default paragraph numbering style (called the numbering definition) includes eight levels of numbers, beginning with the Arabic number 1. For outlines, however, you will probably want to change the numbering definition to Outline, which includes the eight levels shown below:

I. Level 1 = Left Margin

A. Level 2 = First Tab

1. Level 3 = Second Tab

a. Level 4 = Third Tab

(1) Level 5 = Fourth Tab

(a) Level 6 = Fifth Tab

i) Level 7 = Sixth Tab

a) Level 8 = Seventh Tab

Turning on the Outline Feature

To turn on the Outline feature, you would complete the following steps:

1 Choose Tools → Outline. A number *1.* is displayed and the *Outline* Feature Bar appears across the top of the screen.
2 To change the numbering style to Outline, position the arrow pointer on the Definition button (the one containing the word *Paragraph*), then click the left mouse button.
3 At the drop-down menu that displays, position the arrow pointer on *Outline*, then click the left mouse button.

In the *outline mode*, you can access the features provided on the *Outline* Feature Bar by clicking on the desired buttons or by pressing a command on the keyboard. By clicking on the first button ( ), you will see a drop-down menu displaying a list of the keyboard shortcuts.

In the *outline mode* the Enter, Tab, and Indent keys will cause the following to occur:

Enter Moves the insertion point down to the left margin or the tab setting of the previous level and inserts the appropriate level number and indention.

Tab Moves the insertion point to the next tab stop and inserts the level of numbering and indent for that tab stop.

Shift+Tab Releases the margin, moves the insertion point to the previous tab stop, and inserts the previous level outline number and indention.

Indent (F7) Inserts a "hard tab" and moves the insertion point to the next tab stop without changing the paragraph level numbering.

Turning Off the Outline Feature

When all outline information has been keyed, turn off the outline mode by doing the following:

1 Choose **O**ptions on the *Outline* Feature Bar.
2 Click on **E**nd Outline.
3 Click on **C**lose.

As an example of how to use the outline feature, review the following instructions to create the outline shown. Note that the outline is created using the default tab settings of .5". When

7 Drill

Key lines1–6 twice, pushing for speed. Remember to read the numbers as groups.

1 444 47 47 47 47 47 47 47 74 74 74 74 74 74 74 74 4
2 57 57 57 57 57 57 57 75 75 75 75 75 75 75 75 5 666
3 67 67 67 67 67 67 76 76 76 76 67 76 76 76 67 6 777

4 76 74 74 567 567 567 567 567 4567 4567 7 456 457
5 65 45 67 4567 6 777 765 7567 5560 57670 5666 056
6 70 45670 45670 567 5560 5456 6747 44760 547 645

8 Drill

Key lines 1-6 twice, pushing for speed. Read the numbers as groups.

1 555 58 58 58 58 58 58 58 58 85 85 85 85 85 85 58 5
2 58 68 68 68 48 48 48 48 58 78 78 78 78 58 58 6 800 8
3 800 800 807 807 806 805 508 508 408 804 88 876 568

4 468 780 786 807 876 558 558 558 778 78 45678 87654
5 007 80765 876 8888 7787 7877 6778 5678 458 85 8685
6 88458 800 8008 6758 5858 6868 7887 848 776 856 786

9 Drill

Key lines 1–6 twice, pushing for speed. Think of the numbers in groups.

1 69 69 69 69 99 99 99 66 66 66 69 69 69 69 69 66 66 990
2 90 90 90 98 98 98 97 79 79 89 89 69 69 96 96 96 789 78
3 9 456 456 475 678 789 908 908 970 970 987 09 890 890

4 690 906 960 978 589 479 690 978 890 89 6989 6989 697
5 9 6979 69879 69879 69857 96857 456789 9678 9687 898
6 9678 96745 45678 56789 98765 987654 978 8876 99 045

Printing WordPerfect Reinforcement Activities

To save and print the WordPerfect for Windows document you have created, complete steps 1-5 that follow. (***Remember:*** The work you completed up to the WordPerfect Reinforcement section has already been saved automatically.)

1. Choose **F**ile → Save **A**s (or F3).
2. At the *Save As* dialog box, key the new filename, **019wpr.kwp**. Press ***Enter*** or click on the OK button. Your document has been saved to disk, and it also remains on the screen.
3. To print 019wpr.kwp, choose **F**ile → **P**rint (or F5)
4. Click on the **P**rint button or press ***Enter***.
5. Close the file (click on **F**ile → **C**lose).

reference the research sources. The main difference between the traditional and the simplified style is the spacing before and after titles, subtitles, and headings. The traditional format uses a triple space; the simplified format uses a double space, which saves preparation time. For the manuscripts you prepare in this text's assignments, follow the simplified format. If you are keying a manuscript for a specific business or school, however, be sure to follow their guidelines.

OUR PAPER HIGHWAY

The storing of valuable documents and records has had a place in history almost from the beginning of time. Even then, people tried to find a way to preserve and keep important records of their existence. As buying and selling evolved, the need to keep important records of major business transactions also grew. Throughout history, records storage and retrieval has always been an exciting and interesting career field.

Importance of Records Storage

Because of added productivity and the increased volume of business correspondence, the amount of paper used by companies has increased beyond human expectations or imagination. Business records, in spite of computerized data storage, take up more space than any other single item (Holbreck and Marcus 56). Space considerations as well as increased expenses for maintaining records storage have elevated the issue of records storage to a top priority.

One expert indicated that if trends continue, the cost of storing just one document could rise to twenty cents (Dane 38). The storage problem will continue to increase, as one file drawer can hold only a certain number of items. Not only do the records take up precious space, but the need for higher salaries and equipment soars. Quite obviously, any time or effort spent by office workers or any money spent by a business firm is totally wasted if the records are not really needed, or if those records cannot be easily located and retrieved.

Figure 50.1 Bound Educational Manuscript (Simplified Format)

Preparing a Manuscript Outline

WordPerfect contains an outlining feature that automates the numbering in an outline. In Session 49, you used that feature to number paragraphs in a memo report. Remember that the style used by WordPerfect to number an outline automatically is determined by tab positions.

Deleting Files

As you recall, the Paradigm software automatically deletes session files that are more than ten sessions old. However, it is your responsibility to delete your outdated WordPerfect files so that your data disk contains only the ten most current WPR files. To delete the **wpr** document you completed in Session 9, follow these steps:

1 Choose **F**ile → **O**pen
2 Select the file *009wpr.kwp* by clicking on the filename with the left mouse button.
3 With the filename highlighted, choose File **O**ptions → **D**elete.
4 At the *Delete File* dialog box, click on **D**elete.
5 To close the *Open File* dialog box, click on Cancel or press ***Esc***.

Now that you have completed the WordPerfect Reinforcement activities, you are to take several 1-minute timings. Click on the KWP Next Activity button to bring up the Timing screen.

ONE-MINUTE TIMINGS

Goal: 30 WAM with no more than 2 errors

- Take a 1-minute timing on each paragraph.
- Press ***Tab*** to indent the first line.
- If you finish a paragraph before time is up, start over.

1 Traveling in this vast land is a great experience. The endless rivers, vast prairies that stretch as far as the eye can see, and mountains that reach for the sky are all impressive. Rural villages reveal something of the past in terms of how they are laid out. These vivid scenes revive the mind and lift the spirits.

2 During your working life, you will meet and work with people of many different cultures. Although each of us is a member of a racial or ethnic group, our work groups make up one large community. The beliefs we share give us a common base and a list of topics to discuss.

3 A lazy bicycle ride in the country is surely a healthy and worthy activity. A sunny sky and a dry day are good omens to any type of cyclist. Be wary of cloudy and windy days. A daily remedy for a healthy and spry body is a ride on a mountain bike. Both children and adults enjoy the increase in energy.

ENDING THE SESSION

Once you have completed the timings, the KWP program takes you to the next session menu. If you want to print the Session 19 files, however, follow the steps below. Then continue with Session 20 or exit the program.

PRINT

1 Click on Back until you reach the KWP Main Menu.
2 Highlight *Freeform*, then click on OK.
3 Click on the Print button or choose **F**ile → **P**rint.

THREE-MINUTE TIMINGS

Goal: 35 WAM/2 errors

SI: 1.49

- Take two 3-minute timings.

Plants that have been started can also be purchased at all local nursery or garden shops in the spring. Usually, these flowers are in full bloom at the period when they are offered for sale; the gardener can then select the colors and kinds of plants that will look best in the specific garden sites and areas. After the flower garden bed has been prepared, the gardener can simply place the fine blooming plants in the earth and soon there will be a bright garden.

Planning flower displays is a time-consuming but rewarding task. For example, a mass of brilliant colors and textures could brighten a dark corner or highlight darker foliage and shrubs. Some annuals are better suited for border planting or edging. Others that grow quite tall can be used for unique backgrounds or for screening. There are many annuals that make gorgeous bouquets of cut flowers. The gardener can enjoy the fruits of his or her labor with vases of beautiful blossoms placed all around the house.

Growing annuals in containers has become very popular. Creative gardeners will move containers from one place to another to highlight the most beautiful plants in bloom. A movable or mobile green garden allows for the maximum use of color.

PREPARING MANUSCRIPTS

A manuscript is a multiple-page document that is prepared for publication purposes. It might be published as a magazine or journal article, as a research report, or even as a book. In the academic setting, manuscripts are published as reports or term papers that are completed for a particular course.

Manuscripts can be bound or unbound. Unbound manuscripts are generally short—one to four pages. Bound manuscripts are usually five or more pages long and include a title page, a table of contents, the body of the document with footnotes, text notes, or endnotes, and a bibliography.

The most efficient method of preparing a manuscript is to divide the process into the following steps:

- Identify the topic.
- Research the topic for background information.
- Take notes on cards or in some type of electronic format. Include the source of the information (title, author, publisher, publication date, pages).
- Prepare an outline of the major ideas using your PC; edit and revise it.
- Compose a rough draft of the report using your PC; include source notes (footnotes or text notes) for quotations or other information obtained from your research sources.
- Revise the writing and edit the document for punctuation, spelling, and capitalization.
- Prepare a bibliography.

Manuscripts are prepared using a specific format. The format must be consistent, with careful attention to details such as spacing, punctuation, and order. Two formats, the traditional and the simplified, are widely used in colleges and in the workplace. The illustration that follows displays the first page of a bound, simplified-style manuscript. Text notes (author's name plus page) are used to

4. At the *Print* dialog box, select the **D**ocument on Disk option under *Print Selection*. Press ***Enter*** or click on OK.
5. At the *Document on Disk* dialog box, click on the list button at the right of the filename text box.
6. With the mouse pointer, highlight the file to be printed and press ***Enter*** or click on **P**rint.
7. At the *Document on Disk* dialog box, click on **P**rint.

Repeat steps 3-7 to print additional documents on disk.

CONTINUE

1. Print any files, if necessary.
2. If you are working in Freeform, click on the KWP Main Menu button.
3. Highlight *Keyboarding Sessions*, then click on OK.
4. Click on Jump to go to the next session.

EXIT

1. Print any files, if necessary.
2. Click on the KWP Main Menu button on the Toolbar.
3. At the Main Menu, select WordPerfect Only, then click on OK.
4. Click on **F**ile → E**x**it.
5. Exit Windows, if necessary (**F**ile → E**x**it).

UNBOUND MANUSCRIPTS

SESSION GOALS

1-Minute: 40 WAM/2 errors
3-Minute: 35 WAM/2 errors

Steps for completing a manuscript

Centering titles
Numbering pages
Outline numbering
Changing line spacing and top and bottom margins

GETTING STARTED

If you are continuing immediately from Session 49, go to the one-minute timings. If you exited the program at the end of Session 49, do the following:

1. Access Windows, then WordPerfect 6.1 for Windows.
2. Click on the KWP icon to access *Keyboarding with WordPerfect.*
3. Go to the Keyboarding Sessions menu and click on Jump to return to your last activity. Or, access the Session 50 menu and click on OK to begin the session.

ONE-MINUTE TIMINGS

Goal: 40 WAM/2 errors

SI: 1.49

- Take two 1-minute timings.

Firms take time and spend the money to train their workers. Every effort is made to involve employees in decision-making and to allow them to be creative. Employers who train workers are more profitable than those firms who do not. Many studies have shown that one of the best roads to high profits and worker output is to treat those workers as assets to be developed rather than expenses to be cut. Gains to a firm's operation are high when needed changes are made by having training programs that are easy for workers to use on the job. The worker must be given time to absorb the new changes and to start using those changes. Workers must also be given a chance to make decisions that will affect their work.

1, 2, 3

SESSION GOALS

 1, 2, 3

 30 WAM/2 errors

 Review saving, printing, closing, and exiting

GETTING STARTED

1. Access Windows, then *WordPerfect 6.1 for Windows.*
2. Click on the KWP button to access *Keyboarding with WordPerfect.*
3. At the Keyboarding Sessions menu, click on Jump to return to the activity where you left off, or move through the program menus until you reach the Session 20 menu.

If you have already completed part of the session, highlight the desired activity and click on OK to proceed. After you have completed the on-screen instructional activities for the 1, 2, 3 keys, you will be directed to return to the text for the WordPerfect Reinforcement activities.

WORDPERFECT REINFORCEMENT

Earlier in the session you completed new-key drills presented on the screen. Now you will repeat some of those drills to reinforce your keyboarding skills and to practice working in WordPerfect.

Reviewing the 1, 2, and 3 Keys

1 Drill

Key lines 1–6 twice, pushing for speed. Read the numbers in groups and press ***Enter*** at the end of each line.

1 41 14 41 41 41 14 14 14 451 415 514 614 614 716 41

2 61 61 61 51 71 81 91 17 171 171 187 187 191 151 19

3 168 187 187 186 175 177 109 186 101 186 186 19658

5. Upgrade or replace the Centrex system. There are four alternatives:
    a. Leave the Centrex but add features.
    b. Purchase a PBX and network it with Covenant Hospital.
    c. Lease digital Centrex service for both the clinic and Convenant Hospital.
    d. Purchase PBXs for the NorthWest Heyde Clinic and the PersonalCare HMO.

Craig, I think the recommendations our project team has developed provide a variety of options from which the NorthWest Heyde Clinic can choose. I'll call you between 10 a.m. and noon on Friday to set up an appointment for you and the members of the clinic project team to finalize the recommendations report.

xx/049proc.kwp

Document D ← *Block Deleting Activity*

1. At a clear WordPerfect editing window, open **049proc.kwp**.
2. Delete the words "Alternative 1:" at the beginning of paragraph 1.
3. Delete Alternative 2 and all the subparagraphs under it (a, b, c, d, and e)
4. Choose **F**ile → Save **A**s and key **049wprd.kwp** as the filename.
5. Choose **F**ile → **C**lose. This closes Document D and clears the editing window.

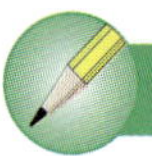

REINFORCING WRITING SKILLS

A vital early step in planning a long document such as a manuscript or a research paper is preparing an outline of the information. By organizing the key points and their subtopics and placing them in order, you know what points to cover and when. Follow these guidelines when preparing outlines:

- Make sure that each major point is equal in importance to the others. If one does not seem as important, perhaps it could be included as a subpoint.
- Each level should have two entries. In other words, do not use an A point if you cannot include at least a B. This is true at all levels.
- Describe each entry within a level using the same language structure. For example, all entries at one level should begin with a noun, or they should all begin with a verb.

Document E ← *Outline*

Assume that you have been asked to write a report on the WordPerfect 6.1 for Windows features that have been covered in Sessions 34-49 of this text. Write a memo to your instructor (use the memo style of your choice) in which you outline the features. Use WordPerfect's paragraph numbering feature to prepare the outline. Your subtopics should include what the feature accomplishes and both the mouse and keyboard commands that access the feature.

Name the memo **049wpre.kwp**. Print and close the file.

ENDING THE SESSION

To end this session, DELETE outdated WordPerfect Reinforcement files, PRINT any files from Session 48 not printed earlier, then CONTINUE with the next session or EXIT the program.

4 145 156 195 157 145 198 966 919 818 717 616 515 41
5 1474 4010 4561 4561 4710 46678 15851 979711 5987
6 919 4111 1444 4568 1787 1679 88981 98871 019 4091

2 Drill

Key lines 1–6 twice, pushing for speed. Read the numbers in groups.

1 52 52 52 52 52 52 25 25 25 25 25 24 24 42 62 72 82 52
2 25 62 72 82 92 02 42 52 27 85 58 85 95 96 90 88 56 24
3 242 252 252 262 852 258 158 148 284 282 272 958 594

4 222 224 225 226 227 228 228 822 922 202 202 212 2169
5 2456 2789 2010 2456 2678 2525 24567 27890 12456 127
6 2222 2525 2582 2582 9792 2728 26267 88771 07862 728

3 Drill

Key lines 1–6 twice, pushing for speed. Read the numbers in groups.

1 63 63 63 63 63 36 36 36 36 36 93 39 39 39 69 69 63 34 35
2 36 73 73 93 83 23 13 30 54 65 63 36 83 49 34 234 354 345
3 456 383 838 938 736 373 369 936 963 33 568 936 947 373

4 464 585 484 737 363 922 291 302 30 4435 4344 3345 3443
5 2343 2334 4873 4848 3929 26282 4844 6673 8733 5663 55
6 43 3323 6788 6733 2343 23343 3443 7979 8520 7963 4873

Printing WordPerfect Reinforcement Activities

To save and print the WordPerfect for Windows document you have created, complete steps 1-5 that follow. (***Remember:*** The work you completed up to the WordPerfect Reinforcement section has already been saved automatically.)

1. Choose **F**ile → Save **A**s (or F3).
2. At the *Save As* dialog box, key the new filename, **020wpr.kwp**. Press ***Enter*** or click on the OK button. Your document has been saved to disk, and it also remains on the screen.
3. To print 020wpr.kwp, choose **F**ile → **P**rint (or F5)
4. Click on the **P**rint button or press ***Enter***.
5. Close the file (click on **F**ile → **C**lose).

Deleting Files

As you recall, the *Keyboarding with WordPerfect* software automatically deletes session files that are more than ten sessions old. However, it is your responsibility to delete your outdated WordPerfect files so that your data disk contains only the ten most current WPR files.

To delete the **wpr** document you completed in Session 10, follow these steps:

1. Alternative 1: Implement an electronic patient records system using Write-Once Read-Many (WORM) optical disk technology. Documents done internally are to be captured via the computer system, and documents from all other sources are to be scanned into the optical disk system.
   a. Paper or microfilm can serve as the system backup. Microfilm reduces records storage space by 98 percent and is recognized as a legal document.
   b. Documents can be converted to film via COM (Computer Output Microfilm), a unit that is attached to the computer system.
   c. Terminals are to be placed throughout the clinic so that doctors and support staff have access to the electronic records.
   d. To eliminate the need to convert existing records, the system can be set to begin at a given time, and from then on all records would be part of the electronic system.
   e. The costs for hardware and software for the above are to be included in computer upgrades/replacements.

2. Alternative 2: Make the following changes in the current medical records system:
   a. Provide access to the file locator software in all medical departments.
   b. Once a medical unit returns a patient's chart to the Medical Records Center, any documents that are to be placed in a patient's chart are to be sent to the Medical Records Center for insertion.
   c. Expand the capacity of the file locator software so that all chart references are in the system, including active, inactive, and recycled charts.
   d. Use a computer-generated list for moving charts to inactive status.
   e. Consider the installation of a track-based shelving system to approximately double the capacity of the Medical Records Center.

3. Centralize the transcription function at both the current clinic and the new clinic to be built next year.
   a. Purchase a software-based dictation system that addresses both the dictation and transcription activities.
   b. The system must include an electronic document-based tracking system with telephone input from internal and external locations.
   c. The system is to have the capacity to retain indefinitely the transcribed documents.

4. Centralize the appointment function for both walk-in and telephone input at the two primary clinic sites.
   a. The computer software used must allow space for doctors to list their preferences.
   b. Automatic appointment reminder software and hardware are to be included in the upgrade/replacement of the computer system so that patients are reminded of scheduled appointments.

Continued on next page

1. Choose **F**ile → **O**pen
2. At the *Open File* dialog box, select the file *010wpr.kwp* by clicking on the filename with the left mouse button.
3. With the filename highlighted, choose File **O**ptions → **D**elete.
4. At the *Delete File* dialog box, click on **D**elete.
5. To close the *Open File* dialog box, click on **C**ancel or press ***Esc***.

Now that you have completed the WordPerfect Reinforcement activities, you are to take several 1-minute timings. Click on the KWP Next Activity button to bring up the Timing screen.

ONE-MINUTE TIMINGS

Goal: 30 WAM with no more than 2 errors

- Take a 1-minute timing on each paragraph.
- Press ***Tab*** to indent the first line.
- If you finish a paragraph before time is up, start over.

1 Students in school today must be prepared to live and compete in a global economy. They must develop a respect for life and work in a society of diverse cultures. Being exposed to the cultures of other countries can open doors to the future in terms of job opportunities.

2 The vessel sank in 510 feet of water in Lake Superior during a raging storm. An adept team of divers salvaged 149,683 parts. Seven local residents were among those who assisted in this job. The additional divers were welcome. The salvage company made a profit on their investment.

3 Max expects to take apart those 147 mailboxes and repack them for a return shipment. This type of exercise helps flex those lax muscles. He plans to exchange the mailboxes for a deluxe model that will be much more appealing to customers. The time and expense for making the switch were not anticipated.

ENDING THE SESSION

Once you have completed the timings, the KWP program takes you to the next session menu. If you want to print the Session 20 files, however, follow the steps below. Then continue with Session 21 or exit the program.

PRINT

1. Click on Back until you reach the KWP Main Menu.
2. Highlight *Freeform*, then click on OK.
3. Click on the Print button or choose **F**ile → **P**rint.
4. At the *Print* dialog box, select the **D**ocument on Disk option under *Print Selection*. Press ***Enter*** or click on OK.
5. At the *Document on Disk* dialog box, click on the list button at the right of the filename text box.
6. With the mouse pointer, highlight the file to be printed and press ***Enter*** or click on **P**rint.

Alternative Numbering Method

In addition to automatically numbering parapraphs with the Outline feature, paragraphs can be automatically numbered with the command, Ctrl + H, When you press Ctrl + H, a number 1 followed by a period is inserted in the document and the insertion point is moved to the next tab setting to the right. The number type defaults to paragraph numbering.

Document C — *Memo Report with Numbered Paragraphs*

1 At the *Production–Session 49 Document C* screen, turn on the Widow/Orphan feature. Before keying the document, create a header for the second-page heading and suppress the header on page 1.
2 To use WordPerfect's automatic paragraph numbering feature to number the paragraphs with Arabic numbers (1., 2., 3., etc.), do the following:
   a Position the insertion point at the left margin where the paragraph number is to appear and press ***Ctrl + H***.
   b Key the paragraph text and press ***Enter***.
3 After keying the last paragraph (e) below 1., press ***Enter*** and then press ***Shift + Tab*** to return to Level 1.
4 After keying the last lettered paragraph (5. d.), press ***Enter***, then turn off automatic paragraph numbering by pressing ***Ctrl + H***.
5 Proofread and correct any errors, then complete a spell check.
6 Click on Check to automatically name **(049proc.kwp)**, save, and check the document.
7 To print with errors highlighted, click on the Print button.
8 To correct errors, click on View Original. Make changes, then recheck the document.
9 Choose **File** → **Close**. This closes Document C and brings up a clear WordPerfect editing window.

Document C

current date

TO: Craig Zachman, Senior Consultant

Mary Traaseth

RECOMMENDED SYSTEM CHANGES

As you read the recommendations, bear in mind the concept of economies of scale. For example, if the NorthWest Heyde Clinic, Covenant Hospital, and PersonalCare were to join together in upgrading or replacing their telephone systems and services, costs would be reduced. Recommendations can also be implemented in phases to minimize interruptions and/or by location as a pilot program so that adjustments can be made based on experience.

Based on the needs analysis, we recommend the following alternatives for NorthWest Heyde Clinic:

Continued on next page

7 At the *Document on Disk* dialog box, click on **P**rint.

Repeat steps 3-7 to print additional documents on disk.

CONTINUE

1 Print any files, if necessary.
2 If you are working in Freeform, click on the KWP Main Menu button.
3 Highlight *Keyboarding Sessions*, then click on OK.
4 Click on Jump to go to the next session.

EXIT

1 Print any files, if necessary.
2 Click on the KWP Main Menu button on the Toolbar.
3 At the Main Menu, select WordPerfect Only, then click on OK.
4 Click on **F**ile → E**x**it.
5 Exit Windows, if necessary (**F**ile → E**x**it).

A. **Negotiations:** Mutual discussions and arrangement of terms do not have to begin on the spot. Ask to return later, perhaps the next day, and work out the details when you have collected your thoughts.

B. **Severance package:** The contents of your severance package depend on the industry you are in, your job level, and how long you have been with the company firing you. There are reasonable things to ask for if they are not offered.

1. **Pay:** A month's pay for each year of service for senior employees; three to six months' pay for shorter-term employees.
2. **Benefits:** Continuation of your benefits, such as health and life insurance, for a specific term.
3. **Reimbursement:** Payment for some of the costs of your job search, such as long-distance calls and secretarial help.
4. **References:** A promise of a decent reference in your search for a new job.

If you are fired and suspect illegal discrimination, contact the Equal Employment Opportunity Commission for help.

xx/049proa.kwp

Document B — Automatic Renumbering of Paragraphs

1 At a clear WordPerfect editing window, open **049proa.kwp**.

2 Choose **T**ools → **O**utline.

3 Select and move the *Negotiations:* paragraph numbered *A.* below *References*, numbered *4.* by completing the following steps:

a Turn on Reveal Codes (press ***Alt + F3***) and position the insertion point to the left of the Para Style: Level 2 code at the beginning of the *Negotiations:* paragraph.

b Press ***F8*** to turn on the Select mode. Move the insertion point immediately past (below) the Para Style Level 2 off code. (This code displays at the end of the paragraph.)

c Click on the Down Arrow on the *Outline* Feature Bar six times to move the paragraph and press ***Enter*** once to adjust the line spacing.

d After moving the paragraph, WordPerfect automatically renumbers the paragraphs. If both paragraphs are numbered A., delete the Par Num: 0 codes at the beginning of the *Negotiations:* paragraph and the letters should adjust to A. and B.

e Check the line spacing to see if it is correct. If it is not, add or delete lines as needed.

4 Select and delete the paragraph labeled *3.* under the new section A (*Reimbursement*).

5 Insert a paragraph between *Pay* and *Benefits* by doing the following:

a Move the insertion point to the end of paragraph *1.* (that ends *shorter-term employees.*), and press ***Enter*** once.

b Key the following paragraph:

Formal notice: Agreement on the wording and timing of the announcement of your departure.

6 Choose **F**ile → Save **A**s and name the document **049wprb.kwp**.

7 Choose **F**ile → **C**lose.

8 Click on the KWP Next Activity button to bring up the Document C screen.

SESSION GOALS

 **Review keys from Sessions 1-20**

 **Review saving, printing, closing, and exiting**

 **10-Key Numeric Keypad: 25 WAM/0 errors**

GETTING STARTED

1. Access Windows, then *WordPerfect 6.1 for Windows*.
2. Click on the KWP button to access *Keyboarding with WordPerfect*.
3. At the Keyboarding Sessions menu, click on Jump to return to the activity where you left off, or move through the program menus until you reach the Session 21 menu.

If you have already completed part of the session, highlight the desired activity and click on OK to proceed. After you have completed the on-screen review of keys from the first 20 sessions, you will be directed to return to the text to create a WordPerfect for Windows document. Watch for the message about "WordPerfect Reinforcement Activities."

WORDPERFECT REINFORCEMENT

Earlier in the session you completed review drills presented on the screen. Now you will repeat some of those drills to reinforce your sense of where the alphabetic, number, and 10-key numeric keypad keys are located. You will create your own WordPerfect for Windows document.

Alphabetic Sentences

Key lines 1–3 twice: first for speed, then for control.

1 It seems that I missed the road; it makes me mad.
2 Those wrecked cars are in the ditch at the curve.
3 Endure the thousand, routine, suspended problems.

Top-Row Numbers

Key lines 1–9 twice: first for control, then for speed.

1 Find 5,000 medium weight legal size file folders.
2 The Merkel 9000 offers 23 channels with .6 watts.
3 Please trace orders 1169, 2978, 67890, and 14989.
4 Return the 420 reams of 16 lb. paper now, please.
5 She is purchasing a Group 4 857 Facsimile system.

Headings, Legal, Legal 2, Numbers, Outline, and Paragraph. For example, to number paragraphs at the left margin with Roman numerals rather than Arabic numbers, do the following:

1. Choose **T**ools → **O**utline.
2. Click on the Definition button on the *Outline* Feature Bar (the one containing the word Paragraph), then click on Outline at the drop-down menu.

Document A ← *Automatic Numbering of Paragraphs*

1. At the *Production–Session 49 Document A* screen, key Document A as a memo report. Use WordPerfect's outlining feature to number the paragraphs as indicated in the document. To number the paragraphs with uppercase letters (A., B., C., etc.), do the following:
   a. Position the insertion point at the left margin where the paragraph is to appear.
   b. Choose **T**ools → **O**utline
   c. Click on the Definition button on the *Outline* Feature Bar, then click on Outline at the drop-down menu.
   d. Press ***Tab*** once to move the insertion point to the first tab stop, then key the text. Tab once before keying the paragraphs preceeded by Arabic numbers (1., 2., 3., etc.).
   e. After keying the last numbered paragraph but before pressing ***Enter***, choose **O**ptions → End Outline.
   f. Choose **C**lose to turn off the *Outline* Feature Bar.
2. Proofread and correct any errors, then complete a spell check.
3. Click on Check to automatically name (**049proa.kwp**), save, and check the document.
4. To print the document with errors highlighted, click on the Print button.
5. To correct errors, click on View Original. Make changes, then recheck the document.
6. Choose **F**ile → **C**lose. This closes Document A and brings up the Document B screen.

Document A

current date

TO: All Employees

Union Representative

OPTIONS WHEN FIRED

The dramatic scene in which the boss calls you in, gives you two weeks' pay, and orders you to be out of the building by sundown is rare. But still, few experiences are more devastating than being fired, whatever the technique. Most Americans work, by common law, at their employer's will, and they can be fired with or without reason.

For most people, the options after being fired are limited. You can accept it and negotiate for the best possible severance package, or you can fight back.

Continued on next page

6 I would like to have 9 shades and 16 gray scales.

7 Send me 13 of Item 4 and 7 of Item 9 immediately.

8 West Arn 20 lb. paper has 99 percent rag content.

9 I have: 360 holders, 75 pencils, and 99 punches.

Printing WordPerfect Reinforcement Activities

To save and print the WordPerfect for Windows document you have created, complete steps 1-5 that follow. (***Remember:*** The work you completed up to the WordPerfect Reinforcement section has already been saved automatically.)

1. Choose **F**ile → Save **A**s (or F3).
2. At the *Save As* dialog box, key the new filename, **021wpr.kwp**. Press ***Enter*** or click on the OK button. Your document has been saved to disk, and it also remains on the screen.
3. To print 021wpr.kwp, choose **F**ile → **P**rint (or F5)
4. Click on the **P**rint button or press ***Enter***.
5. Close the file (click on **F**ile → **C**lose).

Deleting Files

As you recall, the *Keyboarding with WordPerfect* software automatically deletes session files that are more than ten sessions old. However, it is your responsibility to delete your outdated WordPerfect files so that your data disk contains only the ten most current wpr files.

To delete the **wpr** document you completed in Session 11, follow these steps:

1. Choose **F**ile → **O**pen
2. At the *Open File* dialog box, select the file *011wpr.kwp* by clicking on the filename with the left mouse button.
3. With the filename highlighted, choose File **O**ptions → **D**elete.
4. At the *Delete File* dialog box, click on **D**elete.
5. To close the *Open File* dialog box, click on **C**ancel or press ***Esc***.

Now that you have completed the WordPerfect Reinforcement activities, you are to take several 1-minute timings. Click on the KWP Next Activity button to bring up the Timing screen.

TIMINGS: 10-KEY NUMERIC KEYPAD

Goal: 25 WAM with 0 errors

- Take two 1-minute timings on lines 1–5. Then take two timings on lines 6–10.
- If you finish before time is up, start over.
- Press the space bar with your "f" finger.
- Strike ***Enter*** at the end of each line.

1 12 34 56 78 90 123 456 789 987 654 321 4321 8765 9

2 98 76 54 32 10 321 654 897 978 456 123 1234 5678 1

3 76 89 32 12 01 789 564 987 654 545 231 2413 7568 3

4 54 12 12 34 28 897 546 978 123 466 132 1432 6785 2

5 32 54 78 56 58 978 645 789 101 654 213 2431 5867 9

If the insertion point is positioned at the left margin and outlining is turned on, paragraphs are numbered with Arabic numbers (1., 2., 3., etc.). With the insertion point positioned at the first tab stop, paragraphs are numbered with letters (a., b., c., etc.). Each successive tab stop causes numbering to occur as shown on the previous page. This numbering style is the WordPerfect default.

Creating Paragraph Numbers in a Document

Paragraph numbering can be included in a document as the document is being keyed, or paragraph numbering can be inserted in existing text. To insert paragraph numbering at the left margin in a document as it is being keyed, position the insertion point at the left margin of the line where numbering is to appear, then do the following:

1. Choose **T**ools → **O**utline. This inserts **1.** at the left margin and indents the insertion point to the first tab setting.
2. Key the text of the first paragraph.
3. Press ***Enter*** to move the insertion point to the left margin and insert the next paragraph number.
4. Continue keying text and pressing ***Enter***.
5. Press ***Tab*** to move to the next level or press ***Shift*** + ***Tab*** to go back to a previous level. When all paragraphs have been entered, choose **O**ptions → **E**nd Outline at the end of the last line before pressing ***Enter***.
6. Choose **C**lose to close the Oultine Feature Bar.

To insert numbering into existing text, move the insertion point to the margin or tab stop where numbering is to occur and press ***Ctrl*** + ***H*** at the keyboard, or choose the **T**ools → **O**utline to display the *Outline* Feature Bar, then click on the **T** button. If you need to indent text to a tab stop to obtain a particular level of numbering, make sure you are working in the Insert mode.

Deleting or Adding a Paragraph Number

Delete paragraph numbering in a document as you would any other text. Move the insertion point to the first word in the paragraph containing the number and press the ***Backspace*** key. When the number is deleted, the code is also removed from the document. WordPerfect automatically renumbers any remaining paragraphs.

If, after creating numbered paragraphs, you decide you want to insert a paragraph at a different tab stop, move the insertion point to the first word in the paragraph where you want text added and press the ***Tab*** key until you are at the desired level. Key the text at the tab stop level and press ***Enter***. To realign the previous paragraph press ***Shift*** + ***Tab*** until the paragraph is at the correct level. WordPerfect automatically renumbers all remaining paragraphs. If you delete a paragraph number, you can reinsert the number code by positioning the insertion point at the beginning of the paragraph and pressing the **T** button on the *Outline* Feature Bar.

Changing the Paragraph Numbering Style

The numbering style used to number paragraphs or text can be changed in a document. WordPerfect uses the Paragraph numbering definition by default.

The methods described so far cause paragraph numbering styles to be determined by the tab position or left margin. To change the numbering definition, access the Definition drop-down menu on the *Outline* Feature Bar. There are seven definitions to choose from: Bullets,

6 1.3 12.9 14.87 123.456 1.456 14.567 56.21 156.02 4 7
7 8 67.8 67.21 478.231 2.789 27.879 87.90 879.08 56.49
8 42.7 32.56 978.123 3.462 34.620 62.08 620.81 84.8 61
9 72 687.452 4.872 48.729 72.94 729.45 25.2 52.5 98.12
10 187.243 9.678 96.786 78.69 687.89 2 672.3 598 390.26

TIMINGS: ALPHABETIC KEYS

Goal: 30 WAM with no more than 2 errors

- Take a 1-minute timing on each paragraph.
- Press ***Tab*** to indent the first line.
- If you finish a paragraph before time is up, start over.

1 The population of the United States has become more varied culturally. It is extremely important that individuals be made aware of the need to communicate with other cultures in ways that are satisfying to both parties. As people interact on a daily basis, meanings are discovered that form a bond for common understanding.

2 The first thing a visitor notices at the travel agency is a bronze statue of the founder. The agency is merging with another travel group that will give them 4,000 office locations in 125 countries. The merger of their business and information systems will take five years.

3 The clinic is considering a change to centralized appointment scheduling. This would reduce the number of telephone numbers that patients would have to remember to make appointments with different doctors in the same clinic. Some of the doctors are supporting this change; others are not sure it will be effective.

ENDING THE SESSION

Once you have completed the timings, the KWP program takes you to the next session menu. If you want to print the Session 21 files, however, follow the steps below. Then continue with Session 22 or exit the program.

PRINT

1. Click on Back until you reach the KWP Main Menu.
2. Highlight *Freeform*, then click on OK.
3. Click on the Print button or choose **F**ile → **P**rint.
4. At the *Print* dialog box, select the **D**ocument on Disk option under *Print Selection*. Press ***Enter*** or click on OK.
5. At the *Document on Disk* dialog box, click on the list button at the right of the filename text box.
6. With the mouse pointer, highlight the file to be printed and press ***Enter*** or click on **P**rint.
7. At the *Document on Disk* dialog box, click on **P**rint.

THREE-MINUTE TIMINGS

Goal: 35 WAM/2 errors

SI: 1.48

- Take two 3-minute timings.

During every moment of the day or night, all kinds of storms are in the process of raging over land and sea. More than 1,800 thunderstorms or blizzards pelt the earth with rain or snow. Somewhere over a high sea, a hurricane with an awesome wind may be forming. In some areas, the people may be looking at a cloudless sky, but not more than a few hundred miles away other people are sheltering themselves from a wild and furious snowstorm or a pelting rain.

A storm is a disturbance of the upper atmosphere and contains an added element of strong winds. During many storms, destructive winds have been known to cause great damage. During a blizzard on the wide open prairie, snowdrifts pile high and block roads. Ice storms cause widespread damage to telephone and power lines.

Distinctive forms of clouds and precipitation, as well as winds, are common to storms. Precipitation is the weather bureau's name for all forms of water falling from the sky. Clouds are the first signal of an incoming storm. Signals of the hurricane, for example, move in with little or no noise. An alert weather person is well aware of the danger signals. First, the wispy, veil-like cirrus clouds appear and dance on the horizon.

PREPARING MEMO REPORTS

Memo reports often contain numbered or lettered paragraphs to help readers focus on important information. Software programs such as WordPerfect 6.1 for Windows include features that number and format the paragraphs for you.

Paragraph Numbering

With WordPerfect's Outline feature, you can create numbered paragraphs in a document. The Outline default style is paragraph numbering that automatically inserts numbers with the proper indent before paragraphs. One of the advantages of using this feature is that you can insert or delete text later and WordPerfect automatically renumbers the paragraphs. The default paragraph number style includes eight levels:

1. Level 1 = Left Margin
    a. Level 2 = First Tab
        i. Level 3 = Second Tab
            (1) Level 4 = Third Tab
                (a) Level 5 = Fourth Tab
                    (i) Level 6 = Fifth Tab
                        1) Level 7 = Sixth Tab
                            a) Level 8 = Seventh Tab

Repeat steps 3-7 to print additional documents on disk.

CONTINUE

1 Print any files, if necessary.
2 If you are working in Freeform, click on the KWP Main Menu button.
3 Highlight *Keyboarding Sessions*, then click on OK.
4 Click on Jump to go to the next session.

EXIT

1 Print any files, if necessary.
2 Click on the KWP Main Menu button on the Toolbar.
3 At the Main Menu, select WordPerfect Only, then click on OK.
4 Click on **F**ile → E**x**it.
5 Exit Windows, if necessary (**F**ile → E**x**it).

SESSION GOALS

1-Minute: 40 WAM/2 errors
3-Minute: 35 WAM/2 errors

Paragraph numbering

Outlining information

GETTING STARTED

If you are continuing immediately from Session 48, go to the one-minute timings. If you exited the program at the end of Session 48, do the following:

1. Access Windows, then WordPerfect 6.1 for Windows.
2. Click on the KWP icon to access *Keyboarding with WordPerfect.*
3. Go to the Keyboarding Sessions menu and click on Jump to return to your last activity. Or, access the Session 49 menu and click on OK to begin the session.

ONE-MINUTE TIMINGS

Goal: 40 WAM/2 errors

SI: 1.45

- Take two 1-minute timings.
- Use your most recent timing score to set a speed or accuracy goal.

A good keyboarder soon learns how to proofread. Glaring errors will mar the neatness and quality of a good report. Find all the mistakes before printing the final copy. Learn to watch for correct spelling and grammar. Compare the rough draft with the printed copy. You will want to examine your work two or three times and make quite certain it is without mistakes. In the long run, you will be pleased that you have carefully prepared an excellent printed copy. The person who reads your output will have much respect for your ability to prepare accurate documents.

Editing is another task that requires careful attention. Once a document has been prepared, you may need to check it for correct word choice and use. Also, vary the sentence structure so readers enjoy the content.

UNIT 4

PUNCTUATION/ SYMBOL KEYS

Document C ← Copying a File and Printing the Directory

1 Choose **F**ile → **O**pen.
2 Select the file named **048proa.kwp**.
3 Choose File **O**ptions → **C**opy.
4 At the *Copy File* dialog box, key **MIS** in the *To:* text box, then click on **C**opy.
5 To print the directory, choose File **O**ptions → Print File **L**ist.
6 At the *Print File List* dialog box, select Print **E**ntire List, then click on **P**rint.
7 Click on Cancel to exit the *Open File* dialog box.

REINFORCING WRITING SKILLS

Communicating through printed documents or via e-mail offers distinct advantages over communicating by telephone or in person:

- A written (printed) message usually carries more authority.
- The reader can study and reread printed documents containing complicated instructions, but the same information conveyed orally is presented only once.
- A written message provides a permanent record.
- Writing the information gives the writer more control over the tone and desired outcome.

Document D ← Composing a Memo Report

At the clear WordPerfect editing window, compose a memo report that consists of at least one-and-a-half pages, written to your instructor on the subject of A SUMMARY OF THE LANGUAGE ARTS GUIDELINES IN SESSIONS 35-47. Prepare a double-spaced rough draft. Then save, print, and edit your memo report for complete, well written sentences and correct grammar, punctuation, and capitalization. Use subheadings to help direct the reader's attention.

Save the document as **048wprd.kwp**. Then print and close the file.

ENDING THE SESSION

To end this session, DELETE outdated WordPerfect Reinforcement files, PRINT any files from Session 48 not printed earlier, then CONTINUE with the next session or EXIT the program. (If you need help with the specific steps, review the "Ending the Session" section from Session 47.)

HYPHEN, DASH, UNDERSCORE
USING UNDERLINE AND ITALICS, DISPLAYING REVEAL CODES

SESSION GOALS

Hyphen, Dash, Underscore

Underlining and Italics
Displaying Reveal Codes

1-Minute: 30 WAM/2 errors
3-Minute: 25 WAM/2 errors

Hyphenating words
Using dashes

GETTING STARTED

1 Access Windows, then WordPerfect 6.1 for Windows.
2 Click on the KWP button to access *Keyboarding with WordPerfect*.
3 At the Keyboarding Sessions menu, click on Jump to return to the activity where you left off, or move through the program menus until you reach the Session 22 menu.
4 Start with *Warm-Up* or go to the next activity if your fingers are already warmed up.

When you have completed the on-screen activities in Session 22, you will be instructed to return to the text for the WordPerfect Reinforcement activities. Then you will complete Thinking Drills and 1-minute and 3-minute timings before exiting the session.

THINKING DRILLS

This section includes three Thinking Drills that provide practice using the hyphen, dash, and underscore/underline punctuation marks. In addition to practicing the reaches, you will learn to create a dash in WordPerfect. Then you are to apply the punctuation guidelines in response to questions posed in the Thinking Drills. Read the guidelines for each topic before you key the corresponding drills.

General Guidelines for Word Division

A hyphen is a mark of punctuation used to divide words that must be carried over to the next line. Although most word processing programs, including WordPerfect 6.1 for Windows, offer an automatic hyphenation feature, the software sometimes asks the user to make hyphenation decisions during the hyphenating process. The guidelines that follow include the essential rules. However, there are exceptions to the rules. When in doubt, consult a dictionary.

1 The general rule is to leave at least three letters of a word at the end of a line and carry over at least three letters to the next line. The rule has been modified since software packages (including WordPerfect) leave or carry over only two letters of a word when automatic hyphenation is used.

3. Choose File **O**ptions → **P**rint.
4. At the prompt *Do you want to print the selected files?,* click on Print.
5. Now rename the report document with its original name, 048proa.kwp. Follow the steps outlined previously under "Renaming Documents."
6. Click on Cancel to exit the *Open File* dialog box.

Printing the Directory

The directory contains a list of all documents saved on the disk. At times, you may need a hard copy of the directory for record keeping purposes. To print the directory, do the following:

1. Choose **F**ile → **O**pen.
2. At the *Open File* dialog box, choose File **O**ptions → Print File **L**ist..
3. At the *Print File List* dialog box, select Print **E**ntire List.
4. Click on Print.
5. Click on Cancel to exit the *Open File* dialog box.

Copying Documents

With the **Copy** selection from File Options, you can make exact copies of a document and save the document either on the same disk or on another disk. Certain documents you create may be important enough to warrant a backup.

To copy a document on the same disk, choose **F**ile → **O**pen to list your filenames. Select the file to be copied, then choose File **O**ptions → Copy. At the *Copy File* dialog box, the selected filename and path appears in the *From:* text box. Key in a name that is different from the document you are copying, then click on Copy. WordPerfect copies the document and includes the new document in the directory in alphabetic order.

A document can also be copied onto another disk. For example, to copy a document on the disk in drive A to a disk in drive B, do the following:

1. Insert a formatted disk in drive B.
2. Choose **F**ile → **O**pen.
3. Select the file to be copied.
4. Choose File **O**ptions → **C**opy.
5. Key **b:**.
6. Click on **C**opy. WordPerfect saves the document on the disk in drive B with the same name. When entering the drive letter, be sure to enter the colon **(:)**. If you do not, WordPerfect copies the document on the same disk and names it **b** (or whatever drive letter you identified).
7. Click on Cancel to exit the *Open File* dialog box.

You can copy more than one document at a time by selecting the filenames in the directory. For example, to copy several documents onto a formatted disk in drive B, do the following:

1. Choose **F**ile → **O**pen
2. Select the files to be copied.
3. Choose File **O**ptions → **C**opy.
4. At the *Copy Files* dialog box, key **b:** in the *Copy Selected Files To:* text box.
5. Click on **C**opy.
6. Click on Cancel to exit the *Open File* dialog box.

2 Never divide a word that is the last word of a paragraph or a page.

Divide

	Rule	Word		Division
3	Between syllables according to pronunciation	provoke	*may be divided*	pro-voke
4	Between two consonants	napkin	*may be divided*	nap-kin
	unless			
	a root word would be destroyed	billing	*may be divided*	bill-ing (not bil-ling)
5	Between two vowels that are pronounced separately	continuation	*may be divided*	continu-ation
6	**After** a one-syllable vowel rather than **before** (preferable)	benefactor	*may be divided*	bene-factor
	unless			
	the vowel is a part of a suffix	acceptable	*may be divided*	accept-able
7	Between two parts of a compound word	salesperson	*may be divided*	sales-person

8 Do not key more than two consecutive lines ending with hyphens. ***Note:*** Some software packages allow three lines with automatic hyphenation.

Do not divide:

	Rule	Word		Division
9	Words of one syllable	which	*never*	wh-ich
		storm	*never*	sto-rm
10	Words with a one-letter prefix	along	*not*	a-long
		enough	*not*	e-nough
11	A syllable with a silent vowel sound	yelled	*never*	yel-led
		strained	*never*	strain-ed
12	Proper nouns, abbreviations, contractions, or number combinations	Barbara	*not*	Bar-bara
		PSI	*not*	P-SI
		couldn t	*not*	could-n't
		31 Oak Lane	*not*	3-1 Oak Lane
		March 14	*not*	March 1-4

THINKING DRILL

Now you will have an opportunity to apply the word-division guidelines in a Thinking Drill. Follow the instructions on the screen. After you have completed the drill, return to the text and review the information that follows on using hyphens in compound words and numbers.

Renaming Documents

If you decide that a document name needs to be changed, use the Rename selection from File **O**ptions. For example, to rename the document **048proa.kwp** to **report**, do the following:

1. Choose **F**ile → **O**pen.
2. Select **048proa.kwp** in the Filename list box.
3. Click on File **O**ptions → **R**ename.
   Note: The name of the selected file is displayed in the *From:* text box.
4. At the *Rename File* dialog box, key **report** in the *To:* text box.
5. Click on **R**ename. The original document name disappears and is replaced by the new name.
6. Click on Cancel to exit the *Open File* dialog box.

Printing Documents

Documents can be printed by displaying the Print dialog box by choosing **F**ile → **P**rint or by clicking on the Print button in the Toolbar. Up to this point, you have printed the entire document. When you print a document, you can specify particular pages to be printed using the **Multiple Pages** option. The following table illustrates your options for printing pages:

Entry	**Action**
Enter key	Entire document printed
2	Page 2 printed
2-	Page 2 to end of document printed
2-3	Pages 2 through 3 printed
-2	Beginning of document through page 2 printed
2,3	Pages 2 and 3 printed
2-3, 4	Pages 2 through 3 printed and page 4 printed

The hyphen is used to identify a range, and the comma is used to identify specific pages. As illustrated in the last entry, the hyphen and the comma can be used in the same print job. With these options, you can print as little or as much of a document as you wish.

As an example of how to use this feature, you would do the following to print pages 1 and 3 of a document named ***report***.

1. Choose **F**ile → **P**rint or click on the Print button on the Toolbar.
2. At the *Print* dialog box, choose Document on Disk.
3. Click on Print.
4. At the *Document on Disk* dialog box, key **report** in the *Filename* text box.
5. Choose Pa**g**e(s)/Label(s), then key **1, 3**.
6. Click on Print.

You can identify more than one document for printing. To send more than one document to the printer, you would do the following:

1. Choose **F**ile → **O**pen.
2. Select the files to be printed.

General Guidelines for Compound Words and Numbers

A hyphen is used to separate some compound words. It is also used in spelled-out numbers.

1. A hyphen is used as a "combining" mark. Not all authorities agree on which combinations should or should not be hyphenated. If in doubt, consult a reference book or dictionary.
   a. As a general rule, use a hyphen between two or more word combinations used as a unit **before** a noun.
      a 15-story building
      the still-active volcano
      a hard-working person
   b. If the word combinations used as a unit appear **after** a noun, do not hyphenate.
      a building 15 stories high
      the volcano that is still active
      a person who is hard working
   c. words beginning with **ex, self**, and **vice** are usually hyphenated.
      ex-roommate
      self-taught
      vice-principal
2. Hyphenate **spelled-out** fractions and hyphenate **spelled-out** numbers between 21 and 99 if they stand alone or if they are used with numbers over 100. Never hyphenate numerals such as 21 or 66.
   one and one-third
   sixty-six
   one hundred sixty-six

THINKING DRILL

In the Thinking Drill that appears on your screen, you are to apply the guidelines for hyphenating compound words. Follow the instructions on the screen. After you have completed the drill, return to the text and review the information that follows on using dashes.

General Guidelines for the Dash

The dash is often used (1) in place of quotation marks or parentheses, (2) to avoid the confusion of too many commas, (3) for special emphasis, and (4) to indicate a side comment. Study the following examples:

There is a flaw in the plan—a fatal one. [special emphasis]

All books—fiction, poetry, and drama—are on sale. [in place of parentheses]

I cooked the meal—but they got the credit for it. [special emphasis]

I said once—and I will say it again—I disagree. [side comment]

WordPerfect includes a special character for a dash (—). This dash is the kind used in professionally typeset documents, and it is now available to users of word processing programs such as WordPerfect 6.1 for Windows. You can create this dash at the *WordPerfect Characters* dialog box. To create a dash, complete these steps:

1. Choose **I**nsert → **C**haracter.
2. Key 4, 34 and press ***Enter***.

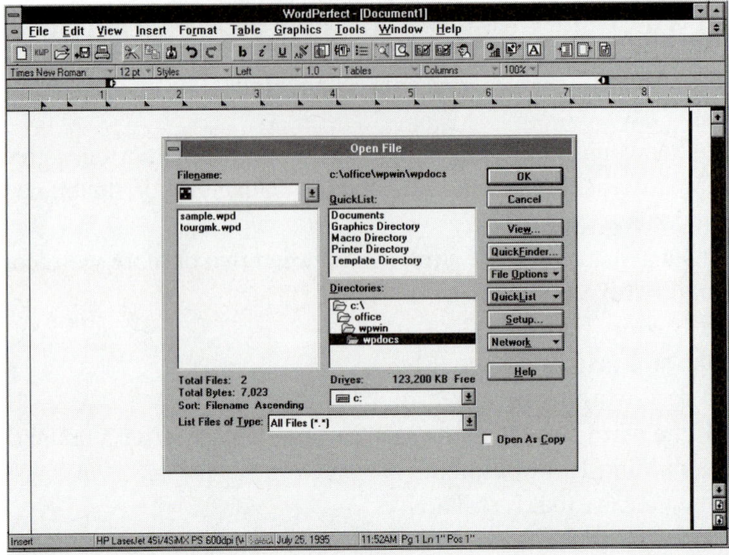

Figure 48.1 Open File Dialog Box

Viewing a Directory

The documents saved on the disk are displayed in alphabetic order. The working drive and directory are displayed at the top of the *Open File* dialog box above the QuickList and Directories. If you do not see both QuickList and Directories, click on the QuickList button located on the right side of the dialog box and choose *Show Both*. The amount of free space available on the disk is shown directly under the Directories list box. The total number of files and bytes used are displayed under the list of filenames.

You can scroll through the list of filesnames using the vertical scroll bars on the right side of the list box. Filenames can be selected by clicking on the name with the left mouse button. Once a filename has been selected, you can also move through the filenames using the Up and Down arrow keys, the Home key, the End key, or the Page Up and Page Down keys.

Deleting Documents

Beginning with Session 11, you have purged (deleted) documents from the disk. If you want to delete more than one document at a time from the directory, select the documents to be deleted by holding down the ***Ctrl*** key while clicking on the filename with the left mouse button. You can also select a *range* of filenames by clicking and dragging the left mouse button to select the range. To delete selected files, do the following:

1. Choose **F**ile → **O**pen.
2. Select the files to be deleted using one of the methods described above.
3. Click on File **O**ptions → **D**elete. (Or press the **Delete** key on your keyboard.)
4. At the prompt, *Do you want to delete the selected files?* click on Delete.
5. Click on Cancel to exit the *Open File* dialog box.

THINKING DRILL

Now you have the opportunity to practice using the dash in a special Thinking Drill that displays on your screen. Follow the directions on the screen. After you complete the drill, you will return to the text for additional key review and WordPerfect instruction.

WORDPERFECT REINFORCEMENT

In the activities that follow, you will learn to use the WordPerfect Underline feature, the Italics feature, and Reveal Codes. After creating, saving, and printing your WordPerfect document, you will complete 1- and 3-minute timings. Follow the directions step by step.

Reviewing the Underscore Key

While WordPerfect provides an automatic underline feature (the ***U*** button on the Toolbar), there are times when using the underscore key on the keyboard is just as fast—for example, when keying a blank line. Both methods of underlining are presented: the ***Underline*** button and the ***Underscore*** key.

Underscore Drill

To practice using the Underscore key, key lines 1–2 twice: first for control, then for speed.

The number of persons who will attend ____________________.

Enter Bette's street address here ________________.

Underlining with WordPerfect

In WordPerfect 6.1 for Windows, the ***U*** button on the Toolbar is used to underline text in a document. To access the underline feature, you would complete the following steps:

1. Click on the Underline button (turns underlining on).
2. Key the text.
3. Click on the Underline button (turns underlining off).

Underlining Existing Text

If you decide to underline existing text in WordPerfect, select the text first, then click on the Underline button. To select text, position the I-beam pointer on the first character of the text to be selected, hold down the left mouse button, drag the I-beam pointer to the end of the text to

but will be adhering to Open Systems standards that a new MPI system will be able to communicate with.

Covenant Hospital's Computer System: Covenant Hospital uses the MediTech software system. MediTech software is used by a significant share of hospitals of Covenant's size throughout the United States. The MediTech software is designed for a proprietary operating system called "Rockets," and it is not compatible with the RAM version of HealthCare. It is, however, compatible with HealthCare for the UNIX operating system due to programming changes by HealthCare. This system is moving toward industry standards with the incorporation of TCP/IP and HL7.

Summary: It appears that the best approach for the NW Heyde Health Clinic, especially considering its plans for expansion, is to replace the internal computer systems with an integrated system that can be linked to the PersonalCare HMO and Covenant Hospital. Our project team has scheduled a meeting with you on Monday at 9 a.m. in the conference room to review alternative hardware and software systems.

xx/048proa.wkp

Document B — *Memo Report Edited with Find and Replace*

1 At a clear WordPerfect editing window, open **048proa.kwp**. Using the Find and Replace feature, make the following changes (check your User's Guide or Session 40 if you need to review the Find and Replace steps):
   a Wherever reference is made to NW Heyde, change it to NorthWest Heyde.
   b Change all references to the RAM 6000 to RAM 6100.
2 Choose **F**ile → Save **A**s to save the document. Name it **048wprb.kwp**.
3 Choose **F**ile → **C**lose to close the document and clear the editing window.

MAINTAINING DISKS

Almost every company that conducts business maintains a filing system. The system may consist of documents, folders, and cabinets; or it may be a computerized filing system where information is stored on tapes and disks. Whatever kind of filing system a business uses, the daily maintenance of files is important to the company's operation. Maintaining the files may include retrieving, deleting, and archiving documents or entire files.

Like a filing system, the disk on which you have been saving documents also needs maintenance. Maintaining a disk may include such activities as deleting unnecessary documents (as you have been doing since Session 11), copying important documents into another file or onto another disk, and renaming documents.

Disk maintenance can be accomplished using the *Open File* dialog box. A directory of files saved on the disk appears at the left side of the *Open File* dialog box and may look like the sample directory that follows.

be selected, then release the left mouse button. (As the I-beam pointer moves through text, the text that is selected displays in reverse video or in a different color.) As a final step, click outside the selected text to deselect it.

General Guidelines for Using Underline and Italics

1. Underline titles of books, magazines, and newspapers. Note, however, that if you have access to an italic typeface (WordPerfect offers the italics button on the Toolbar), you should italicize book, magazine, and newspaper titles rather than underlining them. This is the practice followed by publishers, but until italic typefaces became available on personal computers, underlining was used to stand for italics. To italicize words, follow the same steps as for underlining, except click on the Italics button. (Click on the button to turn on Italics; key the text; click on the button to turn off Italics.) The following examples illustrate situations that call for italics or underlining:
   Gone With the Wind or *Gone With the Wind* (book title)
   Harper's Bazaar or *Harper's Bazaar* (magazine title)
   New York Times or *New York Times* (newspaper title)
   Note: With word processing software, underlining the spaces between words is the accepted practice because it saves time.
2. Underscore (or italicize) the names of ships, trains, and aircraft, but not the names of makes or models:
   the ocean liner Queen Mary or *Queen Mary*
   the train Chicago Sun Streak or *Chicago Sun Streak*
   the aircraft Silver Eagle One or *Silver Eagle One*
3. Underscore (or italicize) technical words that are not part of our normal language:
   The coast redwood, or Sequoia sempervirens or *Sequoia sempervirens*
4. Underscore (or italicize) a word or words in a sentence to provide special emphasis:
   He said there were many problems involved in the contract agreement.
   He said there were *many* problems involved in the contract agreement.
5. Use the Underscore key or WordPerfect's Underline button to create blank lines
   ______________.

Underline and Italics Drill

Key each of the following statements twice, first using the Underline button for the titles, then using italics for the titles:

Quality of Roses by Juan L. Cordoba—a book
He Ran Alone by Barbara Whitter—a book
San Francisco Examiner—a newspaper
Popular Mechanics—a magazine
Chicago Zephyr—a train
the Nautilus—a ship
Air Force One—a jet
panettone—an Italian bread

Staff members from all departments have expressed major complaints about this computer's slow operating speed. The RAM 6000 system is a Model 720 and contains three symmetrical processors. This form of processor lends itself to those programs that are written primarily for on-line transaction processing. They are not efficient in a batch processing mode. The HealthCare software is predominantly a batch mode software, with the exception of the scheduling node.

An example of the numerous limitations of the RAM 6000 system is the people resources required (2.5 staff positions) to handle patient billing under the Oregon Public Assistance (OPA) program. Anywhere from 8,000 to 12,000 *manually* created adjustments need to be made each month. This adjustment is the difference in dollars in what is billed to the OPA and what the OPA actually pays. Additional software is being added to the RAM 6000 that will automate this task; however, it will slow down the system more unless scheduled at off-peak hours.

Laboratory Computer System: The laboratory computer system consists of a microcomputer that functions with a UNIX operating system. The only terminals connected to this system are located in the lab. Medical units throughout the clinic would like to have access to the information on this system but do not have terminals connected to this unit, nor is the system compatible with the RAM 6000. This system does not integrate to the RAM 6000/HealthCare MPI.

Pharmacy Computer System: The pharmacy has a Novell network consisting of PCs located in their area. Because this system is not linked to the RAM 6000 computer system, patient information required when filling our prescriptions must be re-entered into the Novell system. This system is not integrated to any other system within the NW Heyde Clinic.

Medical Records Computer System: The Medical Records computer system consists of a Novell network with PC workstations located in three departments:

- The Medical Records Center
- The Correspondence Department
- The Data Processing Department

This system is yet another Heyde Clinic computer system that is not integrated with the primary computer system, the RAM 6000. Since this system contains record locator software, all medical units have need for the information stored on this system but do not have access to it. The Records Center receives between 400 and 600 calls daily requesting records and/or their whereabouts, yet the Records Center may not know where the records are if the last department sent it to another for referral.

PersonalCare HMO Computer System: PersonalCare has been using its own HealthCare software. However, it is not connected to the clinic's RAM 6000. The PersonalCare computer system is being replaced, and the vendor most likely selected will be operating on an Open Systems platform (UNIX), which is designed primarily for network operations and PC access. The software being purchased for PersonalCare's new computer system is not integrated with the HealthCare software

Continued on next page

Displaying the Reveal Codes Screen

When formatting such as underlining or italics is applied to text, special codes are inserted in the document. These codes and other types of codes can be seen in a special window called Reveal Codes. To display the Reveal Codes window, choose **V**iew, then Reveal **C**odes or press ***Alt + F3***. When Reveal Codes is displayed, a thin, black, double line splits the editing window. Text above the double line displays normally; text below the double line (in Reveal Codes) displays with special codes added. In Reveal Codes, the insertion point displays as a red rectangle.

Codes and text can be deleted in Reveal Codes with the ***Backspace*** key or the ***Delete*** key. The ***Backspace*** key deletes the character or code to the left of the insertion point. The ***Delete*** key deletes the character or code immediately right of the insertion point.

Special codes display in Reveal Codes that identify features. At the end of text lines, you may notice the code (SRt). This code indicates a soft return, which is an end of line created by word wrap. Another symbol, (HRt), identifies a hard return and indicates that the ***Enter*** key has been pressed.

In Reveal Codes, the code Und identifies the beginning of underlined text and the code Und identifies the end of underlined text. If you change your mind and want to remove underlining, display Reveal Codes by choosing **V**iew, then Reveal **C**odes or pressing ***Alt + F3***, then delete one of the underline codes. Underlining codes are paired—if one code is deleted, the other is automatically deleted.

Practice using Reveal Codes by displaying the Reveal Codes window and keying the following paragraph (press ***Alt + F3*** to turn off Reveal Codes when you are finished):

> A career in science involves selecting a path among several options. One could choose to become a doctor in a clinic or a teacher in a medical school. An active search through more than 190 college catalogs will indicate which courses to select. *U.S. News and World Report* also publishes college information annually. Contact campus finance officers to check cost factors.

Saving and Printing WordPerfect Reinforcement Activities

To save and print the WordPerfect Reinforcement activities completed in Session 22, do the following:

1. Choose **F**ile → Save **A**s (or F3).
2. At the *Save As* dialog box, key the new filename, **022wpr.kwp**. Press ***Enter*** or click on the OK button. Your document has been saved to disk, and it also remains on the screen.
3. To print 022wpr.kwp, choose **F**ile → **P**rint (or F5).
4. Click on the **P**rint button or press ***Enter***.
5. Close the file (click on **F**ile → **C**lose).

Deleting Files

As you recall, the *Keyboarding with WordPerfect* software automatically deletes session files that are more than ten sessions old. However, it is your responsibility to delete your outdated WordPerfect files so that your data disk contains only the ten most current WPR files.

To delete the **wpr** document you completed in Session 12, follow these steps:

f. Click on Number on the *Header/Footer* Feature Bar, then click on Page Number at the drop-down menu.
g. Press ***Enter***.
h. Press ***Ctrl + D*** to insert the current date. Press ***Enter*** to add one blank line to the end of your header. ***Note***: WordPerfect leaves only one blank line between the header and the text, so you must press Enter to insert a second blank line.
i. Choose Close.

3. Suppress the printing of the header on the first page by completing the following steps:
   a. Choose Format → **P**age → S**u**ppress.
   b. At the *Suppress* dialog box, choose H**e**ader A.
   c. Choose OK or press ***Enter***.
4. Proofread and correct any errors, then complete a spell check.
5. Click on Check to name **(048proa.kwp)**, save, and check the memo report.
6. To print the memo report with errors highlighted, click on the Print button.
7. To correct errors, click on View Original. Make changes, then recheck the document until there are zero errors.
8. Choose **F**ile → **C**lose. This closes Document A and brings up a clear WordPerfect editing window.

Document A

current date

TO: Craig Zachman, Senior Consultant

Lisa Dachel

THE NORTHWEST HEYDE CLINIC COMPUTER SYSTEMS

Craig, here is an overview of the computer systems being used at the Northwest Heyde Clinic. This information was collected by our project team in our recent visit to the clinic.

Currently the operations at the NW Heyde Clinic involve the use of six different computer systems, none of which are interactive. This minimizes automating operations and increases manual functions. The computer systems include the following:

Primary Computer System: The primary computer system is the RAM 6000, a minicomputer with dumb terminals or PCs utilized as dumb terminals connected by a proprietary cabling scheme. The computer system is used for the Master Patient Index (MPI), for billing from HealthCare, and for a general ledger system from PCI.

This computer system has reached its maximum capacity for the number of ports and sessions available. It is physically not capable of supporting the NW Heyde Clinic's expansion plans. This is not just a processing speed factor; additional terminals cannot be added. In addition, HealthCare is no longer adding software capabilities to the RAM 6000 system.

Continued on next page

1. Choose **F**ile → **O**pen.
2. At the *Open File* dialog box, select the file *012wpr.kwp* by clicking on the filename with the left mouse button.
3. With the filename highlighted, choose File **O**ptions → **D**elete.
4. At the *Delete File* dialog box, click on **D**elete.
5. To close the *Open File* dialog box, click on **C**ancel or press ***Esc***.

Now that you have completed the WordPerfect Reinforcement activities, you are to take several 1-minute timings. Click on the KWP Next Activity button to bring up the Timing screen.

ONE-MINUTE TIMINGS

Goal: 30 WAM, 2 errors

- Take a 1-minute timing on each paragraph.
- Press ***Tab*** to indent each paragraph.
- If you finish a paragraph before time is up, start over.

1 There has been a fantastic growth in the United States in the use of in-line roller skates, sometimes called Rollerblades, which is a trade name. People are using their in-line skates in conjunction with their employment. Couriers in New York City deliver their packages using their in-line skates to move quickly through the crowded streets. USA Hockey created an in-line hockey division in 1994.

2 Two-way radio systems are used by selected groups such as the police, ambulance services, and taxi cab companies. Users are limited to a single, manually selected channel. If the channel is in use, then the person must wait until it is free. There is no privacy for two-way radio systems; all others on your channel can listen to your conversation.

THREE-MINUTE TIMINGS

Goal: 25 WAM, 2 errors

So far all timings have been 1 minute long. Now you will take a 3-minute timing to help prepare you for keying longer documents such as reports. In most cases, speeds drop and errors increase when the length of the timing is extended. Your goal for this timed writing is to reach at least 25 WAM with fewer than three errors per minute. Try to come within 5 WAM of your 1-minute rate while maintaining your accuracy at fewer than three errors per minute. Remember to start over if you finish the paragraph before time is up.

1 Nails date back to 3000 B.C. They have been found in diggings and sunken ships that sailed in the years around 500 A.D. The Romans hand-forged nails and began the new trend toward complete use in building with wood. Most nails were first made in small shops; demand for nails grew so fast that the small, but well made supply of hand-made nails was not quite enough for the demand. Today, most companies that make nails can trace their own beginnings back to those early times.

Using WordPerfect's Header Feature

WordPerfect's Header feature can be used to create a header at the beginning of the document. One advantage of using a header or footer is that the text is keyed in only once, but will appear at the top (or bottom) of every page in the document. Using a header (or footer) also allows you to make editing changes in the text of a document without having to reposition the header. If text is added, deleted, or moved, WordPerfect adjusts the location of the header text accordingly. When using the Header feature for second and following pages of a letter or memo report, the header should be suppressed so that it will not print on the first page of the document.

Creating a Header

To create a header or footer for a memo report, you would complete the following steps:

1 Position the insertion point on the first page of the document.
2 Choose Format → **H**eader/Footer.
3 At the *Header/Footer* dialog box, with Header A selected, choose **C**reate.
4 At the *Header* window, key the receiver's name as the first line, then press ***Enter***.
5 Key the word **Page** followed by a space.
6 Click on Number on the *Header Feature bar.*
7 Select *Page Number* and press ***Enter***.
8 Press ***Ctrl + D*** to insert the current date. Press ***Enter*** to add one blank line to the end of your header. ***Note***: WordPerfect leaves only one blank line between the header and the text, so you must press Enter to insert a second blank line.
9 Choose **C**lose or press ***Ctrl + F4***.

Suppressing a Header

Since the Header should not appear or print on the first page of the memo report, you will need to use the Suppress option on page 1 by completing the following steps:

1 Position the insertion point anywhere on page 1.
2 Choose Format → **P**age → **Su**ppress.
3 At the *Suppress* dialog box, choose H**e**ader A.
4 Choose OK or press ***Enter***.

Document A — *Memo Report with a Header*

1 At the *Production–Session 48 Document A* screen, key Document A as a memo report. Use the WordPerfect margins and justification defaults. Insert the date, and turn on the Widow/Orphan feature.
2 Create a header that appears on page 2 by completing these steps:
   a Position the insertion point on the first page of the document.
   b Choose Format → **H**eader/Footer.
   c At the *Header/Footer* dialog box, make sure Header **A** is selected, choose **C**reate.
   d At the *Header* window, key the receiver's name as the first line, then press ***Enter***.
   e Key the word **Page** followed by a space.

ENDING THE SESSION

Once you have completed the timings, the KWP program takes you to the next session menu. If you want to print the Session 22 files, however, follow the steps below. Then continue with Session 23 or exit the program.

PRINT

1. Click on Back until you reach the KWP Main Menu.
2. At the Main Menu, select *Freeform* and click on OK.
3. Click on the Print button or choose **F**ile → **P**rint.
4. At the *Print* dialog box, select the **D**ocument on Disk option under *Print Selection*. Press ***Enter*** or click on **P**rint.
5. At the *Document on Disk* dialog box, click on the list button at the right of the filename text box.
6. With the mouse pointer, highlight the file to be printed and press ***Enter*** or click on **P**rint.
7. At the *Document on Disk* dialog box, click on **P**rint.

Repeat steps 3-7 to print additional documents on disk.

CONTINUE

1. Print any files, if necessary.
2. If you are working in Freeform, click on the KWP Main Menu button.
3. Highlight *Keyboarding Sessions*, then click on OK.
4. Click on Jump to go to the next session.

EXIT

1. Print any files, if necessary.
2. Click on the KWP Main Menu button on the Toolbar.
3. At the Main Menu, select WordPerfect Only, then click on OK.
4. Click on **F**ile → E**x**it.
5. Exit Windows, if necessary (**F**ile → E**x**it).

You, the Student *second-page header is optional*
Page 2
current date

Types of Advertising Media

Nationwide	**Old London Square Mall**
newspaper	newspaper
television	radio
radio	television
direct mail	direct mail
magazines	magazines

Ranked according to frequency of utilization

Conclusion: The use of advertising media by merchants at the Old London Square Mall closely follows what is being done on a national scale. The only difference occurs in the ranking of television and radio. Television is second in popularity nationwide, and radio is third. At the Old London Square Mall, radio is second in popularity and television is third.

Recommendations: Our agreement called for both a written report and an oral presentation of the findings. This information was given to the merchants at their last monthly meeting. A recommendation was made that the merchants use television more than radio in the future. After discussion, the members in attendance decided to follow this recommendation for the next six months. Accordingly, the mall manager was instructed to change the mall cooperative advertising campaign. We were given another agreement to provide a research follow-up report at the conclusion of the trial period.

Follow-up: Jim Lane will take charge of the follow-up research project. Alice Barnes, June Folton, Bob Arterburn, and Leslie Barth will work with him.

Figure 48.1 Memo report

Creating Headers in Multiple-Page Documents

When a document is longer than one page, it generally has a header on the second and succeeding pages. The placement, content, and formatting of the header depends on the type of document. For letters and memo reports, the header begins one inch from the top of the second page. There should be two blank lines between the header and the body of the letter. The header contains three lines of information: the receiver's name, the page number, and the date.

For manuscripts and research papers (covered in Sessions 50-53), the header information can be included as a header (at the top of the page) or as a footer (at the bottom of the page). The header/footer may include the name of the report section and the page number or the page number alone. The header/footer can be aligned with the right margin or the left margin; or, it can be centered.

APOSTROPHE, QUOTATION MARK

SESSION GOALS

Apostrophe, Quotation Mark

1-Minute: 30 WAM/2 errors
3-Minute: 25 WAM/2 errors

Review creating, saving, printing, and closing

Using apostrophes

GETTING STARTED

1 Access Windows, then WordPerfect 6.1 for Windows, then *Keyboarding with WordPerfect*.
2 At the Keyboarding Sessions menu, click on Jump to return to the activity where you left off, or move through the program menus until you reach the Session 23 menu.
3 Start with *Warm-Up* or go to the next activity if your fingers are already warmed up.

When you have completed the on-screen activities in Session 23, you will be instructed to return to the text for the WordPerfect Reinforcement activities. The final activity in the session is timings (1-minute and 3-minute).

WORDPERFECT REINFORCEMENT: PART ONE

After reviewing the proper reaches to the apostrophe and quotation mark keys, you will use these keys as you complete drills on keying word contractions, conversations, and titles of written works. Read the introductory material for each topic before you key the corresponding drill. You are to create one document containing all the activities from this section. Then you will save and print the file.

Reviewing the Apostrophe and Quotation Mark Keys

current date

double-space between heading parts

TO: You, the Student

Business People of America

MEMORANDUM REPORT PREPARATION

triple-space after subject line

Reports in business are frequently prepared in different forms from those in education. You are looking at a very popular example, the memo report.

Rather than prepare both a report and an accompanying letter or memo, the two are combined. This method is usually used for short reports that are fewer than five pages. You will notice that the style is the same as shown for the simplified-style memo presented in earlier sessions.

double-space between paragraphs

Many times you will find that the report content lends itself to the use of subheadings as shown in the samples that follow.

Summary: The findings of the survey of advertising at Old London Square Mall are similar to the national trends. All the mall stores use some type of outside media in addition to local cooperative advertising. The choice of outside media compares quite closely with national trends, since newspapers are rated most effective and are used most frequently, followed by radio, television, direct mailing, and magazines.

third-level headings may be bolded if there are no second-level heads

Background: Our organization entered into an agreement three months ago with the merchants of the Old London Square Mall to investigate avenues of approach to effective advertising. We assigned methods currently in use throughout the nation, and especially those methods used by businesses in some type of physical location arrangement (shopping centers, malls, and so on). After gathering the evidence used throughout the country, a questionnaire was prepared and administered to all the merchants located in the Old London Square Mall. The results of both the nationwide survey and the mall survey were then compared.

Findings: National merchants agree that individual firms must do more advertising than the cooperative efforts the mall association makes. Cooperative efforts seem to be quite effective when the entire mall conducts some type of sale (usually seasonal), but for the remainder of the time it is the individual firm that must generate sales by individual advertising efforts. The Old London Square Mall merchants agree with this 100 percent. Nationally, the use and popularity of various types of advertising media differ somewhat from what the Old London Square Mall merchants now use.

Continued on next page

Apostrophe Drill

Key lines 1–3 twice: first for control, then for speed.

1 Al's Dad's Ted's Allen's Jane's Jan's Ken's Len's
2 Alfie's neat sedan hasn't had a dent; he's tense.
3 Dale's latest theft hadn't shaken Jeanne's faith.

Quotation Mark Drill

Key lines 1–3 twice: first for control, then for speed.

1 "hello" "Help" "gasp" "Fiddle" "Ha" "Hi" "splash"
2 "At last," said Sal, "is that lad's knee healed?"
3 "At least," said Al, "Jake ate the jelled salad."

Close and save the file as 023wpr.kwp. Then click on the KWP Next Activity button. Before completing the Thinking Drill, read the following guidelines on using apostrophes.

General Guidelines for the Apostrophe

1 An apostrophe is used in a contraction—a shortened spelling of a word, substituting an apostrophe for the missing letter.

cannot	can't
could not	couldn't

2 An apostrophe can be used to show possession by adding an 's.

a hat belonging to John	John's hat
the voices of the people	people's voices
the guess of anybody	anybody's guess

For plural nouns that end in s, add the apostrophe only.

the carts of the golfers	golfers' carts
the clothes of the girls	girls' clothes

3 An apostrophe can also be used as a symbol for feet.

100 feet	100'
255 feet	255'

Note: Some individuals have trouble determining if a word is a personal pronoun or a contraction.

Example: their they're its it's

Remember: The apostrophe indicates a missing letter. Therefore, *they're* indicates *they are*, and *it's* stands for *it is.*

Additional examples:

They're taking their own sleeping bags.

not

They're taking they're (they are) own sleeping bags.

It's a treat to give the dog its bone.

not

It's a treat to give the dog it's (it is) bone.

THREE-MINUTE TIMINGS

Goal: 35 WAM/2 errors

SI: 1.46

- Take two 3-minute timings.
- On your second attempt, try to increase your speed while maintaining your accuracy goal.

In the autumn, when the grass begins to turn brown and the trees begin to lose their leaves, many people turn their attention to the upcoming sports season. Appearing high on the list for sports fans is professional football. Every weekend there are a variety of exciting games to attend, watch, or listen to. As the season progresses, much excitement is evident; the excitement culminates in the last big game of the year. In Canada, it's the Grey Cup; in the United States, it's the Super Bowl Game. The winning team in each country is declared to be "the" football league champion.

Other winter sports games draw the attention of many folks. Ice hockey has grown considerably as a professional sport during the past few years. The whizzing skaters, the delicate skills of the players, and the element of competition will add to a winter spectator's joy.

Basketball draws its share of attention during the long winters. The game of basketball is played at a steady pace and usually is very exciting. As in other professional sports, the teams travel all over the nation, giving the spectators one thrilling game after another.

PREPARING BUSINESS REPORTS

Business reports are typically multiple-page, informative documents written for a specific purpose: to analyze data, to present a proposal, to report on activities, to discuss various solutions to a problem, and so on. There are three categories of reports:

Formal: Formal reports are usually long (from 5 to 50 pages or more) and include a title page, table of contents, the body of the report, footnotes or endnotes, and a bibliography.

Informal: Informal reports often appear in memo form and are thus called *memo reports*. Typically, they are short documents without source notes.

Specialized: This group includes a variety of reports that may be used only in certain occupations. One example is a Request for Proposal (RFP), which is a specifications document sent to equipment or service vendors to get bids.

Report formats vary widely among organizations. The guidelines presented in this and following sessions are general rules that most organizations would accept. However, if your company or organization uses a different report format, follow the company's preferences.

Formatting Memo Reports

The sample memo report that follows illustrates the basic formatting guidelines you should use in preparing memo reports. Note that the purpose of the bolding and centering is to highlight different parts of the report for the reader. Other kinds of formatting, for example, underlining or using a different font, could also be used. The important rule is to choose a format and then use it consistently throughout the report.

THINKING DRILL

Now you have an opportunity to apply the apostrophe guidelines in a Thinking Drill. Follow the instructions on the screen. After you have completed the drill, return to the text and review the information that follows on using quotation marks correctly.

WORDPERFECT REINFORCEMENT: PART TWO

General Guidelines for Quotation Marks

The three most common uses for quotation marks are to indicate conversations, to indicate emphasis, and to highlight titles in published material.

Using Quotation Marks in Written Conversation

1 Quotation marks are used to indicate spoken words in written materials. When each new speaker says something, the text begins on a new line and is indented. Study these examples:

"The weather is really nasty," said Nancy.

Relaxed, Jan yawned and said, "Oh, I really hadn't noticed."

"That's because you have been sleeping all morning," murmured Nancy with a slight sneer in her voice.

2 The comma and period are placed inside the quotation marks. (See the previous examples.)

3 The question mark is placed either inside or outside the ending quotation mark, depending on the sentence logic.

a Place outside if the entire sentence is a question.
When did he say, "I shall not return"?
Did he say, "I saw ten paintings at the exhibit"?

b Place inside if the quotation **only** is a question.
The owner shouted, "Why don't you just leave?"
She asked, "Do you know if the train is late?"

4 The semicolon and colon **always** go outside the end quotation mark.
Last week she announced, "Recreation time will be lengthened"; however, we have not experienced it yet.

Quotation Mark Drill

Retrieve the WordPerfect file you created earlier in the session by clicking on **File** → **O**pen. Highlight the filename *023wpr.kwp*, then click on OK. Go to the end of the file to begin keying the sentences that follow. (The correct answers are shown at the end of the session.)

Key the three sentences, inserting quotation marks where appropriate.

The typewriter is old, stated Mr. Barlow, and must be replaced.

Why did the pilot say, We'll be 30 minutes late?

Catherine sleepily said, Why don't you just be quiet?

Key the following three sentences as conversation, adding quotation marks as appropriate.

We will be landing 30 minutes late, announced the pilot. Deanna muttered, I suppose that means we miss dinner. The flight attendant smiled and said, Perhaps we'll be on time after all.

SESSION GOALS

1-Minute: 40 WAM/2 errors
3-Minute: 35 WAM/2 errors

Writing rough drafts

Renaming and copying documents
Creating headers

GETTING STARTED

If you are continuing immediately from Session 47, go to the one-minute timings. If you exited the program at the end of Session 47, do the following:

1. Access Windows, then WordPerfect 6.1 for Windows.
2. Click on the KWP icon to access *Keyboarding with WordPerfect*.
3. Go to the Keyboarding Sessions menu and click on Jump to return to your last activity. Or, access the Session 48 menu and click on OK to begin the session.

ONE-MINUTE TIMINGS

Goal: 40 WAM/2 errors

SI: 1.45

- Take two 1-minute timings.
- Use your most recent timing score to set a speed or accuracy goal.

Recreation is becoming more and more popular among people of all ages. One particular sport that is growing rapidly is cross-country skiing. If a person makes an effort to get out of the house and put on a pair of skis, cross-country skiing can be a great enjoyment. No specialized skills are needed to learn to cross-country ski. The few basic beginning instructions are simple to master. The excitement of gliding over that snowy countryside, through the magnificent forests, and over the hills is a thrill that no one should miss.

Key the following as conversation, adding quotation marks as appropriate.

The pilot announced, Due to fog, we will be forced to land in Omaha instead of Minneapolis. Deanna's fears were confirmed. Omaha? she blurted. Yes, it's a wonderful city. I vacation there often, replied the flight attendant. The pilot was heard again, We may not be able to leave Omaha for 36 hours. Be prepared to spend the night in the airport. An unexpected treat! exclaimed the smiling flight attendant.

Using Quotation Marks in Titles and for Emphasis

1 Quotation marks are used to enclose titles of works such as poems; short stories; chapters, essays, or articles in magazines and other larger works; radio and television programs; and short musical works.

"The Midnight Ride of Paul Revere" is a good poem.
The last episode of "Star Trek" was really interesting.
The plot of "Last Rays of Daylight" was dull for a short story.
Did the band perform "Stardust" last evening?
I read the article "Thirty Ways to Avoid Work" in the magazine.

2 Quotation marks may be used within a sentence to give a word or words special emphasis, for example, a technical word used in a nontechnical sentence, slang expressions, humorous expressions, or defined words. (In typeset material, defined words are usually set in italics.) Be careful not to overuse the quotation mark in this manner.

The "Aglaonema" is commonly called the Chinese evergreen.
Marvin thought the concert was "far out" and enjoyable.
Their idea of "fast" service is serving one customer at a time.
According to Webster's dictionary, a wren is a "brown singing bird."

Quotation Mark Drill

Key each of the following sentences, inserting quotation marks to enclose titles or special words of emphasis.

The story was a real corker.

The gemot was used largely in early English government.

With friends like you, who needs enemies?

A narrow path or ledge is sometimes called a berm.

The poem entitled Barney's Revenge is not very long.

At midnight, Joan saw The Night of Laughter on television.

The author's last short story, Bars on the Doors, was a mystery.

Her favorite song is Thunder Serenade by Marlo Zahn.

Saving and Printing WordPerfect Reinforcement Activities

To save and print the WordPerfect for Windows document you have created, complete steps 1-5 that follow. (***Remember:*** The work you completed up to the WordPerfect Reinforcement section has already been saved automatically.)

UNIT 9

MANUSCRIPTS AND REPORTS

1. Choose **F**ile → Save **A**s (or F3).
2. At the *Save As* dialog box, the current filename appears in the Filename box. Click on OK.
3. WordPerfect displays a message saying the file already exists and asking if you want to replace it. Click on **Y**es.
4. To print 023wpr.kwp, choose **F**ile → **P**rint (or F5).
5. Click on the **P**rint button or press ***Enter***.
6. Close the file (click on **F**ile → **C**lose).

Deleting Files

Remember that good disk management practices include keeping plenty of space free on your data disk for new files. To delete the **wpr** document you completed in Session 13, follow these steps:

1. Choose **F**ile → **O**pen.
2. At the *Open File* dialog box, select the file *013wpr.kwp* by clicking on the filename with the left mouse button.
3. With the filename highlighted, choose File **O**ptions → **D**elete.
4. At the *Delete File* dialog box, click on **D**elete.
5. To close the *Open File* dialog box, click on **C**ancel or press ***Esc***.
6. Click on the KWP Next Activity button.

Now that you have completed the WordPerfect Reinforcement activities, you are to take 1-minute and then 3-minute timings. Check your screen for directions.

ONE-MINUTE TIMINGS

Goal: 30 WAM/2 errors

- Take a 1-minute timing on each paragraph.
- Press ***Tab*** to indent each paragraph.
- If you finish a paragraph before time is up, start over.

1 The new book called *Fundamentals of Soccer* has an excellent chapter on coaching soccer that offers 14 "awesome" tips to be used in working with young people new to the sport. There are some excellent suggestions on how to get positive support from the parents of the players. It's a great resource for coaches and their assistants.

2 A personal computer's components determine the limitations. For example, a computer without a video adapter and a video "codec" wouldn't be able to store the filming done via a camcorder. What can be done with the right components in today's microcomputers is amazing. It wouldn't take long to think of 101 things that could be done on a computer with the "right" components.

THREE-MINUTE TIMINGS

Goal: 25 WAM/2 errors

- Take a 3-minute timing on the following paragraph.

Document E ← Memo to Instructor

Using a WordPerfect memo template of your choice, compose a memo to your instructor consisting of at least two paragraphs, each with four or more sentences. Select one of the following topics:

- My favorite summer sport(s) and my favorite winter sport(s).
- My hobby.
- If I were to buy a new car today, it would be a ?
- How to stay in shape.

Use the timing feature to have your WAM rate calculated. (When you are ready to start keying, click on WAM Only to start the timer. Click on Stop WAM when you are finished.) Proofread and correct any errors, then complete a spell check with Speller. Save the document as **047wpre.kwp**. Then print and close the document.

ENDING THE SESSION

To end this session, delete outdated WordPerfect Reinforcement files, print any files from Session 47 not printed earlier, then continue with the next session or exit the program:

DELETE

1. Choose **F**ile → **O**pen.
2. Select the Session 37 wpr file.
3. With the filename(s) highlighted, choose File **O**ptions → **D**elete.
4. At the *Delete File(s)* dialog box, click on **D**elete.
5. If you need to print files, go to step 2 under PRINT. Otherwise, click on Cancel or press ***Esc*** to close the *Open File* dialog box.

PRINT

1. Choose **F**ile → **O**pen.
2. Select the files to be printed, then choose File **O**ptions → **P**rint.
3. At the *Print Files* dialog box, press ***Enter*** or click on **P**rint.
4. Click on Cancel or press ***Esc*** to close the *Open File* dialog box.

CONTINUE

1. Print any files, if necessary.
2. Click on the KWP Next Activity button.
3. At the next session menu, click on OK to proceed with the highlighted item.

EXIT

1. Print any files, if necessary.
2. Click on the KWP Main Menu button.
3. At the Main Menu, select WordPerfect Only, then click on OK.
4. Click on **F**ile → E**x**it.
5. Exit Windows (**F**ile → E**x**it), if necessary.

- Press ***Tab*** to indent the paragraph.
- If you finish before time is up, start the paragraph again.
- Take a second 3-minute timing; try to increase your speed while maintaining your accuracy.

1 Fair time is near. Last year, our county had a great fair. Lots of people came to see the fine views and have a good time. Just imagine that 539,437 people attended, which was a record. We are hoping that by the next year we can have over 600,000 at the fair. The new rides were colorful and exciting. Both the young and old had a great time. We hope that the same old amusement company will come back and bring some of those new rides and fun shows that are bigger and better.

ENDING THE SESSION

Once you have completed the timings, the KWP program takes you to the next session menu. If you want to print the Session 23 files, however, follow the steps below. Then continue with Session 24 or exit the program.

PRINT

1. Click on Back until you reach the KWP Main Menu.
2. At the Main Menu, select *Freeform* and click on OK.
3. Click on the Print button or choose **F**ile → **P**rint.
4. At the *Print* dialog box, select the **D**ocument on Disk option under *Print Selection*. Press ***Enter*** or click on **P**rint.
5. At the *Document on Disk* dialog box, click on the list button at the right of the filename text box.
6. With the mouse pointer, highlight the file to be printed and press ***Enter*** or click on **P**rint.
7. At the *Document on Disk* dialog box, click on **P**rint.

Repeat steps 3-7 to print additional documents on disk.

CONTINUE

1. Print any files, if necessary.
2. If you are working in Freeform, click on the KWP Main Menu button.
3. Highlight *Keyboarding Sessions*, then click on OK.
4. Click on Jump to go to the next session.

EXIT

1. Print any files, if necessary.
2. Click on the KWP Main Menu button on the Toolbar.
3. At the Main Menu, select WordPerfect Only, then click on OK.
4. Click on **F**ile → E**x**it.
5. Exit Windows, if necessary (**F**ile → E**x**it).

Answers to Quotation Mark Drills

"The typewriter is old," stated Mr. Barlow, "and must be replaced."

Why did the pilot say, "We'll be 30 minutes late"?

Catherine sleepily said, "Why don't you just be quiet?"

"We will be landing 30 minutes late," announced the pilot.

Deanna muttered, "I suppose that means we miss dinner."

Document C

To: Ben Goldstein/From: Jim Albright/Office Assignments/Attached is a list of the full-time faculty members in the Department of Office Administration and Business Education and their office locations./The department does not have any unfilled positions at this time. For the upcoming school year, our department will have two graduate assistants, Ms. Jean Cannon and Ms. Diane Lawrence, and one full-time researcher, Ms. Marta Gomez. We will have one quarter-time faculty member, Dr. Rena Gibson, who will be teaching courses in management information systems./Ms. Cannon and Ms. Lawrence, our graduate assistants, will be using the office located in Room 420 of Emerson Business Hall, as will Dr. Gibson./Attachment

Document D — *Simplified-Style Letter*

1. At the *Production–Session 47 Document D* screen, key Document D as a simplified-style letter using the default margins and justification. Insert the date. Center the letter on the page.
2. Proofread and correct any errors. Complete a spell check.
3. Click on Check to automatically name (**047prod.kwp**), save, and check the letter.
4. If required by your instructor, print the letter with errors highlighted.
5. Correct errors the software has identified, then recheck the document.
6. Choose **File** → **C**lose. This closes Document D and brings up a clear WordPerfect editing window.

Document D

Ms. Isabelle Martinez, Consumer Representative Supervisor/Office Products Corporation, P.O. Box 3168, Dallas, TX 76231-2218/Dear Ms. Martinez:/our Seminar program speakers have already been contracted for this year's Convention. A list of the speakers and their programs is attached. Should any of them withdraw from the program, I will contact you as a possible alternative./By the way, have you considered renting an exhibit booth at the Convention in Houston? This would give you an opportunity to display your products. Our executive Board is currently making a decision regarding the revision of the Office Techniques Manual. Should this manual be revised, you can be sure that your material will be listed./You referred to the possibility of having your products listed in the "Weekly Division Newsletter." Too my knowledge, there is no such publication; however, there is a monthly organizational report that is sent to all divisions. If you are interested, I can submit your material to the editor for possible inclusion in the report./Dale McNary, Editor/Attachment (Send copies to Francis Jakes and John Walsh.)

Seminar Speakers

The flight attendant smiled and said, "Perhaps we'll be on time after all."

The pilot announced, "Due to fog, we will be forced to land in Omaha instead of Minneapolis."

Deanna's fears were confirmed. "Omaha?" she blurted.

"Yes, it's a wonderful city. I vacation there often," replied the flight attendant.

The pilot was heard again, "We may not be able to leave Omaha for 36 hours. Be prepared to spend the night in the airport."

"An unexpected treat!" exclaimed the smiling flight attendant.

The story was a real "corker."

The "gemot" was used largely in early English government.

With "friends" like you, who needs enemies?

A narrow path or ledge is sometimes called a "berm."

The poem entitled "Barney's Revenge" is not very long.

At midnight, Joan saw "The Light of Laughter" on television.

The author's last short story, "Bars on the Doors," was a mystery.

Her favorite song is "Thunder Serenade" by Mario Zahn.

Document A

Mr. Patrick Shields/3228 Glenview Circle/Staten Island, NY 10302-1620/Dear Mr. Shields:/In accordance with your request, I have enclosed an agreement that sets forth our relationship in helping you find appropriate business investments. Please sign one copy and return it to us for our files./Have you had a chance to review the additional stock information I sent last week? I think there are some excellent investment opportunities available under current market conditions, and I recommend that you take advantage of them. Any communications in this regard will be treated as strictly confidential./We appreciate this opportunity to assist you and hope that our efforts will be successful in achieving your objectives./Sincerely, Robert E. Truax/Senior Vice President/Enclosure

Document B ← *Simplified-Style Memo*

1. At the *Production–Session 47 Document B,* key Document B in the simplified-style format. Use default margins and justification. Insert the date.
2. Proofread and correct any errors. Complete a spell check.
3. Click on Check to automatically name **(047prob.kwp)**, save, and check the memo.
4. If required by your instructor, print the memo with errors highlighted.
5. Correct errors the software has identified, then recheck the document.
6. Choose **F**ile → **C**lose. This closes Document B and brings up the Document C screen.

Document B

To: John Kearney, Editorial Director/ From: Frances Dalton, Administrative Secretary/Subject: Office Systems Seminar/John, here is an updated copy of our Office Systems Seminar outline that we talked about yesterday. This program is offered through our department every quarter as a one-credit course./Also attached is a revised copy of the letter we will send to potential participants. Please review it and call me with any corrections or comments./Thank you for the opportunity to share these thoughts with you and your staff./Attachments

Document C ← *Traditional Block-Style Memo*

1. At the *Production–Session 47 Document C* screen, key Document C in the block-style format using default margins and justification. Insert the date.
2. Proofread and correct any errors. Complete a spell check.
3. Click on Check to automatically name **(047proc.kwp)**, save, and check the memo.
4. If required by your instructor, print the memo with errors highlighted.
5. Correct errors the software has identified, then recheck the document.
6. Choose **F**ile → **C**lose. This closes Document C and brings up the Document D screen.

DOLLAR SIGN, POUND SIGN, AMPERSAND, EXCLAMATION POINT

SESSION GOALS

 $, #, &, and !

 Review creating, saving, printing, closing, and deleting

 1-Minute: 30 WAM/2 errors
3-Minute: 25 WAM/2 errors

 Using exclamation points

GETTING STARTED

If you are continuing immediately from Session 23, go to step 4. If you exited the program at the end of Session 23, do the following:

1. Access Windows, then WordPerfect 6.1 for Windows.
2. Click on the KWP button on the Toolbar.
3. At the Main Menu, click on Jump to return to the activity where you left off, or move through the program menus until you reach the Session 24 menu.
4. Start with *Warm-Up* or go to the next activity if your fingers are already warmed up.

When you have completed the on-screen activities for Session 24, you will be instructed to return to the text for the WordPerfect Reinforcement activities. Then you will complete 1-minute and 3-minute timings before exiting the session.

WORDPERFECT REINFORCEMENT

After reviewing the proper reaches to the symbol keys (dollar sign, number/pound sign, ampersand, and exclamation point), you will use these keys as you complete punctuation drills. Read the appropriate material in the text before you key each drill. You are to create one document containing all the activities from this section. After you save and print the file, you will complete a Thinking Drill on symbols.

Reviewing the Symbol Keys

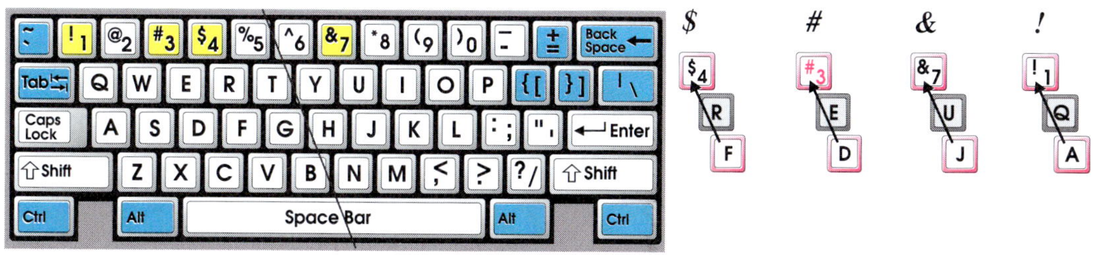

THREE-MINUTE TIMINGS

Goal: 35 WAM/2 errors

SI: 1.48

- Take two 3-minute timings.
- On your second attempt, try to increase your speed while keeping errors at two or fewer per minute.

Since the first moment in time when two people traveled beyond a shouting distance of each other, humans have searched for a method of talking over a long distance. Earlier cultures tried drums and smoke signals for messages. Today, the traffic noises in most places would cover the sounds of a drum; fire engines would arrive on the scene to drown the fire.

People communicate easily today with our telephones. Most of us don't realize how advanced the technology of phone service has become. Old photos show endless miles of phone wires hung on poles; today we would find the wire buried. The switchboard operator has been replaced with automatic dialing handled by a big computer with the sound waves being relayed across the world by satellite. The repair person has now been replaced by a trained service person.

The changes that have taken place are numerous; however, the objective of the service is still the same: to allow people to talk with other people. The next time you have a chance, look for other changes; you will be amazed with what you will find.

PRODUCTION PROGRESS CHECK

Now that you have completed the instruction on formatting memos, letters, and envelopes, it is time to assess how quickly and accurately you can key each of the document types. Each completed document should be "mailable," which means that it could be mailed or sent without any other corrections.

Your goal is to key each document in mailable form at 25 WAM (2.5 lines a minute) or higher. If you are below 25 WAM and/or are missing errors that should have been corrected, your instructor may ask you to repeat documents.

It is your responsibility to review each document before it is keyed. The document may be missing required features such as the date or reference initials and filename. In addition, there may be punctuation or capitalization errors.

Document A — *Block-Style Letter*

1. At the *Production–Session 47 Document A* screen, key Document A in the block-style format with default margins and justification. Insert the date and center the letter vertically.
2. Proofread and correct any errors, then complete a spell check.
3. Click on Check to automatically name **(047proa.kwp)**, save, and check the letter.
4. If required by your instructor, print the document with errors highlighted.
5. Correct errors the software has identified, then recheck the document.
6. Choose **File** → **Close**. This closes Document A and brings up the Document B screen.

Symbols are located on the number keys. You have mastered the necessary reaches; now all you have to do is reinforce the location of each symbol. ***Remember:*** Be sure to press the ***shift*** key.

Dollar Sign Drill

Key lines 1–3 once for control.

1 $1 $2 $3 $4 $5 $6 $7 $8 $9 $10 $11 $120 $16.00 f$
2 Add $1.16, $28.96, $17.44, $18.00, $21.13, $4.26.
3 The gifts cost $1.10, $6.90, $19.89, and $101.13.

Pound/Number Sign Drill

Key lines 1–3 once for control.

1 #33 33# 39 9# #168 168# #106 106# #3 3#3 21# #122
2 Items #10, #7, #3, #6, #4, #12, and #19 are mine.
3 Get #61 weighing 10# and #2299 weighing 189,756#.

Ampersand Drill

Key lines 1–3 once for control.

1 17 & 60 & 9 & 16 & 14 & 71 & 77 & 45 & 61 & 9891
2 Buy gifts from the J & K store and the R & Sons.
3 Jim & Steve & Arlen & Robert were tired & dirty.

Exclamation Point Drill A

Key lines 1–3 once. Space once after the exclamation point (except at the end of the line).

1 Help! Stop! No! Yes! Go! Wait! Begin! Halt! None!
2 Walter, stop right now! You had all better stop!
3 No, you cannot go right now! Listen to them now!

General Guidelines for the Exclamation Point

1 The exclamation point is used to express a high degree of emotion or strong feeling.
2 The exclamation point may be used in any of these situations:
  a One word (space once after the exclamation point)
    What! You mean the flight has been delayed for six hours?
  b A phrase (space once after the exclamation point)
    How frightening! The fire broke out only 10 minutes after we had left.
  c A clause
    The date of the meeting—mark it on your calendar!—is November 10.
  d A sentence (space once after the exclamation point)
    So there you are, you rascal!

PRODUCTION PROGRESS CHECK
CORRESPONDENCE PREPARATION ASSESSMENT

SESSION GOALS

 **1-Minute: 40 WAM/2 errors**
3-Minute: 35 WAM/2 errors

 **Apply features presented in Sessions 34-46**

GETTING STARTED

If you are continuing immediately from Session 46, go to the one-minute timings. If you exited the program at the end of Session 46, do the following:

1. Access Windows, then WordPerfect 6.1 for Windows.
2. Click on the KWP icon to access *Keyboarding with WordPerfect*.
3. Go to the Keyboarding Sessions menu and click on Jump to return to your last activity. Or, access the Session 47 menu and click on OK to begin the session.

ONE-MINUTE TIMINGS

Goal: 40 WAM/2 errors

SI: 1.45

- Take two l-minute timings.
- Use your most recent timing score to set a speed or accuracy goal.

If you enjoy observing the many species of birds, there are many ways of attracting them. A bird requires a shelter, food, and water. Provide fresh, clean drinking and bathing water each day. Place fresh seeds and fruit in accessible feeders that cannot be reached by squirrels. The bird shelters should be quite durable and waterproof. All baths, feeders, and shelters should be kept out of the reach of other animals. Those birds need all the security and safety that you can provide for them. Your new friends will appreciate your efforts and will reward you with singing.

e A quotation that is exclamatory
My brother yelled, "Run for your life!"

f A complete sentence that is exclamatory
I simply do not believe the fiscal report that states, "The absentee rate was increasing by 500 percent"!

Exclamation Point Drill B

Key each sentence, inserting appropriate punctuation. Answers are shown at the end of the session.

Congratulations You won the first prize

Jan shouted What a mess

I emphatically restate my position: I will not resort to underhanded tactics

Help Help I'm locked in

Oh, how ridiculous He's never even seen the inside of a bank

Saving and Printing WordPerfect Reinforcement Activities

To save and print the WordPerfect Reinforcement activities completed in Session 24, do the following:

1. Choose **F**ile → Save **A**s (or F3)
2. At the *Save As* dialog box, key the new filename, **024wpr.kwp**. Press ***Enter*** or click on the OK button. Your document has been saved to disk, and it also remains on the screen.
3. To print **024wpr.kwp**, choose **F**ile → **P**rint (or F5).
4. Click on the **P**rint button or press ***Enter***.
5. Close the file (click on **F**ile → **C**lose).

Deleting Files

To continue building good disk management habits, you should now delete the **wpr** document you completed in Session 14. Follow these steps:

1. Choose **F**ile → **O**pen.
2. At the *Open File* dialog box, select the file 014wpr.kwp by clicking on the filename with the left mouse button.
3. With the filename highlighted, choose File **O**ptions → **D**elete.
4. At the *Delete File* dialog box, click on **D**elete.
5. To close the *Open File* dialog box, click on **C**ancel or press ***Esc***.
6. Click on the KWP Next Activity button to access a Thinking Drill on using symbols. Check your screen for directions.

Finally, begin listing the information you must include in the document to achieve your writing purpose. As you ask yourself questions about your topic and audience, quickly key the words and phrases that come to your mind. When you cannot list any more, clarify your thinking by combining ideas, by moving subpoints under major points, and by rearranging your list to represent a logical flow of ideas. Print this rough outline and use it to write your first draft.

Document E — *Planning a Report*

Using the steps described above, prepare a rough outline on the topic of "Building Improvements Needed at My School." Your reader (audience) is the director or president of your school, and your purpose is to convince that person that your school needs some new facilities and/or that specific buildings should be remodeled.

There is no need to number or letter your points. Just key each one and press ***Enter*** twice to create a blank line between each idea. List ideas as quickly as you can. Then review them and reorganize them, if necessary. Indent subpoints one tab space. Finally, name and save the document as **046wpre.kwp**. Then print and close the file.

ENDING THE SESSION

To end this session, delete outdated WordPerfect Reinforcement files, print any files from Session 46 not printed earlier, then continue with the next session or exit the program:

DELETE

1. Choose **F**ile → **O**pen.
2. Select the Session 36 wpr file.
3. With the filename(s) highlighted, choose File **O**ptions → **D**elete.
4. At the *Delete File(s)* dialog box, click on **D**elete.
5. If you need to print files, go to step 2 under PRINT. Otherwise, click on Cancel or press ***Esc*** to close the *Open File* dialog box.

PRINT

1. Choose **F**ile → **O**pen.
2. Select the files to be printed, then choose File **O**ptions → **P**rint.
3. At the *Print Files* dialog box, press ***Enter*** or click on **P**rint.
4. Click on Cancel or press ***Esc*** to close the *Open File* dialog box.

CONTINUE

1. Print any files, if necessary.
2. Click on the KWP Next Activity button.
3. At the next session menu, click on OK to proceed with the highlighted item.

EXIT

1. Print any files, if necessary.
2. Click on the KWP Main Menu button.
3. At the Main Menu, select WordPerfect Only, then click on OK.
4. Click on **F**ile → E**x**it.
5. Exit Windows (**F**ile → E**x**it), if necessary.

ONE-MINUTE TIMINGS

Goal: 30 WAM/2 errors

- Take a 1-minute timing on each paragraph.
- Press ***Tab*** for each paragraph indent
- If you finish a paragraph before time is up, start over.

1 State, county, and regional fairs provide wholesome entertainment for more than 150 million Americans each year. The Texas State Fair has an annual $160-million-dollar impact on the Dallas-Fort Worth area with more than 3.1 million attendees. From animals to high-tech displays, there's something for everyone, and the price is right!

2 When ordering team jerseys, be sure to include #223-852 in the category box on the order form. JB & K provides an additional 5-percent discount for orders in excess of 15 jerseys. There is a significant savings on two-color jerseys compared to those with three or more colors. Prices are listed on the attached sheet.

THREE-MINUTE TIMINGS

Goal: 25 WAM/2 errors

- Take two 3-minute timings on the following paragraph.
- Press ***Tab*** to indent the paragraph.
- On your second attempt, try to increase your speed while maintaining your accuracy.

1 Why should seat belts be fastened when a car is moving? Seat belts will reduce injuries and deaths. Many tests and studies have been done to prove this point. Half of all the traffic deaths happen within 25 miles from home. Traffic deaths can occur when an auto is moving just 40 miles an hour or less. If a car is moving at 30 miles per hour, the impact is like hitting the ground after hurtling from the top of a building that is three stories high.

ENDING THE SESSION

Once you have completed the timings, the KWP program takes you to the next session menu. If you want to print the Session 24 files, however, follow the steps below. Then continue with Session 25 or exit the program.

PRINT

1. Click on Back until you reach the KWP Main Menu.
2. At the Main Menu, select *Freeform* and click on OK.
3. Click on the Print button or choose **F**ile → **P**rint.
4. At the *Print* dialog box, select the **D**ocument on Disk option under *Print Selection*. Press ***Enter*** or click on **P**rint.
5. At the *Document on Disk* dialog box, click the list button at the right of the filename text box.
6. With the mouse pointer, highlight the file to be printed and press ***Enter*** or click on **P**rint.
7. At the *Document on Disk* dialog box, click on **P**rint.

6. If the ZIP is not displayed in the *POSTNET Bar Code* text box, click inside the text box, then key the ZIP Code.
7. Choose **P**rint Envelope.
8. Choose **F**ile → **C**lose. This closes the document without saving the changes.

Document D — *Creating a Small Envelope*

1. At a clear editing window, choose Fo**r**mat → E**n**velope to open the *Envelope* dialog box.
2. Under Envelope Definitions, see if you have an envelope form available for small envelopes. (This form displays with the measurement 6.5" x 3.5".) If a small envelope form is not available, complete the following steps to create the form:
   a. Choose Create Ne**w** Definition.
   b. Click in the *Paper Name:* text box.
   c. Key **Small Envelope**.
   d. The Paper Type should show *Envelope*.
   e. Click on the down-pointing arrow to the right of the **S**ize text box, then choose User Defined Size.
   f. Key **3.5"** by **6.5"** in the two text boxes under *Paper Size*.
   g. Click on OK.
3. At the *Envelope* dialog box, the new definition *Small Envelope* should be displayed.
4. Remove the X from the *Print Return Address* check box.
5. Select Mailing Addresses by clicking the left mouse button in the Mailing Addresses text box.
6. Key the address for Document D.
7. Click in the *POSTNET Bar Code* text box to insert the ZIP Code from the mailing address.
8. Choose Append to Doc.
9. To print the envelope, choose the Print button on the Power Bar and click on Print.
10. Choose **F**ile → **S**ave and key **046wprd.kwp** as the document name.
11. Choose **F**ile → **C**lose. This closes Document D and clears the editing window.

Document D

MS ROUSHANI MANSOOR
LOS ANGELES CITY COLLEGE
855 NORTH VERMONT AVENUE
LOS ANGELES CA 90029-4571

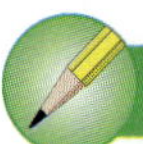

REINFORCING WRITING SKILLS

Probably the most important step in the writing process is planning, which includes defining your purpose, identifying your reader, and deciding what information to include in the document. With short documents—for example, memos of a few lines—planning is usually quite simple and can be accomplished "in your head." However, longer documents such as reports and manuscripts require more planning time, and the planning information should be written down or keyed to ensure that all important information is included.

Planning at the Keyboard

A quick and efficient method for planning longer documents is to use WordPerfect to record your planning information. First, key your writing purpose (what are you trying to accomplish?). Leave a blank line, then key words that identify your audience or your reader.

Repeat steps 3-7 to print additional documents on disk.

CONTINUE
1 Print any files, if necessary.
2 If you are working in Freeform, click on the KWP Main Menu button.
3 Highlight *Keyboarding Sessions*, then click on OK.
4 Click on Jump to go to the next session.

EXIT
1 Print any files, if necessary.
2 Click on the KWP Main Menu button on the Toolbar.
3 At the Main Menu select WordPerfect Only, then click on OK.
4 Click on **F**ile → E**x**it.
5 Exit Windows (**F**ile → E**x**it), if necessary.

Answers to Exclamation Point Drill B

Congratulations! You won the first prize.
Jan shouted, "What a mess!"
I emphatically restate my position: I will not resort to underhanded tactics!
Help! Help! I'm locked in.
Oh, how ridiculous! He's never even seen the inside of a bank.

Options: WordPerfect includes default horizontal and vertical measurements for the return address and mailing address for each envelope definition. To change these options, click on the Options button located at the bottom of the *Envelope* dialog box to access the *Envelope Options* dialog box. You can also change the position of the USPS Bar Code at this dialog box.

Document A — *Creating an Envelope*

1. At a clear editing window, choose Format → Envelope to open the *Envelope* dialog box.
2. Select **R**eturn Addresses by clicking the left mouse button in the Return Address text box.
3. Key your name and address.
4. Select Mailing Addresses by clicking the left mouse button in the Mailing Addresses text box.
5. Key the address for Document A.
6. Click in the *POSTNET Bar Code* text box to insert the ZIP Code from the mailing address.
7. Choose Append to Doc.
8. To print the envelope, click on the Print button on the Power Bar, then click on Print. (Unless instructed otherwise, use plain paper to print the envelope addresses in this session.)
9. Choose **F**ile → **S**ave and key **046wpra.kwp** as the document name.
10. Choose **F**ile → **C**lose. This closes Document A and clears the editing window.

Document A

MS LORETTA BAGLEY CHAIR
DEPARTMENT OF OFFICE EDUCATION
CHICAGO VOCATIONAL HIGH SCHOOL
8700 SOUTH STONY ISLAND AVENUE
CHICAGO IL 60617-1043

Document B — *Adding an Envelope to a Document*

1. At a clear editing window, open **045proa.kwp**.
2. Choose Fo**r**mat → Envelope to open the *Envelope* dialog box.
3. Select **R**eturn Addresses by clicking the left mouse button in the Return Addresses text box.
4. Key the sender's name (Michael Lee) and address if it is not already there. (Make sure the *Print Return Address* has an X in the check box.)
5. Check the Mailing Addresses text box to verify that the address for Mr. William Haggert has been inserted.
6. If the ZIP is not displayed in the *POSTNET Bar Code* text box, click inside the text box, then key the ZIP Code.
7. Choose **P**rint Envelope.
8. Choose **F**ile → **C**lose to close the document **without saving**. The editing window is cleared.

Document C — *Adding an Envelope to a Document*

1. At a clear editing window, open **045prob.kwp**.
2. Choose Fo**r**mat → Envelope to open the *Envelope* dialog box.
3. Select **R**eturn Addresses by clicking the left mouse button in the Return Addresses text box.
4. Key the sender's name (Betty Dawson) and address if it is not already there. (Make sure the *Print Return Address* shows an X in the check box.)
5. Check the Mailing Addresses text box to verify that the address for Mrs. Helen Ryan has been inserted.

SESSION 25

ASTERISK, PERCENT SIGN, BRACKETS, AND PARENTHESES

SESSION GOALS

*, %, [ ], ( )

Use Italics and Underline

1-Minute: 30 WAM/2 errors
3-Minute: 25 WAM/2 errors

Symbols

GETTING STARTED

If you are continuing immediately from Session 24, go to step 4. If you exited the program at the end of Session 24, do the following:

1. Access Windows, then WordPerfect 6.1 for Windows.
2. Click on the KWP button to access *Keyboarding with WordPerfect.*
3. Go to the Keyboarding Sessions menu and click on Jump to return to the activity you left off with. Or, move through the program menus until you reach the Session 25 menu.
4. On the Session 25 menu, *Warm-Up* is highlighted. Click on OK to proceed with the Warm-Up activities.

If you are already warmed up or have completed part of the session, highlight the desired activity and click on OK . When you have completed the on-screen keyboarding drills and the Thinking Drill, you will be instructed to return to the text to complete the WordPerfect Reinforcement activities. The final activity is timings (1-minute and 3-minute).

WORDPERFECT REINFORCEMENT

This section offers a brief review of the proper reaches to the asterisk, percent sign, left and right brackets, and left and right parentheses keys. You will create a WordPerfect document as you key the review drills.

Reviewing the Asterisk, Percent Sign, Brackets, and Parentheses Keys

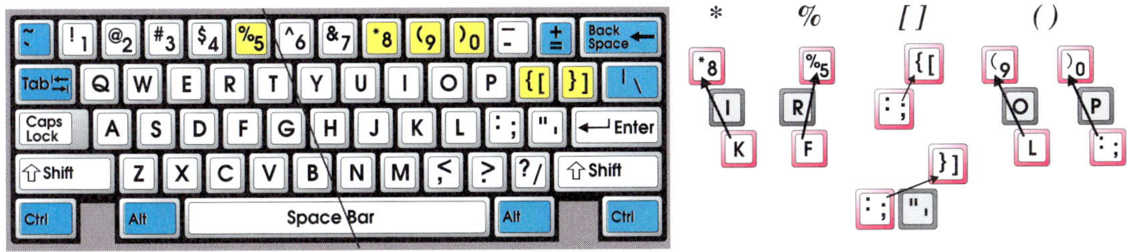

7 Choose **P**rint Envelope to print the envelope or choose Append **t**o Doc to insert the envelope definition code and the return and mailing addresses in the document.

Creating an Envelope in an Existing Document

If you open the *Envelope* dialog box in a document containing a letter, the address is automatically inserted in the **Mailing Addresses** section of the *Envelope* dialog box. For this automatic insertion to occur, the mailing address in the letter must be keyed at the left margin and there must be two hard returns following the address.

To create an envelope in an existing document and append it to the document, complete the following steps:

1 Create or open a document containing a letter.
Note: In order for the mailing address to be inserted in the *Envelope* dialog box, it must be keyed at the left margin and followed by two hard returns.

2 Choose Fo**r**mat → En**v**elope.

3 At the *Envelope* dialog box, verify that the mailing address is correctly inserted in the Mailing Addresses section.

4 Choose Append **t**o Doc to insert the envelope as the last page of the document.

Printing Envelopes

When you choose Append to Doc from the *Envelope* dialog box, the envelope is inserted on a new page at the end of the document. The envelope will be printed as the last page of the document. WordPerfect automatically inserts the page break between the letter and the envelope. If you want to print the envelope without appending it to the document, choose Print Envelope instead of Append to Doc. When you choose the Print Envelope option, the envelope is not added to the text, but is sent directly to the printer. Please refer to your printer manual for specific instructions on printing envelopes with your printer.

Making Changes at the Envelope Dialog Box

The *Envelope* dialog box contains options for turning off the printing of the return address, changing the font of the return and mailing addresses, inserting a POSTNET Bar Code, and changing the envelope size.

Adding/Deleting Addresses: When the *Envelope* dialog box is displayed, WordPerfect inserts the last return address used to create an envelope. You can add several return addresses to the address list if you choose. By default, WordPerfect will print the return address on the envelope. If you do not wish the return address printed, remove the X from the *Print Return Address* check box.

Including a POSTNET Bar Code: You can insert a POSTNET (Postal Numeric Encoding Technique) Bar Code in the mailing address at the *Envelope* dialog box. The bar code speeds mail sorting, increases the accuracy of delivery, and reduces postage costs.

Selecting and Creating Envelope Definitions: If your printer has more than one envelope definition, you can select a different envelope. To do this, Choose *Envelope Definitions*, then select the desired definition. If there are no envelope definitions listed, you can create your own by choosing *Create New Definition*. ***Note***: To delete or edit definitions, you must go to the *Paper Size* dialog box, which is accessed through the Fo**r**mat → **P**age menu option.

Asterisk Drill

In addition to signaling a footnote or indicating spacing, the asterisk serves as a multiplication sign in some programming languages.

Key lines 1–4 twice: first for control, then for speed. (Remember to press the ***left shift*** key.)

1 k8k k8k k8k ki8k ki8k ki8*k k*k K*K k*k k*k *ki*k

2 8*8 8*8 8*8 k8*k ki8*k k*k 8*8*8 *** 8*8 ki8* k*k

3 The check was for $***4.65 and it should be $.46.

4 The * symbol is used in programming: A - B * 38.

Percent Sign Drill

Be sure to press the ***right shift*** key. Place both hands on the home row and practice the move from ***f*** to ***percent sign***.

Key lines 1–4 twice: first for speed, then for control.

1 f5f f5f f5f f5f f5f f%f F%F f5f F%F5 f%f5 f%f f%f

2 55% 555% 5% 5%5% 555% 55% 5% 5% 55% 555% 5%, 555%

3 A 6% discount and a 10% reduction will equal 16%.

4 They made 55% of their shots and 8% of the fouls.

Left Bracket Drill

Key lines 1 and 2 twice: first for control, then for speed.

1 ;[; ;[; ;[; ;[; ;[; ;[; ;[;[;[;[;[; ;[;[; ;[;[;

2 ;[;[;[;[; ;[;[; ;[;[; ;[;[;[; ;[;[; ;[; ;[;[;

Left and Right Brackets Drill

Key lines 1 and 2 twice for control.

1 ;[; ;]; ;[; ;]; ;[; ;]; ;]; ;[; ;]; ;[; ;[; ;];];

2 ;[ ]; ;[; ;]; ;[; [;] [;] [;] [;] [;] [;] [;] [;]

Left Parenthesis Drill

Key lines 1 and 2 twice: first for control, then for speed.

1 l9l l9l l9l l9l lo9l lo9l lo9(l l(1 l(l lo(l lo9(

2 l(l l(l l9l l9l l9(l lo9(l lo(l lo9(l l9Ll l(l l9

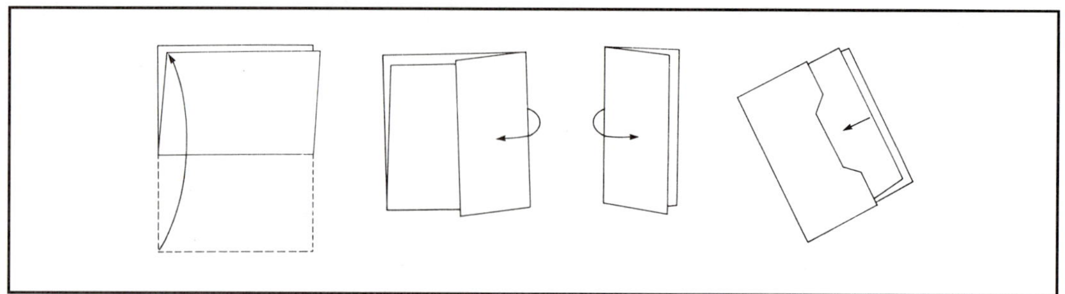

For window envelopes:

1 Place the letter on the desk in the normal reading position.
2 Turn the letter over, with letterhead closest to you.
3 Fold the top third of the letter (farthest away from you) toward you and crease.
4 Fold the bottom of the letter up so that the inside address is on the outside.
5 Insert the letter into a window envelope with the address facing the front. Check to make sure the complete address shows in the window.

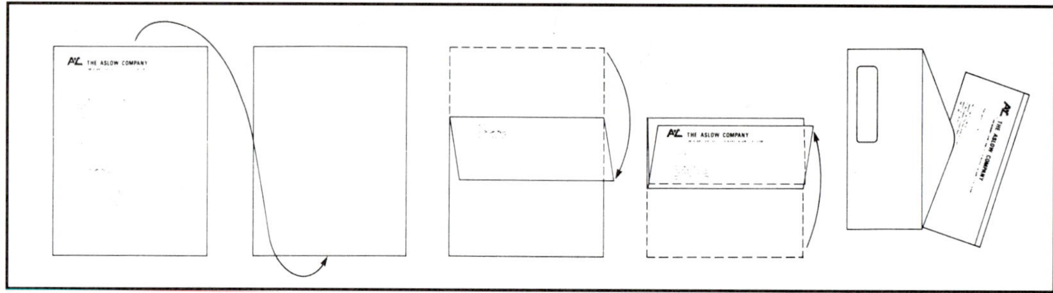

Using Different Form Sizes

When a printer is installed and selected in WordPerfect, a few predesigned paper definitions are available that can be inserted in a document. This paper definition is used to print text on regular-sized stationery, which is 8.5 by 11 inches. This standard form also contains commands specifying where the text prints on the page. Some printers can accept and print text on a variety of paper sizes, while others can print on only a few.

A form is created for special printing needs. For example, some legal documents may need to be printed on legal-sized paper (8.5 by 14 inches). Other documents may need to be printed on half-sized stationery. A special form must also be used to print copy on envelopes.

Creating an Envelope in a New Document

You can use WordPerfect's Envelope feature to print an address in the correct location on an envelope. To create an envelope at a clear editing window, complete the following steps:

1 Choose Format → Envelope.
2 At the *Envelope* dialog box, verify that the correct envelope definition is displayed in the *Envelope Definitions* text box. (Envelope #10 Landscape)
3 Choose **R**eturn Addresses by clicking inside the text box.
4 Key the return address.
5 Choose **M**ailing Addresses by clicking inside the text box.
6 Key the mailing address.

Right Parenthesis Drill

Key lines 1–4 twice: first for speed, then for control.

1 ;0; ;0; ;0; ;0; ;p0; ;p0; ;p0; ;p0; ;p); ;p); ;0;

2 ;); ;); ;); ;); ;); ;0); ;); ;0); ;p0); ;p0); ;);

3 The price ($5.95) was more ($2 more) than I paid.

4 Most of the teams (at least 6) won all six games.

Saving and Printing WordPerfect Reinforcement Activities

To save and print the WordPerfect Reinforcement activities completed in Session 25, do the following:

1. Choose **F**ile → Save **A**s (or F3).
2. At the *Save As* dialog box, key the new filename, **025wpr.kwp**. Press ***Enter*** or click on the OK button. Your document has been saved to disk, and it also remains on the screen.
3. To print 025wpr.kwp, choose **F**ile → **P**rint (or F5).
4. Click on the **P**rint button or press ***Enter***.
5. Close the file (click on **F**ile → **C**lose).

Deleting Files

To continue building good disk management habits, you should now delete the **wpr** document you completed in Session 15. Follow these steps:

1. Choose **F**ile → **O**pen.
2. At the *Open File* dialog box, select the file *015wpr.kwp* by clicking on the filename with the left mouse button.
3. With the filename highlighted, choose File **O**ptions → **D**elete.
4. At the *Delete File* dialog box, click on **D**elete.
5. To close the *Open File* dialog box, click on Cancel or press ***Esc***.

Now that you have completed the WordPerfect Reinforcement activities, you are to take 1-minute and 3-minute timings. Click on the KWP Next Activity button to bring up the Timing screen.

ONE-MINUTE TIMINGS

Goal: 30 WAM/2 errors

- Take a 1-minute timing on each paragraph.
- If you finish a paragraph before time is up, start over.

1 The stock market gets a lot of people's attention. When Standard & Poor's index increases, many people will hold on to their stocks in anticipation of further gains. A 4% drop in durable goods orders would most likely increase short-term interest rates; this has an impact on the Federal Reserve Board's next move.

6 Notations such as *confidential* are keyed in all capital letters three or four lines below the return address.
7 Special mailing instructions such as *registered* and *special delivery* are keyed in all capitals in the upper right-hand corner, below the postage area.
8 Business envelopes usually have the return address printed on the envelope. If not, key it in the upper left-hand corner, block style, single-spaced, approximately two lines down from the top and three spaces in from the left edge.

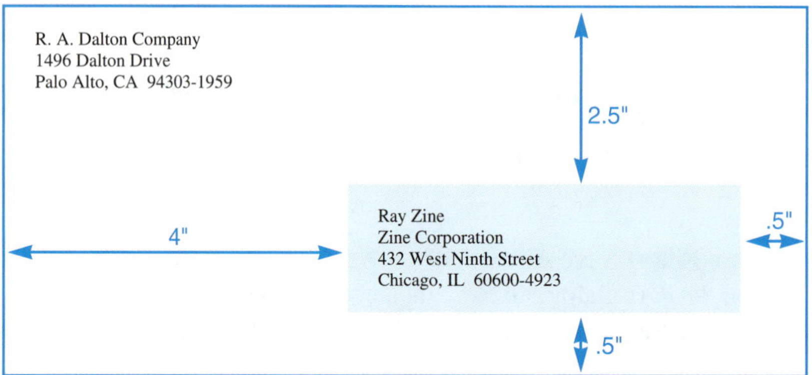

R. A. Dalton Company
1496 Dalton Drive
Palo Alto, CA 94303-1959
2.5"
4"
Ray Zine
Zine Corporation
432 West Ninth Street
Chicago, IL 60600-4923
.5"
.5"

Folding and Inserting Letters

Insert a letter into an envelope so that when it is removed and unfolded it is in a normal reading position.

For the large (business) envelope:

1 Place the letter on the desk in the normal reading position.
2 Fold a little less than a third of the letter up from the bottom and crease.
3 Fold upward again to within 0.5 inches of the top and crease.
4 Insert the last fold into the envelope first. The top of the sheet of paper is at the top of the envelope.

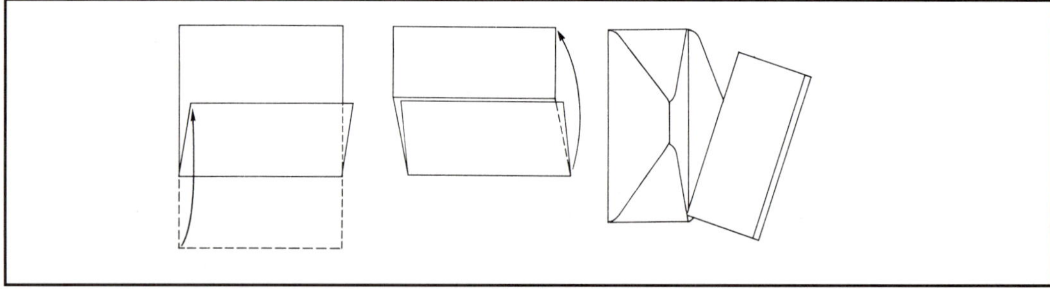

For the small (personal) envelope:

1 Place the letter on the desk in the normal reading position.
2 Fold from the bottom up to 0.5 inches from the top.
3 Fold a little less than the right third over to the left.
4 Fold the left third over to 0.5 inches beyond the last crease.
5 Insert last-creased edge into the envelope first.

2 The Radio Corporation of America (RCA) demonstrated the all-electronic 120-scan line television in the 1930s. In the same decade, Germany began regular TV broadcasting service. In the 1940s, coaxial (copper) cable was introduced as a more efficient method for telephone and television transmission. The progress in TV technology has been dynamic!

THREE-MINUTE TIMINGS

Goal: 25 WAM/2 errors

- Take two 3-minute timings on the following paragraph.
- Start the paragraph again if you finish before time is up.

1 Firms from which persons order items have to charge an amount for shipping and handling. Many firms do pay for the shipping amount if the items you ordered weigh less than a certain amount. If you have to pay the charges, you may wish to have that order sent by UPS. UPS uses varying charges according to the zone in which you live. UPS now has 8 mailing zones. Zone 1 is on the West Coast and Zone 8 is on the East Coast with all the rest of the zones located between these two points.

ENDING THE SESSION

Once you have completed the timings, the KWP program takes you to the next session menu. If you want to print the Session 25 files, however, follow the steps below. Then continue with Session 26 or exit the program.

PRINT

1. Click on Back until you reach the KWP Main Menu.
2. At the Main Menu, select *Freeform* and click on OK.
3. Click on the Print button or choose **F**ile → **P**rint.
4. At the *Print* dialog box, select the **D**ocument on Disk option under *Print Selection*. Press ***Enter*** or click on **P**rint.
5. At the *Document on Disk* dialog box, click on the list button at the right of the filename text box.
6. With the mouse pointer, highlight the file to be printed and press ***Enter*** or click on **P**rint.
7. At the *Document on Disk* dialog box, click on **P**rint.

Repeat steps 3-7 to print additional documents on disk.

CONTINUE

1. Print any files, if necessary.
2. If you are working in Freeform, click on the KWP Main Menu button.
3. Highlight *Keyboarding Sessions*, then click on OK.
4. Click on Jump to go to the next session.

EXIT

1. Print any files, if necessary.
2. Click on th KWP Main Menu button on the Toolbar.
3. At the Main Menu select WordPerfect Only, then click OK.
4. Click on **F**ile → E**x**it.
5. Exit Windows (**F**ile → E**x**it), if necessary.

The upper left-hand corner of an envelope is reserved for the return address (address of the sender). The address of the person or firm to receive the contents of the envelope is keyed in the lower right section.

The Postal Service uses high-speed optical character readers to scan mail electronically. Mail that is not properly addressed is rejected by the machine and set aside until it can be read manually.

Postal Service Guidelines

1 The Postal Service recommends keying the address single-spaced, in all capital letters, omitting all punctuation; block the address in the *read zone* (shaded area shown on the envelope). The address should generally be in three or four lines and should match the inside address.

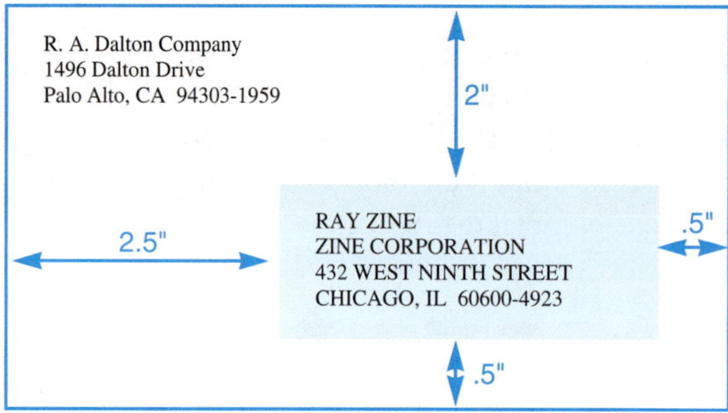

2 Also acceptable is the traditional format shown following. Key the address single-spaced, in capital letters and lowercase letters with normal punctuation; it is also in block form in the *read zone*.

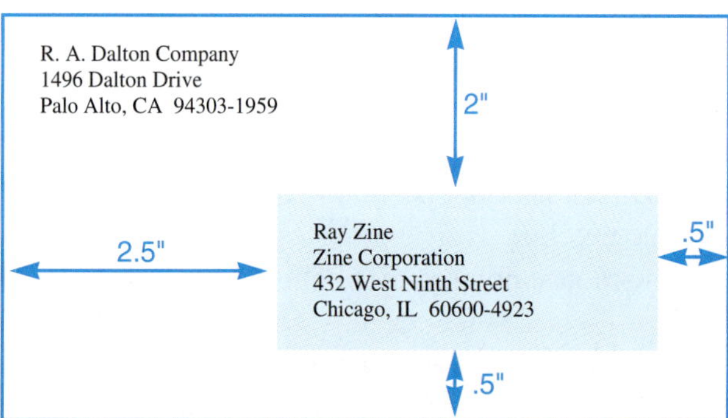

3 For United States addresses, key the two-letter state abbreviation in capital letters with no periods. Space once, then key the nine-digit ZIP Code (ZIP + 4).

4 For Canadian addresses, after keying the city in all capital letters followed by a comma and a space, key the two-letter province abbreviation in capital letters with no periods and one space following. The six-character Canadian Postal Code appears after the city and province, or it may appear with the country name, CANADA, on the last line of the address. The first three characters (consisting of letter, number, letter) are followed by a space and then the last three characters (consisting of number, letter, number).

5 A letter mailed from Canada to the United States includes the initials *USA* as the last line of the address.

SESSION 26 AT, EQUALS, AND PLUS SIGNS

SESSION GOALS

 @, =, and + Keys

 1-Minute: 30 WAM/2 errors
3-Minute: 25 WAM/2 errors

 Review creating, saving, printing, closing, and deleting

 Symbols

GETTING STARTED

If you are continuing immediately from Session 25, go to step 4. If you exited the program at the end of Session 25, do the following:

1. Access Windows, then WordPerfect 6.1 for Windows.
2. Click on the KWP button to access *Keyboarding with WordPerfect.*
3. Go to the *Keyboarding Sessions* menu and click on Jump to return to the activity you left off with. Or, move through the program menus until you reach the Session 26 menu.
4. On the Session 26 menu, *Warm-Up* is highlighted. Click on OK to proceed with the Warm-Up activities.

If you are already warmed up or have completed a portion of the session, highlight the desired activity and click on OK . When you have completed the on-screen Keyboarding drills and the Thinking Drill, you will be instructed to return to the text to complete the WordPerfect Reinforcement activities. The final activity is timings (1-minute and 3-minute).

WORDPERFECT REINFORCEMENT

This section offers a brief review of the proper reaches to the "at" sign, equals sign, and plus sign keys. You will create a WordPerfect document as you key the review drills.

Reviewing the At Sign, Equals Sign, and Plus Sign Keys

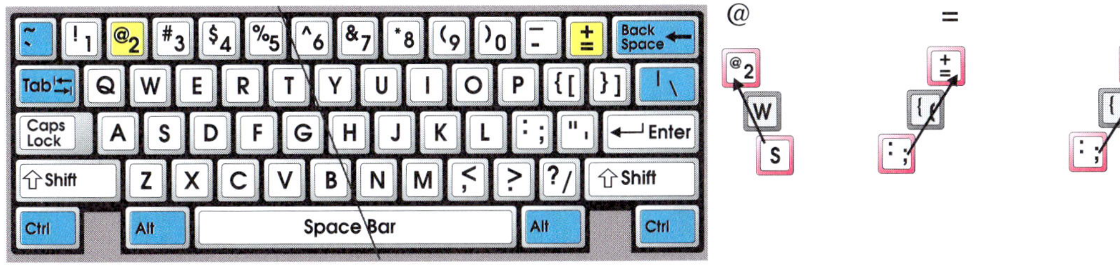

FIVE-MINUTE TIMINGS

Goal: 30 WAM/2 errors

SI: 1.46

- Take two 5-minute timings.
- On your second attempt, try to increase your speed while keeping errors at two or fewer.

A person who owns a home and wishes to sell it has to identify an asking price. Most people who want to sell their homes don't have the background for putting a fair market value on their home. Often, the sale price is based on the original cost plus added improvements to the home. In other cases, sale prices are based on what the owner thinks the property is worth. For most people, their home is their largest investment, and if they plan to sell, it is a good idea to contact a real estate agent or an appraiser for input on the fair market value of a home.

Many factors have to be taken into account when arriving at a property's fair market value. Some of the most important factors are location, size of home, energy efficiency, eye appeal, decorating, age, floor plan, and landscaping, as well as many other minor points. One of the best indicators of the market value of a home is comparable sales, as that is what the buying public is willing to pay. Recent sales of properties that have been sold that are the most similar in size, style, location, and condition are most helpful in establishing a realistic sale price on a home.

No two properties are alike; it is important to review the pros and cons of each property being compared. However, the positives and negatives are really up to the buyer to decide. There are other factors to be considered in setting a sale price on a home. For example, at the time the house is to be listed for sale, is it a seller's or buyer's market? When there is a shortage of homes in a particular category and there are people wanting to buy, this represents a seller's market. Many times, new firms entering or leaving an area will have a direct impact on the market value of homes.

People who are planning to sell their homes should also be aware that at least 90 percent of all buyers will require new financing. Those lending the money to home-buyers will require an appraisal on the property to ensure that the asking price is realistic. In the process of selling a home, the seller wants to get the highest possible dollar for the sale while the buyer wants to purchase at the lowest possible amount. No doubt supply and demand are critical factors in arriving at the sale price of a home.

PREPARING ENVELOPES

In this session, you will be working on preparing envelopes using WordPerfect's automatic envelope addressing feature. All documents are completed in WordPerfect 6.1 alone (Freeform), so there is no automatic checking. Read the instructions for each activity carefully.

Keying Envelopes

There are two popular envelope sizes for letters. The *personal-use* or *small* envelope is approximately 3.5 inches high and 6.5 inches wide. The larger size is approximately 4.25 inches high and 9.5 inches wide; it is known as a *business* or *large* envelope.

At Sign Drill

Key lines 1–4 twice for control. Be sure to press the ***right shift*** key.

1 s2s s2s s2s s2s s2ws sw2s sw2s s@s s@s s2@s sw2@s

2 14 @ $2.50, 16 @ $55.80, 1 @ $17.59, 13 @ $124.66

3 It is better to buy 99 @ 18 rather than 180 @ 10.

4 If you add 1 @ 55 and 1 @ 33 it will cost you 88.

Equals Sign Drill

Key lines 1–4 twice for control.

1 ;=; ;=; ;=; ;=; ;=; ;=; ;=; ;=; =;= =;= =;= =;= ;=

2 a = b c = d e = f g = g j = j k = k l = l ;=; ;=;;

3 A = D C = D J = J K = K L = L A = B C = D E = R =;

4 The = sign is generally used in math problems now.

Plus Sign Drill

Key lines 1–4 twice for control. Remember to press the ***left shift*** key.

1 ;=; ;+; ;+; ;=+; ;+:+:+=; ;=; ;+; ;=; ;+; ;=; :+;

2 The equations were: A = D + F + G and E = E + RT

3 The equations were: A = B + C + E and A = A + BC

4 The computer program stated A = (B + C + C) * AD.

Saving and Printing WordPerfect Reinforcement Activities

To save and print the WordPerfect Reinforcement activities completed in Session 26, do the following.

1. Choose **F**ile → Save **A**s (or F3).
2. At the *Save As* dialog box, key the new filename, **026wpr.kwp**. Press ***Enter*** or click on the OK button. Your document has been saved to disk, and it also remains on the screen.
3. To print 026wpr.kwp, choose **F**ile → **P**rint (or F5).
4. Click on the **P**rint button or press ***Enter***.
5. Close the file (click on **F**ile → **C**lose).

Deleting Files

To continue building good disk management habits, you should now delete the **wpr** document you completed in Session 16. Follow these steps:

1. Choose **F**ile → **O**pen.
2. At the *Open File* dialog box, select the file *016wpr.kwp* by clicking on the filename with the left mouse button.
3. With the filename highlighted, choose File **O**ptions → **D**elete.
4. At the *Delete File* dialog box, click on **D**elete.

ENVELOPES

SESSION GOALS

1-Minute: 40 WAM/2 errors
5-Minute: 30 WAM/2 errors

Using the Envelope feature
Changing line spacing

Planning longer documents

GETTING STARTED

If you are continuing immediately from Session 45, go to the one-minute timings. If you exited the program at the end of Session 45, do the following:

1 Access Windows, then WordPerfect 6.1 for Windows.
2 Click on the KWP icon to access *Keyboarding with WordPerfect*.
3 Go to the Keyboarding Sessions menu and click on Jump to return to your last activity. Or, access the Session 46 menu and click on OK to begin the session.

ONE-MINUTE TIMINGS

Goal: 40 WAM/2 errors

SI: 1.45

- Take two 1-minute timings.
- Take your most recent timing score to set a speed or accuracy goal.

When considering the purchase of any article of clothing, do not let any sales person convince you to take a garment that does not fit well. If you decide to buy something that does not fit, be sure that the store from which you buy the clothing has an excellent alteration department. Make sure that they understand that the clothing must be altered to fit before you make the final arrangements to purchase the item. To be completely assured and satisfied, take a friend along to give you another opinion on how you look.

5 To close the *Open File* dialog box, click on Cancel or press ***Esc***.
6 Click on the KWP Next Activity button.

Now that you have completed the WordPerfect Reinforcement activities, you are to take 1-minute and 3-minute timings. Check your screen for directions.

ONE-MINUTE TIMINGS

Goal: 30 WAM/2 errors

- Take a 1-minute timing on each paragraph.
- Start the paragraph again if you finish before time is up.

1 Symbols are used frequently in computer programming languages. Of course, the plus (+), minus (-), and equals (=) keys are used. The asterisk (*) is used as a multiplication sign, and the diagonal (introduced in the next session) is used for division. It is important that we key symbols just as quickly as we key numbers and letters.

2 Global area networks (GANs) are critical in today's business world. Many U.S. companies are selling their products in overseas markets. It is imperative that communication channels are established with branches, suppliers, and customers wherever they may be. Communication must be instant if a company is to remain competitive.

THREE-MINUTE TIMINGS

Goal: 25 WAM/2 errors

- Take two 3-minute timings on the following paragraph.
- Start the paragraph again if you finish before time is up.

1 There is a new way to lay out a great garden that uses grids of neat 1-foot by 1-foot squares. Then, you plant the seeds and plants with certain spacings. The system is a simple one that allows persons to make the most of a garden space and at the same time conserve water and labor. Talented experts feel that 1-foot by 1-foot garden schemes let you grow the same amount of food as a regular garden does in less than one-fifth of the space.

ENDING THE SESSION

Once you have completed the timings, the KWP program takes you to the next session menu. If you want to print the Session 26 files, however, follow the steps below. Then continue with Session 27 or exit the program.

PRINT

1 Click on Back until you reach the KWP Main Menu.
2 At the Main Menu, select *Freeform* and click on OK.
3 Click on the Print button or choose **F**ile → **P**rint.
4 At the *Print* dialog box, select the **D**ocument on Disk option under *Print Selection*. Press ***Enter*** or click on **P**rint.

CONTINUE

1. Print any files, if necessary.
2. Click on the KWP Next Activity button.
3. At the next session menu, click on OK to proceed with the highlighted item.

EXIT

1. Print any files, if necessary.
2. Click on the KWP Main Menu button.
3. At the Main Menu, select WordPerfect Only, then click on OK.
4. Click on **File** → E**x**it.
5. Exit Windows (**File** → E**x**it), if necessary.

5 At the *Document on Disk* dialog box, click the list button at the right of the filename text box.
6 With the mouse pointer, highlight the file to be printed and press ***Enter*** or click on **P**rint.
7 At the *Document on Disk* dialog box, click on **P**rint.

Repeat steps 3-7 to print additional documents on disk.

CONTINUE

1 Print any files, if necessary.
2 If you are working in Freeform, click on the KWP Main Menu button.
3 Highlight *Keyboarding Sessions*, then click on OK.
4 Click on Jump to go to the next session.

EXIT

1 Print any files, if necessary.
2 Click on the KWP Main Menu button on the Toolbar.
3 At the Main Menu select WordPerfect Only, then click OK.
4 Click on **F**ile → E**x**it.
5 Exit Windows (**F**ile → E**x**it), if necessary.

REINFORCING WRITING SKILLS

Review the letters you completed for Documents A-B. Are there any areas where specific, individualized information would likely catch the eye of a prospective employer? Consider, for example, the information on courses completed and job experiences. Details on the course content and the applicant's particular achievements in those courses could be included on a resume that is sent with the letter. Resumes provide an opportunity to expand on the qualifications noted in the letter of application and to provide concrete examples of how the applicant's skills meet the employer's needs.

In addition to personal data such as name, address, and phone number, a good resume clearly specifies the following information:

- Objectives (short-term and long-term)
- Previous employment (beginning with the most recent job)
- Education (the most recent degree listed first)
- Skills, including academic and athletic

WordPerfect 6.1 for Windows includes three resume templates that include the important information categories in a variety of attractive formats. The templates are available by clicking on the New Document button, then on *resume*, then on either *contemporary, cosmopolitan,* or *traditional*. You are to use the one of your choice as you complete Documents D and E.

Documents D and E — *Letter of Application and Resume*

Using either an actual job advertisement or one you have made up, compose a letter of application and a resume that will attract the attention of the prospective employer and highlight your education, experience, and skills. The letter should be formatted in the block style. For the resume, use one of WordPerfect's resume templates. (You may need to re-enter your personal information.) Be sure to mention in your letter that a resume is enclosed.

When you have finished composing the documents, check them for correct grammar, punctuation, and capitalization. Make sure your sentences are clear and complete. Then complete a spelling check. Save the letter as **045wprd.kwp**. Print, then close the document. Save the resume as **045wpre.kwp**. Print, then close the document.

ENDING THE SESSION

To end this session, delete outdated WordPerfect Reinforcement files, print any files from Session 45 not printed earlier, then continue with the next session or exit the program:

DELETE

1. Choose **F**ile → **O**pen
2. Select the Session 35 wpr file.
3. With the filename(s) highlighted, choose File **O**ptions → **D**elete.
4. At the *Delete File(s)* dialog box, click on **D**elete.
5. If you need to print files, go to step 2 under PRINT. Otherwise, click on Cancel or press ***Esc*** to close the *Open File* dialog box.

PRINT

1. Choose **F**ile → **O**pen.
2. Select the files to be printed, then choose File **O**ptions → **P**rint.
3. At the *Print Files* dialog box, press ***Enter*** or click on **P**rint.
4. Click on Cancel or press ***Esc*** to close the *Open File* dialog box.

DIAGONAL, LESS THAN, GREATER THAN, EXPONENT, BACKSLASH

SESSION GOALS

/, <, >, ^, and \ Keys

Review creating, saving, printing, closing, and exiting

1-Minute: 30 WAM/2 errors
3-Minute: 25 WAM/2 errors

Symbols

GETTING STARTED

If you are continuing immediately from Session 26, go to step 4. If you exited the program at the end of Session 26, do the following:

1. Access Windows, then WordPerfect 6.1 for Windows.
2. Click on the KWP button to access *Keyboarding with WordPerfect.*
3. Go to the Keyboarding Sessions menu and click on Jump to return to the activity you left off with. Or, move through the program menus until you reach the Session 27 menu.
4. On the Session 27 menu, *Warm-Up* is highlighted. Click on OK to proceed with the Warm-Up activities.

If you are already warmed up or have completed a portion of the session, highlight the desired activity and click on OK. When you have completed the on-screen Keyboarding drills and the Thinking Drill, you will return to the text to complete the WordPerfect Reinforcement activities. The final activity is timings (1-minute and 3-minute).

WORDPERFECT REINFORCEMENT

This section provides a review of the proper reaches to the slash/diagonal, less than sign, greater than sign, exponent sign, and the backslash keys. You will create a WordPerfect document as you key the review drills.

Reviewing the Diagonal, Less Than, Greater Than, Exponent Sign and Backslash

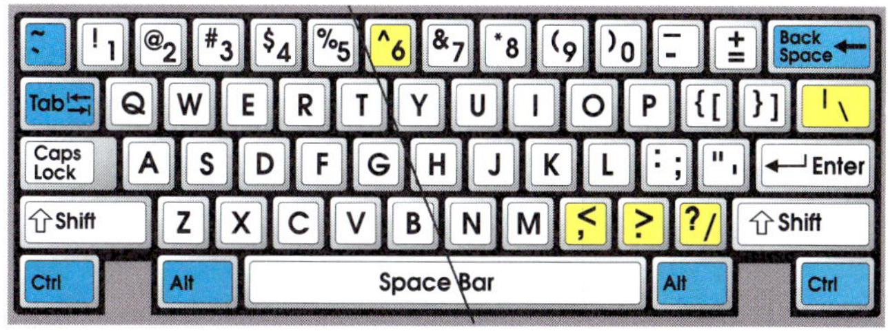

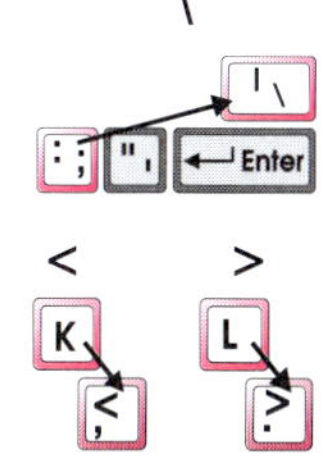

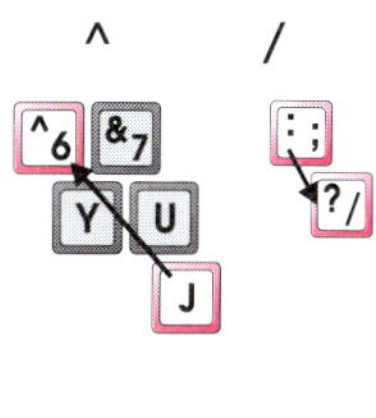

1. During the morning hours, we would present to you and your school administrators an overview of the Microcomputer Applications curriculum and realistic expectations for the students enrolled in your courses. Perhaps we could have lunch together and discuss informally the items that were presented in the morning session.

2. After lunch we would like to meet for one to two hours with your counselors. The emphasis will be on setting up criteria for channeling students into the Office Technology program or into Computer Information Systems.

3. For the remainder of the afternoon, or for however long they can stay, we would like to talk with the Microcomputer Applications instructors. In this portion of the program we would emphasize methodology. We plan to leave on the 9:45 p.m. flight to Chicago so we would be available to talk with the instructors until about 8 p.m. if they would be available.

If you want to change the day's activities around, by all means do so. I know that you may have difficulty getting the administrators together first thing in the morning.

By the way, you might tell Tom that I called Bill Metzger in Milwaukee and suggested some additional texts in the area of telecommunications and the Internet. Some of the best books on the market are available locally. However, with the explosive growth in the information technology area, printed materials become out of date rather quickly.

Also, I have talked with Jim Smola about the new position available on your faculty. With his background at Microsoft and his education credentials, he would make an excellent choice to head up the new technology program. Also, he is interested in moving from industry into the academic arena. He will send you a letter of application and a resume within the next few days. After you have had a chance to look over Jim's application, give me a call if there are any issues or questions I can help clarify.

Sincerely,

Denzel E. Williams
Project Director

xx/045proc.kwp

c Bob Hendrickson

Forward Slash (Diagonal) Drill

The slash is used as a division sign in computer programming languages. It is also used to divide characters such as month, day, and year in the date (i.e., 04/14/97).

Key lines 1–3 twice for control. Remember to use the ***shift*** key.

1 ;/; ;/; ;/; /;/ ;/; ;/; /;/ ;/; /;/ ;/ ;/ ;/;/ ;/

2 a = b/c d = f/g h=j/l t=k/j r = j / k fgh = rty/j

3 The equation: miles/hours will equal speed rate.

Less Than Sign Drill

The < symbol can be keyed with a space before and after it or with no space. Whichever you select, be consistent. Key lines 1–3 twice for control.

1 2<7 3<8 4<9 5<6 8<9 1<2 5<7 6<8 k<l k<l 5<6 1<8<9

2 12 < 43 16 < 58 17 < 89 15 < 28 123 < 456 17 < 77

3 2 < 4, j < k, 1 < m, K < L; S < Z; K < L; JK < LM

Greater Than and Less Than Signs Drill

Follow the same spacing guideline as with the ***less than*** symbol. Key lines 1–3 twice for control.

1 f6f f6f l<l l<l ;<; ;<; 6>f 6>f f>f f>f l>l ;>>;;

2 F>F L>L ;>; 56 > 43 126 > 78 198 > 48 66 > 55 6>>

3 6 > 2 < 6; 6 > 1.2; 78 > 8; 1234 > 678; 56 < 234;

Exponent Sign Drill

Key lines 1–3 twice for control.

1 j6j j6j j6j j^j j^j j^j j^j J^J J^J J^J J^J J^J J^

2 The ^ sign is used to raise an integer to a power.

3 For example, 2^2 is the square of the numeral two.

Backslash Key Drill

Key lines 1–3 twice for control.

1 The \ sign is used to designate a given file path.

2 For example, CD\ will return to the DOS directory.

3 The command, MKDIR\TGRADES, makes a DOS directory.

The experience and skills I could gain working for your company would be a valuable addition to my education. Your organization has a reputation for providing excellent, worthwhile experiences for part-time employees.

I am available for a personal interview at your convenience. Please call me at (714) 555-6832 before 7:30 a.m. or after 3:30 p.m. on weekdays.

Sincerely,

Betty Dawson
12411 Palm Drive
Santa Ana, CA 92650

Document C — *Two-Page Letter with Numbered Text (Review)*

1. At the *Production–Session 45 Document C* screen, turn on the Widow/Orphan feature to prevent an incorrect page break as you key Document C. Press ***Enter*** four times, then enter the date with Insert Date. Press ***Enter*** four times before keying the inside address.
2. Set a tab at 1.75" on the Ruler Bar for the text that follows each number. To indent the numbered items, press ***Tab***, key the number plus period, then press ***F7*** and key the text.
3. Key the second-page heading (name, Page 2, date) and insert a triple-space between the heading and the letter.
4. Proofread and correct any errors, then complete a spelling check with Spell Check.
5. Click on Check to automatically name (**045proc.kwp**), save, and check the document.
6. When checking is complete, the letter is displayed on the screen with errors highlighted.
7. To print with errors highlighted, click on the Print button.
8. To correct errors, click on View Original. Make changes, then recheck the document.
9. Choose **F**ile → **C**lose. This closes Document C and brings up the Document D screen.

Document C

current date

Mrs. Shirley England
Educational Director
Kansas City Occupational Center
2450 Pershing Road
Kansas City, MO 64108

Dear Shirley:

This letter will confirm the agreement we reached in our telephone call earlier this week. Bob Hendrickson and I will spend a day at the Kansas City Occupational Center on Tuesday, August 20. We suggest the following schedule for the day:

Continued on next page

Specialized Punctuation Mark and Symbol Keys

Key each group of five lines once. If you need more practice, choose one or two groups to key again.

1 Two-thirds of the three-fourths are very gifted.
2 John said: *Data Structures* is a great textbook.
3 Jerome's cat ran to Mary's house and said meow!!
4 "Hello," said Jim. "How are you this fine day?"
5 "Help!" yells the old man as the bees followed.

6 If the dress is $35.95, why is the coat $125.75?
7 Take #33 and move it to #66. Move #66 to #1234.
8 Farber & Daughters is the name of my law firm.
9 The check was made out for at least $*******.99.
10 You scored 89% on the exam and 78% on the drill.

11 Now is the time (11:45) for you (Ginny) to move.
12 I make $6 per hour, but I would like to make $9.
13 Sixteen @ $1.23 and 57 @ $23.45 is far too much.
14 If hours = 40 and rate = $5.00 then gross = $200.
15 The equation was A = B + C + F + D + G + H + I + J.

16 Jerry thought that A < B and F < G and JK < JKL.
17 However, Tom knew that A > B and F > G and I I>K.
18 If you raise 2^2 the answer will be squared now.
19 PRINT "THIS IS THE ANSWER: A5$ + TAB(34) + B4S."
20 LET B = A + B + C / D * H * (HH - K) + (HH + JJ)

21 IF TY$ < > "QUACKER" THEN GO TO READ-AGAIN-RTNS.
22 IF GH < AN AND TH > HJ OR TY < TU MOVE TRY TO A.
23 LPRINT TAB(42) "TOTAL" TAB(50) "PER GAME AVER.";
24 PRINT TAB[17] "PLAYER" TAB[34] "FG PERCENT"; FG
25 FIELD 1, 2 AS NUM$, 20 AS NM$, 2 AS D1$, 2 AS Z$

Saving and Printing WordPerfect Reinforcement Activities

To save and print the WordPerfect Reinforcement activities completed in Session 27 do the following.

1. Choose **F**ile → Save **A**s (or F3).
2. At the *Save As* dialog box, key the new filename, **027wpr.kwp**. Press ***Enter*** or click on the OK button.
3. To print 027wpr.kwp, choose **F**ile → **P**rint (or F5).
4. Click on the **P**rint button or press ***Enter***.
5. Close the file (click on **F**ile → **C**lose).

The experience and skills I could attain working for your company would prove most valuable. Your organization has a reputation for providing internship opportunities.

I would like to talk to you in person about the internship program. I can be contacted at (513) 555-9123 before 7:30 a.m. and after 3:30 p.m. on weekdays.

Sincerely,

Michael Lee
9380 Water Street
Cincinnati, OH 45227-8419

Document B ← *Letter of Application*

1 At the *Production–Session 45 Document B* screen, key Document B as a block-style letter. Use the Insert Date feature and vertically center the letter on the page.
2 Proofread and correct any errors. Complete a spell check.
3 Click on Check to automatically name **(045prob.kwp)**, save, and check the letter.
4 When checking is complete, the letter is displayed on the screen with errors highlighted.
5 To print with errors highlighted, click on the Print button.
6 To correct errors, click on View Original. Make changes, then recheck the document.
7 Choose **F**ile → **C**lose. This closes Document B and brings up the Document C screen.

Document B

current date

Mrs. Helen Ryan
California Trust Company
12 Warren Place
Santa Ana, CA 92654-1123

Dear Mrs. Ryan:

Please consider me for any office technology positions you may have available for the summer months of June, July, and August. I am interested in either full-time or part-time employment.

I am presently a full-time student at Santa Ana College where I am completing a degree in administrative management with emphasis in office automation and telecommunications. Previous summer work has given me experience in records management, office management, and the operation of various software packages for personal computers.

Continued on next page

Deleting Files

To continue building good disk management habits, delete the **wpr** document you completed in Session 17. Follow these steps:

1. Choose **F**ile → **O**pen.
2. At the *Open File* dialog box, select the file *017wpr.kwp* by clicking on the filename with the left mouse button.
3. With the filename highlighted, choose File **O**ptions → **D**elete.
4. At the *Delete File* dialog box, click on **D**elete.
5. To close the *Open File* dialog box, click on Cancel or press ***Esc***.
6. Click on the KWP Next Activity button.

Now that you have completed the WordPerfect Reinforcement activities, you are to take 1-minute and 3-minute timings. Check your screen for directions.

ONE-MINUTE TIMINGS

Goal: 30 WAM/2 errors

- Take a 1-minute timing on each paragraph.
- Start the paragraph again if you finish before time is up.

1 Barlow, a shrewd fellow, winked as he waited in the shadows. A whistle warned him of the slow walk of his fellow worker. As he wallowed in the warmth of that workshop, Will worked in the wild, blowing wind. Barlow was worthless.

2 Malaysia is in the process of shifting from an agricultural to an industrial economy. Their government has a plan entitled Vision 2020 that will make them fully industrialized by that year. Many government and business people feel that the ethnic balance of Malay, Chinese, and Indian races must remain intact. Banks are offering low-interest loans for Malay-owned businesses.

3 A lazy bicycle ride in the country is surely a healthy and worthy activity. A sunny sky and a dry day is surely an omen to any type of cyclist. Be wary of cloudy and windy days. A daily remedy for a healthy and spry body is a ride on a cycle. Energy is enjoyed by young and not so young.

THREE-MINUTE TIMINGS

Goal: 25 WAM/2 errors

- Take two 3-minute timings on the following paragraph.
- If you finish before time is up, start the paragraph again.

1 Newer houses seem to cost more and have more space in them. Homes are built with large master bedrooms and have such things as walk-in closets, double sinks, and sitting space. Most homes also have two major rooms: a formal living room and a large family room. Houses that used to sell for reasonable amounts are now priced in the hundreds of thousands of dollars. In parts of the country people pay over $250,000 for a new, average-sized house.

1. **Introduction:** How did you find out about the job opening? Why is the job so interesting to you? What do you know about the company? What can you do for them?
2. **Your qualifications:** What sets you apart from the crowd? Here you can identify educational qualifications, past employment, personal skills, achievements, and/or experiences that make you especially qualified for the job opening. This may require two or three short paragraphs.
3. **Next steps:** What can you do to create a positive reaction to your letter?

Although Documents A and B are letters of application that are keyed for other people, evaluating them in terms of the three parts named above will help you plan how to write your own letter, which is Document D.

Document A — *Letter of Application*

1. At the *Production–Session 45 Document A* screen, key Document A as a block-style letter. Use the Insert Date feature and vertically center the letter on the page.
2. Proofread and correct any errors. Complete a spell check.
3. Click on Check to automatically name **(045proa.kwp)**, save, and check the document.
4. When checking is complete, the letter is displayed on the screen with errors highlighted.
5. To print the letter with errors highlighted, click on the Print button.
6. To correct errors, click on View Original. Make changes, then recheck the document.
7. Choose **File** → **Close**. This closes Document A and brings up the Document B screen.

Document A

current date

Mr. William Haggert
Paragon Laboratories, Inc.
19011 N.E. 36th Way
Redmond, WA 98073-9717

Dear Mr. Haggert:

I recently read your advertisement in the January 20 issue of *The Wall Street Journal*. I was especially interested in the summer internships that your company sponsors. Please consider me as an applicant for one of those internships.

Currently I am a full-time student at the Weber School of Business in Cincinnati. At the end of the current semester, I will have completed two semesters of a four-semester curriculum leading to a certificate in business administration.

My previous work experience has been of a general nature and includes two to three months' (summer-time) work doing the following: swimming pool lifeguard, receptionist for a music store, delivery of newspapers, and helping my father in his small business by waiting on customers.

Continued on next page

ENDING THE SESSION

Once you have completed the timings, the KWP program takes you to the next session menu. If you want to print the Session 27 files, however, follow the steps below. Then continue with Session 28 or exit the program.

PRINT

1. Click on Back until you reach the KWP Main Menu.
2. At the Main Menu, select *Freeform* and click on OK.
3. Click on the Print button or choose **F**ile → **P**rint.
4. At the *Print* dialog box, select the **D**ocument on Disk option under *Print Selection*. Press ***Enter*** or click on **P**rint.
5. At the *Document on Disk* dialog box, click on the list button at the right of the filename text box.
6. With the mouse pointer, highlight the file to be printed and press ***Enter*** or click on **P**rint.
7. At the *Document on Disk* dialog box, click on **P**rint.

Repeat steps 3-7 to print additional documents on disk.

CONTINUE

1. Print any files, if necessary.
2. If you are working in Freeform, click on the KWP Main Menu button.
3. Highlight *Keyboarding Sessions*, then click on OK.
4. Click on Jump to go to the next session.

EXIT

1. Print any files, if necessary.
2. Click on the KWP Main Menu button on the Toolbar.
3. At the Main Menu select WordPerfect Only, then click OK.
4. Click on **F**ile → E**x**it.
5. Exit Windows (**F**ile → E**x**it), if necessary.

FIVE-MINUTE TIMINGS

Goal: 30 WAM/2 errors

SI: 1.48

- Take two 5-minute timings.

From the time we were young, most of us have learned to share. We learned that one result of sharing was gaining new knowledge from some other person. In the world of computers, sharing also takes place as a network. When two computers are linked, the computers are networked.

When computers were first built, they were networked differently. The concept of networking was started with just one computer set up as the sender of information. All the other computers were set up as the receivers of data. The machines that received the data could not send one word to the sender and were known as "dumb" terminals.

Networking today is diverse and unique. Although the concept of a dumb terminal is still in use, the sharing of data has changed. Now, both ends of the network can share; both ends can send and receive data. Users of a network can share files and cut down on the amount of paper used. Networks also let workers who are not in the same place share the same data without ever leaving their cubes. Other hardware in the office, such as printers and scanners, can be used by many persons joined to the network. When office hardware is shared, the result is more money saved.

The concept of a network is not limited to sharing among offices in one building. Many large firms have offices all over the country. It would be impossible to walk down the hall to confer with a fellow worker. Through a worldwide network, large firms can confer with other offices that may be set up in other states or in other countries.

Sharing through computers is done by most large firms in many ways. The phone is the best-known method of sharing with other persons. A message can be sent through e-mail (on the computer). If data is needed, a whole transfer can be done with the tap of a key. Video meetings (with an image of the person on the screen) let the parties see each other as they talk. A lot of people like to use this type of meeting, since it gives them a chance to watch the other person's response and body language.

Networking is an important part of the computer world. New concepts are developed and tried out each day. One day soon, we can look at a watch on our wrist and talk to another person who is thousands of miles away. We can only dream of the exciting future of computing. And, some of us will be part of producing the new things to come.

PREPARING LETTERS OF APPLICATION

A letter of application by itself generally doesn't get you a job. But if the letter is written well, it should get you an interview. The challenge is to prepare a letter and a resume that will make you stand out among all the job applicants. In planning the letter of application, think of it in three parts:

UNIT 5

COMPOSITION

SESSION GOALS

 **1-Minute: 40 WAM/2 errors**
5-Minute: 30 WAM/2 errors

 **Using the Resume template**

 **Writing a letter of application and a resume**

GETTING STARTED

If you are continuing immediately from Session 44, go to the one-minute timings. If you exited the program at the end of Session 44, do the following:

1. Access Windows, then WordPerfect 6.1 for Windows.
2. Click on the KWP icon to access *Keyboarding with WordPerfect.*
3. Go to the Keyboarding Sessions menu and click on Jump to return to your last activity. Or, access the Session 45 menu and click on OK to begin the session.

ONE-MINUTE TIMINGS

Goal: 40 WAM/2 errors

SI: 1.48

- Take two 1-minute timings.
- Use your most recent score to set a speed or accuracy goal.

You can extend the life of your computer by leaving it on during the day. When the switch is turned on, there is a large power surge inside the CPU. You can "save" the switch life by leaving the computer turned on. The temperature inside should stay as even as possible. When you turn the computer off and on many times during the day, the inside temperature will change. This change could cause the joints on the board to become brittle and crack. If you do leave your computer on for a long period of time and you do not have a screen saver, just turn off the monitor.

WORD RESPONSE

SESSION GOALS

Compose and print documents

1-Minute: 35 WAM/2 errors
3-Minute: 30 WAM/2 errors
5-Minute: 25 WAM/2 errors

GETTING STARTED

If you are continuing immediately from Session 27, go to step 4. If you exited the program at the end of Session 27, do the following:

1 Access Windows, then WordPerfect 6.1 for Windows.
2 Click on the KWP button to access *Keyboarding with WordPerfect*.
3 Go to the Keyboarding Sessions menu and click on Jump to return to the activity you left off with. Or, move through the program menus until you reach the Session 28 menu.
4 On the Session 28 menu, *Warm-Up* is highlighted. Click on OK to proceed with the Warm-Up activities.

If you are already warmed up or have completed part of the session, highlight the desired activity and click on OK . When you have completed the on-screen activities for Session 28, you will return to the text to complete the WordPerfect Reinforcement activities. Finally, you will take timings of three different lengths: 1-minute, 3-minute, and 5-minute.

WORDPERFECT REINFORCEMENT

This section provides practice in thinking and composing at the keyboard. Mastering this skill will speed up your preparation of documents.

Composing at the Keyboard

Now that you have learned the keyboard and have further developed your skills, it is time to learn to think and compose at the keyboard so you can use a computer efficiently. The Thinking Drills in previous sessions gave you the opportunity to "think—and key." The next few sessions provide additional practice in composing at the keyboard.

There are four stages in building composition skills:

1 Developing skill at the **word-response** level. (You have already begun working at this level when you keyed the Thinking Drills.)
2 Developing skill at the **phrase-response** level.

ENDING THE SESSION

To end this session, delete outdated WordPerfect Reinforcement files, print any files from Session 44 not printed earlier, then continue with the next session or exit the program:

DELETE

1. Choose **F**ile → **O**pen.
2. Select the Session 34 wpr files.
3. With the filenames highlighted, choose File **O**ptions → **D**elete.
4. At the *Delete File(s)* dialog box, click on **D**elete.
5. If you need to print files, go to step 2 under PRINT. Otherwise, click on Cancel or press ***Esc*** to close the *Open File* dialog box.

PRINT

1. Choose **F**ile → **O**pen.
2. At the *Open File* dialog box, select the files to be printed, then choose File **O**ptions → **P**rint.
3. At the *Print Files* dialog box, press ***Enter*** or click on **P**rint.
4. Click on Cancel or press ***Esc*** to close the *Open File* dialog box.

CONTINUE

1. Print any files, if necessary.
2. Click on the KWP Next Activity button.
3. At the next session menu, click on OK to proceed with the highlighted item.

EXIT

1. Print any files, if necessary.
2. Click on the KWP Main Menu button.
3. At the Main Menu, select WordPerfect Only, then click on OK.
4. Click on **F**ile → **Ex**it.
5. Exit Windows (**F**ile → **Ex**it), if necessary.

3 Developing skill at the **sentence-response** level.
4 Developing skill at the **paragraph**, or "**complete**," level.

Word Response: Yes or No

At your clear WordPerfect window, key answers to the questions that follow. Key the question number, press ***Tab***, then key the letter followed by a period, two spaces, and either **yes** or **no**. Press ***Enter*** and go to the next question. For the second and remaining questions in a group, just press ***Tab***, then key the letter and a period, two spaces, and then the answer. ***Remember:*** Do not hesitate. Key your answer as quickly as possible.

1. a. Do you like the weather today?
   b. Do you like animals?
   c. Are you hungry?
   d. Do you read the newspaper?
   e. Would you like to go into politics?
   f. Do you participate in any sport?
   g. Do you like animals?
   h. Are you hungry?
   i. Do you read the newspaper?
   j. Do you watch television every day?
2. a. Are you tired?
   b. Do you have any brothers?
   c. Do you have any sisters?
   d. Do you have a job?
   e. Are you a "good" speller?
   f. Are you going on vacation soon?
   g. Do you like English?
   h. Do you like coffee?
   i. Would you like to travel overseas?
   j. Do you like to cook?

Word Response: Which One?

Answer the following questions with one of the two choices or with the word **neither.** Follow the same procedure you used in the first drill. Press ***Enter*** after each response. ***Remember:*** Do not hesitate. Key your answer as quickly as possible.

1. a. Would you rather ski or swim?
   b. Would you rather drive or ride?
   c. Would you rather eat or cook?
   d. Would you rather walk or talk?
   e. Would you rather hike or bike?
2. a. Are you a female or a male?

xx/044prob.kwp

Enclosures

c Margaret Lloyd

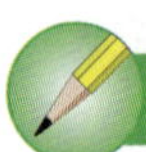

REINFORCING WRITING SKILLS

One of the most common causes of unclear communication is the **misplaced modifier**. Words, phrases and clauses can serve as modifiers. If these modifiers are not placed as closely as possible to the sentence elements they help describe, the meaning of the sentence becomes unclear. The following sentences, for example, are unclear because of the location of the modifiers:

Managing the office last week, the problems piled up for him.

The position of the phrase, managing the office last week, *makes it modify* the problems, *but we know that the writer meant the phrase to describe the person. To correct the problem, rewrite the sentence:* Managing the office last week, he saw the problems pile up. Or: The problems piled up for him when he managed the office last week.

The assistant took his boss to lunch, who was leaving next week.

Who was leaving next week, the assistant or his boss? The sentence construction does not make the writer's meaning clear. To correct the problem, rewrite the sentence so the modifying clause who was leaving next week *is placed as closely as possible to the word it describes:* The assistant, who was leaving next week, took his boss to lunch.

Document C — *FAX Message Edited for Misplaced Modifiers*

The following paragraph is to be faxed to your company's sales representative, Megan Aarmodt, in Plano, Texas, at 709/555-7224. Three of the sentences contain misplaced modifiers that make the meaning unclear. Rewrite the paragraph and key it using WordPerfect's Fax template (click on the New Document button and select *fax* from the list, then select a fax style you like). You may need to re-enter your personal information. Save the completed fax as **044wprc.kwp**. Then print the fax, if requested by your instructor, and close the file.

Megan, we had a meeting last week about some special techniques to use when selling our new software product, *Catalog It!* Here's a brief description of them. We'll send complete information in the next two weeks.

- When giving your presentation, the customer should have a computer to work on.
- Leave plenty of time for questions, which may be difficult in late-afternoon appointments.
- Mention the names of some users of our company's products that are well known.

Watch your mail for samples of a dazzling new brochure that you can send to your best customers.

b. Are you right- or left-handed?
c. Is the instructor of this class male or female?
d. Would you rather drink milk or tea?
e. Would you rather dance or read?

3. a. Would you rather dance or sing?
b. Would you rather eat hot dogs or hamburgers?
c. Would you rather write or read?
d. Would you rather study or play?
e. Would you rather own a dog or a cat?

4. a. Do you like summer or winter best?
b. Would you rather be short or tall?
c. Would you rather be dirty or clean?
d. Would you rather win or lose?
e. Would you rather run or walk?

Word Response: Opposites

Read a word and then key the word's opposite, using the same procedure you followed in the previous drills. If you cannot think of an opposite, key the word shown. Press ***Enter*** after each response. ***Remember:*** Do not hesitate. Key your answer as quickly as possible.

1. a. day
b. salt
c. mother
d. uncle
e. grandmother
f. rich
g. war
h. young
i. love
j. hot

2. a. clean
b. male
c. minus
d. seldom
e. floor
f. stop
g. no
h. winter
i. sick
j. true

Save your document as **028wpr.kwp**. Print and close the file, then click on the KWP Next Activity button to bring up the Timings screen.

6 When checking is complete, the letter is displayed on the screen with errors highlighted.
7 To print with errors highlighted, click on the Print button.
8 To correct errors, click on View Original. Make changes, then recheck the document.
9 Choose **F**ile → **C**lose. This closes Document B and brings up a clear WordPerfect editing window where you will complete Document C.

Document B

CU CONSULTANTS UNLIMITED
806 BOYCE STREET, SALT LAKE CITY, UTAH 84106-9217 801/555-4151

current date

Mr. Timothy Palmer
Wagoner Consultants Corporation
2091 Front Avenue
Rochester, MN 55904-8493

CONTRACT FOR MS. MARGARET LLOYD

Enclosed is a contract for the person listed above. Please sign all four copies of the contract and return them addressed to my attention. We will mail you one copy of the fully executed contract for your records.

Also enclosed is the Requisition for Advertising Materials. The following information must be completed on the form:

- Title of project
- Estimate total cost
- Project completion date

Please fill in the information requested and return the form with the contracts.

We appreciate your prompt attention to these matters and urge you to write or telephone if we may be of any further assistance.

Sincerely yours,

Paul Garcia
Advertising Director

Continued on next page

Syllabic Intensity

Beginning with this session, the **syllabic intensity** (the average number of syllables per word) is listed for all 1-, 3-, and 5-minute timings. Syllabic intensity (SI) is an approximate indication of how difficult material is to key. The lower the S.I., the easier the material is to key; the higher the S.I., the more difficult the material since the words are longer.

When you take timings, your goal is to improve either your speed **or** your accuracy. You must concentrate on one or the other. Your goal will probably change daily—or even during a particular class period. Note that with this session, the speed goals for the 1- and 3-minute timings have been raised by 5 WAM.

ONE-MINUTE TIMINGS

Goal: 35 WAM/2 errors

SI: 1.27

- Take two 1-minute timings on the following material.
- If you finish before time is up, start the paragraph over.

1 Long ago, pilgrims loved to indulge in blunt folklore. Tales, sometimes false, were told with glee daily. One old tale included a blazing clash of sailors in balky sailboats on a bottomless lake. The last sailor alive was a lad that was blind. As he lay clinging to a slim balsa log in filth and slimy silt, the leader's falcon led help to him. Balmy days followed as the lad's leg healed slowly and the salves applied to his eyes let the light in.

THREE-MINUTE TIMINGS

Goal: 30 WAM/2 errors

SI: 1.33

- Take two 3-minute timings on the following paragraph.
- If you finish before time is up, start the paragraph again.

1 To change a U.S. unit of measure to a metric unit of measure takes practice and knowledge. To change back and forth, a table of metric measures and U.S. units of measures is great to have. For instance, 1 mile is equal to a metric measurement of 1.6 kilometers. One yard is about the same as a metric measure of 0.9 meters. One can change a larger metric unit to a smaller one by moving the decimal point one place to the right.

FIVE-MINUTE TIMING

Goal: 25 WAM/2 errors

SI: 1.29

- Take a 5-minute timing on the following paragraph.
- If you finish before time is up, go back to the beginning and continue keying.

Dear Administrator:

We have received from the transfer agent the 150-share certificate of Essex Industries common stock that was donated to your institution by Mr. and Mrs. Verdell R. Jackson of Tampa, Florida.

You have indicated that you would like to sell some of the shares. We will be in a position to proceed with the sale as soon as we receive the following:

1. A resolution stipulating who is authorized to act in such matters for your institution.

2. A stock power signed by the authorized person.

3. A statement of the number of shares you would like to sell.

Please send the materials in the enclosed return envelope.

Yours truly,

Cherlyn Ho
Senior Partner

xx/044proa.kwp

Enc

Document B — *Simplified-Style Letter with a Subject Line*

1 At the *Production–Session 44 Document B* screen, change the left and right margins to 1.25 inches, then key Document B in the simplified style. (See Session 39 or the User's Guide to review this letter style.) Use the Insert Date feature to insert the current date. Triple-space before and after the subject line. (Do not key the letterhead.)

2 For the itemized list, use WordPerfect's Bullet feature with an indent of 0.25 inches between the bullets and the text. With the margins at 1.25 inches, the new tab for the indent between the bullets and text will be set at 1.5 inches. (The new tab setting also affects the copy notation.) Follow these steps to set the tab and insert the bullets:

   a Choose **V**iew → **R**uler Bar or press ***Alt + Shift + F3*** to display the Ruler Bar.

   b Position the arrow pointer just below the 1.5 inches mark, then click the left mouse button.

   c Click on the Insert Bullet button on the Toolbar. With the bullet displayed on the screen, the insertion point should be at Position 1.5" (check the Status Bar).

   d Follow steps a-c to insert the remaining bulleted items. Then double-space to the next paragraph.

3 After keying the letter, vertically center the letter on the page.

4 Proofread and correct any errors. Complete a spell check.

5 Choose **F**ile → Save **A**s to automatically name **(044prob.kwp)** and save the document. The program checks the letter for errors and calculates your WAM rate.

1 The most important piece of furniture in an office is the chair. Workers will spend most of their day doing their work while seated. If people are uncomfortable, they will not be as productive as they could be with the right chair. It has been stated that a person's productivity will increase 15 to 20 percent when using a chair that fits his or her body.

There are several features to look for in selecting a chair to be used in an office setting. First, make sure it has a five-star base so that it won't tip over. Next, make sure that the seat adjusts upward and downward to fit the person using it. The back rest must be adjustable up and down so that it supports the worker's back. The front of the chair must have a "water fall," or downward-curved cushion, so that there is no pressure behind the knees while the worker is seated.

Any adjustments to be made to chair height, back support, or tilt must be easy to do. There are chairs on the market that adjust as the person sits down; no manual adjustments need to be made. Another important part of a chair is the covering. Some coverings are warm (they don't breathe). Chairs can be purchased with arms that drop so that the chair can be moved closer to the desk.

ENDING THE SESSION

Once you have completed the timings, the KWP program takes you to the next session menu. If you want to print the Session 28 files, however, follow the steps below. Then continue with Session 29 or exit the program.

PRINT

1. Click on Back until you reach the KWP Main Menu.
2. At the Main Menu, select *Freeform* and click on OK.
3. Click on the Print button or choose **F**ile → **P**rint.
4. At the *Print* dialog box, select the **D**ocument on Disk option under *Print Selection*. Press ***Enter*** or click on **P**rint.
5. At the *Document on Disk* dialog box, click on the list button at the right of the filename text box.
6. With the mouse pointer, highlight the file to be printed and press ***Enter*** or click on **P**rint.
7. At the *Document on Disk* dialog box, click on **P**rint.

Repeat steps 3-7 to print additional documents on disk.

CONTINUE

1. Print any files, if necessary.
2. If you are working in Freeform, click on the KWP Main Menu button.
3. Highlight *Keyboarding Sessions*, then click on OK.
4. Click on Jump to go to the next session.

EXIT

1. Print any files, if necessary.
2. Click on the KWP Main Menu button on the Toolbar.
3. At the Main Menu, select WordPerfect Only, then click on OK.
4. Click on **F**ile → E**x**it.
5. Exit Windows, if necessary (**F**ile → E**x**it).

The Position option from the *Tab Set* dialog box is used to identify the specific measurement where the tab is to be set. To set a tab, choose **P**osition, key the desired measurement, then choose **S**et. The measurement that you key is a relative measurement. For example, if you set a tab at 3 inches, the tab will appear at the 4-inch mark on the Ruler Bar (if the left margin is at the default setting of 1 inch). In Reveal Codes, the tab would display as **Tab Set: (Rel)+3"L**.

Tab codes take effect from the location of the code to the end of the document or until another tab set code is encountered.

Returning to Default Tabs

If you make changes to the tab settings, then want to return to the default tabs, use the **D**efault option from the *Tab Set* dialog box. This option returns the tabs to the default of a tab set every 0.5 inches.

Document A — *Letter with Attention Line and Numbered Text*

1. At the *Production–Session 44 Document A* screen, change the left and right margins to 1.25 inches. Then key Document A as a block-style letter. Use the Insert Date feature. (Do not key the letterhead.)
2. Before keying the numbered list of items, set a new Left tab at 0.25 inches from the left margin by completing the following steps:
   a. Choose Fo**r**mat → **L**ine → **T**ab Set.
   b. Choose **P**osition, key **0.25**, then click on Set.
   c. Click on OK to return to the document.
3. After keying the numbered list, return the tab settings to the default tabs by clicking on Default at the *Tab Set* dialog box.
4. Finish keying the letter, then vertically center the letter on the page.
5. Proofread and correct any errors. Complete a spell check.
6. Choose **F**ile → Save **A**s to automatically name **(044proa.kwp)** and save the document. The program checks the letter for errors and calculates your WAM rate.
7. When checking is complete, the letter is displayed on the screen with errors highlighted.
8. To print with errors highlighted, click on the Print button.
9. To correct errors, click on View Original. Make changes, then recheck the document.
10. Choose **F**ile → **C**lose. This closes Document A and brings up the Document B screen.

Document A

Waedt-Steiner Investment Services
10 Kearney Drive • Kearney, NE 68847-2817 • (402) 555-6314

current date

Attention: Dean of the Law School
The William Brown School of Law
3209 Virginia Avenue
Orlando, FL 32804-4811

Continued on next page

SESSION 29

SESSION GOALS

Compose and print documents

1-Minute: 35 WAM/2 errors
3-Minute: 30 WAM/2 errors
5-Minute: 25 WAM/2 errors

GETTING STARTED

If you are continuing immediately from Session 28, go to step 4. If you exited the program at the end of Session 28, do the following:

1. Access Windows, then WordPerfect 6.1 for Windows.
2. Click on the KWP button to access *Keyboarding with WordPerfect.*
3. Go to the Keyboarding Sessions menu and click on Jump to return to your last activity. Or, move through the program menus until you reach the Session 29 menu.
4. On the Session 29 menu, *Warm-Up* is highlighted. Click on OK to proceed with the Warm-Up activities.

If you are already warmed up or have completed a portion of the session, highlight the desired activity and click on OK. When you have completed the on-screen activities for Session 29, you will return to the text to complete the WordPerfect Reinforcement activities. Timings of three lengths are the final activities in the session.

WORDPERFECT REINFORCEMENT

In this section you will continue learning to think and compose at the keyboard. You will practice keying whole phrases in response to questions offered in the following drills.

Composing Phrases

Now that you have completed the word-response level, you can move on to the phrase-response level. At a clear WordPerfect screen, read the questions and then answer them by keying the question number; then press ***Tab,*** key the letter, a period, two spaces, then the answer. Press ***Enter*** and go to the next question. For the second and remaining questions in a group, just press ***Tab***, then key the letter, a period, two spaces, and the answer. Do not make complete sentences—just answer the question. If you do not know the correct answer, invent one. ***Remember:*** Do not hesitate. Key your answer as quickly as possible.

Manipulating Tabs with the Tab Set Dialog Box

The Tab Set dialog box shown in figure 44.6 can be used to complete such tasks as clearing tabs and setting a variety of tabs at precise measurements. There are several methods that can be used to display the *Tab Set* dialog box including:

- Choose Format → **Line** → **T**ab Set.
- Position the arrow pointer anywhere on the Ruler Bar, click the *right* mouse button, then click on **T**ab Set.
- Double-click on a tab icon on the Ruler Bar.
- Double-click on any tab code in Reveal Codes.

If the display of the Ruler Bar is on, the Ruler Bar can be seen above the Tab Set dialog box. This is helpful when determining tab settings.

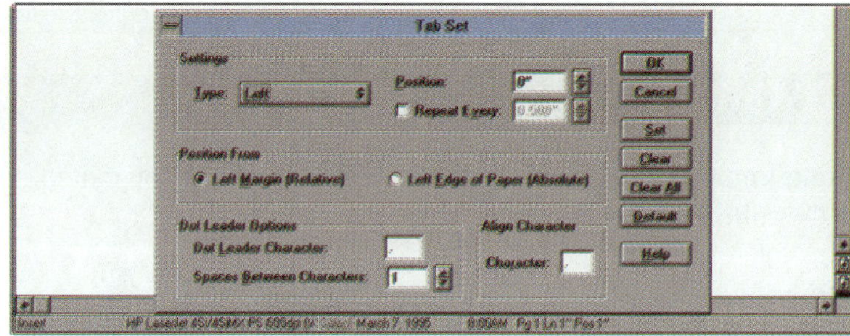

Figure 44.6 Tab Set Dialog Box

Clearing Tabs

At the *Tab Set* dialog box, you can clear an individual tab or all tabs. To clear all tabs from the Ruler Bar, choose Clear **A**ll. To do this with the mouse, click on the Clear **A**ll button in the dialog box. If you are using the keyboard, press ***Alt + A***.

To clear an individual tab, display the *Tab Set* dialog box, choose **P**osition, then key the measurement of the tab to be cleared. If you are using the mouse, you can click on the up-pointing triangle after **P**osition until the desired measurement displays in the ***P**osition* text box. Or, you can select the current measurement in the ***P**osition* text box, then key the desired measurement. With the desired measurement displayed, choose **C**lear.

Tabs in the *Tab Set* dialog box are, by default, *relative tabs*. Relative tabs are measured from the left margin. The Ruler Bar displays *absolute tabs*, which are measured from the left edge of the page.

With tabs that are measured from the left margin, the left margin is 0 inches. Positions to the right of the left margin are positive numbers and positions to the left of the left margin are negative numbers. The distance between tab settings and the left margin remains the same regardless of what changes are made to the document.

With tabs that are measured from the left edge of the page, the left edge of the page is 0 inches. These tabs remain at the fixed measurement regardless of what changes are made to the document.

Setting Tabs

All the tab types available with the Tab drop-down menu are available by choosing **T**ype from the *Tab Set* dialog box. Position the arrow pointer in the *Type* text box, then hold down the left mouse button. If you are using the keyboard, press ***Alt + T***, then press the ***space bar***. With the Type drop-down menu displayed, choose the desired type of tab.

Short Phrases

1. a. What is the name of a town and state/province that you would like to visit?
   b. What is your instructor's first and last name?
   c. What is the president's/prime minister's last name?
   d. What is the name of this book?
   e. What is the name of this course?
2. a. What is your first and last name?
   b. What is your friend's first and last name?
   c. What is the title of your favorite song?
   d. What is the name of the last movie you saw?
   e. What is the name of the last television show you saw?
3. a. Where were you born?
   b. Where did you attend elementary school?
   c. Where did you go on your last vacation?
   d. Where are you going after class today?
   e. Where will you be tomorrow at this time?
4. a. What are your favorite sports?
   b. What are your favorite colors?
   c. What will you be doing five years from now?
   d. What is the name of your favorite class?
   e. What is the name of your best friend?

Longer Phrases

Think of a phrase that completes each sentence. Then key the sentence. Press ***Enter*** after each response.

Because the clock was wrong, I ____________ .
Because the road was icy, I ____________ .
Because the team won, I ____________ .
Because I was late, I ____________ .
Because I can/cannot drive, I ____________ . (Choose either *can* or *cannot*.)

If I pass this test, I ____________ .
If I finish early, I ____________ .
If I get the job, I ____________ .
If the price is right, I ____________ .
If the beach is crowded, I ____________ .

I do/do not like loud music because ____________ .
I do/do not study at the library because ____________ .
I do/do not obey the speed limit because ____________ .
I do/do not like math because ____________ .

The columns displayed in figure 44.4 show text aligned at different tabs. The text in the first column was keyed at a center tab. The second column of text was keyed at a right tab, and the third column was keyed at a decimal tab.

British Columbia	Victoria	34.56
Saskatchewan	Regina	2,314.08
Alberta	Edmonton	368.92

Figure 44.4 Types of Tabs

The four types of tabs can also be set with dot leaders. Leaders are useful in a table of contents or other material where you want to direct the reader's eyes across the page. Figure 44.5 shows an example of leaders. The text in the first column was keyed at a left tab. The text in the second column was keyed at a right tab with dot leaders.

British Columbia . . . . .Victoria
Alberta . . . . .Edmonton
Saskatchewan . . . . .Regina
Manitoba . . . . .Winnipeg
Ontario . . . . .Toronto
Quebec . . . . .Montreal

Figure 44.5 Leader Tabs

Clearing Tabs

Before setting tabs you will probably want to clear the default tabs. You can clear an individual tab, all tabs, or selected tabs. To clear one tab from the Ruler Bar, position the tip of the arrow pointer on the tab icon to be cleared, then hold down the left mouse button. (If the arrow pointer is in the proper position, a vertical dashed line will appear on the screen. This vertical dashed line is called the *ruler guide*.) Drag the tab icon down into the editing window, then release the mouse button.

To clear all tabs from the Ruler Bar, position the tip of the arrow pointer on a tab icon on the Ruler Bar, hold down the *right* mouse button, drag the arrow pointer to Clear **A**ll Tabs, then release the mouse button.

To clear selected tabs, position the tip of the arrow pointer on the Ruler Bar in the gray area below the numbers and to the left of the first tab to be included. Hold down the Shift key on the keyboard, then hold down the left mouse button. Drag the arrow pointer to the right until all tabs to be cleared are selected, then release the mouse button and the Shift key. Point on the selected group of Tab icons and drag them down into the editing window, then release the left mouse button.

Setting Tabs

To set a left tab on the Ruler Bar, position the arrow pointer at the position on the Ruler Bar where you want the tab set, then click the left mouse button.

To set a tab other than a left tab, you must change the type of tab. To do this, position the tip of the arrow pointer on a tab icon, hold down the *right* mouse button, drag the arrow pointer to the desired tab type, then release the mouse button. After changing the tab type, set the tab on the Ruler Bar in the normal manner.

If you change the type of tab at the Tab drop-down menu, the type stays changed until you change it again or you exit WordPerfect.

I do/do not play sports because ____________ .

A hammer is used to ____________ .

A lawn mower is used to ____________ .

Scissors are used to ____________ .

A pencil is used to ____________ .

An eraser is used to ____________ .

Sentences

Read a question and then answer it by keying a complete sentence. The first one is done as a sample. ***Remember:*** Do not hesitate. Key your answer as quickly as possible. Press ***Enter*** after each response.

What does a police officer do? A police officer enforces the laws.

What does a plumber do?

What does a firefighter do?

What does a lawyer do?

What does a teacher do?

What does an auto mechanic do?

What does a medical doctor do?

What does a dentist do?

What does an accountant do?

What does a chef do?

Save your document as **029wpr.kwp**. Print and close the file, then click on the KWP Next Activity button to bring up the Timings screen.

ONE-MINUTE TIMINGS

Goal: 35 WAM/2 errors

SI: 1.27

- Take two 1-minute timings on the following material.
- If you finish the paragraph before time is up, start over.

1 The news on the network newscast might spawn a winning wealth of followers. If the newscaster can draw a wider range of viewers, the rewards are power and wealth. Watchers and followers of a witty newscaster are won when the daily news is written well. It is not a waste to rewrite the worst of interviews when witless words can wreck a well planned show or review. They who dawdle in the newsroom will not work or write very long. Their reward will be awful reviews.

Manipulating Tabs

In previous sessions you created letters that contained lists of numbered items. You used WordPerfect's default tab settings, which are set every one-half inch. Some companies might consider the one-half inch space between a number (and the period) and the text that follows too wide. Professional graphic designers would agree. To create a visually pleasing document, they would probably recommend a space of .25 inches between a number and the text that follows. In this session you will learn how to change tab settings.

WordPerfect offers two methods for clearing and setting tabs. Tabs can be cleared and set at the Ruler Bar or at the *Tab Set* dialog box.

Manipulating Tabs with the Ruler Bar

The Ruler Bar can be used, together with the mouse, to clear, set, and move tabs. To display the Ruler Bar shown in figure 44.1, choose **V**iew → **R**uler Bar; or press ***Alt + Shift + F3***.

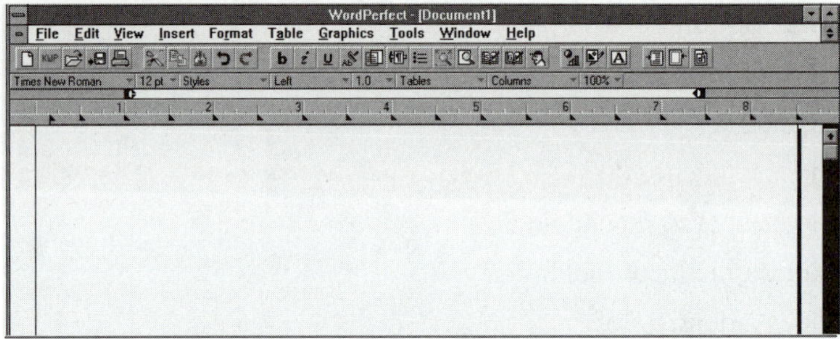

Figure 44.1 Ruler Bar

The Ruler Bar contains left tabs every 0.5 inches. This is indicated by the left triangles below the numbers. At this setting, text aligns at the left edge of the tab as shown in figure 44.2.

Robert Freitas
Bethany Mortensen
Laura Culver
Marina Pasquale

Figure 44.2 Left-Align Tab

The other types of tabs that can be set are Center, Right, and Decimal. You can also set Left, Center, Right, and Decimal tabs with dot leaders (periods). To display the types of tabs available, position the insertion point on any tab icon on the Ruler Bar, then hold down the *right* mouse button. This causes a drop-down menu to display as shown in figure 44.3.

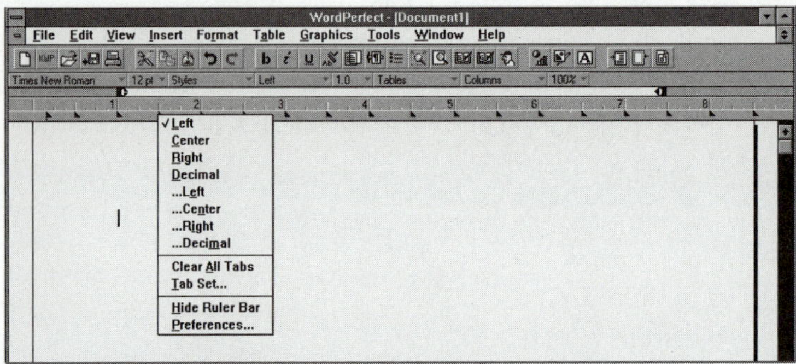

Figure 44.3 Tab Drop-Down Menu

THREE-MINUTE TIMINGS

Goal: 30 WAM/2 errors

SI: 1.33

- Take two 3-minute timings on the following paragraph.
- Remember to start again if you finish keying the paragraph before time is up.

1 Taking photos with a good camera can be fun. Most photo equipment has some method of setting a variety of focal lengths. A focal length setting of 35mm gives a wider picture angle, and it can be used for group portraits or photos of landscapes. A focal length setting of 70mm has a narrow angle for making a portrait or taking a good photo of a good scene or object that is far away. Using the zoom lens requires some practice before a picture can be a work of art.

FIVE-MINUTE TIMINGS

Goal: 25 WAM/2 errors

SI: 1.29

- Take a 5-minute timing on the following paragraphs.
- If you finish before time is up, start over.

1 Education has become a lifelong process. No longer can we say that a person's formal schooling will last for a lifetime. Business spends almost as much for training programs as is spent for our public school system. The average age of students in schools offering programs above the high school level is on the rise.

Adult learners enter school programs with needs and wants that differ from the requirements of traditional students. They are goal-oriented. They are looking for skills and knowledge that will help them keep a job, prepare for a new job, or advance to a higher-level job. Adults don't want to waste time in reaching new skills; they want to spend their time on those things that relate to their goals.

Teachers and trainers of adult learners are faced with a tough task. In most cases, they must narrow the focus of their programs to meet the needs of the learners. Courses must be designed that draw upon the learners' skills and knowledge. To design a good program, you must assess what the learners know and what their goals are.

The next step in the process is to design a performance outcome that shows that the person can demonstrate a mastery of what was presented in the course. Once the outcome has been set, the instructor can choose teaching methods, course length, texts needed, and program content. Problem-solving, learn by doing, and case studies are methods of teaching that help adult students.

FIVE-MINUTE TIMINGS

Goal: 30 WAM/2 errors

SI: 1.45

- Take two 5-minute timings.
- On the second attempt, try to increase your speed while maintaining your accuracy.

As a direct result of the strides being made in telecommunications, the new systems that we have are hard to believe. The number of systems adds to the task we have of knowing how these systems function. It is next to impossible for one person to know about all the systems now being used in transmitting voice, data, and video, much less all of the products and services being developed

One way to help understand telecom systems in use today is to study technical concepts used in sending and receiving all forms of information. While the number of systems is huge, the number of concepts is small by comparison. If one knows the basic concepts used in systems, then that person need not study in detail each device or system by itself. He or she can apply the concepts that relate to the system being reviewed to grasp how and why it works the way it does. This applies not only to current systems but to new ones being released each day.

The concepts of telecom can be divided into six parts. They are encoding, transmitting, receiving, storing, retrieving, and decoding. A person who wants to know how and why a system works can start by dividing the process into each of the six parts noted. This will make it easier to learn and compare since the parts will not be as complex as the whole.

One of the concepts used in telecom systems relates to transmitting. This is the part that moves the data from one point to another point. Often, a signal is sent right after the encoding step is done. This step takes many forms that we use daily, such as the wire that connects our phone to a local telephone office. Other means include radio waves that go between antennas that are found in many places such as towers, cars, homes, and buildings. Satellite networks and fiber optic networks provide another means to send data between and among two or more points.

Whatever system is used, it must move data from its origin to its destination as fast and efficiently as possible. Transmitting is done by putting the data in or through space or by sending it through a copper wire or optical fiber. By being able to break a system into parts, we can digest the concepts for each part.

CREATING LETTERS WITH ATTENTION/SUBJECT LINES

Attention lines are used to direct a letter to an individual and/or to the company as a whole. The attention line is keyed as the first line of the inside address.

In a block-style letter, the subject line follows the salutation. The subject line replaces the salutation in a letter formatted in the simplified style. In either case, this line appears in all capital letters. Watch for the attention and subject lines as you key Documents A-C.

ENDING THE SESSION

Once you have completed the timings, the KWP program takes you to the next session menu. If you want to print the Session 29 files, however, follow the steps below. Then continue with Session 30 or exit the program.

PRINT

1. Click on Back until you reach the KWP Main Menu.
2. At the Main Menu, select *Freeform* and click on OK.
3. Click on the Print button or choose **F**ile → **P**rint.
4. At the *Print* dialog box, select the **D**ocument on Disk option under *Print Selection*. Press ***Enter*** or click on **P**rint.
5. At the *Document on Disk* dialog box, click on the list button at the right of the filename text box.
6. With the mouse pointer, highlight the file to be printed and press ***Enter*** or click on **P**rint.
7. At the *Document on Disk* dialog box, click on **P**rint.

Repeat steps 3-7 to print additional documents on disk.

CONTINUE

1. Print any files, if necessary.
2. If you are working in Freeform, click on the KWP Main Menu button.
3. Highlight *Keyboarding Sessions*, then click on OK.
4. Click on Jump to go to the next session.

EXIT

1. Print any files, if necessary.
2. Click on the KWP Main Menu button on the Toolbar.
3. At the Main Menu, select WordPerfect Only, then click on OK.
4. Click on **F**ile → E**x**it.
5. Exit Windows, if necessary (**F**ile → E**x**it).

SESSION GOALS

1-Minute: 40 WAM/2 errors
5-Minute: 30 WAM/2 errors

Setting tabs
Using the Fax template

Correcting misplaced modifiers

GETTING STARTED

If you are continuing immediately from Session 43, go to the one-minute timings. If you exited the program at the end of Session 43, do the following:

1. Access Windows, then WordPerfect 6.1 for Windows.
2. Click on the KWP icon to access *Keyboarding with WordPerfect*.
3. Go to the Keyboarding Sessions menu and click on Jump to return to your last activity. Or, access the Session 44 menu and click on OK to begin the session.

If your fingers are already warmed up or if you have completed part of the session, highlight the desired activity and click on OK. When you have completed the on-screen activities for Session 44, you will return to the text to complete several business letters in which you will set tabs and use attention and subject lines.

ONE-MINUTE TIMINGS

Goal: 40 WAM/2 errors

SI: 1.45

- Take two 1-minute timings.
- Focus on speed or accuracy, depending on your most recent 1-minute timing score.

You are a consumer. Without you and millions of other consumers in the nation, businesses would have to close. There would be nobody to buy those goods and services that businesses produce. The impact of ceasing all operations would quickly affect every person. Workers would have no jobs and would have no money to continue living. There would be no hustle and bustle of daily life. Every family would have to supply all the necessities in life for themselves. Each family or group would have to grow food, produce clothing, and provide shelter.

SENTENCE/PARAGRAPH RESPONSE
USING SPELL CHECKER AND DOCUMENT TEMPLATES

SESSION GOALS

Compose and create documents
Use Spell Checker and the memo and letter templates

1-Minute: 35 WAM/2 errors
3-Minute: 30 WAM/2 errors
5-Minute: 25 WAM/2 errors

GETTING STARTED

If you are continuing immediately from Session 29, go to step 4. If you exited the program at the end of Session 29, do the following:

1. Access Windows, then WordPerfect 6.1 for Windows.
2. Click on the KWP button to access *Keyboarding with WordPerfect*.
3. Go to the *Keyboarding Sessions* menu and click on Jump to return to your last activity. Or, move through the program menus until you reach the Session 30 menu.
4. On the Session 30 menu, *Warm-Up* is highlighted. Click on OK to proceed with the Warm-Up activities.

If you are already warmed up or have completed a portion of the session, highlight the desired activity and click on OK. When you have completed the on-screen activities for Session 30, you will return to the text to complete the WordPerfect Reinforcement activities. Timings are the last activity in the session.

WORDPERFECT REINFORCEMENT

This section offers more composition activities that include a review of correct word use. In addition, you will learn to use Spell Check and the WordPerfect memo and letter templates.

Choosing the Right Word

One of the most common problems a writer faces is choosing the correct word to convey a certain thought or idea to the reader. Writing must be precise; vague words or the misuse of words may change the author's meaning. Review the *Guidelines for Correct Word Use* that follow. Keep them in mind as you key responses in the composing drills.

General Guidelines for Correct Word Use

1. **Use concrete nouns and descriptive adjectives, adverbs, and phrases; do not use vague or abstract words.** Vague words can mean many different things. Words such as

ENDING THE SESSION

To end this session, print any files from Session 43 not printed earlier, then continue with the next session or exit the program:

PRINT

1. Choose **F**ile → **O**pen.
2. At the *Open File* dialog box, select the files to be printed, then choose File **O**ptions → **P**rint.
3. At the *Print Files* dialog box, press ***Enter*** or click on **P**rint.
4. Click on Cancel or press ***Esc*** to close the *Open File* dialog box.

CONTINUE

1. Print any files, if necessary.
2. Click on the KWP Next Activity button.
3. At the next session menu, click on OK to proceed with the highlighted item.

EXIT

1. Print any files, if necessary.
2. Click on the KWP Main Menu button.
3. At the Main Menu, select WordPerfect Only, then click on OK.
4. Click on **F**ile → E**x**it.
5. Exit Windows (**F**ile → E**x**it), if necessary.

nice, good, bad, thing, and **work** do not give the reader much information. Read each of the following and notice the differences.

Examples:

Vague: The lecture was good, and I learned a lot.

Better: The lecture solved two problems for me. I learned how to balance a checkbook and how to calculate interest.

Vague: a nice color

Better: an emerald green, a vivid scarlet, a dull black

Vague: he said

Better: he shouted defiantly, he muttered, he demanded

2 **Use English idioms correctly.** An idiom is an expression peculiar to a culture and is perfectly acceptable if used correctly.

Examples:

Correct	*Incorrect*	*Correct*	*Incorrect*
acquitted of	acquitted from	in search of	in search for
aim to prove	aim at proving	kind of (+ noun)	kind of a (+ noun)
can't help feeling	can't help but feel	aloud	out loud
comply with	comply to	try to	try and
independent of	independent from	different from	different than

3 **Use the correct word;** the words shown below are often misused.

Examples:

accept *to take or receive*

except *to leave out; aside from*

advice *an opinion*

advise *to recommend*

biannual *twice a year*

biennial *once every two years*

council *a governing body*

counsel *to give advice*

fewer *(use with nouns that can be counted: fewer apples)*

less *(use with nouns that cannot be counted: less noise)*

good *modifies a noun or pronoun*

well *modifies a verb or adverb*

angry at *(things and animals)*

angry with *(people)*

angry about *(occasions or situations)*

In the last session, you practiced composing at the phrase-response and sentence-response level. Now you can move on to the sentence and paragraph level. Read the instructions for each drill; then think of the responses as fast as possible. ***Remember:*** React quickly.

Sentence Response

Drawing from your experience and observations, think of descriptive words or phrases to make the following 20 sentences more interesting. Then key the sentence number, a period, and press ***F7*** (Indent) before keying your revised sentence. After you have keyed all 20 sentences, correct any errors you made. If your sentence goes beyond the right margin, let word wrap work for you. Because you pressed ***F7*** before keying your revised sentence, each sentence will be correctly indented. At the end of each sentence, press ***Enter*** and continue with the next sentence.

1 The last book I read was good.
2 Today is a nice day.
3 My favorite sport is fun.
4 My favorite color is a nice color.
5 My best friend is nice.

REINFORCING WRITING SKILLS

There are a number of words in the English language that have a negative effect on readers. Words such as *hate*, *argue*, *wrong*, *poor*, and *problem* are examples of words that tend to produce an undesirable reaction. Think about how you would react to the following statement in a proposal for automating operations in your organization:

Our project team uncovered numerous problems in the day-to-day operations of your organization . . .

The terms *uncovered* and *problems* immediately convey a negative perception that may cast all the information that follows in a poor light. Are workers trying to cover up something? And, are there that many problems with our system? By rewording the sentence and eliminating the negative words, the reader is more apt to accept what is being presented and to think about it in neutral or objective terms. Here's a more positive way to say the same thing:

Our project team has identified areas where changes can be made in the day-to-day operations of your organization that will make the work flow more smoothly . . .

So, when communicating with others, choose your words carefully. Decide what tone you would like to convey in presenting the information. Then select language that helps achieve that mood or feeling. Put yourself in the position of the reader. Will you cause the reader to take issue with what you are saying before the details are presented? If so, reword your material.

Document C — *Business Memo Edited for Tone*

Review the following memo. Then rewrite the memo using more positive language. You are trying to convince the president of your company that the salary adjustment process needs to be improved.

Check your sentences for clarity and correct grammar, spelling, and punctuation. Save the memo as **043wprc.kwp**. Then print the memo, if required by your instructor, and close the document.

Document C

current date

TO: Michael Chen

(your name)

SALARY ADJUSTMENT PROCESS

Many of the employees feel that the process for increasing our salaries is unfair. Some people seem to get salary reviews more often than others do. People get raises just because their manager likes them better. You've got to make some changes or the staff will get angry. They may even slow down their work and then you won't have products to sell.

A new system should be used that establishes a salary review schedule for all workers. You should also choose who will make the salary decisions and what factors they will use. A new process will make employees feel more satisfied.

Thank you for your consideration. I would be glad to discuss possible changes whenever you have the time.

Select the correct idiom in the following sentences, and key each sentence using the correct words. Check the "General Guidelines For Correct Word Use" if you have a question about which alternative to use.

6 (Try to, Try and) key the data without any errors.
7 Juan went (in search for, in search of) a new printer ribbon.
8 My book is (different from, different than) Harriet's book.
9 I will try to (comply with, comply to) your wishes.
10 This (kind of a, kind of) paper is easier to store.

Select the correct word in the following sentences, and key each sentence using the correct word.

11 (Accept, Except) for Henry, the entire class went on the trip.
12 Our teacher strongly (adviced, advised) us to study for the exam.
13 There have been (fewer, less) absences this winter than last winter.
14 We have (fewer, less) flour than we need.
15 He is a (good, well) student.
16 Martha doesn't feel (good, well) today.
17 Sean plays the violin (good, well).
18 I am angry (at, about, with) my best friend.
19 I am angry (at, about, with) the rising costs of the textbooks.
20 I am angry (at, about, with) Whiskers, my cat.

Compose a complete sentence about each of the following items. Be sure to key the sentence number, period, and press the ***F7*** key before keying your response. Let the sentence automatically wrap to the next line if your sentence extends beyond the right margin. At the end of each sentence, press ***Enter*** and proceed with the next sentence. Be sure to correct any errors.

1 ballpoint pen
2 ice cream
3 gas station
4 bank
5 elevator
6 fire
7 gain
8 dance
9 apple
10 water

Compose a complete sentence about each of the following items:

1 mirror
2 television
3 dollar bill
4 door
5 chair
6 radio
7 shoe

Document B ◄-- *Letter with Indented Text*

1 At the *Production–Session 43 Document B* screen, turn on Widow/Orphan (Fo**r**mat → **P**age → **K**eep Text Together. Click on the check box immediately below *Widow/Orphan,* then click OK).

2 Assume you will print the document on letterhead stationery, which means you should begin keying on about Line 2" (press ***Enter*** until the insertion point is positioned on approximately Line 2").

3 Key Document B. Indent the group of numbered items by pressing ***Tab*** before each number; then key the number and the period and press ***F7*** to indent the text. For indented text beginning with letters a, b, etc., press ***Tab*** twice, key the letter and period, then press ***F7*** and key the text.

4 Proofread and correct any errors. Complete a spell check.

5 Click on Check to automatically name **(043prob.kwp)**, save, and check the document.

6 When checking is complete, the letter is displayed on the screen with errors highlighted.

7 To print with errors highlighted, click on the Print button.

8 To correct errors, click on View Original. Make changes, then recheck the document.

9 Choose **F**ile → **C**lose. This closes Document B and brings up the Document C screen.

Document B

current date/Mr. Gary Wenner/Business Publications/510 Third Avenue/Toronto, ON M2H 2S6/CANADA/Dear Mr. Wenner:/Your letter regarding the proposal by Dr. Darlene Jones of Bailey College arrived while I was on vacation. I've reviewed the proposal carefully and here are my observations./1. The sequence for the proposed textbook is oriented to one job occupation, the administrative services profession. If this is your market niche, then the proposal is right on target./2. Units are not included in the following areas:/a. Desktop publishing/b. Office ergonomics/c. LAN management/3. The business communications chapter does not include anything about oral communications./4. In the electronic office systems chapter, the emphasis is on legal and medical systems applications. However, a large number of administrative assistants today are working for manufacturing firms or in government offices. I recommend that the text include applications in these areas./5. In the filing and records management chapter, nothing was mentioned about electronic filing systems or the cost of maintaining and disposing of recorded information. I believe this information should be added./6. The principles of accounting chapter doesn't seem to cover the basics. No mention is made of the popular accounting software packages./7. The chapter on printers doesn't cover laser color printers. Also, it seems that there should be more emphasis on the range of equipment in use rather than on how to operate specific machines./8. The field of telecommunications is an important topic that should be discussed at length. In particular, all office workers of the future need to understand the Internet system and how to maneuver in it./I hope that these comments will help in your decision to publish in the office education area. I certainly would promote this venture and would be happy to help you in any way possible. If you have any questions, please write, or call me at (312) 555-5622. You may also communicate with me on the Internet at lmissham@reed.com./Sincerely,/Lorraine Misslingham, Editor/your initials and filename

8 building
9 sunset
10 clock

Now you are ready to move on to the paragraph-response level, the fourth stage in building composition skills. Read the following guidelines for composing paragraphs. Study the guidelines and apply them in your composition activities.

General Guidelines for Paragraph Response

A paragraph is a group of related sentences—an organized and meaningful unit in a piece of writing. A paragraph contains a topic sentence and several supporting sentences. The sentences are organized in a logical manner and flow from one to the next. Transitional words connect one paragraph to another.

A **topic sentence** expresses the main idea or subject of the paragraph. The topic sentence usually opens the paragraph, since most readers like to know what the paragraph is about before they read on. The topic sentence is bolded in the following example. **Supporting sentences** describe, explain, or further develop the topic sentence as in this paragraph:

> **In a small office, the receptionist has a wide variety of duties.** Answering the telephone and receiving callers are primary responsibilities of any receptionist. Sometimes an employer asks a receptionist to take an important client to lunch or to contact a business customer. The correspondence in a small office varies from simple letters to complicated reports, and so the receptionist handles many types of communication.

Using Spell Checker

WordPerfect for Windows includes a tool called the **Spell Checker**. You can use the Spell Checker to locate and correct misspelled words in your document. Spell Checker also checks for duplicate words and capitalization errors. Many of the errors in a document can be corrected with a click of the mouse. The Spell Checker uses two dictionaries: a main dictionary containing over 100,000 words and a supplemental dictionary (which you create and customize). When you spell-check a document, the Spell Checker first checks to see if the word or phrase is listed in the supplementary dictionaries. If the word is not found in the supplementary dictionary, the main dictionary is checked. During the spell-check, the following options are listed:

Replace	Replaces the word in your text with the word in the *Replace With* text box or choose any of the additional suggestions in the *Suggestions* list box
Skip Once	Skips the current occurrence of the word or phrase
Skip Always	Skips *every* occurrence of the word or phrase during the current spell-check
Resume	Continues an incomplete spell check
Suggest	Displays additional words or phrases, if any, in the *Suggestions* list box
Add	Adds the word or phrase to the dictionary selected in the pop-up list
QuickCorrect	When this option is activated, all words or phrases with text specified in the *Replace With* text box will be replaced. You may also add words or phrases to the QuickCorrect dictionary.

2. The market conditions at the time of the offering;

3. The filing of a prospectus with the Securities and Exchange Commission and its subsequent notification of effectiveness.

We will not be bound to receive and pay for your shares until Blue Sky qualifications have been met in a reasonable number of states of our mutual selection and a final underwriting agreement satisfactory to each of us is executed.

The exact terms of the underwriting will be set forth in an underwriting agreement to be entered into by IDP Computing and Waedt-Steiner Investment Services. The underwriting discounts and commissions will not exceed 10 percent of the public offering price.

Except for any reimbursement provided for in this letter, Waedt-Steiner Investment Services will pay its own expenses and the expenses of its attorney. The underwriters will also pay the expenses of running the customary advertisements in various publications following the offering.

[insert a hard page break here]

Mr. Mark Shakil
Page 2
current date

IDP Computing will pay the fees and expenses of its legal counsel; all printing charges relating to the registration statement, prospectus, and underwriting agreements; postage; SEC, state, and federal filing fees; and the reasonable costs of a due diligence meeting.

Following the conclusion of the public offering, IDP Computing agrees to furnish quarterly unaudited financial statements to its shareholders and the underwriters with audited reports to be issued annually.

We look forward to working with you and your associates on the proposed public offering. This letter is accepted by IDP Computing and Waedt-Steiner Investment Services as a statement of mutual intent to carry out the proposed transactions, but it does not constitute a firm commitment on the part of either the company or the underwriters.

If this letter sets forth your understanding of our arrangement, please contact us.

Sincerely yours,

Donald F. Steiner
Senior Vice President

xx/043proa.kwp

c Accounting Department Manager

Remember that the Spell Checker will not stop at words that are spelled correctly but used incorrectly. For example, if you key *form* instead of *from*, Spell Checker finds a match for *form* and therefore does not stop to correct it. Spell Checker also contains some common proper names, but not many, so it stops at most proper names for correction. It is very important to proofread your document carefully after you have used Spell Checker.

Spell-Checking a Document

1. Open the document you want to spell-check.
2. From the Menu Bar, choose **T**ools→**S**pell Check or click on the Spell Check button on the Toolbar. (You can also press **Ctrl-F1**.)
3. The *Spell Check* dialog box opens and Spell Check immediately begins checking the document.
4. Make corrections as needed by clicking on the appropriate option (see previous explanation).
5. When the spell-check is completed, close the *Spell Check* dialog box by choosing **Y**es or pressing ***Enter*** at the prompt, *Spell Check Completed. Close Spell Checker?*

Compose a short paragraph using the following topic sentence. Concentrate on content; disregard keyboarding errors. When finished, follow the preceding instructions to use Spell Check to correct errors.

Fast-food containers cause disposal problems.

Saving/Printing WordPerfect Reinforcement Activities

To save and print the WordPerfect Reinforcement activities completed in Session 30, do the following.

1. Choose **F**ile → Save **A**s (or F3)
2. At the *Save As* dialog box, key the new filename, **030wpr.kwp**. Press ***Enter*** or click on the OK button. Your document has been saved to disk, and it also remains on the screen.
3. To print **030wpr.kwp**, choose **F**ile → **P**rint (or F5).
4. Click on the **P**rint button or press ***Enter***.
5. Close the file (click on **F**ile → **C**lose).

Preparing a Memorandum (Memo)

Preparing a widely used document, such as a memo, provides an opportunity to integrate the keyboarding and WordPerfect skills that you have been developing. Other than forms, the memorandum (memo for short) is the most frequently used document in the business world. Employees use memos to communicate within an organization. The traditional memo consists of a four-part heading plus the body (message) as shown in the example that follows:

WordPerfect's Header feature can be used to create this heading at the beginning of the document. However, for a two-page letter, it is probably more efficient to simply key the heading. In later sessions on reports and manuscripts, you will learn to use the Header feature.

Document A — *Two-Page Letter with Indented Text*

1 At the *Production–Session 43 Document A* screen, begin keying Document A on approximately Line 2" (this assumes that the letterhead design takes up about 1 inch of space). Do not key the letterhead.
2 Since this is a long letter, decrease the amount of space between the date line and the inside address to a triple space. (Press ***Enter*** three times after inserting the date with **Ctrl + D**.)
3 Follow the steps below to indent each of the enumerated paragraphs (begin a double-space below the last line of the paragraph preceding the numbered items):
   a Press ***Tab***, then key the paragraph number and the period.
   b Press ***F7***, then key the paragraph. Press ***Enter*** twice.
4 Insert a hard page break where shown in the illustration.
5 Create a heading for the second page, beginning on Line 1". Triple-space after the last line of the heading, then key the remainder of the letter. Press ***Tab*** between the copy notation and the name.
6 Proofread and correct any errors. Complete a spell check.
7 Click on Check to automatically name **(043proa.kwp)** and save the document. The program checks the letter for errors and calculates your WAM rate.
8 When checking is complete, the letter is displayed on the screen with errors highlighted.
9 To print with errors highlighted, click on the Print button.
10 To correct errors, click on View Original. Make changes, then recheck the document.
11 Choose **F**ile → **C**lose. This closes Document A and brings up the Document B screen.

Document A

Waedt-Steiner Investment Services
10 Kearney Drive • Kearney, NE 68847-2817 • (402) 555-6314

current date

Mr. Mark Shakil, President
Dain Bosworth, Inc.
2401 Lincoln Boulevard
New York, NY 10037-6847

Dear Mr. Shakil:

This is to record the mutual intention of IDP Computing and Waedt-Steiner Investment Services to undertake a public offering of common stock of IDP Computing (the "company").

It is our intention to form an underwriting syndicate to purchase up to 250,000 shares of new common stock from IDP Computing and to reoffer the shares to the public at a price mutually agreed upon. This agreement is subject to the following:

1. The assurance that no materially adverse change in the affairs of the company and its prospects occurs which appears sufficient, in our opinion, to threaten the success of our effort;

Continued on next page

DATE: (current date)
ds
TO: (name of the person to receive the memo, person's business title)
ds
FROM: (your name)
ds
SUBJECT: (THE SUBJECT OF YOUR MEMO IN ALL CAPS)
ts

The body includes the information you want to communicate to the receiver. Note that the body is single-spaced with a double space between paragraphs. It is not necessary to indent the first line of each paragraph. The blank space between paragraphs is adequate to show where one paragraph ends and another begins.

The memo starts one inch from the top of the page. Since WordPerfect has a default margin of one inch, you can begin entering the date line on the first line on your screen. **Note:** The introductory headings of the memo (DATE, TO, FROM, SUBJECT) can appear in a different order, depending on the memo style.
ds
your initials/filename

Instructions for Preparing a Memo

Prepare a memo to your instructor indicating the course or courses you have taken that will be the most helpful to you in the future. Explain why this course(s) is important. What content was included in the course(s)? What did you learn that is important in reaching your goals? Your memo is to include at least two paragraphs. You will use a WordPerfect template to create the headings in the memo. The template will format the memo automatically.

Using the Memo Template

WordPerfect includes a number of *template* documents that are formatted for specific uses. You can create a variety of documents with the templates such as business documents, calendars, envelopes, faxes, legal documents, letters, memos, publication documents, reports, and resumes. To display the types of templates available, choose **F**ile, then **N**ew; or click on the New Document button on the Toolbar. At the *New Document* dialog box, you can choose the template on which you want the new document based.

To create a memo using the memo template, complete the following steps:

1. Choose **F**ile → **N**ew or click on the New Document button (not the New Blank Document button) on the Toolbar.
2. At the *New Document* dialog box, click on *memo* in the *Group* list box.
3. Click on *Memo - Traditional* in the *Select Template* list box.
4. Click on Select.
5. At the *Template Information* dialog box, enter the name of your instructor in the *Name of Recipient(s)* text box and the subject of the memo in all caps in the *Subject* text box.

Note: You will have to enter your personal information the first time you use the template. This information will then be automatically inserted whenever you use any of WordPerfect's templates. If you are sharing a computer with other students, this information may have to be entered each time you use the template feature.

Creating Page Breaks

The WordPerfect program assumes that you are using standard-sized paper, which is 8.5 inches wide and 11 inches long. By default, WordPerfect leaves a 1-inch top margin and a 1-inch bottom margin. This allows a total of 9 inches of text to be printed on a standard page.

As you create longer documents, you will notice that when the insertion point nears Line 9.83", a solid black and gray line is automatically inserted at the next line (Line 10"). This line is called a *soft page break*. The soft page break occurs at 10 inches because WordPerfect leaves the first inch on the paper blank and prints text on the next 9 inches. Soft page breaks automatically adjust if text is added or deleted from a document and should be used whenever possible.

There are times when a soft page break may occur in the wrong place in your document, or when a short page is appropriate, for example, a title page. In those situations, a *hard page break* can be created by pressing ***Ctrl + Enter***. The hard page break does not adjust and is therefore less flexible than a soft page break. If you add or delete text from a document in which you have inserted a hard page break, you must make sure the page break is still in an appropriate location after the editing is completed.

To insert a hard page break in a document, move the insertion point to the position where you want the new page to begin and press ***Ctrl + Enter***. This causes a solid black and gray line to appear in the document. (In Page mode, a soft page break and a hard page break display the same.) If you insert a hard page break in a document and then decide you want it removed, display the Reveal Codes window with ***Alt + F3*** or **V**iew → Reveal **C**odes, then delete the [HPg] code.

Keeping Text Together

Options at the Keep Text Together dialog box allow you to create pages that end according to the guidelines listed on the previous page. To display this dialog box, choose Fo**r**mat → **P**age → **K**eep Text Together. The following options at the dialog box let you control WordPerfect's soft page breaks:

- Widow/Orphan
- Block Protect
- Conditional End of Page

Widow/Orphan should be turned on for all multiple-page documents.This feature prevents incorrect paragraph breaks between two pages. The Block Protect and the Conditional End of Page features are similar and are used to prevent page breaks between a heading and the text that follows the heading. They may be used to keep text in a table or chart from dividing between two pages.

Second-Page Heading

When a letter is longer than one page, it must have a heading on the second page. This heading should begin one inch from the top of the second page. There should be two blank lines between the heading and the body of the letter. The heading should contain three lines of information: the addressee, the page number, and the date, as in the following example:

Mr. Neal Chomsky
Page 2 (Use either a number or the word)
June 15, 19xx

6. Click on the *Personal Info* button.
7. At the *Enter Your Personal Information* dialog box, key your personal information in the appropriate boxes. (If you don't have information for a particular box, leave it blank and press ***Tab*** to move to the next box.)
8. After entering your personal information, click on OK.
9. At the *Template Information* dialog box, click on OK.
10. At the document screen, begin composing and keying your memo.
11. When finished, check to be sure that the memo is grammatically correct.
12. Spell-check your document.
13. Save your memo as **030wpra.kwp** and print a copy for your instructor.

Preparing a Personal Business Letter

The business letter is another important communication tool. Although a memo is used to convey information **internally**, a letter is used to transmit information to or from individuals **outside** a company. Just as memos have their distinct parts, so do letters. Study the example that follows:

Current date

Mr. Barth Trimble, Manager
Creative Printing Service
4950 Heights Drive Circle
Denver, CO 80219-1698

Dear Mr. Trimble:

Our communications class is planning a series of intense studies on various aspects of desktop publishing. As part of this series, we would like to visit a printing firm that is known for modern and innovative practices.

Our class meets every day from 8:30 a.m. to 11:30 a.m. Would it be possible for our class to visit your firm sometime during the month of April? If so, please contact me at 555-9462 any day after 3:30 p.m.

Sincerely yours,

Margo Hillman

Margo Hillman, Chair
Communications Series 1190
Mountain Community College
2350 Cataline Drive
Denver, CO 80291

FIVE-MINUTE TIMINGS

Goal: 30 WAM/2 errors

SI: 1.46

- Take two 5-minute timings.

One of the finest fruits on the market today is the mango, which is a fruit found in the tropics. The mango has become more popular all over the nation. The papaya is also a very good tropical fruit that has lots of vitamins and is good to eat. A carambola is quite a strange looking fruit. It has a waxy appearance and contains a solid meat. The cherimoya, or custard apple, is shaped like the strawberry and is green in color and oval in shape. The fruit is not very attractive, but it has a delicious and delicate flavor. Kiwi fruit, the Chinese gooseberry, is grown in New Zealand; thus the name "kiwi" has been given to this fruit in honor of the native kiwi bird. The taste is mild and quite enjoyable.

The celery root has an ugly appearance. The outside of the root is deceiving; inside the ugly wrapping lies a great surprising flavor treat for vegetable lovers. Fine Jerusalem artichokes, also known as sunchokes, have lots of uses. The crispy, crunchy food has a nutlike flavor and makes a great finger food. A jicama is sometimes known as a Mexican or Chinese potato. The brownish vegetable looks like a raw turnip. The crispy and crunchy taste treat is quite good when served with a dip of some sort.

Although all of us seem to be creatures of habit, there is a new world of eating delights right in the produce bins, waiting for us to discover new taste treats. All it takes is some searching and a very sincere desire to try something new. Maybe a recipe or two would add to the variety of these exotic vegetables and fruits. Many cookbooks contain delightful recipes with which to vary our menus.

PREPARING TWO-PAGE LETTERS

Most business letters take up only one page. Even if a sentence or two carry to the next page, you can easily adjust the top and/or bottom margins so that those sentences will print on the first page. However, sometimes you will write or prepare complex letters that require a second or even a third page. For those situations, consider the following guidelines:

- There should be a minimum of two lines (one full line plus three or more words) of a paragraph at the bottom of a page. This prevents orphans from occurring. An *orphan* is the first line of a paragraph that appears at the bottom of a page.
- There should be a minimum of two lines of a paragraph at the top of a page. This prevents widows from occurring. A *widow* is the last line of a paragraph that appears at the top of the next page.
- Do not place a paragraph heading on the bottom of a page and its accompanying text on the next page.
- Do not place the closing and signatures lines on a page by themselves.
- Do not hyphenate words between pages.

With WordPerfect, you can control page endings by inserting your own page breaks ("hard" page breaks) or by using options available under the Keeping Text Together feature.

Most business letters are printed on **letterhead** paper that provides information about the organization (name, address, city, state, ZIP, phone number). Letters from an individual not representing an organization are generally prepared on plain paper. These letters are called *personal business letters*.

The personal business letter begins with the **date line** followed by four to seven lines and then the **inside address**. The **inside address** contains the name of the person receiving the letter, his/her organization, and address. The **inside address** is followed by a double space and then a greeting or **salutation**. In the block-style letter, all of these lines begin at the left margin.

The body of the letter is single-spaced with a double space between paragraphs. At the end of the document, there is a double space followed by the **complimentary closing**. It is customary to allow four lines after the closing to leave sufficient room for the writer's signature. The **signature block,** which contains the writer's name and address, is keyed under the closing.

Using the Letter Template to Prepare a Letter

Using a WordPerfect letter template, you are to compose a ***personal business letter*** to the personnel manager of a company you would like to visit (you can make up a name). Be sure to include a complete inside address (again, you can make it up).

The first paragraph of the letter should include a request to visit the company. Explain who you are, possible dates and times you are available to visit, etc. In the second paragraph, note what you are interested in seeing or learning. In the third paragraph, include information on where and how to get in touch with you to set up an appointment or when you will call this person to confirm the visit.

Complete the following steps to use the template:

1 Choose **F**ile → **N**ew or click on the New Document button on the Toolbar.
2 At the *New Document* dialog box, click on *letter* in the *Group* list box.
3 Click on **Letter - Blank Letterhead** in the *Select Template* list box.
4 Click on Select.
5 At the *Letter* dialog box, enter the name and address of the personnel manager in the *Recipient(s) Name and Address:* text box.
6 Press ***Tab*** to move to the *Salutation* text box.
7 Key the salutation in the *Salutation* text box using the example above the text box but substituting the last name of the personnel manager.
8 Deselect all boxes under *Include* by clicking any check box with an **x**.

Note: You will have to enter your personal information the first time you use the template. This information will then be automatically inserted whenever you use WordPerfect's templates. If you are sharing a computer with other students, this information may have to be entered each time you use the template feature.

9 Click on the Personal Info button, key your personal information, then click on OK.
10 Click on OK at the *Letter* dialog box.
11 Click on OK to close the *Letter Formatting Complete* dialog box and return to the document screen.
12 Begin composing and keying your letter. (Key to approximately Line 8".) Press ***Enter*** only once between paragraphs.
13 When you have completed the body of the letter, press ***Enter***.
14 Choose **I**nsert → Letter Closing. At the *Letter Closing* dialog box, click on OK to accept the default of *Sincerely*.

SESSION 43

SESSION GOALS

1-Minute: 40 WAM/2 errors
5-Minute: 30 WAM/2 errors

Creating page breaks

Choosing positive words

GETTING STARTED

If you are continuing immediately from Session 42, go to the one-minute timings. If you exited the program at the end of Session 42, do the following:

1. Access Windows, then WordPerfect 6.1 for Windows.
2. Click on the KWP icon to access *Keyboarding with WordPerfect.*
3. Go to the Keyboarding Sessions menu and click on Jump to return to your last activity. Or, access the Session 43 menu and click on OK to begin the session.

If your fingers are already warmed up or if you have completed part of the session, highlight the desired activity and click on OK. When you have completed the on-screen activities for Session 43, you will return to the text to complete two-page business letters in which you will insert page breaks and use WordPerfect's Widow/Orphan feature to prevent incorrect page breaks.

ONE-MINUTE TIMINGS

Goal: 40 WAM/2 errors

SI: 1.45

- Take two 1-minute timings.
- Use your most recent timing score to set a speed or accuracy goal.

A very common job today is the home worker. Many people are very happy working at home. They will be more productive doing their tasks at home. It will give them a chance to care for the children and also provide them the opportunity to earn an income. Computer programming, among other occupations, is a typical type of work completed while the worker remains in the home. As more and more of the workers earn more of their income at home, many seem to believe that social problems are going to evolve. Many believe that people have to work in the offices if they are to have the right social surroundings.

15 WordPerfect then inserts your personal information in the signature block. Check it for accuracy and make any necessary changes.
16 Proofread your letter to be sure that it is grammatically correct.
17 Spell-check your document.
18 Save your letter as **030wprb.kw** and print a copy for your instructor.
19 Close the document, then click on the KWP Next Activity button to bring up the Timings screen.

ONE-MINUTE TIMINGS

Goal: 35 WAM/2 errors

SI: 1.35

- Take two 1-minute timings on the following material.
- If you finish the paragraph before time is up, start over.

1 At sunset, it is nice to enjoy dining out on a bank of a pond. Unless uninvited insects and swarms of ants invade the picnic, you will certainly unwind. As those soft night sounds enfold you, frenzied inward nerves and the decisions that haunt you drain from your mind. You may enjoy napping on a nearby bench. Next, swing into action after your rest and inhale much air into your lungs. Unpack the nice lunch and munch away. Don't deny yourself this experience.

THREE-MINUTE TIMINGS

Goal: 30 WAM/2 errors

SI: 1.39

- Take two 3-minute timings on the following paragraph.
- If you finish before time is up, start the paragraph again.

1 Simple salt and pepper shakers are very easy and quite simple to collect today. Lots of "fun" and very colorful pairs are available, either new or pre-owned. The bargains can be found at those family or group sales. Most folks try to see how many kinds they can find and buy. Some collect a mass of shakers that number over 500. The person or persons who are really collectors have shakers that number from 2,000 to 3,000 pairs. If anyone would like to begin the hobby of collecting, just look around and start a collection.

FIVE-MINUTE TIMING

Goal: 25 WAM/2 errors

SI: 1.35

- Take a 5-minute timing on the paragraphs that follow.
- If you finish before time is up, start over.

ENDING THE SESSION

To end this session, print any files from Session 42 not printed earlier, then continue with the next session or exit the program:

PRINT

1. Choose **F**ile → **O**pen.
2. At the *Open File* dialog box, select the files to be printed, then choose File **O**ptions → **P**rint.
3. At the *Print Files* dialog box, press ***Enter*** or click on **P**rint.
4. Click on Cancel or press ***Esc*** to close the *Open File* dialog box.

CONTINUE

1. Print any files, if necessary.
2. Click on the KWP Next Activity button.
3. At the next session menu, click on OK to proceed with the highlighted item.

EXIT

1. Print any files, if necessary.
2. Click on the KWP Main Menu button.
3. At the Main Menu, select WordPerfect Only, then click on OK.
4. Click on **F**ile → E**x**it.
5. Exit Windows (**F**ile → E**x**it), if necessary.

1 Most of the major events in communications grew out of a series of discoveries that took place over many years. Present-day systems can be traced to many great men and women who brought together the tools of their day to meet the needs of people on the job and in the home. The basis of this technology had its start in the 1830s.

One of the first events occurred in Germany when their government built a telegraph network that spanned 8,000 feet. By the next decade, the use of this device had spread to the United.States. Congress funded a line that ran from Washington to Baltimore. During the same time frame, Samuel F.B. Morse finished a new telegraph device and code that came to be known as the Morse Code.

In the next few years, more developments took place. European telegraph wires and underwater cables became widely used. While the telegraph would continue to be used for many more years, other types of technology were taking shape. Bell developed the telephone in 1875, and he and Gray filed for a patent the next year. Bell later offered to sell his patents to Western Union, but they turned him down.

By the late 1880s, there were 140,000 homes in the U.S. with telephone service. The growth of this system has been impressive. Today there are 200 million lines that reach 93 percent of the homes in the U.S. The copper wire that has been used for so many years is being replaced by fiber optic cable that will bring voice, data, and video into our homes.

ENDING THE SESSION

Now that you have completed the timings, you may want to print any session files not printed earlier. Access the Freeform option from the Main Menu, then print the files using the Print button on the Toolbar or by choosing **File** → **Print**, then the *Document on Disk* option. After printing, you may exit the program by returning to the Main Menu and selecting *WordPerfect Only*, then **File** → **Exit**.

Document E ← Block-Style Letter Edited with Cut and Paste

1. At a clear WordPerfect editing window, open **042prod.kwp**.
2. Reverse the order of paragraphs 2 and 3. (If necessary, refer to Session 41 to review the procedures for cutting and pasting.)
3. Choose **F**ile → Save **A**s and name the document **042wpre.kwp**.
4. Choose **F**ile → **C**lose. You are now ready to complete Document F.

REINFORCING WRITING SKILLS

It is human nature to put things off. That trait is called procrastination, and it is the reason you need to write carefully whenever you send someone a letter that contains a request. It is important to phrase your message in words that almost "force" the reader to act. For example, assume that you are sending someone a proposal to automate operations at the company, and you need that person's approval before you can move to the next phase of the project. Review the two sentences that follow. Which one is likely to produce action?

1. After you've had an opportunity to review the attached proposal, please call me so that I can answer questions and get your reaction.

2. Please review the attached proposal; I will call you on Monday between 10 and 11 a.m. to answer any questions you may have and to get your reaction.

In the first example, the person has the option of putting off reviewing the proposal. There is no sense of urgency conveyed in the sentence. In the second example, the person knows that a call for the response will be made on a specific day at a specific time. The person can still put off the review, but chances are the review will be done. As you compose letters and memos that require action, do what you can to stimulate a response within a specified time.

Document F ← Business Letter Keyed in a Letter Template

You are to write a letter to Ms. Lucy Allarie-Gosselin, Manager of the Continental Weston Hotel, 400 Columbus Avenue. Add your city, state, and 9-character ZIP Code. In the letter, explain that you are looking for a hotel at which to hold the annual state convention next fall of the *Society for Records Management*, a student organization with local chapters throughout your state. You need to find out a number of things:

- Are the dates of October 4-6 available?
- Do they have sufficient space to accommodate 300 participants?
- What are the room rates?
- What do they have in the way of meeting room facilities?
- Would the manager be able to give a tour of the hotel to the three members of the Convention Site Selection Committee on the 20th of next month?

Use a letter template of your choice (If necessary, see Session 38 for help in selecting letter templates). Use your school name and address in the letterhead, your name in the signature line, and your initials along with the filename (**042wprf.kwp**).

Remember to use words that require a specific response by a certain time. The response could be a letter or a phone call. Save the document as **042wprf.kwp**. Print and then close the file.

UNIT 6

ALPHABETIC REVIEW

4 Click on Check to automatically name **(042prod.kwp)** and save the letter. The program checks the document for errors and calculates your WAM rate.

5 When checking is complete, the memo is displayed on the screen with errors highlighted.

6 To print with errors highlighted, click on the Print button.

7 To correct errors, click on View Original. Make changes, then recheck the document.

8 Choose **F**ile → **C**lose. This closes Document D and brings up a clear WordPerfect editing window at which you will complete Document E.

Document D

current date

Dr. Gwendolyn S. Brownell
State Department of Education
1831 Gadsden Street
Columbia, SC 29202-1483

Dear Dr. Brownell:

Here is

~~I am enclosing~~ your final class list for the "Basic Statistics" course. This list includes the students who are officially enrolled and for whom tuition is required.

Please return your grades on this roster as soon as the class concludes. Assign each student the appropriate grade and sign the sheet. If an incomplete is assigned, a *Report of Incomplete* form (copies are enclosed) must accompany your roster. ~~We have a fax machine,~~ ~~so~~ you may ~~send~~ your signed grade rosters to (509) 555-3022. fax The last day we may accept grades (for them to be included in the quarterly mailing) is always noon on the Monday following finals week.

If a student requests a withdrawal, please notify us promptly. When paperwork is delayed, it can cause unnecessary hardship to a student. Paperwork that is processed in a timely manner avoids problems with billings and records.

call us

If you encounter a problem, please ~~bring it to our attention~~ prior to the grading cycle. We are available to answer your questions at (509) 555-2598.

We ~~I~~ appreciate your continuing cooperation.

Sincerely,

Wendy Maguire, Coordinator
Continuing Education

xx/042prod.kwp

Enclosures

SESSION 31

SKILL BUILDING: LETTERS A-I

SESSION GOALS

Review A-I, Numbers, and Symbols

30 WAM/2 errors

GETTING STARTED

If you are continuing immediately from Session 30, you should see the Session 31 menu on your screen with the first item highlighted. Click on OK to begin working. If you exited the program during or at the end of Session 30, do the following:

1. Access Windows, then WordPerfect 6.1 for Windows.
2. Click on the KWP button to access *Keyboarding with WordPerfect.*
3. Go to the *Keyboarding Sessions* menu and click on Jump to return to your last activity. Or, access the Session 31 menu to begin the session.

Session 31 provides an opportunity to reinforce your keyboarding skills on the letters **a** through **i**. You may choose to work on selected letters or you may decide to do the activities for all the letters in this session. The directions appear on the screen.

If you decide that additional practice is unnecessary and you want to skip the timings, highlight *WordPerfect Reinforcement* on the session menu. Then follow the directions in the WordPerfect Reinforcement section on the following pages to delete an outdated file.

TIMINGS

Emphasis on A

That happy play has an amazing climax. It affects all 27 watchers. The absorbing last act is majestic with an array of blazing ideas. Many apt actors who speak well may apply and qualify for a part. The author is apt and adept; he is ascending toward a lavish share of awards. He is aware and now aims to avoid mistakes in reaching goals ahead. He had to fire an agent who made absurd demands and squandered all the cash on large purchases. He was a fraud and a hoax.

Document B — *Block-Style Letter with Bold and Italics Text*

1. At the *Production–Session 42 Document B* screen, change the left and right margins to 1.5 inches, then key Document B as a block-style letter.
2. Vertically center the letter on the page.
3. Proofread and correct any errors. Complete a spell check.
4. Click on Check to automatically name **(042prob.kwp)**, save, and check the document.
5. When checking is complete, the letter is displayed on the screen with errors highlighted.
6. To correct errors, click on View Original. Make changes, then recheck the document.
7. Choose **F**ile → **C**lose. This closes Document B and brings up a clear WordPerfect editing window, at which you will complete Document C.

Document B

Mr. John Hepp/1235 Arrowhead Drive/Pittsburg, PA 31645-9882/Dear Mr. Hepp:/If you have the nagging feeling that **your money could be working harder for you**. . . if you want to do more than **hope your dreams come true**. . .you may need a financial plan. With a balanced financial plan, you and your family can enjoy the security and satisfaction that come with taking control of your money./Helping families and individuals achieve financial security through wise planning is our business at IDI. Established in 1894, IDI is America's leading financial planning company. As an IDI personal financial planner, I would like to help you plan for your future./IDI has a wide range of services to help you establish and reach your goals. One financial planning service that has been helpful for many is the *Personal Financial Analysis*. With this analysis, you can assess your current financial situation and establish a plan that includes provisions for available cash, savings, risk management, and investment balance. We can even help you minimize your income taxes each year./I will call you Wednesday morning to set up a short meeting so we can explore the benefits of financial planning for you and your family./Sincerely, /Robert Hasenberg/Personal Financial Planner

Document C — *Business Letter Edited with Find and Replace*

1. At a clear WordPerfect editing window, open **042prob.kwp**.
2. Change all instances of IDI to Investors Diversified International (if necessary, review the information on Find and Replace in Session 40).
3. Choose **F**ile → Save **A**s and name the document **042wprc.kwp**.
4. Choose **F**ile → **C**lose.
5. Click on the KWP Next Activity button to bring up the Document D screen.

Document D — *Block-Style Letter with Wide Margins*

1. At the *Production–Session 42 Document D* screen, change the left and right margins to 1.25 inches, then key Document D as a block-style letter.
2. Vertically center the letter on the page.
3. Proofread and correct any errors. Complete a spell check.

Emphasis on B

While the 15 boys scrambled about, Barb baked a big batch of bars. The bleak cabin needed a good scrubbing. She had been able to buy a bulb for the amber lamp. The bright and probing beam chased the gloom away. A cheery robin sitting on a limb called to other birds. The tasty leg of lamb and herb dressing would soon be ready. The slight haze of that day made the family feel an abounding sense of peace. Soon they would climb aboard the boat and return to urban life.

Emphasis on C

The chief and the crew did concur. That ocean cruiser could be launched at once. It was a fact: The cursed, cruel pirates had discovered their recent acquisition of sacks of gold coins. As the panic arose, the excited crew scanned a curving cedar grove along the coast. Those ancient cypress boards crackled as the excess load caused the boat to crawl and cease almost all movement. The acute crisis excluded a quick chance at a complete escape.

Emphasis on D

Even the steadfast must agree that some birthdays are dandy with abundant kindness and others seem to be dark and dull. Adults have undue qualms when adjusting to becoming 40 and older; a child stampedes through the days with wild abandonment. No doubt a small child full of daring and dynamic energy deals with life in a candid way. All the bedlam and wild dashing dispel any dim attitudes of dour adults. To avoid adverse thoughts on birthdays, spend them with children.

Emphasis on E

That eccentric thief scares me. He swears that he did not steal the wealthy lady's 11 rings. He is either embarking on an evil route of crime, or else he is a cheap cheat. At best, he knows how to effect an illegal entry. Each of his creeping moves suggests a false value. He prizes money and exerts extra effort to obtain it. In any event, it appears that he has the stolen jewelry. He is edgy and tired. His tale may change soon.

Emphasis on F

Often, before we face all the facts, our own fears may begin to defeat us. Life seems filled with deep strife and failures. We become inflamed at ourselves and fuss in 50 futile ways. This is the time to stop fretting and inflate our egos with a firm, fresh start. Swiftly, our spirits are lifted. We have a fine feeling of being free from cares or defeat.

Document A ← Block-Style Letter with Wide Margins

1 At the *Production–Session 42 Document A* screen, change the left and right margins to 1.5 inches, change the justification to Full, then key Document A as a block-style letter. (Do not key the letterhead.)
2 Vertically center the document on the page.
3 Proofread and correct any errors. Complete a spell check.
4 Click on Check to automatically name **(042proa.kwp)**, save, and check the document.
5 When checking is complete, the letter is displayed on the screen with errors highlighted.
6 To print the document with errors highlighted, click on the Print button.
7 To correct errors, click on View Original. Make changes, then recheck the document.
8 Choose **F**ile → **C**lose. This closes Document A and brings up the Document B screen.

Document A

CU CONSULTANTS UNLIMITED

806 BOYCE STREET, SALT LAKE CITY, UTAH 84106-9217 • 801/555-4151

current date

Mr. Ronald A. Christner
Chief Administrator
Lincolnwood Manor
4762 W. Touhy Ave.
Lincolnwood, IL 60646-5121

Dear Mr. Christner:

Enclosed are the resumes, pictures, and outline for the Time Management seminar to be held the last week in January at the Hilton Hotel.

Dr. Joan Kepros of the University of Illinois and I will present a program geared to the needs of nursing home administrators. If you have any special issues you would like us to address, please give me a call. I am confident that all members of your staff will learn some valuable techniques that will make them more productive in their jobs.

Sincerely yours,

Sandra Ferrari
Division Chair

xx/042proa.kwp

Enclosures

Emphasis on G

The boy is going to grab a bag of hamburgers after the game. That last game was grim. The team's energy ought to be higher, for the rough, gripping coughs are gone. The last germs have given way to good health through better hygiene. It is our guess that the girls will get eight goals. Those grounds are genuinely great. The eight dingy lights, which were illegal, glow brighter. When the gala bash is in full swing, the manager will give the guests a grand gift.

Emphasis on H

Those happy chaps hope to hike to the south shore. It is 72 miles from their homes. If harsh weather hinders them, each has a small, tight tent. When they are en route, the head chef can prepare wholesome meals. Breakfast might be ham and eggs or hotcakes. A hearty lunch of milk, fresh fruit, and sandwiches will be eaten in haste. The plans for night meals include hash, mashed chickpeas, and other delights. They are healthy and hearty. The whole group may catch fresh fish.

Emphasis on I

That stadium by the river isn't immune to crime. Last night a thief seized 18 expensive radios from a taxi driver, who was picking up a rider. The thief ditched the radios in the river. A diver fished them out quickly. The weird irony is that the thief is out of jail on bail. It's likely that he bribed an ignorant civil aide. In spite of this, he has been identified. His alibi is nullified. Irate voices are being raised to swiftly close the issue.

WP WORDPERFECT REINFORCEMENT

Practice your file management skills by deleting the file 021wpr.kwp. Follow these steps:

1. Choose **F**ile → **O**pen.
2. At the *Open File* dialog box, select the file *021wpr.kwp.*
3. With the filename highlighted, choose File **O**ptions → **D**elete.
4. At the *Delete File* dialog box, click on **D**elete. ***Note:*** If you want to print any files from this session, print at this point (**F**ile → **P**rint, then **D**ocument on Disk).
5. To close the *Open File* dialog box, click on Cancel or press ***Esc***.

ENDING THE SESSION

You may now continue with the next session or exit the program.

CONTINUE
1. Click on the KWP Next Activity button.
2. At the session menu, highlight the desired activity, then click on OK..

EXIT
1. Click on the KWP Main Menu button.
2. At the Main Menu, select WordPerfect Only, then click on OK.
3. Click on **F**ile → E**x**it.
4. Exit Windows (**F**ile → E**x**it), if necessary.

FIVE-MINUTE TIMINGS

Goal: 30 WAM/2 errors

SI: 1.45

- Take two 5-minute timings.

A letterhead creates an image for a business. It is possible to hire a person or a design firm to design a letterhead for you, or you may decide to use a computer to make your own. By making your own, you have the flexibility to make it a "true picture" of you and your firm. There are several things you should keep in mind while designing your letterhead.

Keep in mind that your letterhead will make a statement about your firm. It will give the reader vital data and also create an image in the reader's mind about your firm. Do you wish the reader to obtain the mental image that your firm is "solid-as-a-rock conservative"? Or, do you wish your firm to be seen as "active, flashy, and fast reacting"? You must decide.

Vital data which must be included on your letterhead is the name of your firm, address, phone and fax numbers. There are certain placement guidelines that should be followed regarding the name and address of a business. For example, the firm's name, address, phone number, and fax number may be centered at the top of the page. Left- or right-justifying at the top of the page is also very popular. When displaying this data, you may simply block the lines, or you may wish to be more creative and try such things as separating the data by bullets, clip art, and so on.

Many businesses have logos and slogans that may be used on the page. These two items may be placed anywhere on the page. A popular location to display a slogan is across the bottom of the page with the logo placed on the left- or right-hand side of the page.

You may wish to use different fonts when displaying your firm's data. Experts warn, however, to not use more than two fonts when designing your letterhead. Consider using both bold and plain fonts for variety. When picking fonts, keep in mind the image you are trying to present. Don't select a "flashy" type font if you are attempting to appear conservative.

The background design also has an impact on the reader. You should know what the background will be before beginning the design of your letterhead. Many people feel that the background and the paper used has more impact than the data contained in the letterhead. If you do select a background, make sure it is simple and does not "hide" the firm's data. There is a large selection of preprinted design papers that you can buy on which to print your letterhead. Remember to select your paper first, then design the letterhead.

PREPARING AND EDITING BUSINESS LETTERS

In this session you will review some of the WordPerfect editing features you have learned previously, including Find and Replace and cutting and pasting text. In addition, the documents give you the opportunity to practice changing margins and use letter templates.

SESSION 32

SESSION GOALS

Review J-R, Numbers, and Symbols

30 WAM/2 errors

GETTING STARTED

If you are continuing immediately from Session 31, you should see the Session 32 menu on your screen with the first item highlighted. Click on OK to begin working. If you exited the program during or at the end of Session 31, do the following:

1. Access Windows, then WordPerfect 6.1 for Windows.
2. Click on the KWP button to access *Keyboarding with WordPerfect*.
3. Go to the Keyboarding Sessions menu and click on Jump to return to your last activity. Or, access the Session 32 menu to begin the session.

Session 32 provides an opportunity to reinforce your keyboarding skills on the letters **j** through **r**. You may select only those letters you think you need to work on or do the activities for all the letters in this session. The directions for completing all keyboarding activities appear on the screen.

If you decide that additional practice is unnecessary and you want to skip the Timings, highlight *WordPerfect Reinforcement* on the session menu. Then follow the directions in the WordPerfect Reinforcement section on the following pages to delete an outdated file.

TIMINGS

Emphasis on J

The object of the jury is to judge that subject and to be just. The adjacent jail adjoins the courtroom. A jaunt to the jail is not enjoyable. The judge's job is to remain judicious when the final judgment must be made. All 12 jurors must be adults; juveniles are not allowed on the jury. The jokers who jeer and jest will be ejected. Adjournment will take place after the judicial question has been resolved.

SESSION GOALS

1-Minute: 40 WAM/2 errors
5-Minute: 30 WAM/2 errors

Review changing margins, Find and Replace, cut and paste, and letter templates

Writing requests that get action

GETTING STARTED

If you are continuing immediately from Session 41, go to the one-minute timings. If you exited the program at the end of Session 41, do the following:

1. Access Windows, then WordPerfect 6.1 for Windows.
2. Click on the KWP icon to access *Keyboarding with WordPerfect.*
3. Go to the Keyboarding Sessions menu and click on Jump to return to your last activity. Or, access the Session 42 menu and click on OK to begin the session.

If your fingers are already warmed up or if you have completed part of the session, highlight the desired activity and click on OK. When you have completed the on-screen activities for Session 42, you will return to the text to complete several business letters in which you will use several WordPerfect features to make editing changes.

ONE-MINUTE TIMINGS

Goal: 40 WAM/2 errors

SI: 1.45

- Take two 1-minute timings.
- Use your most recent 1-minute timing score to set a speed or accuracy goal.

The ceiling fixtures that were standard equipment in many older homes do nothing more than flood the rooms with a harsh, unflattering light. The glaring effect can be greatly softened by bringing lights down to the areas in which they will be used. The direction and also the intensity of the lights can be controlled. The older fixture can be replaced with a newer style such as a hanging swag lamp or a floor lamp. Table lamps can be purchased in a wide variety of sizes, style choices, and colors that blend and harmonize with any decor.

Emphasis on K

That old worker knows his work is risky. His kind of weakness is in his knees. He checks the skyline stockpiles from an airplane cockpit. It is awkward to go backwards or clockwise and keep a keen eye out for cracking walls. When he has checked the skyline, he has breakfast. His business is on the edge of bankruptcy. He needs a workable new plan for a husky bankroll. He hopes he will hit a $100,000 jackpot soon.

Emphasis on L

Long ago, pilgrims loved to indulge in blunt folklore. Tales, sometimes false, were told with glee daily. One old tale included a blazing clash of 94 sailors in balky sailboats on a bottomless lake. The last sailor alive was a lad that was blind. As he lay clinging to a slim balsa log in filth and slimy silt, the leader's falcon led help to him. Balmy days followed as the lad's leg healed slowly and the salves applied to his eyes let the light in.

Emphasis on M

The merger of an academy and the campus may take place in the autumn. It might bring mixed emotions from the 2,000 men and women. The stormy economic issue might make an anatomy class impossible at the academy. Some who must commute for months are not amused; many think that the merger is clumsy and dumb. There is not much warmth among the enemies. The teamwork is not smooth. The amount of stormy mass meetings must be diminished. An amendment must be made.

Emphasis on N

At sunset, around 8:30 p.m., it is nice to enjoy dining out on the bank of a pond. Unless uninvited insects and swarms of ants invade the picnic, you will certainly unwind. As those soft night sounds enfold you, frenzied inward nerves and the decisions that haunt you drain from your mind. You may enjoy napping on a nearby bench. Next, swing into action after your rest and inhale much air into your lungs. Unpack the nice lunch and munch away. Don't deny yourself this experience.

Emphasis on O

An oldtime cowboy often chose a lonely life out on the open range. Hoards of prowling foxes snooped among the 25 old cows and their young ones. Owls often hooted as an obscure and occasional sound annoyed them. The food was often cold and soggy. Cooking his food and boiling his coffee over an orange-hot fire offered some enjoyment, however. Through a long night his mournful songs poured out. He was a proven, loyal worker who overcame obstacles or coped with problems.

Document E — *Composing and Editing Business Letters*

Compose a letter to the manager of the airport that is closest to your school. Request that the manager arrange a meeting for you with one of the airline travel agents so that you can find out what kinds of information are stored in the travel agency's database. You want to know what information is available about passengers and the process that is used to track down lost luggage. Include two or three dates and times at which you would be available.

Write the letter as a block-style letter and include a copy notation to your instructor. Proofread your letter for wordiness and other language errors as well as punctuation and capitalization. When you have finished, save the letter as **041wpre.kwp**. Print, then close the document. Then trade printed copies with a classmate. Edit each other's documents for wordiness, adding your suggestions in pencil or pen. Include the note *Edited by (your name).*

ENDING THE SESSION

To end this session, print any files from Session 41 not printed earlier, then continue with the next session or exit the program. (***Note:*** Since no wpr files were created in Sessions 31-33, no deleting of files is required at the end of Sessions 41-43.)

PRINT

1. Choose **File** → **Open**.
2. At the *Open File* dialog box, select the files to be printed, then choose File **Options** → **Print**.
3. At the *Print Files* dialog box, press ***Enter*** or click on **Print**.
4. Click on Cancel or press ***Esc*** to close the *Open File* dialog box.

CONTINUE

1. Print any files, if necessary.
2. Click on the KWP Next Activity button.
3. At the next session menu, click on OK to proceed with the highlighted item.

EXIT

1. Print any files, if necessary.
2. Click on the KWP Main Menu button.
3. At the Main Menu, select WordPerfect Only, then click on OK.
4. Click on **File** → **Exit**.
5. Exit Windows (**File** → **Exit**), if necessary.

Emphasis on P

If the plan for upgrading the park in the spring would be accepted, the plot could be plowed now. Adept employees can plant the 225 maple and pine trees by the pond with the new equipment. Those sprigs of spindly aspens should be pulled up or snipped off. Most spaces for pleasant picnics should be paved, as well as the paths to the ponds. The chipmunks and other park pets won't be upset and peevish if the plans are to plant all spots with pleasant posies.

Emphasis on Q

At the request of an old acquaintance from the Equator city, quotations for equipment will be sent quickly. Those earthquakes ruined her unique antique aquariums. The 13 techniques of restoring them require liquid lacquer and the equipment in question. Answer her inquiry and quote a good price to her. Ask her to reply quickly as to the quantity. The question of her delinquent account must be settled when the equipment is ordered.

Emphasis on R

A rapid rise in industrial prices is normally absorbed by the consumers. Large firms that need raw materials work hard to realize a profit. It is a marvel that the poor and weary customer can afford to purchase services or products that have increased 15 percent. The grim race to raise prices must be curbed early. Scores of workers who earn small salaries find no mirth in fierce, sharp rises in the market. The rows and rows of bright and sparkling products are a farce to all concerned consumers.

WP WORDPERFECT REINFORCEMENT

Practice your file management skills by deleting the file 022wpr.kwp:

1. Choose **F**ile → **O**pen.
2. At the *Open File* dialog box, select the file *022wpr.kwp.*
3. With the filename highlighted, choose File **O**ptions → **D**elete.
4. At the *Delete File* dialog box, click on **D**elete. ***Note:*** If you want to print any files from this session, print at this time (**F**ile → **P**rint, then **D**ocument on Disk).
5. To close the *Open File* dialog box, click on Cancel or press ***Esc***.

ENDING THE SESSION

You may now continue with the next session or exit the program:

CONTINUE
1. Click on the KWP Next Activity button.
2. At the session menu, highlight the desired activity, then click on OK..

EXIT
1. Click on the KWP Main Menu button.
2. At the Main Menu, select WordPerfect Only, then click on OK.
3. Click on **F**ile → E**x**it.
4. Exit Windows (**F**ile → E**x**it), if necessary.

Document D ◄-- *Business Letter with Double-Indented Text*

1. At the *Production–Session 41 Document D* screen, key the handwritten document as a block-style letter with 1.25-inch left and right margins.
2. Indent the list of numbered items from both margins. After keying each item number, press ***Tab***, then key the text.
3. Vertically center the document on the page.
4. Proofread and correct errors. Complete a spell check.
5. Click on Check to automatically name **(041prod.kwp)** and save the document. The program checks the letter for errors and calculates your WAM rate.
6. When checking is complete, the letter is displayed on the screen with errors highlighted.
7. To print the letter with errors highlighted, click on the Print button.
8. To correct errors, click on View Original. Make changes, then recheck the document.
9. Choose **F**ile → **C**lose. This closes Document D and brings up a clear WordPerfect editing window at which you will complete Document E.

Document D

(current date)/Dr. Carlos Bonner/Department of Business Education/University of Southern Mississippi/Southern Station, Box 83/Hattiesburg, MS 39401-2117/Dear Dr. Bonner:/Dr. Livingston indicated that you would be serving as coordinator for the workshop that Dr. Edith Wenzer and I will be presenting in Hattiesburg in July./For our presentations at the workshop, we will need the following equipment: 1) High-intensity overhead projector 2) Color LCD panel 3) PC with the latest version of Windows./I will send you an outline of the topics we plan to discuss. Also, we will be sending you a copy of the software that will be used in the presentation. Can you arrange to have it installed on the PC?/If there is anything else that you need from us, please drop me a line or give me a call at 505-555-6944./Sincerely yours,/Dennis Czeslaw/President/your initials and filename/c Janet Livingston, Edith Wenzer

REINFORCING WRITING SKILLS

Have you ever read a letter that begins *I would like to take this opportunity to thank you . . .* or *I am writing this letter to tell you about the conference on Aging . . .*? These clauses are examples of using many words for what could be said in a few words. The first clause could be rewritten as *Thank you . . .*. The second clause should be deleted, and the writer should simply begin with *The conference on Aging opens November 15 . . .*.

One of the hazards of using extra "verbiage" (words) is that the writer's message becomes lost. The reader has to plow through meaningless phrases that only cause frustration. And, although most writers can recognize the problem of excessive words, they may omit that editing step because it takes a little extra time. Frequently, writers are satisfied with merely having completed the writing task.

When proofreading and editing your documents, it is critical that you take the time to cut out unnecessary words. Make it a challenge to reduce your sentences to the essential words that convey your meaning clearly and completely.

SESSION 33

SKILL BUILDING: LETTERS S-Z

SESSION GOALS

Review S-Z, Numeric, and Symbol Keys

30 WAM/2 errors

GETTING STARTED

If you are continuing immediately from Session 32, you should see the Session 33 menu on your screen with the first item highlighted. Click on OK to begin working. If you exited the program during or at the end of Session 32, do the following:.

1. Access Windows, then WordPerfect 6.1 for Windows.
2. Click on the KWP button to access *Keyboarding with WordPerfect*.
3. Go to the Keyboarding Sessions menu and click on Jump to return to your last activity. Or, access the Session 33 menu to begin the session.

Session 33 provides an opportunity to reinforce your keyboarding skills on the letters **s** through **z**. You may select only those letters you think you need to work on or do the activities for all the letters in this session. The directions for completing all keyboarding activities appear on the screen.

If you decide that additional practice is unnecessary and you want to skip the Timings, highlight *WordPerfect Reinforcement* on the session menu. Then follow the directions in the WordPerfect Reinforcement section on the following pages to delete an outdated file from a previous session.

TIMINGS

Emphasis on S

The 14 sulky, sad losers are scorned by most of us. A dismal loss or misfortune doesn't have to end in disgrace. Surely most folks in such spots show disgust at a loss. But those persons briskly squelch those feelings and smile because life goes on. There is always a lesson to be learned from every mistake or loss. Stay in the driver's seat and see all the good things that come along. Solving basic problems easily is necessary to reduce tensions.

Document B ← Business Letter with Full Justification

1. At the *Production–Session 41 Document B* screen, change the justification to Full, then key Document B as a block-style letter.
2. Center the letter vertically on the page.
3. Proofread the letter and correct errors. Complete a spell check.
4. Click on Check to automatically save and name **(041prob.kwp)** the letter. The program checks the document for errors and calculates your WAM rate.
5. When checking is complete, the letter is displayed on the screen with errors highlighted.
6. To print the letter with errors highlighted, click on the Print button.
7. To correct errors, click on View Original. Make changes, then recheck the document.
8. Click on **File** → **Close**. This closes Document B and brings up the Document C screen.

Document B

Mr. Howard Young/West, Young & Stern/4200 Exchange Building/new york, NY 10014-3728/ On November 29, a nonqualified stock option was issued to Mr. Del Stewart for 2,500 shares of Life Devices, Inc. common stock. You have informed us that these shares, when issued, bear a two-year restrictive legend./ Life Devices, Inc., engaged in the manufacture and sale of neurological pain-relieving implant devices, has been in business less than five years and has a limited sales and earnings history. The company's common stock is currently trading on the national over-the-counter market. On November 20, the stock closed at 14-5/8 bid and 15-1/8 asked. /Based on the two-year restriction as well as the speculative nature of the company, it is our opinion that the fair market value, for the purpose of the stock option described above, would be a 50 percent discount from the market price. The mean between the bid and asked prices on November 20 was $14,875, resulting in our valuation of $4.44 per share. Donald F. Steiner, Senior Vice President

Document C ← Business Letter Edited with Cut and Paste

1. At a clear WordPerfect editing window, open **041prob.kwp**.
2. Move the sentence that begins *The mean between the bid and asked prices. . .* before the second sentence in the first paragraph, which begins *You have informed us that. . ..*
3. Move the second paragraph that begins *Life Devices, Inc., engaged. . .* to follow the paragraph that begins *Based on the two-year. . ..*
4. Proofread your document and correct any errors, including line spacing.
5. Choose **File** → Save **A**s and name the document **041wprc.kwp**.
6. Choose **File** → **C**lose.
7. Click on the KWP Next Activity button to bring up the Document D screen.

Emphasis on T

Tenseness while keying causes costly mistakes. Take a gentle tip or two and practice them as you key. Watch out for fatigue: A tired receptionist tends to clutch at the keys and doesn't tap them with a gentle touch. Twirling or twisting in your seat is a typical trick at the computer. Talking a lot as you key is first on the list of bad techniques. Do not try too hard, as this often turns those keys into something frustrating. Don't let the keyboarding mistakes continue.

Emphasis on U

The impulse to judge individuals quickly causes faulty results. It is unwise and unfair to jump to conclusions in a hurry. Actually, a useful guide to a sound understanding of humans is to quietly assess the situation. A subtle and thorough query can subdue doubts and evaluate behavior. An ugly and cruel deduction about another's values could cause undue suffering. You are urged to utilize more time (even if it's only 15 to 20 minutes) if you are puzzled and used to useless, quick guesses.

Emphasis on V

A visit to a village in a quiet valley gives vitality, vim, and vigor to the 46 tired individuals. Nothing rivals the vacation voyage to revive the spirits. Heavy problems seem to vanish and vexing tribulations evaporate. Vivid visions of a diverse way of living evoke valuable impressive vistas of rest. Save those fevered nerves and prevent grievous or adverse tribulations. Endeavor to take advantage of events that elevate the spirits; you deserve the very best.

Emphasis on W

The news on the network newscast might spawn a winning wealth of followers. If the newscaster can draw a wider range of viewers, the rewards are power and wealth. Watchers and followers of a witty new reporter are won when the daily news is written well. It is not a waste to rewrite the worst of interviews when 18 witless words can wreck a well planned show or review. Workers who dawdle in the newsroom will not work or write very long. Their award will be awful reviews.

Emphasis on X

An example of a tedious exercise is the flexing of lax muscles daily. Excess anxieties are exhausting to all who are under extreme pressure. A program of extensive, complex exercises is a vexation. Most experts agree that exertion to exhaustion is wrong. A flexible, yet exuberant exercise involves exhaling noxious air and inhaling oxygen. Explore the exotic experience of a brisk 30-minute daily walk. That expended energy will excite you and extend your life.

Copying Text

To copy a block of text from one place to another, you would follow these steps:

1 Select the text.
2 Click on the Copy button on the Toolbar (or press ***Ctrl + C***).
3 Move the insertion point to the location where the text is to be copied.
4 Click on the Paste button on the Toolbar (or press ***Ctrl + V***).

Deleting Text

To delete a block of text, you would following these steps:

1 Select the text.
2 Press ***Delete*** (or press ***Ctrl + X***).

Document A — *Business Letter Edited with Cut and Paste*

1 At a clear WordPerect editing window, open **040prob.kwp**.
2 Move the paragraph located near the bottom of the letter that begins *We plan to work with. . .* between the first and second paragraphs in the letter by doing the following:
   a Position the insertion point anywhere in the paragraph and quickly click the left mouse button four times to select the paragraph.
   b Click on the Cut button on the Toolbar.
   c Position the insertion point at the beginning of the second paragraph (this is the paragraph that begins *It is our intention. . .*).
   d Click on the Paste button.
3 Check the spacing between paragraphs to ensure that it is correct. You may need to insert or delete blank lines to maintain the double spacing between paragraphs.
4 Move the paragraph that begins *3. The completed filing. . .* before the paragraph that begins *1. The assurance that. . .* by doing the following:
   a Position the insertion point anywhere in the paragraph.
   b Click the left mouse button quickly four times to select the paragraph, its number, and the hard return after the paragraph. (You can also select text by dragging with the mouse.)
   c Click on the Cut button on the Toolbar.
   d Position the insertion point at the beginning of the first enumerated paragraph (*The assurance that. . .)* on the number 1.
   e Click on the Paste button on the Toolbar.
5 After pasting the paragraph, renumber the paragraphs.
6 Choose **File** → Save **A**s and key **041wpra.kwp** as the document name.
7 Choose **File** → **C**lose.
8 Click on the KWP Next Activity button to bring up the Document B screen.

Emphasis on Y

A hobby is healthy for nearly everyone. A typical and unhealthy symptom of an extremely busy employer is anxiety. You may enjoy skydiving or flying as an activity. Yet, you might fill joyful and happy days by playing the rhythm of a song on a piano keyboard with its 88 keys. Analyze your daydreams and style your life to trying entirely new ways of living. I usually have enjoyed a foray into the dynamic joy of geology as a hobby. Prying through mystical layers of dirt is always fun.

Emphasis on Z

That wizard of zoology amazes zillions of zoo visitors daily. The dazzling display of the 55 puzzling zebras daze people of all sizes. Lazy lizards zigzag into a dizzy speed on an oozing pond. Monkeys puzzle many folks by the crazy antics on the hazardous horizontal bars. The graceful gazelles in brown graze in the park plazas. After a day at the zoo, it is fun to stop at a bazaar and have a zesty pizza.

WORDPERFECT REINFORCEMENT

Practice your file management skills by deleting the file 023wpr.kwp. Follow these steps:

1. Choose **F**ile → **O**pen.
2. At the *Open File* dialog box, select the file 023wpr.kwp.
3. With the filename highlighted, choose File **O**ptions → **D**elete.
4. At the *Delete File* dialog box, click on **D**elete. ***Note:*** If you want to print any files from this session, print them at this point (**F**ile → **P**rint, then **D**ocument on Disk).
5. To close the *Open File* dialog box, click on Cancel or press *Esc*.

ENDING THE SESSION

You may now continue with the next session or exit the program.

CONTINUE
1. Click on the KWP Next Activity button.
2. At the session menu, highlight the desired activity, then click on OK.

EXIT
1. Click on the KWP Main Menu button.
2. At the Main Menu, select WordPerfect Only, then click on OK.
3. Click on **F**ile → E**x**it.
4. Exit Windows (**F**ile → E**x**it), if necessary.

When cutting and pasting, you work with blocks of text. A block of text is a portion of text that you have selected. A block of text can be as small as one character or as large as an entire page or document.

Selecting Text

Text can be selected using the mouse, the keyboard, or the *Select* option from the **E**dit menu.

To use the ***mouse*** to select text, position the I-beam pointer on the first character of the text to be selected, hold down the left mouse, drag the I-beam pointer to the last character of the text to be selected, then release the left mouse button. The selected text will be highlighted in reverse video.

You can also use the mouse to select a word, sentence, or paragraph quickly. WordPerfect defines (1) a *word* as text that ends with a space, (2) a *sentence* as text that ends with a period followed by a space, and (3) a *paragraph* as text that ends with a hard return (Enter).

To select a ***word*** with the mouse, position the insertion point on any character in the word and double-click the left mouse button. To select a ***sentence***, position the insertion point on any character in the sentence and quickly click the left mouse button three times. To select a ***paragraph***, position the insertion point on any character in the paragraph, and quickly ***click*** the left mouse button ***four times***. If you need to select an amount of text other than a word, a sentence, or a paragraph, use the drag technique described earlier.

To use the ***keyboar***d to select text, use the Select key, F8, along with the arrow keys. Pressing ***F8*** once turns the Select mode on. (The word *Select* should be visible in the Status Bar. When the word is grayed, you are not in the Select mode.) To select text, press any of the arrow keys until the desired text is selected. (You can also key letters or punctuation marks to define your text selection.) Press ***F8*** after text is selected to deselect your text and turn off the Select Mode.

The ***Edit*** menu contains an option that lets you select a sentence, a paragraph, a page, or the entire document. To select a sentence, position the insertion point anywhere in the sentence, choose **E**dit → Select → **S**entence. To select a paragraph, position the insertion point anywhere in the paragraph, choose **E**dit → Select → **P**aragraph. To select a page, choose **E**dit → Select → **P**age. To select the entire document, choose **E**dit → Select → **A**ll.

Note: You can use the Shift + arrow keys to change (lengthen or shorten) the text block. Pressing ***F8*** will also turn the Select mode off and deselect the highlighted text.

Moving Text

To move a block of text from one place to another, you would follow these steps:

1 Select the text.
2 Click on the Cut button on the Toolbar (or press ***Ctrl + X***).
3 Position the insertion point to the location where the text is to be moved.
4 Click on the Paste button on the Toolbar (or press ***Ctrl + V***).

UNIT 7

MEMORANDUMS

FIVE-MINUTE TIMINGS

Goal: 30 WAM/2 errors

SI: 1.42

- Take two 5-minute timings.

Wise managers of money seem to have the ability or the foresight to make their money stretch a long way. Others spend haphazardly and always seem to be short of money long before the next salary check is due. What factors do the wise managers follow?

Food buying takes a large part of the salary check. In the area of buying groceries, one can save a large amount of money by wise and careful buying. There are many fine guides that a shopper can follow to economize and save money.

Probably the one best rule to attempt, at the outset, is to plan ahead. Plan all your meals in detail for a certain period, for example, a week or a month, but never day by day. After making the complete plan for your groceries, you are then ready to prepare your shopping list. Be sure that you have included all of the items required for cooking the meals to come. Many people forget to include the small items such as salt, pepper, and needed condiments. Once you have made a list, additional guides are very useful and helpful.

After making the major shopping list, you should compare prices. You should look at all the local advertisements in newspapers. Quite often, you will save considerable amounts of your money by comparison shopping. However, do not waste time or money for gas by driving your car from store to store. If you do this, you are defeating your purpose. After deciding where to do your shopping, your next step is that of doing the actual shopping.

REVISING BUSINESS LETTERS

Read the following information on *Cutting and Pasting Text*. Then proceed with Documents A-E. Be sure to read the instructions in the text for each document.

Cutting and Pasting Text

Some documents may need to be revised extensively, and those revisions may include deleting, moving, or copying blocks of text. This kind of editing is generally referred to as *cutting and pasting*. WordPerfect offers several ways to cut and paste text, including buttons on the Toolbar, keyboard shortcut commands, and the Edit option on the Menu Bar. Because the Toolbar method is generally easier and more efficient, that method is emphasized in this text.

Cutting and/or *moving* text means that text is deleted from its present location and reinserted in a new location. However, when text is *copied,* it remains in its original location *and* a copy is inserted into the new location. There are two copies of the text in the document.

The basic steps for cutting and pasting text are:

1. Select the text.
2. Choose to move or copy the selected text.
3. Paste the selected text into the new location.

PROOFREADING TECHNIQUES

SESSION GOALS

1-minute: 35 WAM/2 errors

Review error correction methods
Use Spell Check
Split and join paragraphs

GETTING STARTED

If you are continuing immediately from Session 33, you should see the Session 34 menu on your screen, with the first item highlighted. Click on OK to begin. If you exited the program during or at the end of Session 33, do the following:

1. Access Windows, then WordPerfect 6.1 for Windows.
2. Click on the KWP button to access *Keyboarding with WordPerfect.*
3. Go to the Keyboarding Sessions menu and click on Jump to return to your last activity. Or, access the Session 34 menu to begin the session.

If you are already warmed up or have completed part of the session, highlight the desired activity and click on OK. When you have completed the on-screen activities for Session 34, you will return to the text to complete a section of short documents that will provide practice on using WordPerfect's Spell Checker and on splitting and joining paragraphs.

ONE-MINUTE TIMINGS

Goal: 35 WAM/2 errors

SI: 1.36

- Take two 1-minute timings on the following paragraph.
- Set either a speed or accuracy goal, based on your most recent timing score. (Click on the KWP Rep button to review your timings scores on the Student Report.).

Never use a steel hammer to strike a chisel. Utilize either the solid rubber or wooden mallet. You can use the palm of your hand, of course, depending on the particular project. A mallet can be used in cases where the edge to be cut is across the grain. If, however, the cutting edge is with the grain, a mallet could easily split the wood. Remember to angle the chisel slightly when starting a cut. The angle makes smooth or pared cuts easier to do.

SESSION 41

SESSION GOALS

1-Minute: 40 WAM/2 errors
5-Minute: 30 WAM/2 errors

Cutting and pasting text

Cutting unnecessary words

GETTING STARTED

If you are continuing immediately from Session 40, go to the one-minute timings. If you exited the program at the end of Session 40, do the following:

1. Access Windows, then WordPerfect 6.1 for Windows.
2. Click on the KWP icon to access *Keyboarding with WordPerfect.*
3. Go to the Keyboarding Sessions menu and click on Jump to return to your last activity. Or, access the Session 41 menu and click on OK to begin the session.

If your fingers are already warmed up or if you have completed part of the session, highlight the desired activity and click on OK. When you have completed the on-screen activities for Session 41, you will return to the text to complete several business letters in which you will use WordPerfect's cut-and-paste feature to make the letter editing process more efficient.

ONE-MINUTE TIMINGS

Goal: 40 WAM/2 errors

SI: 1.45

- Take two 1-minute timings.
- Use your most recent 1-minute timing score to set a speed or accuracy goal. Note that with this session, the goal has been increased by 5 WAM.

To honor a deserving person in the community is a fine thing. A most interesting factor becomes apparent many times in the ugly form of jealousy for another's accomplishments. Most people can accept a high honor quite well (that is, if they were the ones to win). Those people who did not win may begin to hold a grudge against anyone who was a winner. When something like a community honor causes deep, hard feelings on the part of some people, it becomes an empty prize; the winner may be the loser. Honors and awards must be given and accepted with a generous, happy spirit.

PREPARING BUSINESS DOCUMENTS

Beginning with this session, you will use WordPerfect to prepare a variety of business documents. Most are automatically named, saved, and checked by the KWP software. The program assigns a name that includes four parts: 1) the session number; 2) **pro** for production documents; 3) a document designation (a, b, etc.); and 4) the **kwp** extension. In this session, Documents E, F, and G are named, saved, and checked by the KWP software.

Certain documents, including Documents A-D in this session, must be completed in WordPerfect alone (Freeform). You are instructed to name and save these documents using a system similar to the file-naming system used by the KWP program: the session number, **wpr** for WordPerfect Reinforcement, a document designation (a, b, etc), and the **kwp** extension. The KWP software does not check these documents for errors. However, the program can time your keyboarding speed. You can have your WAM rate calculated by clicking on WAM Only (at the bottom of the screen) before you begin keying the document. Check your User's Guide for a complete explanation of this feature.

Read the following information about Proofreading Techniques. Then prepare Document A. Instructions for subsequent documents also appear in the text.

Proofreading Techniques

Developing effective proofreading techniques is an essential skill whether you are writing your own documents or preparing documents for others. Proofreading requires knowledge and practice. The document is to be read slowly, word for word. For best results, proofread the document three times: (1) for content (check to see that all information from the original document has been included); (2) for punctuation and grammar; and (3) for meaning (this applies particularly to documents you write yourself). Good proofreaders focus on the following guidelines:

1. Know the basics of punctuation and grammar.
2. Pay attention to detail.
3. Use the proofreading method best-suited to the material.
4. Allow sufficient time to proofread.
5. Use standard proofreaders' marks (see the User's Guide) as much as possible.
6. Use an electronic spell checker to catch basic spelling errors.
7. After completing an electronic spelling check, proofread again for errors in word use and other kinds of mistakes that spelling checkers miss.

Correcting Errors: Review

To make corrections to a WordPerfect document, move the insertion point to a specific location within the document and either add text (insert) or remove text (delete). In previous sessions you learned the insertion point (mouse cursor) movement commands. If necessary, review the information on correcting errors in Sessions 2, 3, and 4.

Inserting Text

Once you have created a document, you may want to insert information. By default, WordPerfect is in the "insert" mode. This means that anything new that you key is added at the insertion point location and does not take the place of existing text.

Omit the inside address (assume that it will be added later). Use *Dear Investor:* as the salutation. Use your name and a title of *Marketing Representative*. Save the letter as **040wprf.kwp** and print it, if required by your instructor. Close the file.

ENDING THE SESSION

To end this session, delete outdated WordPerfect Reinforcement files, print any files from Session 40 not printed earlier, then continue with the next session or exit the program:

DELETE

1. Choose **F**ile → **O**pen.
2. Select the Session 30 wpr files.
3. With the filename highlighted, choose File **O**ptions → **D**elete.
4. At the *Delete File(s)* dialog box, click on **D**elete.
5. If you need to print files, go to step 2 under PRINT. Otherwise, click on Cancel or press ***Esc*** to close the *Open File* dialog box.

PRINT

1. Choose **F**ile → **O**pen.
2. At the *Open File* dialog box, select the files to be printed, then choose File **O**ptions → **P**rint.
3. At the *Print Files* dialog box, press ***Enter*** or click on Print.
4. Click on Cancel or press ***Esc*** to close the *Open File* dialog box.

CONTINUE

1. Print any files, if necessary.
2. Click on the KWP Next Activity button.
3. At the next session menu, click on OK to proceed with the highlighted item.

EXIT

1. Print any files, if necessary.
2. Click on the KWP Main Menu button.
3. At the Main Menu, select WordPerfect Only, then click on OK.
4. Click on **F**ile → E**x**it.
5. Exit Windows (**F**ile → E**x**it), if necessary.

If you want to insert or add something, simply key the new text at the desired location. If, however, you want to replace old text with new text, turn Insert off by pressing the Insert key. When you press this key, the message *Typeover* appears in the Status Bar, and the text you key replaces previous text, letter by letter. It is easy to accidentally key over text you want to keep, so be careful about remaining in Typeover mode. Typeover will stay in effect until you press the Insert key again or until you exit WordPerfect.

Deleting Text

WordPerfect includes a variety of commands that can be used to delete text by character, word, or line. In earlier sessions you learned to delete characters.

To delete an entire word, position the insertion point on any character of the word, then press ***Ctrl + Backspace***. The entire word, including any punctuation, is deleted. Any text to the right moves to the left and fills in the gap.

You can delete text to the end of the line by pressing ***Ctrl + Del***. This deletes all text from the location of the insertion point to the end of the line. If you want to delete the entire line, position the insertion point at the beginning of the line, then press ***Ctrl + Del***.

Splitting and Joining Paragraphs

To split a large paragraph into two smaller paragraphs, position the insertion point on the first letter where the new paragraph is to begin and press ***Enter*** twice. The first time you press ***Enter***, the text is taken to the next line. The second time you press ***Enter***, a blank line is inserted between the paragraphs.

To join two paragraphs, you need to delete the lines between them. There are two ways to do this. One is to position the insertion point on the first character of the second paragraph and press the Backspace key until the paragraphs join. (You may have to insert a space to separate the sentences.) The other method is to position the insertion point one space past the period at the end of the first paragraph and press the Delete key until the paragraphs join. When you join the two paragraphs, the lines of the new paragraph are automatically adjusted.

Now you can practice deleting, inserting, and combining text as you complete the following documents using WordPerfect 6.1 for Windows.

Document A — *Paragraphs*

1. At a clear WordPerfect editing window, key the text shown in Document A. Use the WordPerfect default margins.
2. As you key the text, use the insertion point movement commands and the Insert/Delete functions to correct errors.
3. When the text is entered, complete the following steps to practice moving the insertion point:
   a. Press ***Page Up*** to move the insertion point to the top of the screen.
   b. Press ***Ctrl + Right Arrow*** to move the insertion point word by word until you reach the last word at the end of the first paragraph.
   c. Press ***Ctrl + Left Arrow*** to move the insertion point word by word until you reach the beginning of the first paragraph.
   d. Press ***End*** to move the insertion point to the end of the line.
   e. Press ***Home*** to move the insertion point to the beginning of the line.
   f. Press ***Page Down*** to move the insertion point to the bottom of the screen (last line of the document).

emerging medical firms in the city of New York. Please give me a call whenever it is convenient, and I will be pleased to set up an appointment to discuss a mutually satisfying business relationship. Sincerely,/Roberta E. Thomas/Investment Consultant/your initials and filename

Document E — *Business Letter Revised with Find and Replace*

1. At a clear WordPerfect editing window, open **040wprc.kwp**.
2. Search for and delete all bold codes without confirmation by doing the following:
   a. Position the insertion point at the beginning of the document.
   b. Choose **E**dit → F**i**nd and Replace; or press F2.
   c. Choose **M**atch → **C**odes.
   d. At the *Code* dialog box, select Bold On and click on Insert to insert this code in the *Find* text box.
3. Leave the default <*Nothing*> in the *Replace With* text box. (If the *Replace With* text box contains text, choose Replace With, then press Delete.)
4. Click on Replace All to delete all bold codes.
5. Click on Close.
6. Choose **F**ile → Save **A**s. Save the revised document as **040wpre.kwp**.
7. To print the letter, click on the Print button.
8. Choose **F**ile → **C**lose to close the document.

REINFORCING WRITING SKILLS

Identifying your reader is one of the first steps in creating a well written document. Questions to ask yourself include the following:

- Who is my reader?
- What do I know about my reader that will help determine the best approach?
- Is the audience one person or a group?
- Is my reader a co-worker, a subordinate, a superior, or a customer?
- How is the reader likely to feel about my message?
- How much does the reader know already about my topic?

Answering these questions will help you choose the information to include in your document and the words and sentences to convey that information. For example, if you are describing the latest space mission and your readers are scientists or engineers, you will refer to principles of physics and use highly technical words that might be unfamiliar to the general population. You would also include more detail. A description of that space mission written for the local newspaper would have to relate the mission goals and findings in language that the average reader could understand. You would describe results that would affect the everyday person.

Document F — *Rewriting a Letter for a Different Audience*

Retrieve Document 040prob.kwp and rewrite it for potential investors in IDP Computing. Consider their interest in and reaction to the information. How can you make the news attractive to them? Do you need to include all the details outlined in the letter? Consider the financial words used. How can you state the same information in "everyday" language?

4 To save the document, click on the Save button on the Toolbar.
5 At the *Save As* dialog box, key **034wpra.kwp** in the filename textbox and press ***Enter*** or click on OK. Your document has been saved to disk, and it also remains open on the screen. You will add more text to this document in the next exercise.

Document A

Workplace literacy has been targeted as a departmental project for 1997. Interest in the project is driven by expressed need within the organization and increased pressure by regulatory agencies to respond to the literacy needs of employees.

In addition, there is concern about the rapidly and dramatically changing work force and how this changing work force will impact the future viability of our company. Before rushing into any program solutions, literacy needs must be carefully explored.

Document B — *Paragraphs with Proofreaders' Corrections*

With document 034wpra.kwp on the screen, make the corrections shown in Document B, then go to step 4. If you are not familiar with the proofreaders' marks, review them in the User's Guide.

If you are resuming your work in Session 34 with Document B, open 034wpra.kwp by completing the following steps:

1 Choose **F**ile → **O**pen.
2 At the *Open File* dialog box, select the filename *034wpra.kwp* and click on OK.
3 Make the indicated changes.
4 To save the document with the name **034wprb.kwp**, choose **F**ile → Save **A**s (or press F3).
5 At the *Save As* dialog box, you will see the filename *034wpra.kwp* (the file you opened and edited).
6 Move the insertion point to the *a* in the name. Delete the *a* and key the letter **b**. The filename in the textbox should now read *034wprb.kwp.*
7 Press ***Enter*** or click on OK.
8 Choose **F**ile → **C**lose to close the document.

Document B

Workplace literacy has been targeted as a departmental project for 1997. Interest in the project is driven by expressed need within the organization and increased pressure by regulatory agencies to respond to the literacy needs of employees.

In addition, there is concern about the rapidly and dramatically changing work force and how this changing work force will impact the future viability of our company. Before rushing into any program solutions, literacy needs must be carefully explored.

s

we

search string, including words that contain the letters specified. For example, if you enter the string *her* in the *Find:* text box, WordPerfect stops at *there, hers, rather*, and so on, because each word contains the letters *her*. If you want to find a specific word such as *her*, choose **W**hole Word at the Match drop-down menu.

Document C — Business Letter Revised with Find and Replace

1. At a clear WordPerfect editing window, open **040prob.kwp**.
2. Find all occurrences of the word *common* and replace it with the word *preferred* without confirmation by doing the following:
   a. Position the insertion point at the beginning of the document.
   b. Choose **E**dit → **F**ind and Replace; or press F2.
   c. In the *Find* text box, key **common.** (Do not key a period.) Choose **M**atch → **W**hole Word.
   d. In the *Replace With* text box, key **preferred**. (Do not key a period.)
   e. Click on Replace All.
   f. Click on Close.
3. Choose **F**ile → Save **A**s. Save the revised letter with a new name by keying in **040wprc.kwp**.
4. To print the letter, click on the Print button.
5. Choose **F**ile → **C**lose to close the document.
6. Click on the KWP Next Activity button. This brings up the Document D screen.

Document D — Block-Style Letter with Wide Margins and Full Justification

1. At the *Production–Session 40 Document D* screen, change the left and right margins to 1.25 inches (Fo**r**mat → **M**argins). Insert the date with ***Ctrl + D***.
2. Change the justification to Full.
3. Key Document D as a block-style letter. Center the letter vertically on the page.
4. Click on Check to automatically name (**040prod.kwp**) and save the document. The program checks the letter for errors and calculates your WAM rate.
5. When checking is complete, the document is displayed on the screen with errors highlighted.
6. To print the document with errors highlighted, click on the Print button.
7. To correct errors, click on View Original. Make changes, then recheck the document.
8. Choose **F**ile → **C**lose. This exits Document D and brings up a clear WordPerfect editing window.

Document D

Dr. James Moline/Metropolitan Professional Building/5991 Madison Drive/New York, NY 10055-9110/Dear Dr. Moline:/~~It was a pleasure to visit with you on the phone this morning.~~ Truax-Vehlow Investment Services has been in the brokerage and investment banking business for over 25 years and specializes in ~~new~~ growth companies. We firmly believe that such companies represent the greatest profit potential for individual investors. In recent years, we have devoted considerable attention to the medical industry through our research and investment banking activities. We have played an important role in the early stages of several ~~recently~~

Continued on next page

Using Spell Checker

With WordPerfect's spell checking program, you can check words in a document against words in the program for proper spelling. The Spell Checker program contains over 100,000 words and operates by comparing words in the document with words stored in the program. If the word matches, Spell Checker leaves it and moves on. If there is no match for the word, Spell Checker stops and offers you several choices. You can:

1 Replace the word with the word shown in the *Replace With* dialog box.
2 Skip the word, leaving it in its original form.
3 Correct the word using the definition in QuickCorrect.
4 Suggest other words and phrases that are not shown.
5 Add to the Spell Checker supplemental dictionary.
6 Edit the word to correct its spelling.

Spell Checker does not stop at words that are spelled correctly but used incorrectly. For example, if you key *form* instead of *from,* Spell Checker finds a match for *form* and does not stop to correct it. Spell Checker contains some common proper names, but not many, so it stops at most proper names for correction.

Document C ← *Paragraph with Spelling Errors*

1. At a clear WordPerfect editing window, key the text shown in Document C (including misspelled words).
2. Click on the Spell Check button on the Toolbar.
3. Spell Checker highlights *developement* and displays one possible replacement. Click on *Replace* to replace *developement* with the correct spelling.
4. Spell Checker highlights *proirity* and displays two possible replacements. Click on *Replace* to replace *proirity* with the highlighted and correctly spelled word.
5. Spell Checker skips over the word *is* (which should be *are*) and *fore* (which should be *for*) because it found matches. (Do not correct these errors for now.)
6. Spell Checker highlights *employes* and displays possible replacements. In the *Suggestions* box, double-click on the second word in the list, which is **employees,** to replace *employes* with the correct spelling.
7. The checking is complete when the dialog box appears with the prompt, *Spell Check completed. Close Spell Checker?* Click on **Y**es to close the dialog box.
8. Save the document with the name **034wprc.kwp** by clicking on the Save button on the Toolbar.
9. At the *Save As* dialog box key **034wprc.kwp** in the filename box, then click on OK or press ***Enter***. This saves the file to your data disk and keeps the document open so you can add text to this file in the next assignment.

Document C

Staff developement is and will continue to be a top company proirity as restructuring efforts is addressed. Change takes knowledge, time, and ongoing support fore employes in the form of coaching. Calendars and schedules often present obstacles that make supporting change difficult.

We plan to work with management to obtain a distribution of the common stock that will be beneficial to the company, and we look forward to working with you and your associates on the proposed sale of common stock.

Sincerely yours,

Donald F. Steiner
Senior Vice President

xx/040prob.kwp

Using Find and Replace

WordPerfect's Find and Replace feature searches for words, phrases, or codes in your document and replaces them with words or codes you specify. With Find and Replace, you can accomplish the following:

1. Find and replace a misspelled word and replace it with the correct spelling.
2. Save keystrokes by using abbreviations for common phrases, words, names, etc., and replacing them later with complete words.
3. Set up standard documents with general names and replace them with other names to make personalized documents.
4. Find and replace format codes.

To conduct a find and replace in a document, you would do the following:

1. Position the insertion point at the beginning of the document.
2. Choose **E**dit → **F**ind and Replace from the Menu Bar or press F2.
3. At the *Find and Replace Text* dialog box, key the text you want to find in the *Find* text box.
4. Choose Replace **W**ith, then key the replacement text in the *Replace With* text box.
5. From the five command buttons on the right side of the dialog box, click on *Find Next* to find the next occurrence of the search string. Choose the *Replace* button to replace the search string and find the next occurrence of the string. If you are certain that you want all occurrences of the search string replaced in the document, choose *Replace All.* This replaces every occurrence of the search string from the location of the insertion point to the beginning or end of the document.
6. Choose **C**lose to close the *Find and Replace Text* dialog box.

The Find and Replace feature includes several options that allow you to customize your search. For example, you may need to limit your search to instances of whole words, which is what you will do in Document C. In a later session, you will learn to use other options.

Conducting Whole Word Searches

The Match menu allows you to search for a whole word, a specific case, a specific font, or a code. If you do not specify *whole word*, WordPerfect will stop at all occurrences that match the

Document D ← Paragraph Added to Document C

1. With Document C on the screen, key the paragraph shown in Document D. Begin a double-space below the text of Document C. (If you are resuming your work in Session 34 at this point, open file **034wprc.kwp**.)
2. Proofread both paragraphs and correct any errors you find.
3. Use the WordPerfect Spell Checker program to see if you have found all your errors. Remember, Spell Checker will not find errors in word use.
4. Choose **F**ile → Save **A**s to save the document with a new name.
5. At the *Save As* dialog box, the filename *034wprc.kwp* displays. Delete the letter *c* in the filename, then key **d**. The new filename should read *034wprd.kwp*. Press ***Enter*** or click on OK.
6. Choose **F**ile → **C**lose to close the document.
7. Click on the KWP Next Activity button to bring up the Document E screen.

Document D

The implimentation of Information Proocessing Systems in busniess offices requires secretariel and clerical personnil to haev a greater knowledge of a veriaty of keyboarding applications, since thier responsibility is too process the keyboarding of material from many authors.

Common Errors Found During Proofreading

Errors	**Examples**
Confusion of similar words	now/not; on/of/or; than/that; yes/yet
Confusion of suffixes and word endings	formed/former; pointing/point; type/types
Omissions in sequence of enumerated items	a/b/d/e; 1/2/4/5
Transposition of digits in numbers	451/541; 1998/1989
Transposition of letters within words	form/from
Misspelled names and words that sound alike	Clark/Clarke; Reed/Reid; knew/new
Errors in capitalization	capitalizing articles and conjunctions in titles
Errors in punctuation	missing or misplaced commas
Errors in word use	principal (head of a school) vs. principle (rule); advise (to suggest) vs. advice (a suggestion)
Errors in words that fall near margins	(because beginnings and endings of lines are often skimmed more rapidly)
Omission of an entire line when a word appears in the same place in two consecutive lines	Turning it on is accomplished by moving the lever in. Turning off is done by moving the lever out. Turning it on is accomplished by moving the lever out.
Errors occurring at the bottom of a page	(Because the eye is tired or the reader skims too rapidly at the end of the page)
Omission of short words	(Short words such as **if, is, it,** and **in** when the preceding word ends in a similar letter or the following word begins with the same letter)

Document B ← Business Letter with Bolded and Indented Text

1. At the *Production–Session 40 Document B* screen, key Document B in the block-style format, inserting the date with ***Ctrl + D***. Make the following changes:
   a. Bold the name *IDP Computing* wherever it appears in the document.
   b. Indent the numbered items one tab stop from both the left and right margins (***Ctrl + Shift + F7***). Indent the text after each number (***F7***).
2. Center the letter vertically on the page.
3. Proofread and correct any errors, then complete a spell check.
4. Click on Check to automatically save and name (**040prob.kwp**) the document. The program checks the letter for errors and calculates your WAM rate.
5. When checking is complete, the letter is displayed on the screen with errors highlighted.
6. To print the letter with errors highlighted, click on the Print button.
7. To correct errors, click on View Original. Make changes, then recheck the document.
8. Choose **File** → **Close**. This closes Document B and brings up the Document C screen.

Document B

current date

Mr. Mark Ogrel
Dain Bosworth, Inc.
1440 East McKinley Avenue
New York, NY 10037

Dear Mr. Ogrel:

This letter records the intentions of IDP Computing and Waedt-Steiner Investment Services to undertake a public offering of common stock of IDP Computing (the "company").

It is our intention to form an underwriting syndicate to purchase up to 250,000 shares of new common stock from IDP Computing and to reoffer the common shares to the public at a price mutually agreed upon. This agreement is subject to the following:

1. The assurance that no change takes place in the company and in the common stock that would threaten success.
2. The market condition for common stock at the time of offer.
3. The completed filing of a prospectus for the common stock with the Securities and Exchange Commission.

We will not be bound to receive or pay for your common shares until conditions for common stock have been met in several states and a final underwriting agreement concerning the common stock has been met.

Continued on next page

Document E ← *Sentences with Spelling Errors*

1. At the *Production–Session 34 Document E* screen, key the sentences that follow.
2. Proofread the sentences and correct any errors you find. Watch for errors in word use.
3. Click on the Spell Check button on the Toolbar to check for spelling errors.
4. Click on Check. The Paradigm software saves and names the document as **034wpre.kwp** and checks it for accuracy and keyboarding speed.
5. When checking is complete, you will see the WAM and Error counts displayed at the bottom of the screen. This score has been saved in your Student Report and is the score used for grade calculation.
6. To print the document with the errors highlighted, click on the Print button on the Toolbar. Otherwise, you may print all Session 34 documents at the end of the session.
7. To see your original document, click on View Original.
8. With the original document displayed, you may correct the errors and have the document checked again (click on Check), repeating the process until there are zero errors. Remember, however, that the first score is the one saved in the Student Report.
9. Choose **File** → **C**lose. This closes the document and brings up the Document F screen.

Document E

He paid me a great complement.

Please except our apology for the delay in shipping your order.

Many of our correspondence request literature on the subject.

In the United States and Canada, each state and province has a capitol city.

Far to many errors are made as a result of our failure to listen to directions.

The personal in the Marketing Department planned an office party.

I strongly advice you to consult your attorney before signing the papers.

I do think that their are advantages to be gained from a variety of media.

Honesty is it's own reward.

The base of the bookend is weighted with led to prevent sliding.

Document F ← *Paragraphs with Spelling Errors*

1. At the *Production–Session 34 Document F* screen, key the paragraphs that follow.
2. Proofread the paragraphs and correct any errors you find.
3. Click on the Spell Check button on the Toolbar to check for spelling errors.
4. Click on Check to save the document as **034wprf.kwp** and to have it checked for speed and accuracy.
5. Once checking is complete, your WAM and Error counts are displayed at the bottom of the screen.
6. To print the document with errors highlighted, click on the Print button on the Toolbar. Otherwise, you may print all Session 34 documents at the end of the session.

Document A — *Block-Style Letter with Wide Margins*

1 At the *Production–Session 40 Document A* screen, change the left and right margins to 1.75" by completing the following steps:
   a Click on Format → **M**argins or press ***Ctrl + F8***.
   b At the *Margins* dialog box, key **1.75** in the left margin text box. Press ***Tab***.
   c Key **1.75** in the right margin text box. Click on OK or press ***Enter***.
2 Key Document A, using ***Ctrl + D*** to insert the current date.
3 Center the letter vertically.
4 Proofread the document, correct any errors, and complete a spell check.
5 Click on Check to automatically name **(040proa.kwp)** and save the document. The program checks the letter for errors and calculates your WAM rate.
6 When checking is complete, the letter is displayed on the screen with errors highlighted.
7 To print the document with errors highlighted, click on the Print button.
8 To correct errors, click on View Original. Make changes, then recheck the document.
9 Choose **F**ile → **C**lose. This closes Document A and brings up the Document B screen.

Document A

current date

Ms. Madeline Serro
Office Systems Publishing Company
280 Fulton Avenue
Hempstead, NY 11550-1624

Dear Ms. Serro:

Our department administrative assistant, Cynthia Brummond, has talked with you on two occasions about the bills you have submitted for some video cassettes and CD-ROMs we ordered on a preview basis.

I have reviewed these materials and although the basic instruction is adequate, the format and visual design are not of the caliber we had in mind. In fact, the interface in the CD-ROMs would probably be difficult for users to understand.

We returned the materials more than 45 days ago; therefore, there should be no charge outstanding on our account.

Sincerely yours,

Barbara Caserza
Research Assistant

xx/040proa.kwp

7 To correct errors, click on View Original. Make the changes in your original document, then recheck the document (click on Check); repeat the process until there are zero errors.

8 Choose **File** → **C**lose to close the document and bring up the Document G screen.

Document F

You may not no this storey, but it is told by hunters talking about thier hunting experiences.

Every hear, during the deer hunting season, a certain farmer lost one or two cows to overzealous hunters. In their enthusism to bring back a prize buck or doe, some hunters would shoot at anything that moved or didn't mover.

It got so bad that the farmer and his family were afraid to come out of their house, for fair of being shoot. At first, the farmer put up signs warning the hunters not to hunt on his propety. This was not very succesful beuse the hunders would shoot at the signs. All that mattered to the poor famer is that he new something had to be done or he would go broke, or get kilt.

One year, after a trip to the local hardware stor, the farmer beleived he had the solution to his problm.

With the usually excitement, the hunters invaided the area with the thoughts of bagging a prise dear. Of course, the first place they headed for was the the farmer's property. But this time, they were in for a surprise. The farmer had taken the precauiton of identifying everything he owed with large letters painted with bright yellow paint. Each cow had the word "cow" painted on it side, and the house and the bard and the tracter were also marked with yellow paint identify them

Needless to said, the hunters got the massage and the farmer stopped losing his cows.

Tips for Proofreading Technical Material

- Proofread technical or difficult material ***at least twice.*** Read slowly; check for content (words left out or the wrong word), numbers, initials, and technical terms that may not be in the Spell Checker program. Also, read for errors in punctuation and grammar.
- Proofread with another person; one person should read from the original while the other makes proofreading changes on the keyed document. When reading from the original, indicate difficult spelling, paragraphing, format, and decimal points. Read numbers digit by digit; for example, 4,230.62 should be read aloud as "four, comma, two, three, zero, point, six, two."
- Proofread statistical tables by adding the numbers on the material from which you are copying. Then add the numbers on your keyed copy. If totals do not agree, check the figures on your copy with the ones on the original to locate the error.

Document G ← *Paragraph of Technical Material*

1 At the *Production–Session 34 Document G* screen, key the paragraphs shown in Document G.

2 Use Spell Checker to check for spelling errors.

THREE-MINUTE TIMINGS

Goal: 30 WAM/2 errors

SI: 1.43

- Take two 3-minute timings.
- On the second attempt, try to increase your speed while maintaining your accuracy.

Many of the metal articles in everyday use are made of brass. A bookend or candlestick made of brass is quite common. But no one has ever heard of brass mines, because there are none. Brass is a blend, or mixture, of metals. Copper and zinc are usually mixed when making brass. These two metals are heated to their melting points, at which time they are joined together. After the mixture cools, it begins to harden. The copper and zinc have blended and formed a new metal with which one can make many creations.

There are quite a few other alloys. In fact, almost none of the metal items we have are made of a single pure metal. The most common alloy by far is steel. Steel is chiefly iron. Since iron is not the strongest metal in the world, it must be combined with just the right amount of carbon for strength. The steel is then used to construct a number of objects such as cars, bridges, skyscrapers, and rails. The iron is also mixed with chromium and nickel to form stainless steel.

Bronze is another common alloy. Bronze is made from the mixture of copper and tin. We call our pennies copper, but actually they are made of bronze. Another alloy called pewter is made of tin.

REVISING BUSINESS LETTERS

As you learned in previous sessions, the block-style letter is formatted with WordPerfect's default margins of 1 inch. These defaults work well for most correspondence. However, there are times when you will need to change the left and right margins to visually balance the letter on the page. For example, a very short letter of ten lines would look better with wide margins. The larger areas of "white space" more closely match the white spaces above and below the text, creating a visually pleasing appearance.

Changing Margins

To change the left and right margins in WordPerfect, you would complete the following steps:

1. Choose Format → **M**argins or press ***Ctrl + F8***.
2. At the *Margins* dialog box, the setting for the left margin (1") is highlighted. Key the new setting or click on the up- or down-pointing triangle at the right of the text box until you reach the setting you want.
3. Press ***Tab*** to move to the right margin setting.
4. Key the new setting or click on the up- or down-pointing triangle at the right of the text box until you reach the setting you want.
5. Click on OK.

3 After you complete the spell check, ask another student to read the paragraph to you while you proofread the text on the screen. Make any needed corrections.
4 Click on Check to save the document as **034wprg.kwp** and to have it checked automatically by the KWP program.
5 When checking is complete, your WAM and Error counts are displayed at the bottom of the screen.
6 To print the document with errors highlighted, click on the Print button on the Toolbar. Otherwise, you may print all Session 34 documents at the end of the session.
7 Click on View Original to see your original document. Correct any errors and recheck the document, repeating the process until there are zero errors.
8 Choose **F**ile → **C**lose. This exits Document G and brings up a clear WordPerfect editing window where you can complete the end-of-the-session activities.

Document G

Mr. Smythe suggested that our selling price on Item #16-780-32 was entirely too high. He recommends that we reduce the price approximately 5 percent, from $14 to $13. I feel he has a good idea, but I would like you to check it with Sandra Dennis in accounting. Perhaps she may have some additional recommendations that should be considered. Please get back to me as soon as possible. The new catalogs will have to go to the printers within the next two weeks. If something unexpected comes up, contact me at 734-1617. Thanks. George Aspick

ENDING THE SESSION

To end this session, delete the Session 24 WordPerfect Reinforcement (wpr) file and print all files created in Session 34. Then continue with the next session or exit the program:

DELETE
1 Choose **F**ile → **O**pen
2 Select the Session wpr 24 file by positioning the mouse pointer on the filename and clicking the left mouse button.
3 With the filename(s) highlighted, choose File **O**ptions → **D**elete.
4 At the *Delete File(s)* dialog box, click on **D**elete.
5 If you need to print files, go to step 2 under PRINT. Otherwise, click on Cancel or press *Esc* to close the *Open File* dialog box.

PRINT
1 Choose **F**ile → **O**pen.
2 At the *Open File* dialog box, select the files to be printed, then choose File **O**ptions → **P**rint.
3 At the *Print Files* dialog box, press ***Enter*** or click on Print.
4 Click on Cancel or press ***Esc*** to close the *Open File* dialog box.

CONTINUE
1 Print any files, if necessary.
2 Click on the KWP Next Activity button.
3 At the next session menu, click on OK to proceed with the highlighted item.

EXIT
1 Print any files, if necessary.
2 Click on the KWP Main Menu button.
3 At the Main Menu, select WordPerfect Only, then click on OK.
4 Click on **F**ile → E**x**it.
5 Exit Windows (**F**ile → E**x**it), if necessary.

SESSION GOALS

1-Minute: 35 WAM/2 errors
3-Minute: 30 WAM/2 errors

Changing margins
Using Find and Replace

Writing for the reader

GETTING STARTED

If you are continuing immediately from Session 39, go to the one-minute timings. If you exited the program at the end of Session 39, do the following:

1. Access Windows, then WordPerfect 6.1 for Windows.
2. Click on the KWP icon to access *Keyboarding with WordPerfect.*
3. Go to the Keyboarding Sessions menu and click on Jump to return to your last activity. Or, access the Session 40 menu to begin the session.

If your fingers are already warmed up or if you have completed part of the session, highlight the desired activity and click on OK. When you have completed the on-screen activities for Session 40, you will return to the text to complete several business letters in which you will change margins and use WordPerfect's Find and Replace feature to speed up editing.

ONE-MINUTE TIMINGS

Goal: 35 WAM/2 errors

SI: 1.43

- Take two 1-minute timings.
- Use your most recent timing score to set a speed or accuracy goal.

Roller blading can provide hours of exciting fun. If there is a nearby paved lot, you are ready. Roller blades and protective equipment are needed. Skating requires lots of energy or zest to keep moving for a long period of time. The beginning skater should only skate for a short time and not get too tired. After some time has passed, the skater should be able to skate for hours without ever getting tired.

SESSION GOALS

1-Minute: 35 WAM/2 errors
3-Minute: 30 WAM/2 errors

Writing at the keyboard

Aligning and indenting text
Changing justification
Inserting the date

GETTING STARTED

If you are continuing immediately from Session 34, go to the one-minute timings. If you exited the program at the end of Session 34, do the following:

1. Access Windows, then WordPerfect 6.1 for Windows.
2. Click on the KWP button to access *Keyboarding with WordPerfect.*
3. Go to the Keyboarding Sessions menu and click on Jump to return to your last activity. Or, access the Session 35 menu to begin the session.

If you are already warmed up or have completed part of the session, highlight the desired activity and click on OK. When you have completed the timings, you will return to the text for instructions on preparing memorandums (memos).

ONE-MINUTE TIMINGS

Goal: 35 WAM/2 errors

SI: 1.36

- Take two 1-minute timings on the following paragraph.
- Set either a speed or accuracy goal, based on your most recent timing score. (Click on the KWP Rep button to review your timings scores on the Student Report.)

Your ability to key at a very rapid rate will be a skill that you will never forget. It will be a skill that you will use almost all of the time if you work with computers. It will be an important skill if you end up using it only to access the Internet to do research, send e-mail messages, and interact with others in real time.

REINFORCING WRITING SKILLS

Well written paragraphs begin with a topic sentence and build to a clear conclusion. Each sentence should tie in with the one before and after it, creating a sense of *unity*. Every sentence should also add information that helps explain or support the topic sentence.

The paragraph that follows contains both essential and unnecessary information. Read it carefully and decide which sentences should be omitted because they do not help explain the topic sentence. Then rekey the paragraph as you have changed it. If you notice some weak word choices, edit those as well. Save the file as **039wprd.kwp**. Then print, if required by your instructor, and close the file.

> The applicant's job interview went well. She had a difficult time finding a parking place. Within minutes after meeting the personnel manager, she began to ask thoughtful questions about the company. She was told that the company was previously located five blocks away. The personnel manager talked a lot about the company's history, its achievements, and its future plans. The applicant worried that someone else had already gotten the job. This company had been researching ways to recycle its products before most people had ever heard about recycling. It also won a presidential award for outstanding customer service. By the time the interviewer began asking her questions, she knew a lot about the company. This knowledge helped her answer the personnel manager's questions about her potential role in the company, and she got the job.

ENDING THE SESSION

To end this session, delete outdated WordPerfect Reinforcement files, print any files from Session 39 not printed earlier, then continue with the next session or exit the program:

DELETE

1. Choose **F**ile → **O**pen.
2. Select the Session 29 wpr file.
3. With the filename highlighted, choose File **O**ptions → **D**elete.
4. At the *Delete File(s)* dialog box, click on **D**elete.
5. If you need to print files, go to step 2 under PRINT. Otherwise, click on Cancel or press ***Esc*** to close the *Open File* dialog box.

PRINT

1. Choose **F**ile → **O**pen.
2. At the *Open File* dialog box, select the files to be printed, then choose File **O**ptions → **P**rint.
3. At the *Print Files* dialog box, press ***Enter*** or click on Print.
4. Click on Cancel or press ***Esc*** to close the *Open File* dialog box.

CONTINUE

1. Print any files, if necessary.
2. Click on the KWP Next Activity button.
3. At the next session menu, click on OK to proceed with the highlighted item.

EXIT

1. Print any files, if necessary.
2. Click on the KWP Main Menu button.
3. At the Main Menu, select WordPerfect Only, then click on OK.
4. Click on **F**ile → E**x**it.
5. Exit Windows (**F**ile → E**x**it), if necessary.

THREE-MINUTE TIMINGS

Goal: 30 WAM/2 errors

SI: 1.42

- Take two 3-minute timings on the following paragraphs.
- Set either a speed or accuracy goal, based on your most recent 3-minute timing score.

Each spring thousands of gardeners declare war on one bothersome weed that seems to plague everyone. This weed is the lowly dandelion plant. In earlier times, people savored all the virtues of this many faceted plant. Rather than referring to it as a weed, folks utilized the very fine herbal qualities. Some broths and tonics were made and utilized to restore health to persons who were ill. Even now, modern pharmacies continue to use extracts of this springtime plant in quite a number of medicines on the market for our use.

As a food, the dandelion is a big source of nutritious, healthy, and delicious food. It is quite rich in proteins, calcium, and iron. The plant contains more Vitamin A than spinach or green peppers. The durable leaves, which may be used in many delicious salads, should be picked before the first blossoms appear. The tender leaves, although tangy in taste, are very nutritious. If you carefully dry the leaves and boil them correctly, you can make delicious teas. You might wish to consume the new blossoms and make wines, salad garnishes, and snacks made from blossoms that have been dipped in a very tasty batter.

PREPARING PRINTED AND ELECTRONIC MEMORANDUMS

Memorandums (memos) continue to be the most frequently produced type of business correspondence. They are used to communicate internally with other individuals or groups within an organization. Memos can vary in length and formality, from handwritten messages to multi-page printed reports.

Memos are keyed; printed on a laser, inkjet, or dot matrix printer; and then placed in an internal mail delivery system. The development of local area networks (LANs), wide area networks (WANs), and e-mail software has produced an alternative to the traditional method of preparing and delivering memos: the e-mail memo. Instead of printing the memo, the writer sends it electronically in a few seconds to the receiver's electronic mail box, where it is then retrieved through the receiver's computer. The memo can then be read, stored, deleted, and/or printed.

Memo Styles

Throughout this text, the terms "traditional memos" or "memos" mean internal documents that are keyed, printed, and delivered via an organization's internal mail system. Electronic memos refer to documents that are transmitted electronically (e-mail).

Traditional memos may be prepared on preprinted memo forms, letterhead, or plain paper. The standard format is the block style, with guide words (DATE, TO, FROM, SUBJECT) and the message starting at the left margin (see the examples that follow). The order and placement of the guide words may vary from one organization to the next and among software packages that include preformatted document templates. For example, WordPerfect's memo templates (introduced in Session 30) place the date last, rather than first, in the heading.

Document C

current date

Mr. Dale Egland, Division Director
Sacred Heart Hospital
900 Clairemont Avenue
Dubuque, IA 52003-0524

Dear Mr. Egland:

Lynn Gullicksrud, Director of Medical Records at Sacred Heart Hospital, really helped us out on Monday evening. I teach Office Automation Systems at Bradford University. There are 36 students in the class, and they were divided into team of 4 each. They were to submit a strategic plan for automating office operations in a law firm. After reviewing the projects over the weekend, it was obvious that there was one area where all the groups seems to have difficulty and that was in the area magnetic disk dictation/transcription systems.

On Monday morning I called Lynn Gullicksrud and asked her it there was any way that I could bring the class to Sacred Heart Hospital on a really short notice. I wanted her to explain and demonstrate how your centralized dictation/transcription system funcitons. It was important for the class to see rather than just read about these systems.

Lynn came back to work on Monday evening at 6:30 p.m. and spent the next hour with our students demonstrating, explaining, and answering questions about your system. She did a fantastic job helping our students understand how these systems function and their value to an organization. Sacred Heart Hospital can certainly be proud of Lynn Gullicksrud. Please convey our thanks to Lynn.

Sincerely,

Jordan Leno, Chair
Office Technology Division

xx/039proc.kwp

In this session, two styles of printed memos are introduced: traditional and simplified. The order of the guide words for these memos is DATE, TO, FROM, SUBJECT.

Formatting a Traditional Memo

The examples that follow show the format for a block-style memo and a simplified-style memo prepared on plain paper. Follow the guidelines as you prepare Documents A-D, which are traditional block-style memos, and Document E, which is a simplified-style memo.

DATE: current date

ds

TO: Receiver's name *(first and last) plus title (optional)*

ds

FROM: Sender's name *(first and last) plus title (optional)*

ds

SUBJECT: TOPIC OF MEMO KEYED IN ALL CAPITAL LETTERS

ts

This is the first line of the message, or body, of the memo. Typically, memos are short forms of communication, perhaps one or two paragraphs. The message should be written in clear, direct sentences using correct grammar, capitalization, and punctuation.

Notice that there is a double line space between paragraphs. If a memo includes a list, the list should be set off by a double line space above and below. Use numbers or bullets to highlight each item. Indenting the list is optional, although if you use WordPerfect's bullet feature, the bullets align at the left margin and there is one tab space between the bullet and the text:

ds

- Item 1
- Item 2
- Item 3

ds

xx/memo *[your initials and the filename]*

ds

Attachment

ds

c Person 1
Person 2
Person 3

Figure 35.1 Traditional block-style memo

Business, Government, and Education." The evaluations of your presentation were absolutely outstanding. I have enclosed a summary prepared by my assistant.

We need your kind of guidance and expertise to help our students prepare for full-time employment. You can be sure that we will ask you to return to our school for a repeat performance.

Rosemary has told me a little about her discussion with you. We hope that your new endeavor will bring you the rewards and satisfaction that you anticipate. My staff members and I agree that you have the skills, knowledge, and dedication required for the new position.

We look forward to seeing you soon.

Sincerely,

Joan LaMavia
Administrator

send copies to Dr. Ross Byrd and Dr. Kim Freier

Document C — *Block-Style Letter with Proofreaders' Corrections*

1. At the *Production–Session 39 Document C* screen, key Document C using the block-style letter format.
2. Use ***Ctrl + D*** to insert the date, and make the corrections indicated with the proofreaders' marks.
3. Proofread and correct any errors, then complete a spell check.
4. Center the letter on the page.
5. Click on Check. The document is automatically saved and named **039proc.kwp**. The program checks the letter for errors and calculates your WAM rate.
6. When checking is complete, the letter is displayed on the screen with errors highlighted. Move the insertion point to the end of the document to display the number of errors and your WAM rate.
7. To print the document with errors highlighted, click on the Print button. Otherwise, print at the end of the session.
8. To correct errors, click on View Original. Make changes, then recheck the document.
9. Choose **F**ile → **C**lose. This closes Document C and brings up a clear WordPerfect editing window, at which you are to prepare Document D.

current date

TO: Receiver *(first and last names) plus title (optional)*

Sender *(first and last names) plus title (optional)*

TOPIC IN ALL CAPITAL LETTERS

As with the traditional block-style memo, all lines in the simplified memo begin at the left margin. The same guidelines for writing clear, direct sentences apply. As with all communication, it is important to use correct punctuation, capitalization, and spelling.

Many people prefer using the simplified memo style because it uses fewer guide words and therefore is faster to prepare. Follow the style preferred by your company or organization.

xx/simple

Attachment

c Person 1
Person 2
Person 3
Person 4

Figure 35.2 Simplified-style memo

Inserting the Date Automatically

Another time-saving feature available with WordPerfect is the ability to enter the current date automatically into a document. To insert the date, you would press ***Ctrl + D*** or choose **I**nsert → **D**ate → Date **T**ext. As you complete documents throughout this text, be sure to use this feature unless instructed otherwise.

Document A *Traditional Printed Memo*

1. At the *Production–Session 35 Document A* screen, key Document A using WordPerfect's default margins. Begin by keying **DATE:,** then press the ***Tab*** key once to move the insertion point to position 2". Press ***Ctrl + D*** (or choose **I**nsert → **D**ate → Date **T**ext) to insert the current date into the document.
2. Tab to position 2" after keying the other headings (**TO:, FROM:,** and **SUBJECT:**). The Tab key properly aligns the information after each heading.
3. Key the remainder of the memorandum. Add your initials and the filename a double space below the last line. Press ***Tab*** between the copy notation and the names.
4. Proofread and correct any errors, then complete a spell check.
5. Click on Check to automatically name, save, and check the memo. Note that the program names the memo **035proa.kwp** and saves it to your data disk.

extended for another full year when you accrue 70,000 credited Transcontinental actual flight miles between January 1 and December 31.

Transcontinental Gold was recently named the "Best U.S. Airline Frequent Flyer Program" by one of America's leading consumer reporting agencies and in the current issue of the *World Traveler* magazine. We appreciate your business and look forward to serving you often.

Sincerely yours,

Jan Gould
Managing Director

xx/039proa.kwp

Enclosures

Document B ← *Block-Style Business Letter*

1. At the *Production–Session 39 Document B* screen, key Document B using the block-style letter format.
2. Use ***Ctrl + D*** to insert the date, and remember to include your initials, the filename (039prob.kwp), and other notations where applicable.
3. Proofread and correct any errors, then complete a spell check.
4. Center the letter on the page.
5. Click on Check. The document is automatically saved and named **039prob.kwp**. The program checks the letter for errors and calculates your WAM rate.
6. When checking is complete, the letter is displayed on the screen with errors highlighted. Move the insertion point to the end of the document to display the number of errors and your WAM rate.
7. To print the document with errors highlighted, click on the Print button. Otherwise, print at the end of the session.
8. To correct errors, click on View Original. Make changes, then recheck the document.
9. Choose **F**ile → **C**lose. This closes Document B and brings up the Document C screen.

Document B

Dr. Paul Mazza
140 Moloney Building
University of Kentucky
9868 Cooper Drive
Lexington, KY 40507-0235

Thank you for coming to our school to conduct an in-service program for faculty and students on the "Impact of Technology on

Continued on next page

6 When checking is complete, the memo is displayed on the screen with errors highlighted. Move the insertion point to the end of the document to display the number of errors and your WAM rate. This score is automatically recorded in the Student Report.
7 To print the document with errors highlighted, click on the Print button. Otherwise, you may wait until the end of the session to print all Session 35 documents.
8 To view the original document and correct errors, click on View Original. Make your changes and recheck the memo until you have zero errors.
9 Choose **File** → **Close**. This closes Document A and brings up the Document B screen. Read the information on "Indenting Text" before completing Document B.

Document A

DATE: current date

TO: Ron Decker, Editorial Department

FROM: Bill Walczak, Educational Consultant

SUBJECT: SEMINAR OUTLINE

Ron, attached is the revised seminar outline for the program on Organizational Communication.

Ned Ostenso, Bill Sauro, Juanita Jimenez, and I collaborated on this revision. Please note that we changed the name of the program. We feel that the new title describes the seminar content more accurately.

Please let us know when you are ready to review the program.

xx/035proa.kwp

Attachment

c Ned Ostenso
Bill Sauro
Juanita Jimenez

Indenting Text

By now you are familiar with the word wrap feature of WordPerfect. This feature ends lines according to the program's line length and moves the insertion point to the next line. If you want several lines of text to be indented to a tab stop, you must use the Indent key, **F7,** or the Double Indent command, **Ctrl + Shift + F7**. The Indent key indents text from the left margin only, whereas the Double Indent command indents text from the left and right margins.

Document A ← Business Letter with Bullets

1. At the *Production–Session 39 Document A* screen, key Document A using the block-style letter format. Use the Insert Date feature to insert the current date.
2. To create the bulleted list, complete the following steps:
   a. Change the bullet style to Large Circle (follow the steps outlined on the previous page).
   b. Position the insertion point at the left margin on the line you want the first bulleted item to appear.
   c. Click on the Insert Bullet button on the Toolbar. WordPerfect inserts a bullet and moves the insertion point to the first tab stop.
   d. Key the text, then press ***Enter***.
   e. Repeat steps c and d to insert the remaining bulleted items.
3. Center the letter on the page. (Fo**r**mat → **P**age → **C**enter).
4. Click on Check. The document is automatically saved and named **039proa.kwp**. The program checks the letter for errors and calculates your WAM rate.
5. When checking is complete, the letter is displayed on the screen with errors highlighted.
6. To print the document with errors highlighted, click on the Print button. Otherwise, print at the end of the session.
7. To correct errors, click on View Original. Make changes, then recheck the document.
8. Choose **F**ile → **C**lose. This closes Document A and brings up the Document B screen.

Document A

current date

Ms. Teri M. Podgorski
140 Third Street South
West Orange, NJ 07052-2772

Dear Ms. Podgorski:

Congratulations! As one of Transcontinental's most loyal customers, you have qualified for membership in Transcontinental Gold. This elite membership entitles you to the following benefits:

- Unlimited domestic First Class Upgrades on any published Transcontinental fare, confirmable one day prior to departure.
- Periodic First Class Companion Upgrades that treat your traveling companions to the same luxury you enjoy.
- A 100 percent mileage bonus on credited Transcontinental mileage.
- First Class check-in and preboarding, even when you're traveling Coach Class.

Enclosed are your Transcontinental Gold membership credentials and your Gold Benefits Guide. Your Gold membership is valid for one calendar year. It will be

Continued on next page

Indenting with the Indent Key

To use the Indent key, position the insertion point at the left margin of the paragraph to be indented and press ***F7*** or choose Format → Paragraph → Indent. This causes the insertion point to move to the first tab stop. As text is keyed, it will wrap to the first tab stop rather than the left margin. The indent stays in effect until ***Enter*** is pressed.

Text is indented to a tab stop each time the Indent key is pressed. For example, pressing the Indent key, ***F7,*** three times causes text in the paragraph to be indented to the third tab stop, or 1.5 inches from the left margin.

The paragraph below would be created with the following steps (this is an example—do not key):

1 Position the cursor at the left margin.
2 Key **1** and then the period.
3 Press ***F7***.
4 Key the paragraph.

1. This paragraph was created with the Indent key, F7. The number 1 and the period were keyed, then the F7 function key was pressed.

Indenting with the Double Indent Command

The command **Ctrl + Shift + F7** is used to indent text an equal distance from both the left and the right margins. For example, text can be indented 0.5 inches from the left and right margins by pressing ***Ctrl + Shift + F7*** once. Or, text can be indented 1 inch from the left and right margins by pressing ***Ctrl + Shift + F7*** twice. The paragraph that follows was created by pressing ***Ctrl + Shift + F7*** once. While **Ctrl + Shift + F7** indents from both margins, the Indent key, **F7**, indents only from the left margin.

When either the Indent key, **F7,** or the Double Indent command, **Ctrl + Shift + F7,** is used to indent text, additions and deletions can be made and the text adjusts so the lines remain correctly indented. However, if the Tab key is used to indent text and then words are added or deleted, the tab stop may wrap to the middle of a line, causing blank space to appear in the middle of the line.

Document B — *Traditional Block-Style Memo witih Indented Text*

1 At the *Production–Session 35 Document B* screen, key Document B as a block-style memo. Begin by keying **DATE:,** then press the ***Tab*** key once to move the insertion point to position 2 inches. Press ***Ctrl + D*** to insert the current date.
2 Tab to position 2 inches after keying each heading (**TO:, FROM:,** and **SUBJECT:**).
3 Create the enumerated paragraphs in the memorandum by completing the following steps:
   a Position the insertion point at the left margin where the first enumerated paragraph is to begin.
   b Key **1** and then the period.
   c Press ***F7***.
   d Key the paragraph.
   e Repeat these steps to create the other enumerated paragraphs.
4 Proofread and correct any errors, then complete a spell check.
5 Click on Check to save, name, and check the memo as **035prob.kwp**.

Letter Styles

A variety of letter styles are used today for both personal and business letters. The letter format presented in this section is the *block style.* In the block-style letter, all parts of the letter begin at the left margin. The block-style letter is popular because it is comparatively easy to learn and it is the fastest letter style to set up. Once you have mastered the block-style letter, you will have little difficulty adjusting to other letter styles.

Using Bullets and Numbers to Highlight Items

Sometimes letters include a list of items (words, phrases, or sentences) that should be set apart from the body of the letter for special emphasis. These items can be numbered, or they can be preceded by a symbol called a *bullet*, which may take the shape of a circle, a square, or even a diamond. If you number the list of items, you may begin at the left margin or you may indent the list. For bulleted lists, it is efficient to use WordPerfect's bullet feature, available on the Toolbar by clicking on the Insert Bullet button. This feature inserts a bullet at the left margin and automatically indents (one tab stop) the text that follows.

Inserting Bullets

To use WordPerfect's bullet feature, you would complete the following steps:

1 Position the insertion point at the left margin on the line you want the first bulleted item to appear. ***Note:*** Bulleted or numbered lists should be set apart from the text by a double-space before and after the list.

2 Click on the Insert Bullet button on the Toolbar. WordPerfect inserts a bullet and moves the insertion point to the first tab stop.

3 Key the text, then press ***Enter***.

4 Repeat steps 2 and 3 to insert additional bulleted items. The completed list should resemble the example that follows:

- This is an example of how bullets can be used to highlight material within a document.
- Use either a single space or a double space between bulleted items, but be consistent throughout the document.

Changing Bullet Style

WordPerfect offers five bullet styles, as shown below:

- • Small Circle (the default)
- ● Large Circle
- ◆ Diamond
- ■ Square
- ▲ Triangle

You may change the bullet style by clicking on **I**nsert on the Menu Bar. From the drop-down menu, click on Bullets & **N**umbers, highlight the new symbol choice, then click on OK. That style will remain in effect for all bullets in every document until you change it.

6. When checking is complete, the memorandum is displayed on the screen with errors highlighted. Move the insertion point to the end of the document to display the number of errors and your WAM rate.
7. To print the memo with errors highlighted, click on the Print button. Otherwise, you may print all Session 35 documents at the end of the session.
8. To view the original document and correct errors, click on View Original. Make changes and recheck the memo until you have zero errors.
9. Choose **F**ile → **C**lose to close the document. This closes Document B and brings up the Document C screen.

Document B

DATE: current date

TO: Marilyn Donaldson, Computer Systems

FROM: Jill Mersereau, Information Processing

SUBJECT: SOFTWARE TRAINING

I have talked with the employees of the Information Processing Department about the type of computer training they would like. The employees said they would like training in the following areas:

1. Internet Browsers: The employees would like more training on the use of GUI and text-based browsers for accessing information on the Internet.

2. Spreadsheet Program: Since the company is changing to a new spreadsheet program, the employees would like some immediate training on the software.

3. Desktop Publishing: One of the employees attended a half-day seminar on desktop publishing and thinks it would be valuable for the other employees of the department to attend similar training.

Please consider these areas when determining the training budget for the Information Processing Department.

xx/035prob.kwp

Document C — *Block-Style Memo with Double-Indented Text*

1. At the *Production–Session 35 Document C* screen, key Document C as a block-style memo. Use the Tab key to properly align the text after the headings.
2. Double-indent the second paragraph in the memorandum by doing the following:
   a. Position the insertion point at the left margin where the second paragraph is to begin.

Common Letter Notations

In addition to the major sections of a business letter, there are several notations that are used if they are appropriate to a particular letter, as shown in figure 39.1.

1. **Enclosure/attachment**: Indicates that a document or another item is included with the letter. Several styles are acceptable, including the abbreviation *Enc*.
2. **Copy (c)**: Lists in alphabetical order the additional people who will receive copies of the letter. Either the word *copy* or the letter *c* is acceptable. This text uses the letter *c*.

Special Letter Notations

Occasionally, there is a need for one or more special notations, as shown in figure 39.2.

1. **Attention**: Used when the letter is addressed to an entire organization rather than to an individual or when the sender is unsure of who in the company should receive the letter.
2. **Subject or Reference**: Indicates the topic; used most often in the simplified-style letter.
3. **Delivery Notation**: Indicates a special delivery method, such as registered mail.
4. **Postscript**: Expresses an aside, an afterthought, or a personal note.

current date

5 Enters - may be adjusted for short and long letters

Attention: Communications Coordinator
First Interstate Travel Company
6567 Postoria Avenue
Wichita, KS 67207-5938

ts

OPTIONAL FEATURES OF BUSINESS LETTERS

At our client's suggestion, we have prepared this letter illustrating the recommended use, placement, and formatting of optional features of business letters. This information is based on U.S. Postal Service guidelines.

ds

In particular, note the placement of the attention line and the subject line. If you need any additional information, don't hesitate to call me at 555-2399.

4 Enters

Jeannette Brownson
Public Relations Specialist

ds

rt/optparts.let

ds - but use a single-space if not enough room

By registered mail *delivery notation*

ds

Don't forget to reserve space at the upcoming seminar, "You and Your Words."

postscript - the letters PS: are optional

Firure 39.2 Simplified-style letter

   b. Press ***Ctrl + Shift + F7***. (Hold down the Ctrl and Shift keys while pressing F7.)
   c. Key the paragraph.
3. Proofread and correct any errors, then complete a spell check.
4. Click on Check to name, save, and check the document as **035proc.kwp**.
5. When checking is complete, the memo is displayed on the screen with errors highlighted. Move the insertion point to the end of the document to display the number of errors and your WAM rate.
6. To print the memo with errors highlighted, click on the Print button. Otherwise, you may print all Session 35 documents at the end of the session.
7. To view the original document and correct errors, click on View Original. Make changes and recheck the memo until you have zero errors.
8. Choose **F**ile → **C**lose. This closes Document C and brings up the Document D screen. Read the information on "Changing Justification" before completing Document D.

Document C

DATE: current date

TO: Joshua Redmond, Public Relations Department

FROM: Raye Dearborn, Human Resources Department

SUBJECT: EMPLOYEE RETIREMENT

After 22 years as an employee at the hospital, Nancy Ruschner is retiring. For the past five years, Nancy has worked as the personnel director for the Human Resources Department. When asked about her retirement, Nancy stated:

> Leaving the hospital after 22 years is going to be very difficult. I have made wonderful friends over the years whom I will miss very much. I haven't made any future plans, but I do hope to spend time reading, relaxing, and doing some traveling with my family.

Please have one of your staff members write an article about Nancy's retirement for the next hospital newsletter. The above quote should be included.

xx/035proc.kwp

Changing Justification

By default, WordPerfect prints a document with left justification, which means that all text aligns evenly at the left margin but is uneven, or "ragged," at the right margin. Justification can be changed with the *Justification* option from the **F**ormat menu by clicking on the Justification button Left on the Power Bar. The Justification can also be changed by using the Shortcut keys: ***Ctrl + L*** for Left Justification; ***Ctrl + R*** for Right Justification, ***Ctrl+E***

9 **Reference initials and filename**: Initials of person who keyed the document (included only if this person is not the sender) plus the name of the electronic file where the document is stored.

Ohio Medical Society
15 Medford Avenue ▪ Toledo, OH 57089 ▪ (108) 555-1717

Use WordPerfect's default margins of 1" on all sides

June 15, 1997 *keyed at line 1" or 3 lines below the last line of the letterhead; increase this space for short letters*

5 Enters - but may be adjusted depending on length of letter

Dr. Denise Armstrong *Use the WordPerfect default of left justification*
Cleveland Medical Clinic
8900 University Avenue
Cleveland, OH 44102 *1 space between the state abbreviation and ZIP Code*

2 Enters

Dear Dr. Armstrong:

2 Enters

Thank you for submitting a paper to be presented at the Ohio Medical Society in Toledo on September 15. I read your paper with great interest and applaud the diligence you have applied to your research on treating heart disease with aspirin.

2 Enters

Unfortunately, a similar study was submitted three weeks ago. While I wish we could allow both papers to be presented, the program committee has decided that due to the large number of papers, we must limit each topic to one presentation.

2 Enters

You may wish to contact Drs. Teresa Lopez and Lee Wong at the Akron Cardiology Center, the researchers who are conducting studies similar to yours. Perhaps you can exchange some information.

2 Enters

Thank you again for supporting your professional society. I have enclosed your paper along with a list of the meeting presenters.

2 Enters

Sincerely yours,

4 Enters

Kirsten Danforth
Executive Secretary

2 Enters

cm/armstrng.ltr

2 Enters

Enclosures

2 Enters

c *tab* Dr. Margit Bergren
tab Dr. Keith Holmes

Figure 39.1 Traditional block-style letter

for Center Justification, and ***Ctrl + J*** for Full Justification. To change the justification of text in a paragraph, you would complete the following steps:

1 Click on the Justification button on the Power Bar (or Choose Format → **J**ustification).
2 Choose the desired Justification (Left, Right, Center, Full, All).

Changes in justification can be made throughout a document. When a change is made, a code is inserted in the document that can be seen in Reveal Codes. Changes made to justification affect text from the location of the code to the end of the document or until another justification code is encountered. Justification changes affect only the document in which you are working. If you save a document and begin a new one, justification reverts to the default setting of Left.

Left-Justified Paragraph

The paragraph that follows is left-justified. Left justification is the WordPerfect default and the preferred style for business documents because it is easy to read.

The Justification option from the Format menu contains a variety of selections that affect the appearance of the document. How the document looks when it is printed is called the format. Attributes such as bold, italics, underlining, and font changes are examples of formatting options.

Center-Justified Paragraph

On the Power Bar, click on the Justification button. From the drop-down menu click on *Center* (or press ***Ctrl + E***) to center each line in a paragraph between the left and right margins. This results in both the left and right margins being uneven or ragged as shown below.

The Justification option from the Format menu contains a variety of selections that affect the appearance of the document. How a document looks when printed is called the format. Attributes such as bold, italics, underlining, and font changes are examples of formatting options.

Right-Justified Paragraph

On the Power Bar, click on the Justification button. From the drop-down menu click on *Right* (or press ***Ctrl + R***) to justify the right margin and leave the left margin ragged as shown below.

The Justification option from the Format menu contains a variety of selections that affect the appearance of the document. How a document looks when printed is called the format. Attributes such as bold, italics, underlining, and font changes are examples of formatting options.

Full-Justified Paragraph

On the Power Bar, click on the Justification button. From the drop-down menu, click on Full (or press ***Ctrl + J***) to justify text at both the left and right margins.

The Justification option from the Format menu contains a variety of selections that affect the appearance of the document. How a document looks when printed is called the format. Attributes such as bold, italics, underlining, and font changes are examples of formatting options.

THREE-MINUTE TIMINGS

Goal: 30 WAM/2 errors

SI: 1.42

- Take two 3-minute timings.

To avoid consumer problems, some decisions should be made before buying a product. The first major point is to decide if you and your family really need that new product or new service. If the answer is yes, then the next step is to shop around and compare prices. A good library will have publications that give helpful comparisons among similar products. Check on the firm with which you are dealing; call the Better Business Bureau for more information. Make certain that a guarantee is in writing. Before you sign a contract, read it to make sure that you understand it fully. If you have any doubts at all, it would be wise to wait and think about the purchase a little longer.

When you buy a product or a service, be sure that you understand the method of payment if it is to be a credit purchase. Know exactly when each payment is due, how much interest is being charged, and how many months the payments are to be made. Read all tags and labels to learn all about the product before you use it. If you have any problems with the product or service, speak with the seller first. If you find that a seller does not give the proper satisfaction to a problem, there are many consumer protection groups and agencies you can contact.

PREPARING BUSINESS LETTERS

As you learn to prepare letters and envelopes, work toward the following goals:

- Prepare a document that conveys a favorable image. This requires learning style and format guidelines.
- Prepare correspondence free from errors in spelling, punctuation, and word use.
- Prepare correspondence in mailable form at job-ready production levels of at least 25 WAM.

Parts of a Business Letter

A business letter has nine major parts, as shown in the illustration that follows:

1 **Letterhead**: Company logo, including the name, address, and phone number(s).
2 **Date line**: Current date written as month, day, year (April 15, 1997). The international format lists the day, the month, then the year with no commas (15 April 1997).
3 **Inside address**: Receiver's name, title, department, company name, and address.
4 **Salutation**: Greeting that includes the receiver's name followed by a colon. In the *open punctuation* style, no punctuation is used after the salutation or the closing.
5 **Body**: Message of the letter, consisting of one or more single-spaced paragraphs with a double space between them.
6 **Closing**: Short farewell followed by a comma. The open punctuation style uses no punctuation.
7 **Signature line**: First and last names of the sender.
8 **Title line**: Sender's business or professional title. If the person's name and title are short, they may be combined on the signature line.

All-Justified Paragraph

The last selection on the Justification drop-down menu from the Power Bar is *All*, which justifies all lines of text, a character at a time, as shown below.

> The Justification option from the Format menu contains a variety of selections that affect the appearance of the document. How a document looks when printed is called the format. Attributes such as bold, italics, underlining, and font changes are examples of formatting o p t i o n s .

Document D — *Block-Style Memo with Full Justification*

1 At the *Production–Session 35 Document D* screen, change the justification to Full by doing the following:
   a Click on the Justification button on the Power Bar.
   b At the drop-down menu, click on *Full.*
2 Key Document D as a block-style memo. Use the Tab key to align the text after the headings. ***Note:*** In this document and in certain documents in later sessions, the diagonal slash is used to indicate separations between heading parts or to indicate new paragraphs.
3 Proofread and correct any spelling errors, then complete a spell check.
4 Click on Check to save, name, and check the document as **035prod.kwp**.
5 When checking is complete, the memo is displayed on the screen with errors highlighted. Move the insertion point to the end of the document to display the number of errors and your WAM rate.
6 To print the memo with errors highlighted, click on the Print button. Otherwise, you may print all Session 35 documents at the end of the session.
7 To view the original document and correct errors, click on View Original. Make changes and recheck the memo until you have zero errors.
8 Choose **F**ile → **C**lose. This exits Document D and brings up the Document E screen.

Document D

(current date)/TO: Ms. Pat Ganser, Editorial Department/FROM: Amos Grant, Research Director/SUBJECT: ABSTRACTS OF OFFICE RESEARCH STUDIES/The National Business Educator's Association (NBEA) is calling for abstracts of research studies that were completed in office systems during the past calendar year. If you are interested in submitting your abstract, note the attached directions from Oscar Byrnside, Executive Director of NBEA./All abstracts must reach NBEA headquarters within the next 30 days./your initials and filename/Attachments

Document E — *Simplified-Style Memo*

1 At the *Production–Session 35 Document E* screen, key the memo that follows. Use the simplified style as shown on page 180.
2 Click on the Italics button before keying the name of the journal in the first paragraph. After keying the journal name, click on the button again to turn Italics off.
3 Create the indented paragraph in the memo by doing the following:
   a Position the insertion point at the left margin where the indented paragraph is to begin.
   b Press ***Ctrl + Shift + F7***.

SESSION 39

BUSINESS LETTERS

SESSION GOALS

1-Minute: 35 WAM/2 errors
3-Minute: 30 WAM/2 errors

Creating bullets

Building paragraphs

GETTING STARTED

If you are continuing immediately from Session 38, go to the one-minute timing. If you exited the program at the end of Session 38, do the following:

1. Access Windows, then WordPerfect 6.1 for Windows.
2. Click on the KWP icon to access *Keyboarding with WordPerfect.*
3. Go to the Keyboarding Sessions menu and click on Jump to return to your last activity. Or, access the Session 39 menu to begin the session.

If your fingers are already warmed up or if you have completed part of the session, highlight the desired activity and click on OK. When you have completed the on-screen activities for Session 39, you will return to the text to complete several business letters, including one with bullets created by WordPerfect.

ONE-MINUTE TIMINGS

Goal: 35 WAM/2 errors

SI: 1.38

- Take two 1-minute timings.
- Use your most recent timing score to set a speed or accuracy goal.

Most clouds move usually from west to east as they cross an area of land. If there should be a high pressure system holding around the West Coast, it will divert the clouds and moisture northward into the Canadian Rockies. Many experts think that the climate over the whole earth is becoming warmer and drier. These experts state that the one thing that will suffer most will be rainfall.

c Key the paragraph.

4 Proofread and correct any errors, then complete a spell check.

5 Click on Check to save, name, and check the document as **035proe.kwp**.

6 When checking is complete, the document is displayed on the screen with errors highlighted. Move the insertion point to the end of the document to display the number of errors and your WAM rate.

7 To print the memo with errors highlighted, click on the Print button. Or, you may wait until the end of the session to print all Session 35 documents.

8 To view the original document and correct errors, click on View Original. Make changes and recheck the memo until you have zero errors.

9 Choose **F**ile → **C**lose. This exits Document E and brings up a clear WordPerfect editing window where you can complete the "Reinforcing Writing Skills" activities.

Document E

(current date)/TO: Leslie McKay, Training and Education/Pat Iverson, Human Resources/WORKPLACE LITERACY/How are you doing on the workplace literacy project? Workplace literacy appears to be an important topic for all businesses in the United States. Yesterday, I read an article in the August 1993 edition of *Training and Development Journal.* I thought the following quote had an element of truth for our company.

> With foreign competition challenging American businesses, U.S. industrial plants are pushing to improve worker productivity, often by using more advanced equipment. But many companies have introduced sophisticated, computer-driven machinery, only to find that workers do not have the basic reading and math skills required to operate the equipment.

Are you still on target with the project? I am anxious to read the final research results and the recommendations you will make.

xx/035proe.kwp

REINFORCING WRITING SKILLS

Many students and office workers handwrite documents and then key them on their computers. This process can be shortened if you can think and key at the same time—you don't need to prepare the handwritten copy first. The average individual writes at the rate of 10-12 WAM. You can double this speed if you use the keyboard. It takes practice, but perfecting this skill is well worth the effort.

Beginning with Session 35, most of the sessions include an optional writing activity that strengthens your writing and grammar skills while giving you an opportunity to compose at the keyboard. With practice, you will find that it is much easier to create documents directly at the keyboard.

5 If you need to print files, go to step 2 under PRINT. Otherwise, click on Cancel or press ***Esc*** to close the *Open File* dialog box.

PRINT

1 Choose **F**ile → **O**pen.
2 At the *Open File* dialog box, select the files to be printed, then choose File **O**ptions → **P**rint.
3 At the *Print Files* dialog box, press ***Enter*** or click on Print.
4 Click on Cancel or press ***Esc*** to close the *Open File* dialog box.

CONTINUE

1 Print any files, if necessary.
2 Click on the KWP Next Activity button.
3 At the next session menu, click on OK to proceed with the highlighted item.

EXIT

1 Print any files, if necessary.
2 Click on the KWP Main Menu button.
3 At the Main Menu, select WordPerfect Only, then click on OK.
4 Click on **F**ile → E**x**it.
5 Exit Windows (**F**ile → E**x**it), if necessary.

Document F ← Simplified-Style Memo

At a clear WordPerfect editing window, compose a memo to the director of your school using the simplified-style format. The subject is "School Evaluation." Include the following in your memo:

- In the first paragraph, state your purpose (evaluating the strong and weak points about your school). Then identify two or three things you like about the school (for example, the curriculum, the buildings, the computer software and hardware, the faculty, the students, the administration).
- In the second paragraph, note two or three things you would like to see changed. Be sure to explain how/when these changes can be made and their impact on the school. ***Note:*** If you list items, use the Indent or Double Indent feature.

Proofread your memo, then complete a spell check. Save the memo as **035wprf.kwp**. Then print (check with your instructor) the memo and close the file.

ENDING THE SESSION

To end this session, delete the Session 25 WordPerfect Reinforcement file and print any Session 35 files not printed earlier. Then continue with the next session or exit the program:

DELETE

1. Choose **F**ile → **O**pen
2. Select the Session 25 wpr file by positioning the arrow pointer on the filename and clicking the left mouse button.
3. With the filename(s) highlighted, choose File **O**ptions → **D**elete.
4. At the *Delete File(s)* dialog box, click on **D**elete.
5. If you need to print files, go to step 2 under PRINT. Otherwise, click on Cancel or press ***Esc*** to close the *Open File* dialog box.

PRINT

1. Choose **F**ile → **O**pen.
2. At the *Open File* dialog box, select the files to be printed, then choose File **O**ptions → **P**rint.
3. At the *Print Files* dialog box, press ***Enter*** or click on Print.
4. Click on Cancel or press ***Esc*** to close the *Open File* dialog box.

CONTINUE

1. Print any files, if necessary.
2. Click on the KWP Next Activity button.
3. At the next session menu, click on OK to proceed with the highlighted item.

EXIT

1. Print any files, if necessary.
2. Click on the KWP Main Menu button.
3. At the Main Menu, select WordPerfect Only, then click on OK.
4. Click on **F**ile → E**x**it.
5. Exit Windows (**F**ile → E**x**it), if necessary.

like to meet with you in the afternoon to discuss the purchase of a lot and to review the floor plan choices. I have some questions about changing certain room sizes.

I will arrive in Tucson via Northwest Airlines Flight 107 at 11:10 a.m., and I have rented a car to use during my stay. I will be available anytime after 1:30 p.m. Please call me at 612/555-4320, or send me an e-mail message at **xxxxxxxx@umd.edu** with the time I should meet you.

Sincerely,

(your name)
(your address)

REINFORCING WRITING SKILLS

Have you ever seen a document containing a paragraph that is half a page or more in length? Research demonstrates that most people will read a long paragraph quickly, paying little attention to detail. Yet those details frequently contain information that is important for the reader.

Technical reports, scientific research, and other academic documents often include long paragraphs due to the complexity of the information. However, general correspondence, business documents, and college assignments usually can be structured with shorter paragraphs of up to nine or ten lines. As with short sentences, brief paragraphs tend to increase readability.

Document D — *Personal Business Letter*

Using the Letter - Blank Letterhead template, compose a letter to a friend or relative living in another city. Your purpose is to get information on the job market. Are jobs available, and if so, what types of jobs are they? What are the experience and education requirements? Explain what kind of a job you are seeking. Describe your qualifications and include when you could start working.

In your letter use some of the WordPerfect features you have learned so far, including indenting, underlining, italicizing, and bolding. Pay particular attention to your word choice and paragraph length. Are your words accurate and short? Are the paragraphs of ideal length?

Proofread and correct any errors, then complete a spell check. Save the letter as **038wprd.kwp** and print a copy, unless you are to print all documents at the end of the session. Finally, close the document.

ENDING THE SESSION

To end this session, delete outdated WordPerfect Reinforcement files, print any files from Session 38 not printed earlier, then continue with the next session or exit the program:

DELETE

1. Choose **F**ile → **O**pen.
2. Select the Session 28 wpr file.
3. With the filename highlighted, choose File **O**ptions → **D**elete.
4. At the *Delete File(s)* dialog box, click on **D**elete.

SESSION 36

MEMO TEMPLATES

SESSION GOALS

1-Minute: 35 WAM/2 errors
3-Minute: 30 WAM/2 errors

Ideal sentence length

Memo templates, bolding
Review indenting, Reveal Codes and inserting the date

GETTING STARTED

If you are continuing immediately from Session 35, go to the one-minute timing. If you exited the program at the end of Session 35, do the following:

1. Access Windows, then WordPerfect 6.1 for Windows.
2. Click on the KWP button to access *Keyboarding with WordPerfect.*
3. Go to the Keyboarding Sessions menu and click on Jump to return to your last activity. Or, access the Session 36 menu to begin the session.

If you are already warmed up or have completed part of the session, highlight the desired activity and click on OK. When you have completed the timings, you will return to the text for instructions on preparing memos.

ONE-MINUTE TIMING

Goal: 35 WAM/2 errors

SI: 1.38

- Take a 1-minute timing on the following material.
- Use your most recent timing speed to set a speed or accuracy goal. (If you don't remember that score, click on the KWP Rep button to view the scores on your Student Report.)

Rain is quite welcome when the land is dry. The earth's surface holds quite a bit of water, but in times of very dry weather it always seems to be in the wrong place, or it is of the type that can't be used. Normally, all regions of the United States receive adequate amounts of rain; however, there are particular periods when clouds don't release their moisture for long amounts of time.

Document C ← Personal Business Letter Using a Letter Template

1. At a clear WordPerfect editing window, click on the New Document button on the Toolbar or choose **F**ile → **N**ew.
2. At the *New Document* dialog box, click on *letter* in the *Group* list box.
3. Click on *Letter - Blank Letterhead* in the *Select Template* list box.
4. Click on Select.
5. At the *Letter* dialog box, enter the receiver's name and address in the *Recipient(s) Name and Address:* text box.
6. Press ***Tab*** to move to the *Salutation* text box, then key the salutation.
7. Deselect all boxes under *Include* by clicking on any check box that displays an *x*.
8. Click on the Personal Info button, key your personal information, then click on OK.
9. Click on OK at the *Letter* dialog box.
10. Click on OK to close the *Letter Formatting Complete* dialog box and return to the document screen.
11. Key the letter, pressing ***Enter*** only once between paragraphs. For the Internet address, replace the x's with the first letter of your first name followed by the first seven letters of your last name. (If there are fewer than seven letters in your last name, your userid will be shorter.) Bold the complete Internet address.
12. Proofread and correct any errors, then complete a spell check.
13. When you have completed the body of the letter, press ***Enter***.
14. Choose **I**nsert → Letter Closing. At the *Letter Closing* dialog box, click on OK to accept the default of *Sincerely*.
15. WordPerfect then inserts your personal information in the signature block. Check it for accuracy and make any necessary changes.
16. Click on **F**ile → Save **A**s and name the letter **038wprc.kwp**.
17. To print the letter, click on the Print button (or print at the end of the session).
18. Click on **F**ile → **C**lose to close the document.

Document C

current date

Ms. Michele Woggon
13643 N. Pima Spring Way
Tucson, AZ 85736-4891

Dear Michele:

Thank you for showing me the new homes being built in the Vistoso Planned Community north of Tucson. I was especially impressed with the mountain view and the way the new homes blended into the surroundings. The quarter-acre lot you showed me is my first choice. I hope it is still available.

Would you please send me a map that includes the street names and lots available in the new addition? I will be returning to Tucson on the 15th of next month and would

Continued on next page

THREE-MINUTE TIMING

Goal: 30 WAM/2 errors

SI: 1.38

- Take one 3-minute timing on the following paragraphs.

Changes are often the cause of stress, whether you wanted these changes or they are thrust upon you. Change can be frightening and may call for some adjustment on your part. Change and stress are closely knit. You may experience stress as the result of changes that occur on a regular basis. These changes can be good or they can cause problems. Some of the common changes that cause stress are the death of a parent, the death of a child, the start of a new job, enrollment in a new school, asking someone for a date, or giving a speech.

You may also encounter stress by getting married or by having children. There are many other causes as well. It is best to confront stress when you have a problem managing it. Do not keep feeling bad about something that has happened to you on the job or at home. Work through the problems. Keep a positive outlook, and be prepared for the usual ups and downs in feelings. Work to handle your relationships with care. Learn to control stress.

PREPARING MEMOS USING MEMO TEMPLATES

Memo templates (introduced in Session 30) are another WordPerfect feature that can increase your efficiency in preparing documents, especially if you are working on your own computer. If you are not sharing the computer with anyone else, you need to enter your personal data only once; otherwise, as in a school situation, you may have to enter this information each time you use the template feature. The memo template feature offers the following efficiencies:

- The heading (*Memo* or *Memorandum*) is printed automatically.
- The guide words *To, From, Subject*, and *Date* are printed for you.
- Your name and the date (plus title, company address, and phone number—if you have included it as part of your personal information) are entered automatically.

WordPerfect includes four memo template styles: Contemporary, Cosmopolitan, Traditional, and Trimline.

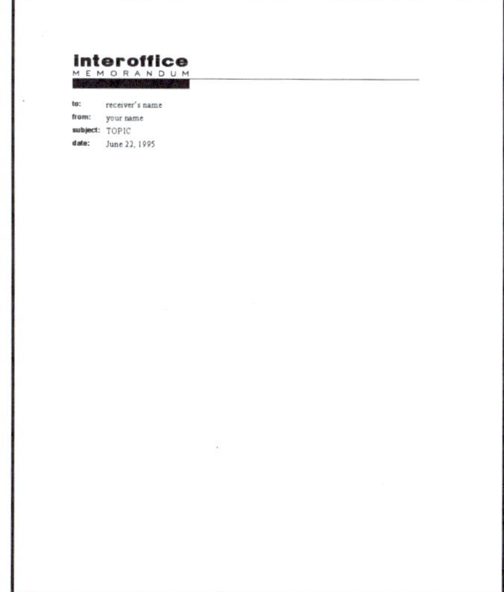

Figure 36.1 Contemporary Memo Template

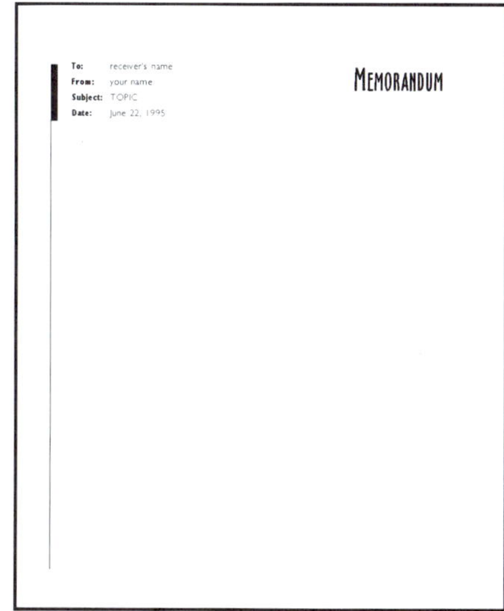

Figure 36.2 Cosmopolitan Memo Template

6 When checking is complete, the letter is displayed on the screen with errors highlighted.
7 To print the document with errors highlighted, click on the Print button. Otherwise, you may print at the end of the session.
8 To correct errors, click on View Original. Make changes, then recheck the document
9 Click on **F**ile → **C**lose. This closes Document B and brings up a clear WordPerfect editing window, at which you will prepare Document C.

Document B

current date

Mr. Tom Torrence
General Wolfe Secondary School
55 McCraney Street East
Oakville, ON K1A 0B1
CANADA

Dear Mr. Torrence:

For the presentation in Toronto on March 8, I would like to have the following equipment: an **LCD**, a **high-intensity overhead projector**, a **35mm carousel slide projector**, and a **large screen**. I will bring my own laptop computer and software.

You need not worry about sending an advance for the cost of airfare as I will put the ticket on my credit card. It takes approximately 30 days for the bill to catch up.

By the way, can you estimate the number of people attending the workshop? I want to ensure that I have sufficient materials for each participant.

Sincerely yours,

Paula Goldberg
1964 Showgate Way
Denver, CO 80219

Using WordPerfect's Letter Templates

Letter templates provide the same efficiencies as memo templates. In Session 30 you prepared a personal business letter using the Letter - Blank Letterhead template. You will use this template again as you prepare Document C.

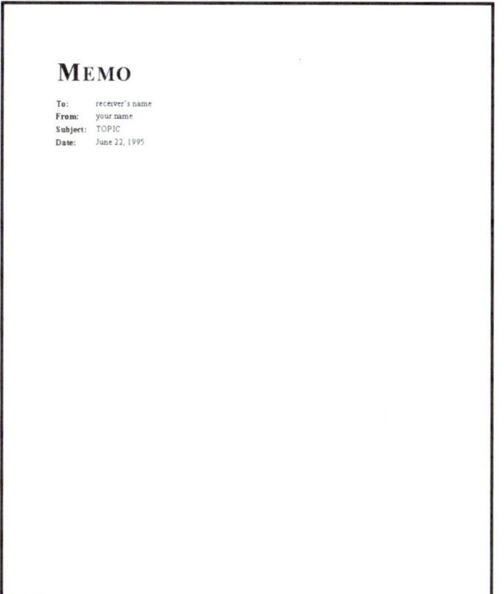

Figure 36.3 Traditional Memo Template

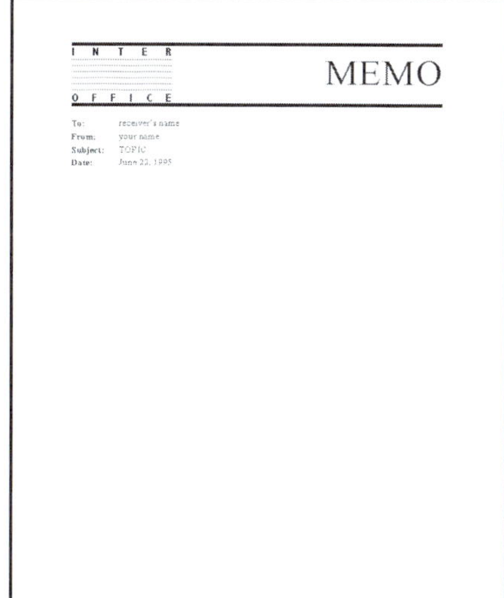

Figure 36.4 Trimline Memo Template

As you compare the memo template examples, note that the order of the guide words (To, From, Subject, and Date) differs from the illustrations of traditional block-style and simplified-style memos shown in Session 35. Although the block-style format is probably the most widely used style in the work place, every organization or business has its own preference. Check the company's policies and procedures manual to determine the memo style preferred.

In Documents A and B, which follow, you will use the Cosmopolitan memo template and the Trimline memo template to prepare memos.

Document A — *Block-Style Memo Using the Cosmopolitan Memo Template*

1. At a clear WordPerfect editing window, click on the New Document button on the Toolbar.
2. At the *New Document* dialog box, click on *memo* in the *Group* list box.
3. Click on *Memo - Cosmopolitan* in the *Select Template* list box.
4. Click on Select.
5. At the *Template Information* dialog box, key **Leslie McKay, Training and Education** in the *Name of Recipient(s)* text box and **WORKPLACE LITERACY** in the *Subject* text box. (Do not use bold; it is used in the instructions only to highlight the words.)
6. Click on the *Personal Info* button.
7. At the *Enter Your Personal Information* dialog box, key your personal information in the appropriate boxes. (If you do not have information for a particular box, leave it blank and press ***Tab*** to move to the next box.)
8. After entering your personal information, click on OK.
9. At the *Template Information* dialog box, click on OK.
10. At the document screen, begin keying the body of the memo.
11. When you are finished, check the sentences for correct grammar.
12. Spell-check the memo.
13. Click on **File** → **Save** to save the memo.
14. At the *Save As* dialog box, key the filename **036wpra.kwp**. Press ***Enter*** or click on OK.
15. To print the file, choose **File** → **Print** (or F5). Otherwise, print at the end of the session.
16. Click on **Print** or press ***Enter***.
17. Close the file (click on **File** → **Close**).

5 When checking is complete, the letter is displayed on the screen with errors highlighted.
6 To print the document with errors highlighted, click on the Print button. Otherwise, print at the end of the session.
7 To correct errors, click on View Original. Make changes, then recheck the document.
8 Choose **F**ile → **C**lose to close the document. This closes Document A and brings up the Document B screen.

Document A

current date

Ms. Bobbi Ray, Director
Personal Development Division
Office Systems Publishing Corporation
3839 White Plains Drive
Bronx, NY 10467-1910

Dear Ms. Ray:

Thank you for the brochures describing programs that are available through Office Systems Publishing Corporation.

Please send me, on a ten-day free inspection basis, the following video programs. The first is *How to Face an Audience with Poise* (Cat. No. 14-2.1.8), and the second is *The Employment Interview* (Cat. No. 14-5.4).

These programs will be viewed for possible use in workshops and seminars for business and office education.

Sincerely yours,

Kathy Aarons
3103 Eddy Lane
Eau Claire, WI 54701

Document B ← *Personal Business Letter*

1 At the *Production–Session 38 Document B* screen, key Document B following the same format used in Document A.
2 Bold the equipment names (but not the words *a, an, and*).
3 Proofread and correct any errors, then complete a spell check.
4 Center the letter vertically on the page (Fo**r**mat → **P**age → **C**enter).
5 Click on Check to automatically save and name the document as **038prob.kwp**. The program checks the letter for errors and calculates your WAM rate.

Document A

To: Leslie McKay, Training and Education

From: (your name)

Subject: WORKPLACE LITERACY

Date: current date

Because of rapid advances in computer technology over the past decade, it is essential that employees at all levels have at least a fundamental understanding of computer hardware and software. In the past, only those employees in the Information Processing and Computer Systems departments received regular computer training. With the integration of computer technology at all levels of the company, we need to provide training seminars focusing on basic computer operations. This is just one facet of the overall workplace literacy that will make our company competitive in today's global economy.

xx/036wpra.kwp

Document B *Block-Style Memo Using the Trimline Memo Template*

1 At a clear WordPerfect editing window, click on the New Document button.
2 At the *New Document* dialog box, click on *memo* in the *Group* list box.
3 Click on *Memo - Trimline* in the *Select Template* list box.
4 Click on Select.
5 At the *Template Information* dialog box, key **Dr. Robert Fraser, Dean of Arts and Sciences** in the *Name of Recipient(s)* text box and **ADDITION OF MIS 240 TO GENERAL STUDIES** in the *Subject* text box. (Do not use bold; it is used in the instructions only to highlight the words.)
6 If you have not previously entered your personal information, click on the *Personal Info* button.
7 At the *Enter Your Personal Information* dialog box, key your personal information in the appropriate boxes. (If you don't have information for a particular box, leave it blank and press ***Tab*** to move to the next box.)
8 After entering your personal information, click on OK.
9 At the *Template Information* dialog box, click on OK.
10 At the document screen, begin keying the body of the memo.
11 When you are finished, check the sentences for correct grammar.
12 Spell-check the memo.
13 Click on **File** → **Save** to save the memo.
14 At the *Save As* dialog box, key the filename **036wprb.kwp**. Press ***Enter*** or click on OK.
15 To print the file, choose **File** → **Print** (or F5). Otherwise, print at the end of the session.
16 Click on **Print** or press ***Enter***.
17 Close the file (click on **File** → **Close**).

Another error concerns the amount you charged for moving our underground service line. When I called to arrange this service, I was told that the charge would be $75. However, the bill includes a charge of $95. Again, please check your records and correct this mistake. If you have any questions, you may reach me at 555-0963.

I appreciate the prompt way you have dealt with my questions in the past, and I look forward to receiving a statement showing an accurate amount due for last month's electrical service.

Sincerely yours,

Ms. Maria Hill
2350 Skyline Drive
Denver, CO 80291

Figure 38.1 Personal business letter

Centering Text on the Page

Text can be centered vertically on the page with the Fo**r**mat → **P**age → **C**enter command from the Menu Bar. This selection can be used, for example, to center a report, a letter, a table, or an illustration.

To center text vertically on the page, you would do the following:

1. From the Menu Bar, choose Fo**r**mat → **P**age → **C**enter.
2. At the *Center Page(s)* dialog box, select Current **P**age, then click on OK.
3. Key the text. ***Note:*** You can also center the page after you have finished keying. The command can be entered before or after you key the document.

The text then prints vertically centered on the page. To ensure that the text is centered properly, do not press ***Enter*** before you begin keying text or at the end of text. If you do, WordPerfect uses the blank lines when centering the text on the page.

To see how *Center Current Page* works, key Document A. As usual, follow the document instructions step by step; however, refer to the preceding directions before printing the document.

Remember: It is your responsibility to watch for—and correct—any intentional errors in spelling, spacing, or arrangement that appear in the documents. This helps you become a **thinking** keyboarder.

Document A — *Personal Business Letter*

1. At the *Production–Session 38 Document A* screen, change the justification to Full. Then key Document A as a personal business letter. Press ***Ctrl + D*** to insert the current date.
2. Proofread and correct any errors, then complete a spell check.
3. Center the letter on the page. (See the above instructions on "Centering Text on the Page.")
4. Click on Check. The document is automatically saved and named **038proa.kwp**. The program checks the letter for errors and calculates your WAM rate.

Document B

current date

To: Dr. Robert Fraser, Dean of Arts and Sciences

From: (your name), Dean of the School of Business

Subject: ADDITION OF MIS 240 TO GENERAL STUDIES

Many faculty members of the School of Business are concerned because MIS 240 is not included on the recently published list of additions to the general studies program. From past experience, we are convinced that selected courses offered in our school are beneficial to all students, regardless of their major. MIS 240 is one of those courses. Its emphasis on general computer literacy is important for all students.

Please investigate the possibility of adding MIS 240 to the general studies program. I would be glad to meet with you to discuss this issue further.

xx/036wprb.kwp

c Dr. Jack Hamilton
Dr. John Schillak

Using WordPerfect's Bold Feature

Underlining, italicizing, enumerating, and indenting are text formatting options that draw the reader's attention. Another way to emphasize words or lines of text is to use the *Bold* feature. Bolding is often used to make key words and phrases stand out within a body of text. Bolding is also used in report headings to help set them apart from the text.

WordPerfect's Bold feature can be used to bold text as you key or to bold previously keyed material. To bold words as you key, you would complete the following steps:

1. Click on the Bold button **b** on the Toolbar to turn bolding on. (Or press ***Ctrl + B***.)
2. Key the word or words to be bolded.
3. Click on the Bold button to turn bolding off. (Or press ***Ctrl + B***.)

To bold previously keyed text, you would complete the following steps:

1. Select the text to be bolded (position the I-beam on the first character, hold down the left mouse button, drag to select the block of text, then release the button).
2. Click on the Bold button.
3. Position the I-beam pointer outside the selected text and click the left mouse button to deselect the text.

THREE-MINUTE TIMINGS

Goal: 30 WAM/2 errors

SI: 1.39

- Take two 3-minute timings.

Many people are growing herb gardens. The herb plants provide a variety of new seasonings, fragrances, and flavorings. Growing herbs is quite similar to growing a vegetable garden. You should select an area for your herb garden that is sunny, as herbs demand an abundance of sunlight to make them sweet and flavorful.

To supply enough herbs for a family of four, you would need a garden space of at least 12 to 18 square feet. If you do not have enough room, it is always easy to grow an abundance of herbs in an ordinary window box or in small clay flower pots. If grown inside, the herbs should be placed in a window that receives full sunlight at least half of the day. In cases where sunlight is not available, a fluorescent-light garden will give you a plentiful harvest of herbs. To promote compact growth, it is a good idea to snip the plants back on a regular basis.

Herbs placed with other plants add charm and grace with the rich foliage. Freshly picked herbs can either be dried or frozen for future use. Many good cookbooks offer directions for using a variety of herbs.

PREPARING PERSONAL BUSINESS LETTERS

In Session 30 you learned that the personal business letter is a letter from an individual to a business. Examples of personal business letters are the letters individuals write to companies requesting information or complaining about a product.

In this session, you will review the formatting guidelines for preparing personal business letters. In the illustration that follows, note that the return address is placed below the keyed sender's name. Note also that the personal business letter is keyed on plain paper, not on company letterhead. The letter is centered on the page for a visually pleasing appearance.

This is a sample. Do not key.

current date

Mr. Warren Chen, Manager
New Age Electric Company
4950 Scenic Heights Ridge
Denver, CO 80219-1698

Dear Mr. Chen:

My recent electric bill contains some errors that need correcting. For one thing, the bill shows a past-due balance of $59.98. However, I sent a check for that amount three weeks ago. Please review your records and make the necessary adjustment.

Continued on next page

Reviewing the Reveal Codes Feature

In Session 22, you learned how to display the Reveal Codes window. This feature is especially helpful during the editing process because it displays embedded formatting codes such as margin settings, tabs, underlining, bolding, italicizing, hard returns, soft returns, and spacing between words. For example, when the *Keyboarding with WordPerfect* software identifies an error that you cannot see in the printed document, you can often locate the problem by opening the file and displaying Reveal Codes.

To display the Reveal Codes window, press ***Alt + F3*** or choose **V**iew → Reveal **C**odes. The Reveal Codes window displays in gray and is separated from the editing window by a thin, black, double line. Text above the double line displays normally; text below the double line displays with the formatting codes included. The insertion point displays as a red rectangle, and spaces between words display as diamonds. To turn off Reveal Codes, press ***Alt + F3*** again or choose **V**iew → Reveal **C**odes.

Document C — *Block-Style Memo Using the Cosmopolitan Memo Template*

1. At a clear WordPerfect editing window, click on the New Document button.
2. At the *New Document* dialog box, click on *memo* in the *Group* list box.
3. Click on *Memo - Cosmopolitan* in the *Select Template* list box.
4. Click on Select.
5. At the *Template Information* dialog box, key the name of the recipient and the subject.
6. If you have not previously entered your personal information, click on the *Personal Info* button and key your personal information in the appropriate boxes.
7. After entering your personal information, click on OK.
8. At the *Template Information* dialog box, click on OK.
9. At the document screen, begin keying the body of the memo.
10. Double-indent the list of Internet tools and bold each tool name by completing the following steps:
    a. Create an extra line space before beginning the list by pressing ***Enter***.
    b. Press ***Ctrl + Shift + F7*** to double-indent the first tool, Browsers.
    c. Click on the Bold button, key **Browsers**: then click on the bold button again. Key the text that follows. Press ***Enter***.
    d. Follow the same steps for the remaining items. Press ***Enter*** twice after keying the last item.
11. When you are finished with the entire memo, check the sentences for correct grammar.
12. Spell-check the memo.
13. Click on **F**ile → **S**ave to save the memo.
14. At the *Save As* dialog box, key the filename **036wprc.kwp**. Press ***Enter*** or click on OK.
15. To print the file, choose **F**ile → **P**rint (or F5). Otherwise, print at the end of the session.
16. Click on **P**rint or press ***Enter***.
17. Close the file (click on **F**ile → **C**lose).

(*Note:* In the memo that follows and in other unformatted documents used throughout this text, diagonals [/] are used to separate lines in an address or to indicate the beginning of a new line.)

SESSION 38

SESSION GOALS

1-Minute: 35 WAM/2 errors
3-Minute: 30 WAM/2 errors

Centering text on a page
Using letter templates

Ideal paragraph length

GETTING STARTED

If you are continuing immediately from Session 37, go to the one-minute timings. If you exited the program at the end of Session 37, do the following:

1. Access Windows, then WordPerfect 6.1 for Windows.
2. Click on the KWP icon to access *Keyboarding with WordPerfect*.
3. Go to the Keyboarding Sessions menu and click on Jump to return to your last activity. Or, access the Session 38 menu to begin the session.

If your fingers are already warmed up or if you have completed part of the session, highlight the desired activity and click on OK. When you have completed the on-screen activities for Session 38, you will return to the text to complete several personal business letters in which you use WordPerfect's centering feature to center the text on a page.

ONE-MINUTE TIMINGS

Goal: 35 WAM/2 errors

SI: 1.40

- Take two 1-minute timings.
- Work on improving either speed or accuracy, depending on your most recent timing score.

> A good keyboarder soon learns how to proofread. Glaring errors will mar the neatness and quality of a good report. Find all the mistakes before you key the final copy. Learn to watch for correct spelling, grammar, and word use. You might wish to examine your printed copy two or three times to make certain that it is without mistakes. In the long run, you will be pleased that you have carefully prepared an excellent copy. The person who reads your material will respect your ability to key and proofread. Aim for high-quality output.

Document C

To: Todd Stewart/From: (your name)/INTERNET TOOLS/(current date)/Todd, for your presentation to Corporate Marketing personnel on Internet tools for a variety of applications, please cover the following:/Browsers: Be sure to include examples of both graphic browsers as well as text-based browsers./Home page: Please identify how home pages can benefit the corporation and the steps involved in creating home pages, including setting up firewalls./List servers: Note examples of worthwhile lists and the amount of information that can be received./News groups: Give examples of news groups that would have information on the products we are marketing./E-mail: Point out that this feature gives us access to clients outside our corporation./The networked microcomputer laboratory in the west wing has been reserved for your presentation next Wednesday from 1 to 4 p.m. There will be 20 participants, so each person will have access to a PC for any hands-on applications you might want to use. Call Mike Baldwin at 4320 or e-mail him a message (mbaldwin) if you have any questions or special equipment needs./your initials/036wprc.kwp

Document D — *Block-Style Memo Using the Trimline Memo Template*

1. At a clear WordPerfect editing window, click on the New Document button.
2. Select the Trimline memo template.
3. At the *Template Information* dialog box, enter the appropriate information.
4. If you have not previously entered your personal information, do so now. Then click on OK.
5. At the *Template Information* dialog box, click on OK.
6. At the document screen, begin keying the body of the memo.
7. Bold Dr. Carl Bishop's name wherever it appears in the document.
8. When you are finished with the entire memo, check the sentences for correct grammar.
9. Spell-check the memo. Did you remember to add the Attachment notation?
10. Save the file as **036wprd.kwp**.
11. Print the memo (or print all documents at the end of the session).
12. Close the file.

Document D

To: State BEA Presidents/From: (your name)/THE SEARCH IS OVER FOR YOUR NEXT PROGRAM SPEAKER/We would like to introduce you to one of America's outstanding motivational speakers, Dr. Carl Bishop. His acceptance by industry across the United States and Canada has been exceptional. We invite you to read the attached letter of recommendation from Mr. John B. Suter of Pilgrim Industries describing Dr. Bishop's impact on his audiences./Dr. Bishop can make a valid contribution to your next conference or convention program. He speaks to the critical issue of skill application, which is a primary concern to every industrial leader. You will appreciate the humor he incorporates into his presentation and his ability to speak the technical language of your people./As we have done with more than a thousand previous clients, we would like to work with you to add a touch of brilliance and zeal to your convention program. Write or call today about arranging a personal appearance by Dr. Carl Bishop.

xx/036wprd.kwp

UNIT 8

LETTERS

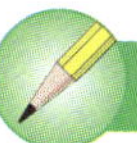

REINFORCING WRITING SKILLS

Communicating with people in writing is much more difficult than communicating in person. On a face-to-face basis, the speaker knows immediately if the message is not being communicated correctly. Body language, facial expressions, and questions provide instant and ongoing feedback. But a writer does not enjoy that advantage. Instead, the writer must rely on clear sentences and carefully chosen words to convey the intended meaning.

One simple way to help the reader get your message is to keep sentences at a reasonable length—15 to 25 words. Readers tend to get lost in sentences that are too long, and very short sentences create a "choppy" rhythm.

Focus on creating sentences of the target length as you complete the next document. First, compose the memo at the computer. Then edit your document for clear meaning, correct punctuation, and accurate word choices. Check the sentence length and edit accordingly.

Document E — *Block-Style Memo Using a WordPerfect Memo Template*

Select one of the memo templates. Then compose a memo to the instructor of this class identifying which of the WordPerfect features you have used to date that have been the most helpful. Explain how and why. In a second paragraph, talk about the WordPerfect features that have been the most difficult to master and why. Include any suggestions you have for making that learning easier.

In your memo, use some of the WordPerfect features you have learned—for example, bolding and indenting. Check your sentence length and make adjustments. Then proofread the memo, complete a spell check, and save and print the file (name it **036wpre.kwp**). Finally, close the document.

ENDING THE SESSION

To end this session, delete Session 26 files and print any Session 36 files not printed earlier. Then continue with the next session or exit the program:

DELETE

1. Choose **F**ile → **O**pen.
2. Select the Session 26 wpr file by positioning the arrow pointer on the filename and clicking the left mouse button.
3. With the filename(s) highlighted, choose File **O**ptions → **D**elete.
4. At the *Delete File(s)* dialog box, click on **D**elete.
5. If you need to print files, go to step 2 under PRINT. Otherwise, click on Cancel or press ***Esc*** to close the *Open File* dialog box.

PRINT

1. Choose **F**ile → **O**pen.
2. At the *Open File* dialog box, select the files to be printed, then choose File **O**ptions → **P**rint.
3. At the *Print Files* dialog box, press ***Enter*** or click on Print.
4. Click on Cancel or press ***Esc*** to close the *Open File* dialog box.

CONTINUE

1. Print any files, if necessary.
2. Click on the KWP Next Activity button.
3. At the next session menu, click on OK to proceed with the highlighted item.

EXIT

1. Print any files, if necessary.
2. Click on the KWP Main Menu button.
3. At the Main Menu, select WordPerfect Only, then click on OK.
4. Click on **F**ile → E**x**it.
5. Exit Windows (**F**ile → E**x**it), if necessary.

PRINT

1. Choose **File** → **Open**.
2. At the *Open File* dialog box, select the files to be printed, then choose File **Options** → **Print**.
3. At the *Print Files* dialog box, press ***Enter*** or click on Print.
4. Click on Cancel or press ***Esc*** to close the *Open File* dialog box.

CONTINUE

1. Print any files, if necessary.
2. Click on the KWP Next Activity button.
3. At the next session menu, click on OK to proceed with the highlighted item.

EXIT

1. Print any files, if necessary.
2. Click on the KWP Main Menu button.
3. At the Main Menu, select WordPerfect Only, then click on OK.
4. Click on **File** → **Exit**.
5. Exit Windows (**File** → **Exit**), if necessary.

TRADITIONAL AND E-MAIL MEMOS

SESSION GOALS

1-Minute: 35 WAM/2 errors
3-Minute: 30 WAM/2 errors

Choosing effective words

Review memo templates, automatic date insertion, indenting, bolding, italics

GETTING STARTED

If you are continuing immediately from Session 36, go to the one-minute timing. If you exited the program at the end of Session 36, do the following:

1. Access Windows, then WordPerfect 6.1 for Windows.
2. Click on the KWP icon to access *Keyboarding with WordPerfect*.
3. Go to the Keyboarding Sessions menu and click on Jump to return to your last activity. Or, access the Session 37 menu to begin the session.

If you are already warmed up or have completed part of the session, highlight the desired activity and click on OK . When you have completed the on-screen activities for Session 37, you will return to the text to complete a variety of memos, including some done with the templates and one prepared for e-mail.

ONE-MINUTE TIMINGS

Goal: 35 WAM/2 errors

SI: 1.35

- Take two 1-minute timings.
- Work on improving either speed or accuracy, depending on your most recent timing score.

Snowshoes add two dimensions to the feet. Snowshoes are big and add a lot of weight. To compensate for size, you must use your eyes, as well as your brain, to pick the way. Normally, in walking through the forests, most of us look ahead about ten feet. When walking with snowshoes, it is best to look ahead about 20 or 30 feet. The size of the shoes requires that a person turn bigger corners and also allow more room to maneuver. Most brush and bramble bushes are a big problem and should be avoided.

- You do not need to enter your "userid" (user identification) and date when sending an e-mail memo; this is done by the software. A userid generally is a name of eight or fewer characters that identifies the sender.
- E-mail messages can be created in WordPerfect (where documents can be edited) and then uploaded to the e-mail system for electronic delivery.
- If the memo is to be sent to one person, you must include the receiver's userid. If the memo is to reach several people, you need not send it to each person individually. Rather, you would list a filename for the distribution list and all people on the list would receive the memo.

At a clear WordPerfect editing window, prepare an e-mail memo according to the instructions in Document E. Use the block style, but note that you will not include a FROM or DATE entry. For the TO: and SUBJECT: entries, include two spaces after the colon. When you have finished keying the document, proofread your work and complete a spell check. Save the memo as **037wpre.kwp**. Print the memo, if required by your instructor, and then close the document. At the clear WordPerfect editing window, complete the end-of-session activities.

This is a sample. Do not key.

TO: (userid of person who is to receive the memo)

SUBJECT: (topic in all capital letters)

This part of the electronic memo is the body of the document. For Document E, compose a memo to your instructor. Create a userid made up of the first initial of the instructor's first name and the first seven letters of the instructor's last name. The topic is AN IDEAL VACATION. The memo should include at least two paragraphs.

Write about where you would like to go for an ideal vacation and what you would do. Include names of places, the length of the vacation, the time of year, and transportation. Finally, be sure to explain why you consider this to be an ideal vacation.

Some parts of the format are determined by the particular e-mail software you are using. Thus e-mail memo styles may vary somewhat from company to company.

YOUR NAME (keyed in all capital letters)

Figure 37.1 Sample e-mail memo

ENDING THE SESSION

To end this session, delete outdated WordPerfect Reinforcement files, print any files from Session 37 not printed earlier, then continue with the next session or exit the program:

DELETE

1. Choose **F**ile → **O**pen
2. Select the Session 27 wpr file.
3. With the filename highlighted, choose File **O**ptions → **D**elete.
4. At the *Delete File(s)* dialog box, click on **D**elete.
5. If you need to print files, go to step 2 under PRINT. Otherwise, click on Cancel or press ***Esc*** to close the *Open File* dialog box.

THREE-MINUTE TIMINGS

Goal: 30 WAM/2 errors

SI: 1.39

- Take two 3-minute timings.

A wood chisel may be used to remove extra wood when another tool will not do the job efficiently. The wood chisel can also be used to make precision wood joint cuts.

Never use a steel hammer to strike a chisel. Use either a solid rubber or wooden mallet. You can also use the palm of your hand, of course, depending on the particular project. A mallet can work in cases where the edge to be cut is across the grain. If, however, the cutting edge is with the grain, a mallet could easily split the wood. Remember to angle the chisel slightly when starting a cut. The angle makes smooth or pared cuts easier to do. Cutting on the angle leaves the piece of wood much smoother when cutting either with or against the grain.

To make a vertical cut against the grain, tilt the chisel off to one side to initiate a sliding action to the flat cutting edge. A surface that is wider than the chisel is easier to cut if the chisel is pressed against the cut-out portion. The procedure will provide a guide for that portion of the chisel when cutting out the new portion or edge. Always remember to cut with the grain so that any excess or extra wood will split away in a straight line and not cause a further problem to the woodcutter.

FORMATTING TRADITIONAL AND SIMPLIFIED-STYLE MEMOS

Although using WordPerfect's memo templates is an efficient, quick way to prepare memos, there are times and situations when you may not want to use this feature. For example, if your company prefers a simplified-style memo or has its own in-house style, you will need to prepare documents that match that style.

Many companies prefer the simplified-style memo because formatting is cut to a minimum. The only guide word included is *To:* followed by two spaces, then the receiver's name. No text alignment is required in the heading.

Document A — *Simplified-Style Memo*

1. At the the *Production–Session 37 Document A* screen, change the justification to Full (click on the Justification button on the Power Bar, then click on *Full* at the drop-down menu).
2. Key the memo in a simplified-style format. Insert the current date by pressing ***Ctrl* + *D*** or by clicking on **I**nsert → **D**ate → Date **T**ext.
3. Proofread and correct any errors, then complete a spell check.
4. Click on Check. The program automatically names and saves the document as **037proa.kwp**, then checks for errors and calculates your WAM rate.
5. When checking is complete, the document is displayed on the screen with errors highlighted. Move the insertion point to the end of the document to display the number of errors and your WAM rate.
6. To print the memo with errors highlighted, click on the Print button.
7. To correct errors, click on View Original. Make changes and recheck the document.
8. Click on **F**ile → **C**lose to close the document and bring up the Document B screen.

5 To print the memo, click on the Print button. Or, you may wait until the end of the session to print all the Session 37 files.

6 Choose **File** → **Close**. This closes Document D and brings up a clear WordPerfect editing window, where you will prepare Document E.

Document D

To: Jack MacPearson, Finance/From: (your name)/Subject: Operations Report/Please prepare a spreadsheet for the past six months that includes the following information:

1. *Agency trades: Be sure to include trades that took place in our five-state area and the province of Ontario.*
2. *Listed trades: Include trades in all 50 states as well as the 10 provinces of Canada.*
3. *Underwriting trades: How many trades of this type took place in our five-state area plus Ontario?*
4. *Margin trades: In addition to the number of trades in both the U.S. and Canada, what is the average margin spread?*
5. *Bond trades: Report only those bond trades that took place within the U.S., including Puerto Rico and the U.S. Virgin Islands.*

From now on, this report is to be updated on a quarterly basis so that we can be fully aware of the income generated in the various categories.

REINFORCING WRITING SKILLS

In Session 36, you read that for readability and comprehension purposes, the ideal sentence length is 15 to 25 words. Another factor that promotes clear communication is word choice. In addition to choosing words that accurately say what you mean, it is important to choose simple, common words that everyone understands. Do not fall into the trap of selecting long, obscure words just to make your message seem more important. Some of the most powerful written statements consist of very short words, as in the following example:

If it is to be, it is up to me.

As you complete Document E, concentrate on keeping sentences in the 15- to 25-word range and use simple words that communicate directly and forcefully.

Document E ← *E-Mail Memo*

The instructions for preparing this electronic memo and all e-mail memos in this text are based on the following assumptions:

- You are using an e-mail software package that does not have editing capabilities.

Document A

current date

TO: Ronald Decker

Fred Waedt

SMALL BUSINESS DEVELOPMENT SEMINAR

On Wednesday, we will be making the final plans for next month's seminar on new marketing techniques. Would you have time to stop by the office to show Connie the layout for your handouts? We need to send the information to the printer by Friday. We also will need an estimate of your expenses for travel, lodging, meals, etc.
I think this marketing seminar will be one of our most effective presentations. The topic is vital to business people, and more than 30 small-business owners have sent in their registration materials.

xx/037proa.kwp

Document B ← *Block-Style Memo*

1. At the *Production-Session 37 Document B* screen, key Document B as a traditional block-style memo. Insert the current date by pressing ***Ctrl + D***.
2. Format the title Small Business Computing in italics (replaces the underlining).
3. When you have finished keying the memo, proofread the document and correct any errors. Then complete a spell check.
4. Click on Check to automatically name (**037prob.kwp**), save, and check the memo for errors.
5. When checking is complete, the document is displayed on the screen with errors highlighted. The number of errors and your WAM rate are displayed at the end of the document.
6. To print the memo with errors highlighted, click on the Print button. Otherwise, you may print all Session 37 documents at the end of the session.
7. To correct errors, click on View Original. Make changes and recheck the document.
8. Click on **F**ile → **C**lose. This closes Document B and brings up the Document C screen.

Document B

Memo to Ms. Betty Mathiason, Editor/from John Melrose, Printing Department/subject: PRINTING OF SMALL BUSINESS COMPUTING

The deadline for receiving the disk files for Small Business Computing is approaching quickly. We need to know as soon as possible if you will be able to meet the deadline. If you cannot, it will mean rescheduling the project for next month. At this time, the schedule for next month looks quite open, so we have some flexibility.

We should get together sometime in the coming weeks to set up our printing schedule for next year. Give me a call, and we'll choose a date that's mutually convenient.

xx/037prob.kwp

Document C ← Simplified-Style Memo

1 At the *Production–Session 37 Document C* screen, key Document C as a simplified-style memo. Include your name as Dean.
2 In paragraph 2, bold Bob MacDonald's name, and in paragraph 3 bold Dave Armbruster's name.
3 For the copy notation, key **c**, press ***Tab***, then key the name(s).
4 Proofread and correct any errors, then complete a spell check.
5 Click on Check to automatically name (**037proc.kwp**), save, and check the document for errors.
6 When checking is complete, the document is displayed on the screen with errors highlighted. The number of errors and your WAM rate are displayed at the end of the document.
7 To print the memo with errors highlighted, click on the Print button. Or, you may choose to print all Session 37 documents at the end of the session.
8 To correct errors, click on View Original. Make changes and recheck the document.
9 Choose **File** → **Close**. This closes Document C and brings up a clear WordPerfect editing window, at which you are to complete Document D.

Document C

Memo to Otis Franke, Space Coordinator/from (your name), Dean/Subject: CHANGE IN OFFICE ASSIGNMENTS

Because of some recent course changes, we have assigned new office locations to various faculty members. These changes are effective on the first of next month.

Bob MacDonald has been transferred to the Computer Science Center. He will move to an office on the south side of the fourth floor. Larry Ozzello will indicate which office it will be.

Please note that **Dave Armbruster** will now work in the office that Bob had been assigned, which is 43.

xx/037proc.kwp

c Dave Armbruster
Bob MacDonald
Larry Ozzello

Document D ← Block-Style Memo Using the Trimline Memo Template

1 At a clear WordPerfect editing window, access the Trimline memo template and key Document D as a block-style memo. You may need to re-enter your personal information.
2 For the numbered items, key the number at the left margin, then press ***Ctrl + Shift + F7*** to indent the text from both margins.
3 Proofread and correct any errors, then complete a spell check.
4 Click on **File** → Save **As**, then name the document **037wprd.kwp**.

INDEX

Use the two checklists below whenever you write your own documents. Evaluate your first draft according to the checkpoints. Then make any necessary changes before you print the final draft.

Composition Checklist

- ☐ Did I order my thoughts in a sensible way?
- ☐ Did I group related paragraphs together?
- ☐ Did I group related pieces of information in a single paragraph?
- ☐ Did I start a new paragraph for each new idea?
- ☐ Did I begin each paragraph with a topic sentence or a connecting sentence?
- ☐ Did I vary sentence structure and length?
- ☐ Did I break up overly long sentences?
- ☐ Did I make my subject and verb agree?
- ☐ Did I use pronouns correctly and without bias?
- ☐ Did I use adjectives sparingly, without being flowery or opinionated?
- ☐ Did I take care not to split verb phrases?
- ☐ Did I put modifiers next to the words they modify?
- ☐ Did I use correct punctuation?

Style Checklist

- ☐ Did I use language suitable for my intended reader?
- ☐ Did I use everyday language?
- ☐ Did I avoid slang, cliches, and phoniness?
- ☐ Did I avoid sexist language?
- ☐ Did I use strong, lively words?
- ☐ Did I use concrete rather than abstract words?
- ☐ Did I use the active voice?
- ☐ Did I eliminate redundancies?